Religion of a Different Color

Religion of a Different Color

Race and the Mormon Struggle for Whiteness

W. PAUL REEVE

OXFORD
UNIVERSITY PRESS

UNIVERSITY PRESS

Oxford University Press is a department of the University of Oxford.
It furthers the University's objective of excellence in research, scholarship,
and education by publishing worldwide.

Oxford New York
Auckland Cape Town Dar es Salaam Hong Kong Karachi
Kuala Lumpur Madrid Melbourne Mexico City Nairobi
New Delhi Shanghai Taipei Toronto

With offices in
Argentina Austria Brazil Chile Czech Republic France Greece
Guatemala Hungary Italy Japan Poland Portugal Singapore
South Korea Switzerland Thailand Turkey Ukraine Vietnam

Oxford is a registered trade mark of Oxford University Press
in the UK and certain other countries.

Published in the United States of America by
Oxford University Press
198 Madison Avenue, New York, NY 10016

Library of Congress Cataloging-in-Publication Data
Reeve, W. Paul, author.
  Religion of a different color : race and the Mormon struggle for whiteness / W. Paul Reeve.
    p. cm.
  Includes bibliographical references and index.
  ISBN 978-0-19-975407-6 (hardcover : alk. paper) 1. Race relations—Religious aspects—
Church of Jesus Christ of Latter-day Saints—History. 2. Whites—Race identity—United States—
History. 3. Race relations—Religious aspects—Mormon Church—History. 4. Indian
Mormons—History. 5. African American Mormons—History. I. Title.
  BX8611.R44 2015
  305.6'893—dc23
                              2014027391

9 8 7 6 5 4 3

Printed in the United States of America on acid-free paper

To Mom, Dad, and Roene
for teaching me to look on the heart

CONTENTS

ACKNOWLEDGMENTS

Scholarship on the Mormon past is flourishing, perhaps as never before, nourished by a vibrant community of scholars. I am the beneficiary of that community's collective generosity and those fellow researchers who shared sources and insights with me. Their kindnesses greatly enriched the texture of this book and made it far better than it would have been had I fumbled along on my own. My colleagues also convinced me that I was indeed on to something, especially at the early stages of the project when some friends suggested there would not be enough sources available to sustain an entire book. A trickle soon turned into a flood, and I ended up gathering far more references than could be included here. I am grateful for friends and colleagues who shared sources, time, wisdom, and knowledge with me: including Sam Brown, Jared Tamez, Christopher Jones, Stan Thayne, Ben Park, Max Mueller, Melissa Coy, Russell Stevenson, Alan Morrell, Michael Van Wagenen, Andrea G. Radke-Moss, Nathan Oman, Ben Cater, Nathan Jones, Brent Rogers, Blair Hodges, Michael Paulos, Cassie Clark, Janiece Johnson, Ed Jeter, Tom Kimball, Stephen Fleming, Todd Compton, Connell O'Donovan, Matthew Basso, Jon Moyer, Ed Blum, Darius Gray, J. B. Haws, Nadja Durbach, John Turner, and Arvella George. Ardis Parshall continues to be a generous scholar with a keen eye for detail: she shared so many of her obscure "finds" with me that the end product is richer for having her as a friend. Other people (Patrick Mason, Quincy Newell, Barbara Jones Brown, Michael Shamo, David Grua, Margaret Blair Young, Jonathan Stapley, Christopher Rich, Heather Stone, and Colleen McDannell) were generous enough to read chapters and offer feedback. I am grateful for the collective wisdom of the many scholars who contributed to this project. The oversights and misinterpretations that persist are mine.

Christopher Rich deserves special mention. Early in the project I submitted a request at the LDS Church History Library to see if there was a Pitman shorthand version of Brigham Young's speech to the territorial legislature, either on 5 January or 5 February 1852. I wanted to clear up the ambiguity of the timeline of Young's speeches to the legislature and get as close as possible to his original words, rather than rely on Wilford Woodruff's truncated summary. I also wanted to know if his most important speech was delivered on 5 February or 5 January. The only response I received from the Church History Library was that there was no shorthand version of a 5 January speech and no mention of 5 February. Not entirely satisfied, I decided to try again later. In the meantime, I thought I had solved the chronology problem of Young's speeches, yet I still had lingering questions. I sent a version of chapter 5 to Christopher Rich to read. He believed that Young's most fully enunciated rationale for a race-based priesthood denial was delivered on 5 February, not 5 January. His feedback prompted me to again inquire at the Church History Library, so this time I requested a shorthand version of a 5 February speech. This new request led not only to the discovery of shorthand for Young's speech but also to speeches by Orson Pratt and Orson Spencer that had never been transcribed, as well as a vigorous debate over the Indian indenture bill. These discoveries led to a meeting and a new friendship with LaJean Purcell Caruth, the first person to transcribe some of these speeches since they were originally recorded by George D. Watt in 1852. Information from the speeches also led to new insights into the beginnings of the race-based priesthood ban in Mormonism that have never been considered before. LaJean and Christopher have since joined me in coediting and contextualizing the 1852 legislative bills, debates, and speeches for publication for the first time. The result of this editorial collaboration is slated to appear as a book of its own entitled *"Enough to cause the Angles in Heaven to Blush": Race, Servitude, and Priesthood at the 1852 Utah Legislature.*

I also thank the Church History Library and the group of dedicated professionals who made my research there rewarding. Richard Turley, Bill Slaughter, Matthew Grow, Michael Landon, LaJean Purcell Carruth, Silvia Ghosh, Elder Marcus Nash, and Jed Woodworth were all generous with their time and resources. Robin Jensen was always helpful with quick answers to questions and insights into sources which saved me countless hours. I especially honor former LDS Church Historian Elder Marlin Jensen for creating an inviting atmosphere for scholarly inquiry and for his encouragement on this project.

My friends and colleagues at the J. Williard Marriott Library at the University of Utah were also helpful, especially Greg Thompson, Paul Mogren, Peter Kraus, Walter Jones, and Luise Poulton.

The Tanner Humanities Center at the University of Utah, under the leadership of Bob Goldberg, honored me with a Virgil C. Aldrich Research Fellowship at the early stages of this project and offered me a rewarding intellectual space in which I could test my ideas. My research was also supported by a Mayers Fellowship at the Huntington Library at San Marino, California, where I benefitted from the guidance of William Deverell and Peter Blodgett. The University of Utah History Department, under the leadership of Jim Lehning, and the College of Humanities under Robert Newman, supported a semester-long sabbatical leave, which, combined with a University Faculty Fellowship, provided the time to write the bulk of the manuscript.

I am especially grateful to Susan Ferber at Oxford for her interest in this project. Her editorial skills polished my prose, and her professionalism enhanced the final product. I am thankful to my colleagues Eric Hinderaker and Becky Horn for suggesting that Susan visit with me while she was in Salt Lake City and to Susan for knocking on my door.

My strongest thanks go to my family. They have endured the most and have kept me grounded over the last seven years, especially with their less-than-inspiring questions: "When are you going to be done with that thing?" "Are you still working on the same book?" "How long does it take to write a book?" "Shouldn't you be done by now?" And, most pressingly, "Am I going to be in your book?" Porter, Eliza, Josh, Rebecca, Emma, and Hunter, you are in my book, but more importantly you are in my life. You brighten my days and give me hope. Thank you for being captives on my journey into race and religion and for tolerating my moralizing about treating all people with respect. And for Beth, I am lucky to have you as my partner and friend. Thanks for making me laugh. I am now "done with that thing."

ABBREVIATIONS

BYC   Brigham Young Collection, CHL.

CHL   Church History Library, the Church of Jesus Christ of Latter-day Saints, Salt Lake City, Utah.

FHL   Family History Library, the Church of Jesus Christ of Latter-day Saints, Salt Lake City, Utah.

HBLL   Harold B. Lee Library, Brigham Young University, Provo, Utah.

HL   Huntington Library, San Marino, California.

JH   Journal History of the Church of Jesus Christ of Latter-day Saints (chronology of typed entries and newspaper clippings, 1830 to the present), CHL.

JWML   J. Willard Marriott Library, University of Utah, Salt Lake City, Utah.

LTPSC   L. Tom Perry Special Collections, HBLL.

USHS   Utah State Historical Society, Salt Lake City, Utah.

Religion of a Different Color

Introduction
All "Mormon Elder-Berry's" Children

On 28 April 1904, less than two months after the president of the Church of Jesus Christ of Latter-day Saints, Joseph F. Smith, spent a withering six days as a witness before a US Senate committee, *Life* magazine published a political cartoon that offered a profound pictorial vision of what Mormonism looked like at the dawn of the twentieth century.[1] Cartoonist C. J. Rudd simply labeled his drawing "Mormon Elder-Berry—out with his six-year-olds, who take after their mothers" (see figure 0.1). As was typical of period magazines, there was no text or story to accompany the cartoon. There was only Rudd's short caption and the picture itself.[2]

The image seems incongruous with present-day expectations of what a Mormon family looked like in 1904. Apart from the blatant attack on polygamy explicit in the image, if the cartoon were to appear in 2014 the LDS Church's public affairs department might well embrace Elder Berry's racially diverse international family. The church might even recruit several of Elder Berry's children for its "I'm a Mormon" media campaign, which is an effort to promote a heterogeneous and global identity for Mormonism in the twenty-first century.[3]

In 1904, however, the *Life* magazine cartoon was certainly not meant as a compliment, nor was it intended as a celebration of Mormon diversity. In fact, it was intended as a lingering critique, a holdover from the nineteenth century when politicians, Protestant ministers, journalists, news editors, overland migrants, dime novelists, graphic artists, and others contributed to the construction of mythic mixed-race Mormon families similar to that of Mormon Elder Berry's.

Life's publication came at the very moment when Mormon leaders were attempting to orchestrate a new image for the faith and to make the transition from a polygamous and racially suspect past toward a monogamist and racially pure future. Following his testimony before the US Senate, Joseph F. Smith

Figure 0.1 "Mormon Elder-Berry—Out with His Six-Year-Olds, Who Take After Their Mothers." Reprinted from *Life*, 28 April 1904, 404.

returned to Salt Lake City and on 6 April 1904, issued what historians refer to as the "Second Manifesto." Smith, in essence, enforced the first manifesto delivered almost fourteen years earlier by then church president Wilford Woodruff, who had promised to use his influence to ensure Mormon compliance with the laws of the land and to end Mormon polygamy. Insisting he would keep that earlier promise, Smith warned the LDS faithful that any "officer or member" of the church who entered into any future plural marriage would be "deemed in transgression against the Church" and subject to excommunication.[4]

The *Life* cartoon was part of an effort to trap Mormons in a racially suspect past even as Mormon leaders attempted to shape a whiter future. This profound moment of transition played out on a national stage with intense media scrutiny. The Senate hearings in Washington, DC generated curiosity and at times appealed to the nation's prurient interests. The hearings dragged on for three years as the US Senate decided if it would allow Reed Smoot, a sitting LDS apostle, a monogamist, and a Republican, to retain his seat. In this setting and beyond, the nation attempted to come to terms with Mormonism, to situate this uniquely American-born faith within a broader religious landscape and to decide if it belonged.[5]

The Utah state legislature elected Smoot in 1903, but reports of continuing plural marriage among the Mormons, church interference in politics, and lingering questions over Mormon loyalty to the nation prompted the Senate investigation. The Reed Smoot hearings were the culmination of an Americanization process that began with the Woodruff Manifesto in 1890, continued through Utah statehood in 1896, and finally solidified when the Senate voted in 1907 to allow Smoot to retain his seat.[6] It was an important period of transition for Mormonism, from the nineteenth to the twentieth century, from polygamy to monogamy, from outsider to insider, from communalism to capitalism, from isolation to integration, and perhaps even from insular to global. Those transformations were gradual and messy, and they left lingering vestiges of the old mixed with the new. Nonetheless, Mormonism was in fact "in transition" and the Smoot hearings served as an important harbinger of change.[7]

This book argues that one of those transitions was racial: from not securely white in the nineteenth century to too white by the twenty-first century. Being white equaled access to political, social, and economic power: all aspects of citizenship in which outsiders sought to limit or prevent Mormon participation. At least a part of those efforts came through persistent attacks on the collective Mormon body. Outsiders suggested that Mormons were physically different and racially more similar to marginalized groups than they were to white people. Mormons responded with aspirations toward whiteness. It was a back-and-forth struggle between what outsiders imagined and what Mormons believed. The process was never linear and most often involved both sides talking past each other. Yet, Mormons in the nineteenth century recognized their suspect racial position. One leader complained that Mormons were treated as if they were "some savage tribe, or some colored race of foreigners" while another acknowledged that the Saints were not "considered suitable to live among 'white folks.'"[8]

Although much has been written about the economic, cultural, doctrinal, marital, legal, religious, and political differences that set Mormons apart from mainstream nineteenth-century America, much less is known about the ways in which Protestants believed Mormons were physically different.[9] The Mormon body in fact became a key battleground in the conflict between church and state that played out among the Mormons.[10]

In many regards, the Mormon struggle for whiteness is a microcosm of the history of race in America, this time taught through the lens of religion. Mormons were conflated with nearly every other "problem" group in the nineteenth century—blacks, Indians, immigrants, and Chinese—a way to color them less white by association. In telling the Mormon racial story, one ultimately tells the American racial story, a chronicle fraught with cautionary tales regarding whiteness, religious freedom, and racial genesis.

As the historian David R. Roediger contends, "In the United States of a century ago people did not talk about race in the way we do."[11] Ever shifting and frequently contradictory definitions of race and racial hierarchies functioned at all levels of American society. Race operated as a hierarchical system designed to create order and superiority out of the perceived disorder of the confluence of peoples in America. Race could variously be marked by language, national origin, religion, laws and government, marital relationships, and a variety of cultural characteristics. In general, "race" was a loosely used word that sometimes referred to nationality more than skin color, especially in reference to immigrants from Europe. Nineteenth-century writers did not simply refer to "the Irish," they discussed "the Irish race." Yet, race as nationality increasingly became entangled with race as skin color, especially in the power dynamics that played out between the white majority and black, red, and yellow minorities. In the case of the Mormons, such distinctions blurred dramatically. Latter-day Saints were white-skinned and often native born. If they had not converted, they would have been categorized as Nordic or Anglo-Saxon people and placed at the top of the racial hierarchy. Instead they were labeled "Mormons," a derogatory term used to define an ever shifting set of group characteristics similar to the ways in which "Celt" and "Dago" were sometimes used to delineate people of Irish-Catholic and Italian descent. In defining a group identity for Mormons, outsiders frequently conflated believers with other marginalized groups to imagine them as more red, black, yellow, or less white than white. Race, then, was a socially invented category and not a biological reality. It was employed by the white Protestant majority to situate Mormons at various distances away from the top of a racial hierarchy and thereby justify discriminatory policies against them.[12]

The significance of whiteness in American history has largely been taught through an immigration and labor lens. It is a story that typically involves the arrival of immigrant groups, foreigners who underwent an Americanization process as they transitioned from not-white to white. Immigrants experienced racialization in their neighborhoods and more often in America's factories, mines, and smelters as they "worked toward whiteness."[13]

Mormonism challenges that story. No longer is it solely a tale about immigration and labor. Whiteness was also a powerful mediator between the Protestant majority and the Mormon minority. The intriguing racial twist to the story lies in the fact that the Protestant majority gave birth to its own despised offspring. Nineteenth-century Mormons came from the same stock as the white Protestant majority who quickly turned on its own and then cast about for ways to warrant its behavior. A fluid, illogical, and highly charged American racial context offered a variety of readymade justifications.

Outsiders were convinced that Mormonism represented a racial—not merely religious—departure from the mainstream, and they spent considerable effort attempting to deny Mormon whiteness. Mormons thus became "inbetween peoples," somewhere between "hard racism and full inclusion," "neither securely white nor nonwhite."[14] Mormons in turn fought to maintain and ultimately claim their white identity, a fact that underscores the ways in which race was both "ascription" and "aspiration."[15] While the Mormons aspired to define themselves, outsiders ascribed certain characteristics to the Mormons. The Mormon experience, in fact, highlights both halves of that formulation uncommonly well. The consistent denial of the blessings of whiteness emphasized for Mormons the ways in which Americans essentialized skin color and found them wanting. Although Mormons initially challenged the white status quo, they eventually participated in it. It was a struggle from which they ultimately emerged triumphant—but certainly not unscathed.

* * *

When the Mormons arrived in the Salt Lake Valley in July 1847, they were fleeing almost two decades of persecution in New York, Ohio, Missouri, and finally Illinois. Suspicion, mistrust, and outright animosity followed Joseph Smith from the time in 1820 when he announced Mormonism's genesis miracle, a visitation from God the Father and his son Jesus Christ. Smith's audacious claims to heavenly intervention grew to include ancient American prophets such as the angel Moroni, as well as biblical luminaries such as Moses, Elijah, Noah, John the Baptist, Peter, James, and John. Smith went on to publish the Book of Mormon, new scripture he claimed to translate from gold plates. The text narrated God's dealings with peoples in the Americas long before Columbus arrived. In 1830 Smith formally organized the Church of Christ—later renamed the Church of Jesus Christ of Latter-day Saints—and declared it a pure restoration of the primitive church established by Jesus Christ. Persecution only intensified as adherents to the new religion gathered together for strength, unity, and worship. Driven from their homes at the hands of angry vigilantes, Mormons followed a frontier trajectory, attempting to find solace as a people apart, at the very edges of the American republic. Following the murder of Smith and his brother Hyrum in 1844, Mormons fled the United States altogether and sought refuge in isolated northern Mexico.

Less than seven months after their arrival in the Great Basin, Mexico signed the treaty of Guadalupe Hidalgo, ceding 55% of Mexican territory to the United States. The Mormons found themselves once again on American soil. Before that transfer took place, however, in late December 1847 and early January 1848 John C. Calhoun, US Senator from South Carolina, introduced a resolution into the Senate that held far-reaching and unintended implications for the Mormon refugees. US military forces then occupied Alta California or northern Mexico as well as Mexico City itself. Some of America's most ardent expansionists even clamored for the annihilation of Mexican nationhood and for the annexation of the entire country. In Calhoun's mind, to do so would have been inconsistent with the war's objectives and with America's "character and genius." More importantly, Calhoun feared that swallowing Mexico whole would be "subversive of our free and popular institutions." He made it clear that he did not have a problem with the United States taking land from Mexico as indemnity for US losses during the war, but he did object to "the annihilation of the nationality of Mexico" and the potential for "eight or nine millions of Mexicans, without a government, on our hands, not knowing what to do with them." In other words, it was not so much the acquisition of land that Calhoun opposed as it was the people on that land.[16]

Calhoun later detailed the racial ideology that lay at the heart of his concern: "We have never dreamt of incorporating into our Union any but the Caucasian race—the free white race. To incorporate Mexico, would be the very first instance of the kind of incorporating an Indian race; for more than half of the Mexicans are Indians, and the other is composed chiefly of mixed tribes. I protest against such a union as that! Ours, sir, is the Government of a white race."[17] Calhoun feared incorporating new "races" into the United States and being forced to create territorial governments for them. To do so, he fretted, would place "them on an equality with the people of the United States." He went on to suggest that in the entire history of humankind "there is no instance whatever of any civilized colored races being found equal to the establishment of free popular government." Calhoun wondered, "Are we to associate with ourselves as equals, companions, and fellow-citizens, the Indians and mixed race of Mexico?" "We make a great mistake . . . when we suppose that all people are capable of self-government." Only "people advanced to a very high state of moral and intellectual improvement are capable, in a civilized state, of maintaining free government."[18] For Calhoun, only white people possessed the race, morals, intellect, and democratic capacity necessary for self-rule.

Ironically, Mormons of mostly white American and Euro-American descent, about 17,000 strong by 1850, were then living in northern Mexico.[19] Even though their skin color conformed to Calhoun's definition of whiteness, it was not enough. Protestant America over the course of the nineteenth century constructed elaborate illogical arguments that struck at the morals, intellect, and the heart of a fabricated Mormon body. In doing so their disparate arguments gave rise to the idea that Mormonism was spawning an entirely "new race."

So rather than being an anomaly in frontier history, the Mormons helped to define America's racial and religious identity. In doing so they fit well with the people living in the last four contiguous states admitted into the United States, three of which came from land acquired as a result of the US-Mexican War. As Calhoun suggested, Congress and the federal government were the gatekeepers and as such held the power to decide who was fit for democracy. Calhoun's "Indians and mixed race of Mexico" applied to Oklahoma, initially created as Indian territory, and to the large Hispanic populations of New Mexico and Arizona. But what of the mostly white Mormons of Utah? The United States was a Protestant nation and the Constitution a Protestant document.[20] Congress and the American people made decisions along religious as well as racial lines.

Sometimes with the Mormons, however, that distinction blurred and even disappeared altogether.

In the eyes of the Protestant majority, members of the "Mormon race" were incapable of democracy. Mormons from Utah applied seven times for statehood between 1849 and 1896 but were deliberately kept at bay until the end of the nineteenth century. Polygamy, theocracy, and Mormon clannishness were deemed too un-American to allow Utah into the sisterhood of states. In building its rhetorical barriers against full citizenship for Mormons, the Protestant majority racialized a predominantly white religious group alongside Indians, blacks, Chinese, and immigrants. The Mormon experience can thus be recast as one of race, citizenship, civil rights, identity, and equality, much like that of other peoples living on land acquired from Mexico as a result of the US-Mexican War. It is only in viewing Mormon whiteness as a contested variable, not an assumed fact, that makes such a paradigm shift possible.

In nineteenth-century America, whiteness dominated the social, political, and economic life of the country. Politicians equated being white with citizenship and fitness for self-rule. It was a socially imagined category that was taken for granted, deemed normal or natural, and functioned as the preferred condition in American history. In 1790 the US Congress established a precedent when it passed a naturalization act that limited citizenship to "free white persons." Senator Calhoun reinforced that principle in his 1848 speech. The US Supreme Court in its Dred Scott decision in 1857 expressed a similar sentiment when it declared that blacks possessed no rights "which the white man was bound to respect." Even Abraham Lincoln, the future "great emancipator" announced in 1858 that he was not in favor "of making voters or jurors of negroes, nor of qualifying them to hold office, nor to intermarry with white people." As he saw it, as long as blacks and whites coexisted, "there must be the position of superior and inferior." In such a situation he favored "the superior position assigned to the white race." Following the Civil War and the demise of federal Reconstruction in the South, the Supreme Court sided with those who attempted to reassert white supremacy. In 1896 it ruled that separate-but-equal facilities were constitutional, a decision that legalized a color barrier and condoned Southern attempts to segregate most facets of American life.[21]

Even still, historian Nell Irvin Painter contends that "hatred of black people did not preclude hatred of other white people," especially those "considered different and inferior." Mormonism's founding decades coincided with a period in which whiteness itself came under question. Between the 1840s and 1920s, America underwent a dramatic industrial transformation which in turn produced a demand for cheap labor. Immigrants swarmed to America to meet that demand. Corresponding nativist backlashes also permeated the same period, especially as older Americans perceived the new influx of immigrants as threats to a smooth-functioning republic. As a result "a fracturing of monolithic whiteness" occurred, shored up by "scientific doctrines of race" which blended with "political concerns over the newcomers' fitness for self-government." These forces all combined to produce an emerging hierarchy of whiteness, with Anglo-Saxons on top and other undesirable less-white "races" situated at various lower rungs on the racial ladder.[22] Immigrants from Ireland were singled out for their "physical traits, their moral character and their peculiar customs." Their "wild look and manner, mud cabins and funeral howlings," all conjured "the memory of a barbarous age" in the mind of one observer.[23]

It was not just the Irish, however, who complicated ideas about whiteness in America. Racial schemes flourished as early as the eighteenth century with each one "offering a different number of races, even a different number of Caucasian races." Mormons, like their Protestant neighbors, tended to draw upon biblical genealogy, specifically Noah's sons, Shem, Ham, and Japheth, to divide the globe into three racial groups: yellow, black, and white, respectively. For Judeo-Christian believers, Noah's three sons repopulated the globe following the great flood and thereby accounted for racial differences. However, by the 1840s, "science" also informed racial understanding and gave rise to competing ideas regarding whiteness, a process that further complicated the racial landscape. White, Caucasian, Nordic, Anglo-Saxon, Celt, Slav, Alpine, Hebrew, Mediterranean, Iberic, Latin, and other such identifiers emerged to additionally blur racial categories. This fracturing of whiteness sent racial thinkers and the popular imagination scurrying to invent an ordered hierarchy out of a growing multiplicity of "races," with Anglo-Saxons generally at the top.[24] Mormonism was born into this era of fracturing whiteness and did not escape its consequences.

Regardless of the racial scheme employed, outsiders were uncertain where to situate Mormons. Were they more nonwhite than white, or were they more black, yellow, or red? Even though outsiders could never fully agree where to place Mormons on competing racial hierarchies, some were, nonetheless, convinced that Mormonism represented a backward racial descent. Some social evolutionists focused upon "development," contending that as societies progressed from savagery to barbarism to civilization, they left behind such barbaric practices as polygamy and a devotion to authoritarian rule.[25] Mormonism, in contrast, represented a fearful decline, especially as supposedly civilized Americans and western Europeans joined the new faith and then devolved into polygamy and despotism. As one commentator warned, if America failed to eradicate polygamy from its soil, a debilitating process would only end "in animalizing man, in corrupting the very founts of virtue and purity, and, finally, in barbarism."[26]

Rather than being an undesirable immigrant group, however, Mormons were already American insiders who were first generation converts from America or western Europe. Yet the Protestant majority repeatedly called into question their whiteness and capacity for self-rule. The Mormon experience therefore high-lights the racialization process at work from the very birth of a suspect group. Among other things, it shows how "native-stock" Americans imagined religious conversions among their own neighbors as somehow a sign of racial decline. As early as the 1840s, some cultural observers began to speak of a "Mormon race" but always in terms of racial regression, never racial progress.

In this light, Mormon Elder Berry's family violated existing American norms in a variety of ways. Elder Berry's marriages represented blatant abuses of anti-miscegenation laws then in force in most states, including Utah, that made one form or another of white and black, white and red, and/or white and yellow marriages illegal. Elder Berry's failure to segregate whiteness and his unabashed flaunting of race mixing marked him as not just religiously suspect but racially suspect as well. Clearly Mormons were not only a threat to America's religious life but also a racial threat to American democracy. The irony, of course, was that nineteenth-century Mormons were overwhelmingly white and should have easily blended into the racial mainstream. Yet their ability to blend only seemed to exacerbate anxiety among outsiders, so much so that they grew increasingly intent upon seeing a difference where none existed.

George A. Smith's experience as a Mormon missionary in 1838 is illustrative. When Smith learned of mob activity against his coreligionists in Missouri, he left his proselyting work in Kentucky to join the main body of Saints and assist them in their time of need. On his way through Missouri he stopped for the night at the home of a man who lived near DeWitt in Carroll County. Smith wisely did not identify himself as a Mormon so that his host would feel at liberty to speak to him about the Mormon expulsion then taking place. As Smith recounted it, the man "was very bloodthirsty toward the Mormons. He said he hated them worse than he did the Indians, for he could tell an Indian when he saw one, but he could not always tell a Mormon."[27] To compensate, outsiders became preoccupied with distinguishing Mormons from their neighbors. As one late-nineteenth-century memoir recounted, Missouri Mormons were "clannish, traded together, worked together, and carried with them a melancholy look." Their appearance was distinct enough "that one acquainted with them could tell a Mormon when he met him by the look upon his face almost as well as if he had been of a different color."[28] Although outsiders could never fully agree upon the color, they conjured a variety of Mormon bodies upon which to inscribe their hatred: red, black, yellow, and "not white." Mormonism thus became a religion of a different color, a pariah faith with racially aberrant adherents.

In this regard, Mormon Elder Berry's fictional family represented a culmination of nineteenth-century efforts to racialize Mormons. Their interracial solidarity underscored a blatant violation of legal segregation, antimiscegenation laws, societal norms, Protestant ideals, and generally understood standards of decency. In seeking to understand the historical roots of Elder Berry's family, a myriad of sources give life to the branches of his family tree. News clippings, editorials, pictures, stories, speeches, letters, laws, journals, diaries, and commentaries each offer a small piece in a much larger montage of efforts designed to exclude Elder Berry's family from the broader American family. That montage accentuates the intricacies of religious discrimination cloaked in racial garb and a way for outsiders to justify discriminatory policies against Mormons and mark them as unfit for self-rule. America's religious *and* racial purity were at stake.

For their part, the Mormons were by no means willing to leave the definition of their identity to others. The Mormon body, thus, became a battleground on which the LDS hierarchy and the federal government grappled to inscribe very different values, laws, and morality signifying either racial ascendancy or racial deterioration. Mormon leader George Q. Cannon, for example, asserted that "here in these [Utah] valleys, we shall raise a race of men who will be the joy of the earth, whose complexions will be like the complexions of angels—full of health, purity, innocence and vitality." Rather than racial regress, Mormons imagined racial progress through efforts to fashion an equally mythical yet racially pure family for themselves designed to counter that of Mormon Elder Berry.[29]

Mormons tapped into then-current notions of "British Israelism" and "Anglo-Saxon Triumphalism" as one means of claiming racial purity for themselves. The idea that the peoples of Great Britain were direct lineal descendants of the ten lost tribes of Israel predated Mormonism but was still current in Britain and America throughout the nineteenth century and found expression as the British-Israelism movement. At the same time, some thinkers argued that the Anglo-Saxon "race" represented the triumph of Western civilization as it marched across Europe to Britain and from Britain to America. The fact that the bulk of Mormon missionary success came from England and the "Nordic" or Scandinavian nations of Europe offered ready evidence to Mormons that their proselyting efforts were doing more than winning converts: they were redeeming ancient Israel. Mormons became convinced that the lost descendants of Israel possessed "believing blood," a condition inherent in a convert's character—in his or her blood—that prepared proselytes to respond favorably when they heard the Mormon gospel.[30] In 1851 there were more Mormons in the United Kingdom and Ireland than there were in Utah Territory. An estimated 32,000 British and Irish Latter-day Saints immigrated to the Great Basin between 1847 and 1869. As Mormon revelation put it, "The field is white already to harvest" (Doctrine and Covenants, 4:4). The white conversions that followed only added certainty to the ways Mormons constructed a triumphal Anglo-Saxon identity for themselves.[31]

British Israelism and Anglo-Saxon triumphalism as Mormon identity markers take on a different hue, however, when placed in dialogue with the negative racial identities outsiders imagined for Mormons. In this light, Mormon efforts at asserting Anglo-Saxonism can profitably be reconsidered as one facet of the Mormon move toward whiteness: it was an attempt to position Mormons at the top of America's racial ladder while others tried to push them several rungs down. It was that attack on Mormon Anglo-Saxon triumphalism that Mormon Elder Berry's imagined 1904 family captured so well.

The chapters that follow trace each of Elder Berry's children: where they came from, how they found their way into such a mythical multiracial and international Mormon family, and what that means for the history of race in America. The chronological focus is on the nineteenth-century roots of Elder Berry's family, although the concluding chapter considers what happened to Elder Berry's hypothetical descendants in the twentieth and twenty-first centuries, culminating with Mitt Romney.

Perhaps as typical in most families, not all of Elder Berry's children receive equal treatment. The six white children are considered collectively in chapter 1. Even though they were immigrants from western and northern Europe, their conversion to Mormonism marked them as suspect in the popular American imagination, so much so that outsiders perceived Mormonism as a foreign and alien problem on American soil. It was also a racial problem, an argument that unfolded in stages over time with an assumed set of group characteristics coming to define "the new race."

Chapters 2 and 3 consider Mormon Elder Berry's Indian daughter, the third child from his right (see figure 0.1). Chapter 2 traces her story up through the Mormon expulsion to the Great Basin and chapter 3 from 1847 to the end of the century. Mormon theological views of Native Americans certainly affected how outsiders imagined Mormon race mixing between red and white. Mormon leaders did in fact encourage Mormon men to marry Native American women as a means of racial uplift, even as outsiders envisioned those same marriages as evidence of racial decline. Beyond intermarriage, outsiders persistently imagined Mormons conspiring with Indians against white Americans and sometimes descending below the level of savages themselves.

The third child from Elder Berry's left, the black pickaninny girl, is the focus of chapters 4 through 7. This attention is indicative of how the black-white binary dominated racial thought in nineteenth-century America and the way it dramatically impacted Mormonism. It also indicates how fully the Mormon racial story was both ascribed from the outside and something that Mormons aspired to from within. The first black convert joined Mormonism in 1830, its founding year, and other blacks trickled in over the course of the century. At least two black men were ordained to the faith's highest priesthood before Joseph Smith's death in 1844. Yet the space for full black participation gave way, in fits and starts, across the course of the nineteenth century. By the early twentieth century Mormon leaders had put firm policies in place that racially segregated the Mormon priesthood and temples. That story is situated here within a broad national context wherein Mormons were depicted as facilitators of race mixing despite forceful internal policies to the contrary. Chapter 4 demonstrates that dialectic at work when outsiders racialized Mormons as black during the faith's first two decades and Mormons moved away from black toward white, with the two processes informing and shaping each other. Chapters 5, 6, and 7 shift to monologues with each side alternately speaking past the other. Chapter 5 focuses on the internal story, the beginning of a priesthood ban, and the way Brigham Young theologized and practiced race. Chapter 6 shifts back toward outside perceptions as interracial polygamous families and the "Mormon coon" animated public opinion, this despite Mormonism's internal policies to the contrary. Chapter 7 returns to the view from within as Mormon leaders enacted temple restrictions designed to bar black women and men from the faith's crowning rituals, solidified a race-based priesthood ban, and curtailed missionary efforts among blacks.

Chapter 8 explores Elder Berry's oriental child, the second child to his right (see figure 0.1). Muslims, Turks, and Chinese immigrants on the West Coast all provided opportunities for outsiders to orientalize Mormonism and heighten fears of civilization's backward descent. In the view of some thinkers, polygamy was racial and Eastern, marking Mormons as incapable of shouldering the blessings of democracy. In 1879 the US Supreme Court utilized such a rationale when it upheld antipolygamy legislation. Mormons, in short, represented an oriental threat on American soil and put the nation's democratic experiment at risk.

By the early decades of the twentieth century, Mormons had successfully passed as white. Yet, as the concluding chapter explores, whiteness for Mormons came at a significant cost. During the civil rights era, the price of that passage began to manifest itself as Mormons yet again found themselves on the wrong side of white. This time, segregated priesthood and temples marked them as too white, especially as LDS leaders dug in their heels in efforts to shore up black-white racial barriers. The faith's passage back toward universalism began in 1978 when it reintegrated its priesthood and temples and ushered in a racially diverse and global future, despite a persistent effort among outsiders to trap it in a pre-1978 whiteness.[32]

Elder Berry's family thus provides a useful lens into a moment of racial transition for Mormons. In this book his fabricated children serve as guides for an exploration into the intersections among race, whiteness, and religion in the nineteenth century. While Elder Berry's children act as organizational tools, this method conceals the messiness of the historical record, suggesting a systematic approach to a topic that was not systematic in its creation. Those Americans who racialized Mormons did not neatly organize their views in ways that always fit into one child or another's family tree. In 1836 Mormon missionaries in Tennessee, for example, faced rumors that they "walk[ed] out with colored women" and that their church had "long communion with the Indians."[33] Americans did not always know how to think about Mormons and race; many of the sources discussed here shift almost randomly between racial groups with no firm notion of a specific racialization in mind. Even still, evidence abounds to give life to each branch of Elder Berry's family tree.

Focusing so intently upon race also has the potential to obscure other ways in which Mormons were marginalized. The evidence presented here does not seek to supplant the argument that Mormons were denigrated as religiously different but to enrich it.[34] Racialization is an additional facet of the Mormon story that helps explain how outsiders justified discriminatory policies against this American-born faith. Although it is impossible to know how deeply the racialization rhetoric deployed against Mormons penetrated the average American mind, or what readers thought or listeners heard when they read an editorial or listened to a sermon, the evidence of racialization is overwhelming. Moreover, that evidence comes from most segments of American society, from diaries of overland immigrants to newspaper columns, from Protestant tracts and sermons to Supreme Court decisions and Congressional debates, from political cartoons to dime novels, and from letters and journals to presidential speeches. In total these sources reveal new insights into the place of whiteness and religion in America's racial history.

CHAPTER 1

"The New Race"

The northern and western European children in Elder Berry's family, the children who one might logically believe were white and acceptable, were instead subject to scorn. The Scottish boy, the wild Irish girl, the two British street urchins seemingly straight out of *Oliver Twist*, the Dutch girl, and the spinster in the making, were all at least white, children who should have drawn no special attention and been easily assimilated. Such was not the case.

In 1857, just ten years following the arrival of the Mormons as religious refugees in the Great Basin, they gained a profound understanding of the depth of suspicions then percolating in Washington, DC, about them. In what would come to be called the "Utah War," the most extensive and expensive military expedition between the US-Mexican War and the Civil War, President James Buchanan ordered a 2,500-man army to Utah to suppress a reported Mormon rebellion and replace Brigham Young as territorial governor.[1]

The Utah War left lingering fears and prejudices on both sides of the already strained relationship between the Mormons and the federal government. It further shaped and solidified long-standing public opinion about Mormons as distinct, peculiar, suspicious, and potentially dangerous outsiders. One military physician in the Utah War moved the discourse on Mormon differences firmly into the realm of the racial as he constructed an explicit description of Mormons as a degenerate and deformed race. Dr. Roberts Bartholow's first significant assignment as an army doctor was with the Utah expedition in 1857. Bartholow spent a challenging and uncomfortable winter bivouacked with the Fifth Army outside the burned-out remains of Fort Bridger in present-day southwestern Wyoming. Then in June 1858 he entered the Salt Lake Valley and caught his first glimpse of the Mormon people. In a report to the US Senate printed in 1860, he detailed his observations of the Mormons over the course of his two-year stay in Utah.[2]

"The Mormon, of all the human animals now walking this globe, is the most curious in every relation," Bartholow wrote. He called Mormonism a great social blunder that seriously affected "the physical stamina and mental health" of its adherents. As a result of their isolated location, their "grossly material" religion, and the practice of plural marriage, he concluded that "the Mormon people have arrived at a physical and mental condition, in a few years of growth, such as densely-populated communities in the older parts of the world . . . have been ages in reaching." Polygamy, in Bartholow's estimation, was the central issue, especially as it created a "preponderance of female births," high infant mortality, and a "striking uniformity in facial expression," which included "albuminous and gelatinous types of constitution" and "physical conformation" among "the younger portion" of Mormons.[3]

In Bartholow's view, polygamy forced Mormons to unduly interfere with the normal development of adolescence and was in sum a "violation of a natural law." Mormon men were at the heart of the problem, constantly seeking "young virgins, [so] that notwithstanding the preponderance of the female population, a large percentage of the younger men remain unmarried." To sustain this system Bartholow claimed that girls were married to the waiting patriarchs "at the earliest manifestations of puberty" and when that was not soon enough, Mormons made use of "means" to "hasten the period." The result was high fertility among polygamous wives, but there was also an equally high infant mortality rate, natural evidence of the wrongs bound up in polygamy. In fact, the progeny of the "peculiar institution" demonstrated its "most deplorable effects" in "the genital weakness of the boys and young men." Polygamy created a "sexual debility" in the next generation of Mormon men, largely because their "sexual desires are stimulated to an unnatural degree at a very early age, and as female virtue is easy, opportunities are not wanting for their gratification."[4]

All of this, to Bartholow, combined to create a distinct, even degraded, Mormon body. Bartholow could not tell if it was due to "the practice of a purely sensual and material religion," the "premature development of the passions," or simply to Great Basin "isolation," but no matter the reason, he observed a unique body type among the Mormons: "An expression of countenance and a style of feature, which may be styled the Mormon expression and style; an expression compounded of sensuality, cunning, suspicion, and smirking self-conceit. The yellow, sunken, cadaverous visage; the greenish-colored eyes; the thick, protuberant lips; the low forehead; the light, yellowish hair; and the lank, angular person, constitute an appearance so characteristic of the new race, the production of polygamy, as to distinguish them at a glance." "The degradation of the mother follows that of the child," Bartholow concluded, "and physical degeneracy is not a remote consequence of moral depravity."[5]

In Bartholow's mind the consequences of polygamy manifested themselves quite literally in the next generation of Mormons. Because of the "genital weakness" he observed among the men, Bartholow suspected that if Mormons received no additional converts from "outside sources," the so-called Mormon problem would "eventually die out" and solve itself. The "Mormon problem" or "Mormon question," as it was variously known in nineteenth-century politics, was cultural shorthand for the national debate over Mormonism and what to do about it. Bartholow pushed that debate in new directions as he suggested that the stream of converts, especially from the lowest stratum of European society, provided an influx of "new blood" and perpetuated "the new race" into the future.[6]

Fear of Mormon foreignness emerged early in the new faith's history and only grew more intense as the century progressed. In this regard, Bartholow both summarized and foreshadowed the Mormon question as an immigrant issue that would eventually take on international dimensions. Bartholow additionally evidenced the characteristics that outsiders frequently ascribed to the male, female, and child Mormon bodies: the men were painted as lecherous and lascivious patriarchs, the women as helpless victims enslaved in a system against their will, and the children as the deformed offspring of moral depravity.

In sum, Bartholow's report synthesized prevailing cultural ideas regarding the existence of a "Mormon race," as well as moved them squarely into the realm of racial science and medicine. His report, filed just thirty years after the founding of Mormonism, offers significant insight into the ways in which Mormon racial purity was called into question by mid-century. Despite being overwhelmingly white, Mormons were imagined as a racial deterioration from the advances of Western civilization. Even though Mormon converts hailed from America and western Europe, the very fact that they joined a suspect and hierarchical religion signaled their racial susceptibility to superstition and despotic rule. After the Mormons openly acknowledged polygamy in 1852, it confirmed to the outside world a conclusion already made, that Mormonism represented both a religious and a racial decline.

Bartholow's report was reprinted almost without critique in the *Boston Medical and Surgical Journal*, the *Georgia Medical and Surgical Encyclopedia*, the London *Medical Times and Gazette*, the *St. Louis Medical and Surgical Journal*, and *The Pacific Medical and Surgical Journal* in 1860 and 1861. This "unusually wide distribution" certainly had an impact on the way outsiders viewed the Mormon body.[7]

By December of 1860 Bartholow's report was the topic of discussion at the New Orleans Academy of Sciences meeting, where it encountered at least some resistance from one member of the medical community. Dr. James Burns was skeptical of Bartholow's methods and his conclusions. Burns resisted "speaking of any people as a new 'race,'" especially a group whose "origin did not date more than thirty years back." As Burns saw it, Mormon existence was more dependent on immigration than reproduction, a fact that complicated any notion of racial genesis. Rather than an entirely separate species, he wondered instead if Mormons were "only a variety" in the human family.[8]

As he made clear, Burns had no sympathy for Mormonism, especially "its fanaticism, its impostures, its misery, and its polygamy." Nonetheless, he could not accept Bartholow's conclusion that "in consequence of polygamy, the Mormon community has degenerated." Burns noted that "it is scarcely more than thirty years since Joe Smith, the founder, was first heard of. It is incredible, that, in so brief a period has been produced a well-marked inferior 'race,' with salient facial angles, low and retreating forehead, thick lips, green areola about the eyes, gelatinous or albuminous constitutions, and the other alleged characteristics of 'race.'" He was "at a loss" to guess what Bartholow meant by a "gelatinous or albuminous constitution" and was especially concerned with Bartholow's methodology. In Burns's estimation, Bartholow's observations had not met the "rigorous requirements of science" and were based more on impressions than the systematic gathering of data. Mormons and their offspring would need to be studied for a decade or more in an empirical manner before the existence of a new race could be verified.[9]

In contrast to Burns, other members of the New Orleans Academy pushed Bartholow's conclusions forward with inferences of their own. Professor C. G. Forshey accepted Bartholow's observations to be "just and true" and then offered collateral remarks designed to amplify their significance. "The European (or white race of men) has never been a polygamist before," Forshey asserted, "it is contrary to his nature and his instincts." The white race was "created, manifestly, for a higher destiny—an instinctive abhorrence of the brutality of promiscuous intercourse is impressed upon the males and especially the females of the race," he declared. This was true "through untold centuries and through every state of barbarism and civilization." Mormons were thus a "temporary and local exception, sustained by craft and power on the one hand, and by religious bigotry, fear, and ignorance, on the other." The isolation of the Great Basin and the Mormons' violation of the "natural law" of whiteness, he assured listeners, would eventually work out the "extinction" of the new race. As Forshey saw it, monogamy was "the normal condition of the white race of mankind" and the Mormons' violation of that normality would lead to its demise.[10]

Dr. Samuel A. Cartwright supported Forshey and Bartholow with his own observations. Polygamy not only impacted the "outward or physical form" of those who practiced it but also had a "blighting influence upon the mind and morals of the white race." The "nations and tribes" who were "most addicted to polygamy" were also "most deficient in physical prowess." "Polygamy is too injurious to the mind and body to be tolerated among a progressive and Christian people," Cartwright concluded.[11]

Members of the New Orleans Academy ultimately voted to publish Cartwright's and Forshey's papers along with excerpts from Bartholow's report in

DeBow's Review, the antebellum South's "most prominent economic journal."[12] *DeBow's* printed the entire proceedings as "Hereditary Descent; Or, Depravity of the Offspring of Polygamy among the Mormons." Dr. Burns's criticisms notwithstanding, the Academy's publication added to the growing sense in the medical community that polygamy was producing a "new race" in the American West.[13]

In 1863, after visiting Utah himself, Dr. Charles Furley, assistant surgeon of the Second California Calvary, followed Bartholow's report with one of his own. For Furley, "a marked physiological inferiority strikes the stranger, from the first, as being one of the characteristics of this people." As he observed, "a certain feebleness and emaciation of person is common amongst every class, age, and sex; while the countenance of almost all are stamped with a mingled air of imbecility and brutal ferocity." Mormon faces exhibited "a general lack of color" with "sallow and cadaverous" cheeks signaling "an absence of good health." "The eye is dull and lusterless—the mouth almost invariably coarse and vulgar." In fact, Furley concluded that "the features—the countenance—the whole face, where the divinity of man should shine out, is mean and sensual to the point of absolute ugliness." Furley's report, like Bartholow's before it, found a wide audience in a variety of medical journals.[14]

Bartholow did not retract or refine his views over time but went on to amplify them. As a professor at the Medical College of Ohio he addressed the Cincinnati Academy of Medicine in 1867 on the "Physiological Aspects of Mormonism." This time he referred to the Mormon people as a "congress of lunatics" without offering additional evidence to support his conclusions. "Lean and weak of body, depraved of mind, precocious manhood and womanhood are the characteristics of the new population," Bartholow contended. "The cadaverous face, the sensual countenance, the ill-developed chest, the long, feeble legs, and the weak muscular system . . . are recognized as the distinctive feature of the Mormon type," he said. The *Cincinnati Lancet and Observer* published his lecture in its entirety and then excerpts were reprinted in the *Boston Medical and Surgical Journal*.[15]

Bartholow and Furley were reasonable, intelligent men and medical professionals with respected reputations. Their arguments fit well within one aspect of nineteenth-century notions about race: that it was based upon phenotype or physical appearance. Race was, in part, what one could see with the eye, and both doctors were convinced that Mormons were physically peculiar. Bartholow and Furley also fed into then-current ideas about sexuality and the perceived debilitating impact that lustful desires had upon conception and the development of an unborn child. They both pointed to the "sensual" nature of Mormon countenances and alluded to the inherently lustful aspects of polygamy, which they believed passed on a carnal weakening to the next generation. Other observers would make similar claims. It is impossible to know which Mormon people the doctors observed or why they arrived at the conclusions they did. Dr. Burns was clearly skeptical of Bartholow's initial assessment, yet medical journals republished his reports and spread his findings. In sum, the doctors promulgated with scientific certainty a growing sentiment that polygamy produced physical decline.

It was only later, in 1875, that US Army surgeon E. P. Vollum filed a government report to contradict those of Furley and Bartholow. Vollum, like Burns before him, believed that it was "too early" to arrive at a solid conclusion regarding the impact of polygamy upon the "health or constitution or mental character of the Anglo-Saxon race as seen in Utah." Vollum could detect no difference between the offspring of polygamy and monogamy in Utah. Polygamy furnished "no idiocy, insanity, rickets, tubercles or struma, or other cachexia, or debasing constitutional conditions of any kind." In his estimation, the "polygamous children are as healthy as the monogamous, and the proportion of deaths is about the same." In fact, because he perceived the polygamous families he observed to be of a higher socioeconomic class, he believed any difference fell in their favor. Vollum's commentary did not receive the same type of wide distribution as the earlier reports from Bartholow and Furley and did little to stem the tide of popular opinion regarding degraded Mormon bodies.[16]

Bartholow's and Furley's reports and the subsequent attention they received marked a midpoint in the Mormon racialization process and not its beginnings. Mormon racialization began much earlier, almost with the birth of the faith, and developed deep roots in a fertile and inventive American racial culture. Like "race" in general, however, it existed solely in the minds of those who imagined it, not in a physical or biological reality. For the Mormons, the consequences were nonetheless real.

As outsiders described it, "race" was also cultural, something that Mormons created in being Mormon. Their fanaticism, perceived ignorance, lower-class status, susceptibility to despotic rule, and ultimately polygamy marked them as inferior. Some of these distinctions emphasized religious aberration more than racial.[17] Nonetheless, when typically religious markers such as fanaticism or superstition were used to stain an entire group and the implication was that these attributes were somehow inborn in those who were attracted to the Mormon message, the religious bled into the racial. In a circuitous argument, outsiders posited that Mormons were degraded because they did not act white and that they did not act white because they were degraded. Rather than race producing undesirable characteristics, outsiders implied that the undesirable characteristics of the Mormons produced a new race. The pseudosciences of phrenology and physiognomy offered ready evidence to shore up such claims and to push Mormons farther and farther away from whiteness. As the influx of "undesirable" immigrants from Europe fractured American whiteness, Mormons found themselves caught in the same nativist crosshairs as the Irish and other less-white peoples. Despite the effort of Mormon leaders to assert an Anglo-Saxon-Israelite identity for themselves, outsiders were not convinced.

* * *

The Mormon racialization process began early with a label. Outsiders quickly coined the term "Mormonite" and then "Mormon" to distinguish adherents to the new faith from their neighbors. Even then the label was useful only insofar as it accrued meaning. Initially it centered upon religious distinctions, especially belief in the Book of Mormon. Over time it facilitated the assumption that Mormons shared a group identity bound by characteristics that stretched beyond a common set of religious beliefs to include notions of physical degeneration, foreignness, intellectual inferiority, susceptibility to superstition and delusion, and ultimately racial decline.

Within a year and a half of the founding of the new faith, outsiders described "Mormonites" as a distinct subgroup of people with shared although inconsistent traits. Sometimes the descriptions were positive, but even then they served to reinforce a collective identity for Mormons shorn of individuality. One 1831 account published in the *New York American* entitled "Latest from the Mormonites" described "an active, intelligent and enterprising set of people" among whom were "many intelligent and respectable individuals." More often, however, the portrayals were negative.[18] Another 1831 report described "a sect of people called Mormonites" who were "ignorant" followers of Joseph Smith and "dupes who put implicit confidence in all his words." Other accounts variously described Mormonites as "silly sheep," "infatuated people," "a community of vagrants, lovers of idleness," "haters . . . of manual labor," "strange people," "poor fanatics," "a class of simple and credulous people," and "fanatical and deluded beings" who "degraded themselves" when they agreed to follow the "false prophet" Joseph Smith. In each case, the articles attempted to characterize a "set" or "sect of people" according to an assumed group identity.[19]

Over time, that shared identity was used to justify the expulsion of Mormons from Missouri and Illinois. A significant portion of the distinction was religious, but it frequently included racialization as an underlying rationale. In 1833, 1836, and 1838 respectively, Mormons were expelled from their homes in Jackson County, Missouri; Clay County, Missouri; and from the state of Missouri altogether. Much of the racialization that took place in these expulsions conflated Mormons with Indians and blacks as justifications for driving white people from their homes. Yet a growing sense that Mormons were degraded whites bound together by a shifting set of degenerate traits or that they were "foreigners" or "aliens" also permeated the discussion. In every situation "Mormon" became a distinct nomenclature employed by outsiders to differentiate between themselves as "citizens," people with rights to life, liberty, and property—or the blessings of whiteness—and "Mormons" as people shorn of those same basic rights.

Jackson County "citizens" described their Mormon neighbors as "deluded fanatics or weak and designing knaves." Had they been "respectable citizens in society" and thus merely religiously "deluded," they "would have been entitled to our pity rather than to our contempt and hatred," one removal petition declared. However, some old settlers found that, with few exceptions, the physical appearance, manners, and conduct of the Mormons signaled that they "were of the very dregs of that society from which they came, lazy, idle and vicious."[20] Another account charged Jackson County Mormons with "gathering together the scum of the earth" and deemed it "extremely natural" that Missourians would "feel disposed to rid themselves of such a pest." The large majority of Jackson County residents, by contrast, were "fearless, honest, and independent citizens."[21]

Similar distinctions were drawn in both Ohio and Missouri as tension between Mormons and their neighbors again escalated in the mid-1830s. One outsider from Kirtland, Ohio, admonished Missourians to protect themselves from "the incursions of [Mormon] savages" who were then on their way to Missouri. He bemoaned the fact that Kirtland was "completely over run" with Mormons or, more precisely, "cursed with them." As he put it, "no greater curse could befall any people than to have these fiends in human shape settle among them." He called the Mormons a "scourge" and warned Missourians of an impending "immense swarms of them." They were people "mostly from the New England States [and] Upper & Lower Canada," yet despite their generally favorable geographic origins, their collective character was deemed "indolent," "vicious," and "unprincipled." The movement of these Mormons represented a transfer of the "worst part of the population of the East to the West," a group of people to whom "the inmates of the Ohio Penitentiary" were deemed "respectable" by comparison.[22]

Missourians used similar rhetoric to expel Mormons from Clay County in 1836. One petition drew a distinction between the "people commonly called Mormons" and the "citizens" of Clay County. The Mormons, it insisted, were "Eastern men, whose manners, habits, customs and even dialect, are essentially different from our own." It urged them to "seek a home where they may obtain large and separate bodies of land, and have a community of their own." If, instead, the Mormons insisted on "flooding the county," civil war would be the "inevitable consequence."[23] It was a clear signal that some Clay County residents deemed removal the only option for dealing with their Mormon neighbors.

In response, the state of Missouri attempted to relegate Mormons to their own county by 1836. Yet over the next two years a continuing influx of Mormons to other counties again raised the ire of Missourians and led to a complete Mormon expulsion. This time Missourians elaborated upon the perceived foreign and alien aspect of Mormons as one justification for their ouster. Residents of DeWitt in Carroll County complained that "a large portion of the people called Mormons . . . [were] from different parts of the world" and they were therefore justified in "waging a war of extermination" against them or removing them from the state.[24] DeWitt residents also asked for the cooperation of their Howard County neighbors "in expelling the fanatics," people who they deemed "mostly aliens by birth, and aliens in principle from the county."[25]

So within ten years of the founding of this new American faith, outsiders derisively labeled its adherents and began to invent for them a variety of degraded identities. In defining a shared set of Mormon characteristics outsiders began a prolonged process by which they replaced Mormon individuality with traits they assumed applied to all members of the group.

Some Latter-day Saints acknowledged this process and were cognizant of their growing pariah status. In 1834 one Mormon described the Saints as a people "few in number" compared with "the multitudes" that surrounded them. He fully recognized that they were deemed a "by-word and the but[t] of ridicule," a group collectively denigrated as "deluded and deceived."[26] Mormon leaders sometimes attempted to push back against such criticism such as when they asserted that the Saints were "neither deluded nor fanatics." Instead, they were similar to other Americans who had a "claim on the world for land and for a living." Despite the "false reports" which vilified them as "meaner than the savages," Mormons, like their "venerable fathers" before them, were in search of "Independence and liberty."[27]

Following the Mormon eviction from Missouri, apostle Parley P. Pratt best articulated the ways in which the rhetoric of expulsion became racialized. He complained that as the Mormons were driven from their homes "most of the papers of the State" described them as "Mormons, in contradistinction to the appellation of citizens, whites, &c., as if we had been some savage tribe, or some colored race of foreigners."[28]

Nonetheless, Mormon racialization continued unabated. In 1841 the process began in Illinois when outsiders and former Latter-day Saints referred to Mormons as somehow different from white. That year the *New York Herald* reported that "excitement" against the Mormons was "increasing very fast" in the vicinity of Nauvoo. As the *Herald* described it, "The conduct of Jo. Smith and the other leaders, is such as no community of *white men* can tolerate." It was "the entire absence of all moral and religious principle" which rendered them "obnoxious to the Gentiles of all denominations, wherever they reside."[29]

One resident of La Harpe, Illinois, about twenty-five miles East of Nauvoo, expressed a similar sentiment. As he put it, Joseph Smith surrounded himself with "thieves aduterers [sic] fornicaters [sic] pick . . . pockets cut throats knaves & Murders [sic]." They were a disparate and unseemly gathering of hangers-on, people of "all nations and colours [sic] such as could not stay any where else."[30]

"The population of the holy city . . . is rather of a mixed kind," another observer of Nauvoo commented. "The general gathering of the saints has . . . brought together men of all classes and characters. The great majority of them are uneducated and unpolished people," he wrote. "A great proportion of them consist of converts from the English manufacturing districts, who were easily persuaded by Smith's missionaries to exchange their wretchedness at home for ease and plenty in the promised land."[31]

As outsiders perceived it, then, Mormons were far too inclusive in the creation of their religious kingdom. They accepted "all nations and colours," they welcomed "all classes and characters," they included "aliens by birth" and people from "different parts of the world" as members of God's earthly family. Edward Strutt Abdy, a British official on tour of the United States in 1833 and 1834, pointed to this very openness as one potential source of tension between the Mormons and broader society. He noted that the Mormons lived in common and honored the principles of "equality and harmony" in their interactions with each other, including with Indians and blacks. Abdy specifically pointed to the Book of Mormon's lofty ideal that "all are alike unto God," including black and white, bound and free, male and female, and heathen, Jew, and Gentile (2 Nephi 26:33). With such an expansive vision articulated in the Mormons' new book of scripture, it was no wonder that they were persecuted, Abdy wrote. The perception that they were too inclusive earned them fear and scorn in a national culture that favored exclusion, segregation, and even the extermination of undesirable "races."[32]

When John C. Bennett, one time confidant of Joseph Smith Jr. and an influential Mormon in Nauvoo, left the faith, he tapped into that national culture and turned its rhetoric against the Mormons. His 1842 exposé expressed a growing sentiment designed to racialize the Mormons and call their whiteness into question. He told his readers of the Mormons' plan to one day return to Jackson County, Missouri, where "in that delightful and healthy country they expect to find their Eden, and build the New Jerusalem." This religious vision was too much for the embittered Bennett to stomach. "Joe had better take another look through his peep-stone," Bennett wrote, because the Lord intended that "white folks, and not *Mormons*, shall possess that goodly land."[33]

By the mid-1840s, as outsiders were making a case for the Mormon expulsion from Illinois, the descriptions of Latter-day Saints morphed into that of a "Mormon race." Although "race" in these accounts was applied loosely and did not equate to its later usages by the medical community, it was nonetheless a step in that process and a way to collectively mark Mormons peculiar and worthy of extermination. The *New York Herald* in 1843 reported on a growing animosity in Illinois toward the Saints, so much so that the *Herald* believed it "threatened the extirpation of the whole Mormon race." The St. Louis *New Era* argued that the growing crisis might be averted "if the Mormons as a religious body, will but eschew politics and amalgamate with our citizens." The paper feared that it was too late for such a remedy, however, so wide had the chasm grown between "Mormons" and "citizens."[34]

The following year, on the very day that a mob with blackened faces murdered Joseph and Hyrum Smith at Carthage, Illinois, the *Cleveland Herald* ran a story on the so-called Mormon War in Illinois. It noted that in recent weeks outsiders were "all breathing extermination to the whole Mormon race."[35] Similarly in 1845, when Illinois Governor Thomas Ford recounted his version of events surrounding the murder of the Smith brothers, he recalled the heightened desire among the most rabid outsiders "for the extermination of the Mormon race."[36]

Although extermination was not the outcome in Illinois, vilification and expulsion were. Mormons again recognized their pariah status and even began to desire a separation from their neighbors. By 1845 they were searching for land upon which "a white man's foot never trod" and a place where no one could "molest and make us afraid."[37] Apostle Heber C. Kimball told a Mormon audience that because they were not "considered suitable to live among 'white folks'" they would grow their own crops and make their own clothes and thereby insulate themselves from outsiders. He also noted that outsiders considered Mormons to be "the offscouring of the earth," but he countered that they were "the best people of the age, and God knows it, and the devil knows it, and everybody else knows that this is not a bad people." In his mind it was only a matter of washing their faces, combing their hair, and wearing their finest clothes and then people would say "we are the best looking fellows in the world."[38] A few months later Kimball again acknowledged, "We are not accounted as white people, and we don't want to live among them. I had rather live with the buffalo in the wilderness," he insisted.[39]

* * *

By the 1840s outsiders began to imagine physical differences associated with the Mormon body and to assume that Mormons were an oddity to gawk at. In 1846, following their expulsion from Illinois, Mormons were strung out in various camps across Iowa where they became a peculiarity, something to look at but also to fear: "It is quite a curiosity for the inhabitants here to see a 'Mormon.' The women and children all came running to the doors to look at us as we passed by," Mormon Warren Foote recorded in his diary. "The most of their talk is about the 'Mormons' coming down and killing them all off."[40]

Such curiosity even stretched across international borders. An American visitor to Germany in the 1850s reported that the interest of Germans was "about equally divided between Negroes, Indians, and Mormons." In fact, he said, "on hardly any subject have I been more questioned than concerning the

Mormon. . . . If I had a live one to exhibit I could make a small fortune among these speculative, philosophic, meditative *Deutschen*."[41] Indeed, travelers from across Europe made a point of visiting among the Mormons as a part of their journeys to America.[42] French writer and feminist Olympe de Joaral Audouard made her way to Utah in 1868. "We were very curious to see these famed Latter-day Saints," she recalled. When she and her fellow passengers received word that a Mormon family would host them upon their arrival in the territory, they were thrilled. "At last we were going to contemplate these seventeen-strong families with only one man!" she wrote.[43] Other European and American travelers were also curious to visit among the Mormons. As late as the 1880s, one travel narrative recounted a passenger train's arrival at Salt Lake City filled with "a host of tourists . . . all rife to see a Mormon with his retinue of wives."[44]

Even before Mormons openly acknowledged polygamy as a practice, however, popular perceptions suggested that they were physically distinct. The pseudoscience of physiognomy, along with the related field of phrenology, grew in popularity in the 1840s and even gained support from a few prominent intellectuals.[45] These two disciplines created scientific context within which nineteenth-century Americans could look at the Mormon body and find it racially suspect.

As a field of inquiry physiognomy suggested that one could assess a person's mental and moral disposition, as well as his character and personality traits, through a study of his facial features. Those who practiced physiognomy, for example, believed that "inquisitiveness" was manifest in a "wedge-shaped face and protruding nose indicative of a prying disposition." "Ambitiousness or desire of pre-eminence" was evident in those with "coarse, strong, well-defined features," such as Napoleon the Great. "Autohegemony or self-esteem" carried a disposition "to draw the head backwards and upwards." "Tonireceptionality" or "the ability for appreciating sounds" could be detected in a person with a "round, outstanding ear."[46]

In contrast, phrenologists focused primarily upon the brain and skull and believed that certain "faculties" were localized in specific areas of the brain. As one phrenology publication explained, the forehead was seen as "the seat of intellect," while the lower back of the head was the site for "the affections." The sides of the head housed "the executive, propelling, constructive, and economical powers," and the top of the head was the location "of the moral, spiritual, and religious sentiments." Within each of those areas were further subdivisions into more specific faculties such as "friendship," "hope," "spirituality," "veneration," "firmness," "cautiousness," and "inhabitiveness" ("a desire for a home, place of abode, or haven of rest"). Of particular applicability in the Mormon case was "conjugal love" or the "monogamic faculty, giving the desire to reciprocate the love of *one* in matrimony." A person with an excess of this faculty exhibited a "morbid fervor of attachment," while someone deficient experienced an "aversion to permanent union." The faculty of "amativeness" involved "connubial love" and created an "attractiveness to the opposite sex, and a desire to unite in wedlock." Those with an excess of "ama-tiveness" demonstrated a tendency to "grossness and licentiousness," and those with a deficiency were indifferent "toward the other sex."[47]

Phrenologists believed that the localized areas of the brain varied in size ac-cording to a person's capacity for the corresponding faculty. They measured, physically examined, and otherwise assessed the size, shape, and various bumps and contours of a person's head as a means to determine his or her propensity for a given faculty. Skeptics and detractors sometimes derisively labeled the practice "quackery" or "bumpology," but it nonetheless influenced racial thought in Amer-ica, especially as phrenologists used their discipline to rank the races according to the characteristics of the brain. Indians and blacks were deemed inferior in such rankings, but they were not the only "races" under scrutiny.[48] Physiognomy and phrenology helped to inform public perceptions of Mormons as well.

On three occasions Joseph Smith allowed different phrenologists to ex-amine his head. He assented to one of the resulting charts being published in the Nauvoo *Wasp* newspaper in order to satisfy "a large number of persons in different places" who had "manifested a desire to know the Phrenological de-velopment of Joseph Smith's head." He was willing to "let the public judge for themselves whether Phrenology proves the reports against him true or false." He included the same chart in his history, but he did so, he said, only "for the gratification of the curious, and not for respect to Phrenology."[49]

The published chart ranked Smith with an extreme susceptibility for the fondness for the "company of the other sex" as well as high in "secretiveness." He also ranked high in "ambition for distinction," "aspiration for greatness," "kind-ness, goodness, tenderness, sympathy," "firmness," "hope," and "Marvelousness" or "belief in the supernatural." Brigham Young, Willard Richards, Hyrum Smith, and other Mormon leaders also had phrenological readings, and some Latter-day Saints subscribed to *The Phrenological Journal* or became phrenologists themselves. In fact, after the Saints' migration to the Great Basin there developed a somewhat friendly relationship between some Mormons and phrenologists.[50]

Perhaps one reason for such an accord was unwillingness on the part of phre-nological publications to endorse the popular sentiment that polygamy produced degraded offspring. The *Phrenological Journal,* for example, sometimes included articles favorable—or at least relatively moderate—in their tone toward the Mormons. "As regards offspring," the *Journal* wrote in 1871, "it may be said that the Mormon children are not physically degenerated through polygamy." The reason, the *Journal* said, was that "the associations of the sexes are regulated by religious motives and for the purpose of offspring." Unlike most publications that essentialized polygamy, the *Journal* downplayed its importance: "It should always be borne in mind that after all the attention given to the polygamic, the vast majority of Mormon society are practically in the monogamic state."[51] It was an effort to deemphasize polygamy and normalize Mormon marital practices, which was rare in the nineteenth century.[52] Nonetheless, the *Journal* argued that monogamy was the result of civilization's long progress and thus became the "institution of the superior races." Polygamy, in contrast, was only "found in the primitive states of society" and was never the "*result* of social progress."[53]

As for "phrenological and physiological considerations," the *Journal* noted that phrenologists had "examined the heads of hundreds of the representative men and women of the Mormons" and otherwise became acquainted with them. Their findings varied between American and European Mormons as well as between leaders and followers. Among the leaders, their phrenological developments were deemed "rather powerful," especially in the "religious and moral regions" even though they lacked "high culture." The "pioneering" class of Mormons were similar in "rugged appearance" to their counterparts in "any part of America." The European converts, in contrast, were "simple minded people from the working-classes, both of the cities and agricultural districts." Even though some classified the Mormon Elders as "knaves" and their converts as "dupes," the *Journal* argued that "they have the capacity and weight of the Anglo-Saxon head, and are wonderfully adopted for the formation of the body of a new society of a hardy, industrious, conservative people."[54]

Even though the *Phrenological Journal* was atypical in its relatively balanced perspective toward the Mormon body, the very fact that Mormons were included in its pages at all only added weight to the nineteenth-century perception that Mormons were physically distinct from the broader American population. The *Journal* sometimes featured prominent "Christian" or Protestant leaders in its pages, but it did not typically treat mainstream Protestant religious adherents as a separate people the same way it did the Mormons.[55] In 1871 the *Journal* ran five articles on Mormons or Mormon-related topics. That same year it also examined Tasmanians, Japanese, Chinese, Jews, Italians, Grecians, and American Indians but never Methodists, Presbyterians, or Baptists. It was another indication of the ways in which Mormons entered the scientific mind, not merely as a religion, but as a physically peculiar people.[56]

Even though phrenologists tended toward a moderate assessment of the Mormon body, at least one advocate of physiognomy, Dr. Joseph Simms, used the Mormons to physically distinguish the face of a polygamist from that of someone who favored monogamy. As Simms argued, a person's inclination toward "Monoeroticity" or "Monogamy" versus "Polyeroticity" or "polygamy" was evidenced in the shape and vertical opening of the eye. "The amount of love for the opposite sex may be known by the fullness of the eyes," he wrote, "and its quality by the shape of the commissures, or opening between the lids of the eyes. When the opening is quite almond-shaped, promiscuous love prevails in that form; if the commissure has great vertical measurement, the love is connubial."[57]

To illustrate his point, Simms's book featured the face and eyes of Brigham Young and Mrs. Margaret Fuller Ossoli, a prominent journalist and woman's right advocate (see figure 1.1). Young's eye was almond shaped, flat, and the lid partially closed, a shape and narrow opening most comparable to that of a hog. For Simms it was clear and physical evidence of Young's "disposition to love many." Ossoli died tragically in a shipwreck and was said to have chosen to drown rather than be separated from her lover, a sign of her strong devotion to one man. Her eyes were large and round with a wide vertical opening, similar to the eye of a dove—a bird that mates for life (see figure 1.2). Simms thus concluded, "In the range of Physiognomy everything partakes of a lower nature when built upon the wide and low form." The almond-shaped eyes with their "less vertical measurement" produced an "exhibition of love" that was "more bestial in its nature, and has little in common with Monoeroticity, which is pure and angelic in its tone."[58]

Other observers also pointed to the eyes, faces, and countenances of Mormons as distinct, generally in negative and ominous tones. A writer for *Harper's Weekly* claimed in 1858 that he had "never yet seen a Mormon but that something ailed his eyes. They are sunken, or dark, or ghastly, or glaring. There is certainly some mania in all Mormon eyes; none of them can look you straight

Figure 1.1 "Monoeroticity Large—Mrs. Margaret Fuller Osoli, who preferred to drown rather than to leave her husband. Monoeroticity Small—Brigham Young, the noted polygamist." Reprinted from Joseph Simms, *Nature's Revelations of Character; or, Physiognomy Illustrated: A Description of the Mental, Moral and Volitive Dispositions of Mankind, as Manifested in the Human Form and Countenance*, 3d ed. (New York: D. M. Bennett, Liberal and Scientific Publishing House, 1879), 158.

Figure 1.2 "Polyeroticity Small—The eye of Mrs. Margaret F. Osoli; Polyeroticity Large—The eye of Brigham Young. Polyeroticity large—The head of a Hog; Polyeroticity Small—the head of a Turtle-dove." Reprinted from Joseph Simms, *Nature's Revelations of Character; or, Physiognomy Illustrated. A Description of the Mental, Moral and Volitive Dispositions of Mankind, as Manifested in the Human Form and Countenance,* 3d ed. (New York: D. M. Bennett, Liberal and Scientific Publishing House, 1879), 163.

or steadily in the face."[59] Another *Harper's* reporter described Mormon apostle Heber C. Kimball's face in similar terms: "Under projecting eyebrows roll two bright, cunning eyes. Their expression is sly and rat-like, vivid and repulsive."[60] Another account described Kimball with a "very keen, sharp eye" who was most notorious for his "vulgar and coarse speech." Among the Mormon leadership, it noted, two or three had "fine faces—such as you would meet in intellectual or business society in Boston or New York—but the strength of most of the party seems to lie in narrowness, bigotry, obstinacy."[61]

Joseph Smith and Brigham Young became popular targets of efforts to scrutinize Mormon faces. One observer described Smith's eyes as "grey and unsteady in their gaze, and his face and general physiognomy coarse and unmeaning."[62] Another account claimed that from a young age Smith "appeared dull and utterly destitute of genius," while a different report alleged that "his countenance exhibits a curious mixture of the knave and the clown. . . . He has a downcast look, and possesses none of that open and straightforward expression which generally characterizes an honest man."[63] "Never did we see a face on which the hand of Heaven had more legibly written—rascal," a different critic said of Smith. "That self-complacent simper, that sensual mouth, that leer of vulgar cunning, tell us at one glance the character of their owner."[64]

Meanwhile, a visitor to Salt Lake City in 1865 found Young to be "a very hale and hearty looking man, young for sixty-four, with a light gray eye, cold and uncertain, a mouth and chin betraying a great and determined will—handsome perhaps as to presence and features, but repellent in atmosphere and without magnetism."[65] Five years later, a visitor described Young with "as clear an eye and as bright a complexion as if he were a hale English farmer," yet there was still "something fox-like or cunning lurking under the superficial good nature and kindliness of the face." The "expression of his face, especially of his eyes," conjured for the visitor "a strange blending of vanity, craft and weakness."[66] Another report called Brigham Young's brain "foul and lustful" and described polygamy as Young's way of gratifying his "sensual bestiality."[67]

One local satirical magazine carried the animalistic nature of Mormonism to its extreme when it imagined Brigham Young's body as a new species (see figure 1.3). The cartoon featured Young as the "cephalopod of the Great Basin,"

Figure 1.3 "The Cephalopod of the Great Basin—Genus Polypi Mormoni Priesthoodi." Reprinted from *Enoch's Advocate*, 11 May 1874. Special Collections, J. Willard Marriott Library, University of Utah, Salt Lake City.

a riff on an octopus-like marine animal with a prominent head and armlike tentacles extending from it. The newspaper called it "one of the most horrible and repulsive sea monsters" known to exist and noted that it was sometimes called the "Devil Fish," a fitting metaphor for the Mormon prophet. In Young's case the tentacles of polygamy, cooperation, consecration, blind obedience, temple endowments, blood atonement, and tithing corrupted the Mormon body into its own scientific classification, "Genus Polypi Mormoni Priesthoodi." This visual depiction of the degrading and physically transformative power of Mormonism tapped into current efforts to classify and order the animal world according to a scientific taxonomy.[68]

Such descriptions of Young, Smith, and other Mormon leaders were typical. Their eyes and faces exhibited their true characters. If there was something positive in the Mormon face, it was merely a mask hiding more sinister features. One visitor suggested that Mormons wore a "thin disguise of loyalty and disposition to succumb," which was used to obscure the lurking reality of Mormon disloyalty and defiance of federal authority.[69]

Other observers looked to the Mormon followers themselves for additional evidence of deterioration in their faces and bodies. A visitor to a Mormon worship service, for example, called it a "strange assemblage" and focused upon the faces of the people she saw. "If I were a scientific phrenologist, I would undertake some classification," she wrote. "There were a few intelligent countenances, interspersed with sly cunning and disgusting sensuality; in both male and female, a large mass of credulity, and an abundance of open-mouthed, gawky stupidity."[70] Sensuality and ignorance were common themes to which outsiders repeatedly returned to reinforce the ways in which traditional Protestant morality was at stake and also to assert that truly intelligent people would never fall for such a religious fraud as Mormonism.

Most commentators focused on the deteriorating impact of polygamy on Victorian expectations of masculinity and femininity. A gendered reading of Mormon bodies emerged with men as despots and tyrants and women as helpless, sensual, and depraved victims. Children also received attention, both for their sheer numbers and for the perception that polygamy produced a gender imbalance with more girls than boys—despite considerable evidence to the contrary. Outsiders also believed that polygamy produced sickly, deformed, cursed, or immoral children, clear evidence of the ways in which Mormonism created racial decline. As one critic put it, those who practiced it were "moral lepers" who filled the "land with a degenerate race."[71]

Former Mormon John Hyde Jr. published an attack on the faith in 1857 in which he described the deteriorating impact of polygamy upon Mormon men, women, and children. As Hyde saw it polygamy made men "heartless," "liars," and "brutes." It also turned "old men with white hair and wrinkled faces" into lechers who, instead of "thinking of God and their graves," went "hunting after young girls." Once married, it further deteriorated the men so that they lost "all decency or self-respect, and degenerate[d] into gross and disgusting animals. Many of them frequently sleep with two of their wives in the same bed," Hyde reported with considerable contempt.[72]

Mormon men were so driven by lust that observers imagined convoluted marital relations in Utah as the result. One sensationalized novel recounted one man who married a divorced woman with "three little girls, all under the age of seven. When the girls grew up he married all three, thus becoming the husband of four women, though he had but one mother-in-law, that mother-in-law being his own wife." If that were not bad enough, the same source described a different man who married a woman with an adolescent daughter. When the daughter reached womanhood "she was married to the father of her mother's husband, making him his step-daughter's step-son, and when a son was born to the father, the mother's husband became half brother to his own grandchild." Another account described a sixteen-year-old girl with a two-month-old deformed baby who was "the wife of her own father."[73]

Others described Mormon men as "slave drivers" who had no feeling toward their wives. One antipolygamy publication told of a particularly ruthless patriarch who would lash his wife as if she were "a refractory horse or mule." In fact, "he often whipped her more severely than he would his animals, for he held a mule in far higher estimation than he did a woman." Replacing his wife would be easy, "but it cost money to get a mule."[74] Mormon men were thus presented as brutal, lascivious patriarchs—men who violated the liberty and morality of the American family.

As for the women, Hyde contended that polygamy had different impacts on first wives than subsequent wives. The first wife's face showed the marks of sorrow and despair once her husband took additional wives. It ruined her body and soul and in many instances she lost control of her home, her marital bed, and her freedom. Hyde described one such first wife as a "wasted and sallow wreck of a woman." Some resorted to whisky in an effort to "kill feeling," while others tried to be indifferent to avoid becoming "depraved." Others still were blindly obedient, Hyde said, "degraded into slavery by this Mormon stepback into barbarism."[75]

A variety of outside observers concurred. One account described a cruel and demanding second wife, a "coarse, blowzy, greasy specimen of womanhood" who moved in and usurped the first wife's authority and ruled the home "with a rod of iron."[76] Another first wife, after being "robbed of the affections of a once kind and loving husband," wore "suffering and blasted hopes" in "every feature of her face." So great was her "life of torture that her countenance plainly said to the world, 'I am heartbroken.'"[77] Still another woman bore upon "her face the marks of the great suffering she has passed through."[78] Polygamy, in short, was a "degradation of womanhood" that turned plural wives into cowering shells of their former selves.[79]

Beyond polygamy, outsiders tended to characterize Mormon women by their perceived ugliness. Mark Twain most famously called them "poor, ungainly and pathetically 'homely' creatures." He was so taken aback by their appearance that he posited that the man who was willing to marry one of them "has done an act of Christian charity which entitles him to the kindly applause of mankind, not their harsh censure." Even more so, the man who married sixty of them performed "a deed of open-handed generosity so sublime that the nations should stand uncovered in his presence and worship in silence."[80]

This theme was already in circulation before Twain popularized it. "There is not a handsome woman in the country; they are the worst looking . . . I ever saw," one news account proclaimed.[81] Mormon women were specimens of "the lowest class of ignorance," another visitor wrote. The elderly females "were destitute of those mild, refined, and softened feelings which often form such an agreeable relief to old age." Instead, they were of "the wrinkled, spiteful, hag-like order." The younger women were "more repulsive still—there was no youthful vivacity of appearance or manner. They were stupid, and sensuality had swallowed up all pure womanly feelings."[82] One overland traveler who stopped in Salt Lake City found the women "to belong to an ignorant class & all of them wear a sad & dejected look."[83] A US Army soldier found the men to be "fine looking fellows," but called the women "ugly." He opined that if the women he met were representative of what Mormonism had to offer, then one woman was more than enough for him.[84] Another visitor confessed that he was "not favorably impressed with the beauty of the Mormon ladies" and found them to be "ugly and deformed females."[85] "There are no handsome women in Utah" another report declared; "the great body of Mormon women are rough field laborers" who lead "a purely animal life."[86]

In the popular imagination polygamous unions also had a negative impact upon the children. "Monogamic countries" produced more boys than girls, Hyde claimed, while "polygamic countries" produced the opposite. "Were the inhabitants of Utah, therefore, to grow up, intermarry without any mixture from other incoming people and practice polygamy as they now practice it, the male race in a few generations would become extinct," he argued. In his observation, the more wives a man had "the greater proportion of female to male children" he produced. Mormon children, he believed, were sickly and suffered from high rates of infant mortality. "I think I can say, more children die in Salt Lake City, notwithstanding the salubrity [sic] of its climate, than in any other city of its size in the Union."[87]

Other commentators worried about Mormon fertility and the number of children that polygamy produced. One overland traveler was struck by "the number of little towheaded 'Saints' running about." As she feared, "Mormonism was evidently on the increase" and it would take many years before "the race would be extinct." Another critic decried Mormon parents who, in the guise of "modern vermin," perpetuated "their kind in the disgusting ratio of other loathsome creatures." The children of "such paternity" constituted a "Pariah race" on American soil.[88]

Other detractors referred to Mormon children as the "putrid production" of polygamy, "ugly," "ungovernable," "vicious, profane, and obscene." John Hyde said they were filled with "mischievous cruelty," "cheating" dispositions, "pompous bravado," and "manly talk." As he put it, every visitor to Salt Lake City proclaimed them to be "the most whisky-loving, tobacco-chewing, saucy and precocious children he ever saw." Other observers variously described Mormon children as "wretches" who possessed a "dull & in numerous instances, almost an idiotic expression of countenance." They were "a neglected, uncared-for set, generally dirty and ill clad," urchins who were "suffered to grow up in ignorance and vice." As one critic put it, polygamy was a "curse bequeathed to children," a system "that makes marriage a by-word and puts the brand of shame on the innocent foreheads of little children."[89]

The Mormon family was clearly a departure from the ideal American family, a point made abundantly clear in a depiction published in the pictorial magazine *Wild Oats* in 1872 (see figure 1.4). The cartoon was sardonically titled "Brigham Young the Great American Family Man," an effort to portray how far Young's family departed from American ideals. It featured a mockingly large Young in the foreground holding two sickly and poorly clad children. A string of toddlers and older children followed behind; the first clutched Young's coattail dressed only in a nightshirt and stovepipe hat. A homely wife stood behind Young, noticeably pregnant—again—despite her advanced age. She puffed smoke from a tobacco pipe, seemingly oblivious to the throng of children that surrounded her. The cartoon captured many of the ideas then in circulation about the Mormon family, especially its debilitating impact upon the "Great American Family."[90]

* * *

A common theme that percolated throughout the nineteenth century went beyond the eyes and face to suggest that Mormons were more animalistic or devilish than human, especially as they were sometimes described with cloven feet and horns. In 1834 the first anti-Mormon book claimed that when a person truly understood Mormonism "the cloven foot is uncovered—the deformity brought into open day light."[91] This notion was likely borrowed from Christian descriptions of Jews as spiritually and physically corrupt dating back to medieval Europe. Jewish cloven feet and horns offered evidence of that corruption and equated Jews with Satan's minions or devils.[92] The messages were similar among

Figure 1.4 "Brigham Young: The Great American Family Man." Reprinted from *Wild Oats*, 28 March 1872. L. Tom Perry Special Collections, Harold B. Lee Library, Brigham Young University, Provo, Utah.

the Mormons. As one outsider put it in 1841, "The absurdities of Mormonism, and the wickedness of its spirit and design" were "palpable matters in which the cloven foot of the great beast has been displayed."[93]

Mormons themselves were aware of such descriptions, and some of the earliest evidence of the growing denigration of the Mormon body emerged from inside sources. At Nauvoo, Joseph Smith's older brother Hyrum Smith noted in April 1844 that outsiders were then moving to the city, something they felt safe to do only after they confirmed "that the Mormons had not got horns."[94]

William Smith, Mormon apostle and younger brother to Joseph and Hyrum Smith, complained later that year that outsiders imagined a variety of negative stereotypes associated with the Mormon city of Nauvoo and by extension the Mormon people. He protested that travelers and others gave "many faint and incorrect descriptions" of Nauvoo so that "some have thought the temple built upon moonshine, and the city a barbarian—ugly, formal with head and horns." What was it, Smith rhetorically wondered, that "smote the daughters of Zion with scabby heads, and numbered the thousands of saints . . . with goats, and cursed them above all horned cattle?"[95]

Two years later, as Mormons fled Illinois, one Saint faced such misperceptions firsthand. As Warren Foote and other Mormons searched in rural Iowa for a mill to grind their grain, Foote stopped at a fork in the road to ask a man plowing his field the way to the mill. The man asked if they were Mormons, to which Foote responded that they were. He then yelled to his boys "to come and see some 'Mormons.'" As Foote recalled, "They all came up to the wagon, although the boys were very shy. After looking at us he said to the boys 'They haven't got any horns have they' 'and they look like other folks don't they.' This he said laughing as he told us that the boys had thought that the 'Mormons' were terrible looking creatures."[96]

In 1858 the popular pictorial magazine *Yankee Notions* picked up on this theme to depict Brigham Young as an authoritarian mountain ram who presided over fawning followers (see figure 1.5). The picture mocked the supposed "Liberty" of the Mormons as they all bowed in subservience before their horned leader. Two years later *Vanity Fair* magazine again gave Young horns and cloven feet, this time depicting him as a half-human, half–Greek God Pan, a mythical deity known for his sexual prowess and seductive reed flute (see figure 1.6). In this picture, Young was blindfolded with only one eye open to the corruption and murderous exploits of his followers, even as he warned outsiders away by threatening execution if they trespassed on Mormonism. As *Vanity Fair* saw it, Utah Territory under Brigham Young was more savage than when "primitive bears and indigenous buffaloes" freely roamed the region. The "Valley of the Lake of Salt" had never witnessed "half so beastly a sight as that of the grizzly goat-head, Brigham, leading his hoofed and horned flock to the sound of his Pandean, polygam pipe." The refrain continued throughout the century, becoming a cultural shorthand for Mormon distinction, sometimes lore to be dismissed in its absurdity even as the very dismissal reinforced Mormon peculiarity. The hoof and horn continued to symbolize corruption, animalistic degradation, and, as *Vanity Fair* put it, the "demi-semi-demoniac" aspects of Polygamutah.[97]

Figure 1.5   "Ye Popular Idea of Brigham Young and his Followers." Reprinted from *Yankee Notions*, April 1858.

As federal prosecution of polygamy increased during the 1880s, so too did outside perception of Mormon corruption. In 1883 the *Austin Weekly Statesman* announced that "there are some Mormons who do not wear visible horns and display cloven feet" but still warned its readers that "a smiling and insidious foe is none the less to be feared."[98] Two years later *Sam the Scaramouch,* a short-lived Cincinnati, Ohio, tabloid, published a biting cartoon designed to offer its readers "one way to solve the Mormon Problem" (see figure 1.7). The picture featured a determined Uncle Sam kicking a horn-headed and beastly looking Mormon patriarch into the Great Salt Lake. By then the lake was already crowded with the floating bodies of other Mormons sent to their watery graves. The Salt Lake Tabernacle was engulfed in flames in the background. Meanwhile a string of "Danites"—Brigham Young's band of rumored hit men—hung from a line of gallows. A ghoulish Mormon with horns certainly deserved such treatment, and the American public would expect no less from its leaders than to rid the nation of such a devilish threat to its safety and democracy.[99]

The *Salt Lake Herald,* a Mormon news source, did its part to push back against such ideas and to promote a normalized image for the Saints. It noted that "there were many foolish stories extant in relation to the Mormons—that they had

Figure 1.6 "The Veiled Prophet of Polygamutah." Reprinted from *Vanity Fair,* 11 February 1860.

horns and tails and were different from the rest of mankind." The *Herald,* however, asserted that actual visitors to Salt Lake City learned the truth, that Mormons were "like other people."[100] On another occasion the *Herald* poked fun at the eastern press for various reports "that the Mormons wear horns, eat babies, are lunatics and walk backwards."[101] These were minor examples of a broader effort among the Mormons to assert a racially pure identity for themselves in the face of the barrage of attacks on that same purity.

* * *

Very early in the history of the new faith, Mormons imagined a chosen identity for themselves and a way to assert a special relationship to God via ancient Israel. The founding of Mormonism coincided with a broader Protestant belief among some thinkers that Europeans in general (and the British specifically)

Figure 1.7 "One Way to Solve the Mormon Problem." Reprinted from *Sam the Scaramouch*, 23 May 1885. L. Tom Perry Special Collections, Harold B. Lee Library, Brigham Young University, Provo, Utah.

may have been the descendants of the biblical lost ten tribes of Israel.[102] This religiously motivated "British Israelism" sometimes merged with and/or coexisted with a secular Anglo-Saxon triumphalism. This triumphalism served to bolster British imperialism as a means of spreading liberty and self-rule, which were the special preserves of the Anglo-Saxon "race." In the United States, the story of civilization itself became intertwined in the Anglo-Saxon narrative of progress, uplift, freedom, and racial superiority. Anglo-Saxons, it held, preserved the flame of liberty as they marched westward across Europe to Britain and then to North America. As Anglo-Saxons and the Western world in general progressed, they abandoned savagery and barbarism along with polygamy and an inclination toward authoritarian rule. In the United States, some politicians and thinkers became so convinced of the inevitability of Anglo-Saxon progress that by the 1840s they called it America's "manifest destiny" to spread from the Atlantic to the Pacific Coast.[103]

At the same time, the Irish potato migration began to complicate the triumphal narrative by bringing an influx of less desirable "white" people from Europe. As the Irish immigration increased, racial thinkers created a variety of categories designed to reorder a hierarchy of "white races," with the Anglo-Saxons at the top. The Irish Celts, Germanic Teutons, Slavs, Nordics, Welsh, Scotch, Alpine, Iberic, and others were no longer seen as part of a unified "white" race as scientists attempted to organize the various peoples of the world according to their innate capacity for self-rule. In practice, any "race" under scrutiny was often judged according to shifting standards of what it meant to be white. More often than not it devolved into a subjective judgment of a given group's ability to act in the ways that white people were supposed to act. The perception that Mormons were superstitious, fanatical, and prone to despotism marked them well outside the bounds of whiteness. After polygamy became an acknowledged fact, it only solidified outsiders' previous determination that Mormons were a deterioration of whiteness.[104]

Mormonism's birth into this splintering racial landscape certainly impacted Mormons' attempts to define their own identity. Beginning in the 1830s leaders developed notions of an Israelite identity, tapping into current cultural understandings that inherited traits were transmitted in a person's blood. As they came to view it, when a person responded to the Mormon message it was due in part to "believing blood" in their veins and evidence of a chosen Israelite lineage. The large number of converts to Mormonism in Britain and Scandinavia only confirmed the Mormon sense that they were gathering the modern-day descendants of scattered Israel, especially the descendants of Joseph through his son Ephraim.

So convinced were early leaders of the literal nature of Israelite heritage that Joseph Smith even claimed that a person who converted to Mormonism who was not already of Israelite descent would undergo a miraculous physical change of blood. A person's conversion, in Smith's words, would "purge out the old blood and make him actually the seed of Abraham." Mormon patriarchal blessings—a bestowal of promises and blessing from God through the medium of an ordained "Patriarch" via the inspiration of the Holy Ghost—added spiritual certainty to a person's Israelite identity. Such blessings sometimes declared to which tribe a recipient belonged, generally a lineage through Ephraim. Thus Mormonism's unique religious vision added theological weight to its very own emerging sense of a chosen British Israelism.[105]

By the 1860s Brigham Young most fully enunciated an Anglo-Saxon-Israelite identity for the Saints. By that point tens of thousands of British converts offered living proof in his mind of the "believing blood" among the British peoples. Young told the Saints that they were in the midst of "gathering the children of Abraham who have come through the loins of Joseph and his sons, more especially through Ephraim, whose children are mixed among all the nations of the earth." Even though they were "wild and uncultivated, unruly, ungovernable" and the "spirit in them is turbulent and resolute; they are the Anglo-Saxon race." On other occasions he similarly declared that "most of the Anglo-Saxon races will be . . . of the blood of Israel" and that the "Anglo Saxon race were the pure Ephraimites."[106]

In addition to an Ephraimite Anglo-Saxon identity, Mormons developed notions of a physically healthy and vigorous body for themselves to combat outsiders' descriptions of them as degraded. Especially after the open acknowledgement of polygamy in 1852, Mormons entered into a national debate with their detractors. Both sides stretched and contorted the Mormon body into either a deformed atrocity or an improved celestial being. "It is marvelous to the world," Brigham Young declared, "that the poor, ignorant, deluded 'Mormons,' as they call them, can make so much real improvement. Is there another people on the earth," he queried, "with the same facilities, that can do what the Latter-day Saints can? There is not," he answered.[107] It was typical Brigham Young hyperbole, yet it represented the ways in which Mormons signaled an awareness of the charges against them and then responded directly to these charges.

The offspring of polygamy became a key battleground between the Mormons and their antagonists. As one critic observed, the Mormons "expect to obtain the hardy bodies and sound minds of the Saxons from the worst practices of effeminate Asiatics."[108] Mormons were just as convinced of the healthy physical benefits of polygamy as their opponents were of its debilitating impact. "There are no healthier, or better developed children than those born in polygamy," one Mormon mother asserted. In her estimation plural marriage was a principle "established by revelation for the regeneration of mankind."[109] George Q. Cannon, a counselor in the LDS First Presidency, contended that "the children of our system are brighter, stronger, [and] healthier [in] every way than those of the monogamic system." Other Mormons praised the offspring of plural marriages for giving rise to a "more perfect type of manhood, mentally and physically," and a "fine healthy race."[110]

The improved condition of Mormon children came in part, Mormons argued, from the solution plural marriage offered to a nineteenth-century Victorian sexual conundrum. Some medical and scientific thinkers argued that a person's lustful desires could be imprinted upon a developing and unborn fetus during gestation or while nursing and therefore suggested that sexual continence for women was most appropriate during those times.[111] Brigham Young argued in 1847, for example, that when a woman was pregnant she should "never be crossed in anything, but treated as gentle as an infant, her mind guided and ruled by the principles of righteousness and kept continually upon Holy things." If she instead gave in to the temptation to "steal, get drunk, or any other evil," then her "offspring will partake of the same qualities." If the expecting mother would "continually resist all temptation," Young promised that she would be blessed and that the "body of her child will be larger, more strong and robust." In this way, Young said, "our race will become improved until the age of man Shall be as the age of a tree."[112]

As Mormons saw it, Victorian sexual ideals forced non-Mormon men to look outside the bounds of marriage to satisfy their sexual desires and thereby led to prostitution and adultery. Polygamy offered a solution. Its primary purpose, according to some leading Mormons, was for procreation, not to satisfy lustful desires: therefore, the sexual union was marked by a more pure drive than mere physical gratification. As Charles W. Penrose, one Mormon leader viewed it, the monogamic system was producing "puny, spindly, and easily prostrated" offspring, children with feeble constitutions who were easy prey to disease and "physical decay." The cause for such "degeneracy," Penrose wrote, "lies in the spirit of lasciviousness . . . and in the absence of proper regulations for the marital relations of the sexes." While the rest of the world was traveling a slow road "to decay and death," the Mormons were "commencing the great work of physical regeneration." In Penrose's estimation the proof was in the fruits of plural marriage: "the stalwart sons and fair and robust daughters of Zion."[113]

Mormon leader Albert Carrington agreed. In monogamy, the "intercourse of the sexes is not confined . . . to the perpetuating of the species," he complained. "Long after that end has been attained the same communion is continued, robbing the future mother of that vigor which should nourish her embryotic offspring, and giving intensified sensual desires to that offspring." In contrast, plural marriage "produces a higher condition of physiological existence. Continence, from conception until the term of gestation ceases, gives to the dawning generation stronger and healthier organizations, purer desires, and a higher condition of physical and mental excellence." Such arguments were not mere speculation, he claimed, but "scientific truth."[114]

George Q. Cannon and Orson Hyde added another unique Mormon twist to the argument. Mormons believed that before birth they existed as spirit beings in a premortal state where they waited for their turn to come to earth and to receive bodies. The most noble and righteous spirits waited for opportunities to be born into the most noble and righteous families. As apostle Hyde rhetorically wondered, "Do good spirits want to partake of the sins of the low and degraded? No," he answered. "They will stay in heaven until a way is opened for purity and righteousness to form a channel in which they can come and take honorable bodies in this world." If Mormons adhered to such principles and set standards of "purity and righteousness" in their homes, then Hyde promised that their "offspring will be the fairest specimens of the work of God's hand." As he put it, it was a way for Mormons to "improve our own race."[115]

Cannon took the argument even further. He maintained that "as long as monogamy is the law, bastardy, whoredom, and degeneracy will exist." To combat such vices he advocated the legalization of polygamy, the eradication of "whoredom," and the death penalty for adultery. Only then would "numberless evils both physical and moral . . . disappear from the land" and "a superior race of men" emerge to form a "purer state of society."[116] In many regards, such arguments anticipated the eugenics movement that gained national and international prominence decades later. Mormon bodies continued to serve as fodder in those later debates, yet the most immediate context for racially pure and physically improved Mormon bodies from the 1850s through the 1880s was the consistent attacks from outsiders who imagined just the opposite.

*   *   *

The foreign nature of the "new race" did not escape scrutiny, especially as Americans attempted to situate Mormons among a splintering of "white races." By the 1850s the racialization of Mormons as foreigners became more refined. Even though the bulk of Mormon immigrants originated in Great Britain and Scandinavia, generally desirable parts of Europe, the simple fact that they had converted to Mormonism made them racially suspect and undesireable. No true Anglo-Saxon would fall prey to such a regressive trap as Mormonism. European converts were thus sometimes described as intellectually inferior, from the lowest classes of European society, poor, and deluded. As one Protestant minister warned in 1853, a heterogeneous collection of Mormons was then "swarming" to Utah "from the dark lanes, and crowded factories, and filthy collieries of the old world,—the sewerage and drainings [*sic*] of European population."[117]

In 1856 a reporter for the *New York Times* visited Castle Garden, America's first immigration station (which predated Ellis Island) to survey for his readers what the Mormon immigrants from Liverpool were like. He counted 454 Mormons who had recently arrived on the packet ship *Caravan* "from England, Wales, Scotland, Ireland and Denmark." As the *Times* put it, "Our reporter saw these people, conversed with them, and estimated them, intellectually and otherwise. They all belong to the lower, almost to the lowest classes of society." A typical "Welsh peasant is notably clean," the *Times* declared, whereas the Mormon "Welsh peasants were dirty." Typical Welsh girls were distinguished by their "very ruddy" complexions, "very wholesome" appearance, and "very staid and chaste . . . manners," but the Welsh Mormons "were neither ruddy, wholesome nor staid." The English and Scotch Mormons were no different. "Their countenances were imbruted with ignorance and dirt—not the material dirt of a sea voyage, but the moral dirt of a life of imbecility and indolence. The Apostles of Joe Smith and Brigham Young found them an easy prey." The *Times* declared that "[a]mong the whole four hundred and fifty, there was scarcely one face that showed that its possessor was greatly elevated above the animal. Dissipation had done its work with many." All of this left the *Times* to predict, "if Salt Lake

City is wholly peopled by individuals of the average of intellect possessed by the newly-arrived emigrants, we should, following the law of depreciation, expect that in a century it would be merely a congregation of apes with tails."[118]

Another description, this one from a congregation in Wales, portrayed Mormon women favorably, even as it denigrated the men for their lecherous intentions. A visitor described the worshippers as working-class people but noted that some were "very respectably dressed, and the women generally clean and well looking." The young men in the room, however, were "lank and gaunt" with a "self-satisfied smirk on their countenances, as if they were looking forward to the bliss of having a dozen wives." The older men, in contrast, were "worn" and "haggard," and "looked as though they actually had the wives and did not find it a bliss at all." One of the preachers, despite being "thoroughly earnest," was "a little dark grubby man" who was "rude, unpolished, and unlettered." The other speaker that day was "a mean, yellow, dirty man . . . [who] looked the incarnation of a vulgar hypocrite." As the reporter put it, if such men were typical of the Mormons in Wales, it was no wonder that "the women have some excuse for being in such haste to get to Utah."[119]

The theme of lecherous men seeking new female converts to ship to Utah to join the harems of the waiting patriarchs grew in outsiders' imaginaries. Once in Utah, however, women would find themselves trapped in a life of servile drudgery. In the process Mormons facilitated the dumping of "an inferior class of foreigners" upon American shores.[120]

Dr. Roberts Bartholow's report of a "new race" and the corresponding response from the medical community in the 1860s added to the growing national concern over Mormon immigration. Bartholow worried about Mormon conversions abroad because they perpetuated the Mormon problem into the future. "The strength and vigor of the population is maintained by constant infusions of new blood," he complained. The source of that "new blood" was particularly problematic, coming as it did from the "deluded rank and file" of European society: "English, Welsh, Swedish, Danish and Norwegian poor, chiefly, of that class of ignorant religionists who are looking in every age for startling revelations."[121] Other members of the medical community agreed. A Mr. Thomassy from the New Orleans Academy of Sciences believed that the Mormon recruits "from every nation in the world to whom they had access" were usually "from the very worst specimens of each people," a fact he supposed could not help but have a negative impact upon the offspring of polygamy. Dr. Charles C. Furley also pinpointed "European immigration" as the true source of the population increase among the Mormons.[122]

Such concerns did not fall on deaf ears. By 1879 US Secretary of State William M. Evarts, under President Rutherford B. Hayes, became convinced of the crucial role that foreign immigration played in the Mormon problem. That

August he issued a circular letter to American consuls throughout Europe seeking the aid of foreign governments in stemming the tide of the "large numbers of immigrants [who] come to our shores every year from the various countries of Europe for the avowed purpose of joining the Mormon community at Salt Lake." As Evarts viewed it, polygamy in Utah rested upon a foundation of European immigration. Tapping into a well-worn theme, he contended that the Mormon immigrants were "drawn mainly from the ignorant classes, who are easily influenced by the double appeal to their passions and their poverty."[123] Since the United States had already outlawed polygamy, Evarts asked his European counterparts to take measures to cease the arrival of future lawbreakers. It was his hope that such actions might prevent Utah Territory from "becoming a resort or refuge for the crowds of misguided men and women whose offenses against morality and decency would be intolerable in the land from whence they came."[124]

The response in Europe varied from country to country. Some governments expelled Mormon missionaries, others agreed to cooperate as best they could, while still others said that they could not prevent people from emigrating simply because they belonged to a particular religion. Because restricting the emigration of any religious group was difficult at best, most countries that responded did so with a promise to curtail Mormon missionary activities or to expel the missionaries from their countries. France promised to arrest, punish, or oust anyone who preached polygamy there, while other countries denied passports to missionaries. The Austro-Hungarian Empire imprisoned one missionary, and Bavaria arrested and expelled others.[125]

Evarts's circular continued to impact Mormon missionary work in Europe throughout the 1880s and reinforced public opinion about Mormon immigrants. One particular episode played out in the pages of the *New York Times* in 1883. The *Times* reported on a dispatch from the US consul at Basel, Switzerland, warning that the *Nevada* was on its way to New York with a group of Swiss "pauper polygamists" on board. The Mormons were described as "poor degraded creatures, most of whom are women," and as "poor, ignorant, and in many cases imbecile people." As the *Times* reported it, the crux of the matter was that Mormon immigrants from Europe would perpetuate plural marriage in America: "Polygamy can probably never be exterminated in Utah while its harems can be freely recruited from the dregs of European society," the Swiss consul worried.[126]

Based upon such concerns, immigration agents in New York thoroughly investigated the *Nevada*'s passengers upon arrival. Rather than finding paupers, imbeciles, and degraded creatures, the agents and a *Times* reporter found the Mormons with ample money to support themselves and that there was nothing in their character or physical condition that might "justify any objections to their landing." The *Times* reporter found them to be principally composed of families who "looked healthy" and were "comfortably clad, and many of the children showed bright and intelligent faces." Most were "clean" and there was nothing to indicate that they were "imbecile or depraved." Even though the reporter did not find any "particularly attractive women in the party," he nonetheless described them as "rugged and thrifty."[127]

In the end, the investigation found no legal grounds for excluding the Mormon immigrants, and they were allowed to continue their journey to Utah. The *Salt Lake Tribune* nonetheless objected, deeming the newcomers "just about as bad material as any that drifts to our shores." As the *Tribune* argued, even though they might not become public burdens as paupers "they are as great a burden to this country—morally—as any pauper Irishmen who have ever reached America."[128]

Thus by the 1880s there was a growing moral outrage turning the arrival of Mormon immigrants at New York into a cultural discourse readily expressed in pictorial form. Most outsiders imagined that foreign converts were overwhelmingly female victims of male seduction who were promised prosperity in the new world as a way to trap them into sexual bondage and white slavery—the ultimate signs that they could not be of true freedom-loving Anglo-Saxon stock. As one British observer put it, Mormon missionaries were sent to Britain "for the very purpose of securing prostitutes for their hellish dens of infamy in Utah."[129]

In 1882 *Harper's Weekly* poked fun at the "Pure White 'Mormon Immigration' on the Atlantic Coast" (see figure 1.8). Rather than immigrating to enjoy a life of freedom as Anglo-Saxon heritage suggested, these women immigrated as "cheap 'help-mates' for Mr. Polygamist." In 1883 Frank Leslie, a prominent nineteenth-century New York publisher, added a more sexual and sinister nature to the Mormon immigration, calling it the twin relic of barbarism and depicting the anxious male patriarchs as lecherous wolves waiting to sexually devour the latest flock of innocent lambs (see figure 1.9).[130]

A cover image from *Frank Leslie's Illustrated* for March 1882 offered a telling visual depiction of how outsiders imagined the Mormon system to work. First the Mormon "agent" lured unsuspecting females by offering them the "promise of a happy home out west" (see figure 1.10). But the "happy home" was only a trap with sharp metal claws that would capture the female immigrants and funnel them into polygamy and ultimate degradation. Once they arrived in Utah they would be employed as slave labor and kept hostage by the ball and chain of ignorance held by an uncaring patriarch (see figure 1.11). That patriarch used the whip of intimidation to keep his enslaved immigrant wives under his power and only cared about his financial bottom line. The account sheet he held pleased him as he contemplated the amount of money he had saved in farmhands by importing cheap foreign labor in the form of wives. Even black slavery was not as degraded as the white slavery practiced in Utah, as the black man looked on with the Emancipation Proclamation tucked securely under his arm.

Figure 1.8 "Pure White 'Mormon Immigration' on the Atlantic Coast. More *Cheap* 'Help-mates' for Mr. Polygamist." Reprinted from *Harper's Weekly*, 25 March 1882, 191. Courtesy of the Library of Congress.

Even he was racially superior and more free than white women among the Mormons. The women, in contrast, bore the marks of degradation and sorrow on their faces, with one in the foreground wearing Dutch wooden shoes to remind readers of her foreignness. Mormon immigrants in this depiction, even if coming from England and northern Europe, were still not fully white.[131]

The term "white slave" grew out of a much broader antebellum context in which wage laborers described themselves as white slaves in order to emphasize their sometimes deplorable working conditions. As early as the 1830s, however, workers themselves began to reject the metaphor in part because it "detract[ed] from the dignity of the laborer." Northern workers especially rebuffed the term "white slave" when deployed by Southerners to attack northern wage labor. In essence, "to be a slave, even a white slave, was to be associated with degradation." Factory women in the North recognized this when they spurned the term, especially as slavery implied sexual exploitation and a "connection with blackness."[132]

Figure 1.9 "'The Twin Relic of Barbarism.'—The Wolves and the Lambs—Arrival of Scandinavian Converts, in Charge of Mormon Missionaries, at Castle Garden, en route for Salt Lake City." Reprinted from *Frank Leslie's Illustrated Newspaper*, 15 December 1883.

In fact, Republican advocates of free white labor argued in 1857 that in deploying the term "white slave" Southerners essentially degraded free white labor to nothing "but the counterpart of the negro." It put "the white pioneer in Kansas" on par with a black slave in the plantation South, a conflation that Northerners disdained before the Civil War but one that they and others turned on the Mormons with zeal after the war.[133]

To be sure, "white slave" was a term fraught with paradox simply because on the surface it seemed to reify the whiteness of the person so labeled. In its application, however, it implied that a white slave was not free and therefore not fully white—a way to deny whiteness without ever defining what the white slave actually was. As deployed against Mormon immigrant women, the rhetoric of white slavery also highlights the ways in which nineteenth-century Americans viewed polygamy as a sacrifice of liberty, something that no true Anglo-Saxon would do. As white slaves, Mormon women acted black and in the process abandoned their racial heritage.

In September 1890 Mormon president Wilford Woodruff issued what came to be called "The Manifesto," an announcement that signaled the beginning of the end for plural marriage among the Mormons. It was a watershed moment in Mormon history with far reaching implications, even for overseas immigration. After 1890 the US State Department no longer encouraged foreign governments to restrict

Figure 1.10 "The Mormon Agent's Delusive Bait." Reprinted from *Frank Leslie's Illustrated Newspaper*, 11 March 1882. Church History Library, The Church of Jesus Christ of Latter-day Saints, Salt Lake City, Utah.

Mormon immigration or to curtail Mormon missionary activity abroad. In fact, in 1895, when the French-controlled Pacific Island of Tahiti closed the proselyting offices of several American churches, including the LDS and Seventh Day Adventists, the US State Department protested. Once polygamy was dropped as a "chief tenet of Mormonism," the State Department argued, Latter-day Saints had "the same civil rights" as other religious groups in the United States. So long as missionaries in Tahiti did not preach or practice the violation of law or morality, the State Department deemed them worthy of the "same impartial protection as other American citizens." In a dramatic reversal the State Department considered Mormons to be citizens with rights worthy of defending.[134]

As Mormons began the process of abandoning polygamy and integrating into the national mainstream, other voices also signaled a change in perceptions. Although notions of Mormon physical "otherness" continued well past 1890, a

Figure 1.11 "Woman's Bondage in Utah. The Mormon Solution of the 'Cheap Labor' Question." *Frank Leslie's Illustrated Newspaper*, 11 March 1882. Church History Library, The Church of Jesus Christ of Latter-day Saints, Salt Lake City, Utah.

makeover was underway. In 1893 Julian Ralph, a reporter for *Harper's Weekly*, shared a previous exchange that had taken place between a Mormon in Utah Territory and a stranger. When the stranger learned that his new acquaintance was a Mormon, the stranger replied, "'You don't say so! I thought Mormons were queer-looking people and had horns.'" To set the record straight, Ralph described Mormons as "precisely like the people of the West generally—the Americans being very American indeed, the Germans being more or less German, the Scandinavians being light-haired and industrious as they are at home, and so on to the end." On his visit to Utah Ralph met Angus Cannon, a local Mormon leader of "Scotch stock," and other leaders from New York, Virginia, Kentucky, and New Jersey. Ralph could not help but conclude that "such blood as that is apt to be good." He described Bishop William B. Preston, a Virginian, as a "fine type of sturdy American manhood—a middle-aged, kindly man, gentle but firm and strong in appearance, speech, and methods." At a lunch hosted by a large Mormon family, Ralph found a first wife, who he described as of "prim and ma-tronly appearance . . . with great strength of character deep-lined in her face," and her daughter, "very beautiful . . . full but graceful of figure, with nut-brown hair and great dreamy eyes." For Ralph at least, the degraded bodies of popular perception had disappeared, and in their place he found Mormons who were "very American indeed." It was a sign of the growing peace between the nation and the Mormons.[135]

In 1897 the *Denver Post* ran a similar story simply titled "Only Human," which attempted to soften and refine perceptions of Mormons. After interviewing a land appraiser who had recently visited Mormon settlers in Conejos County in south-central Colorado, the *Post* announced that the Mormons there "do not wear horns nor have two wives." Even though "many people are inclined to imag-ine the Mormons are exaggerated specimens of the human race," the *Post* as-sured its readers that "Mormons are like other people." Rather than "beards of abnormal length, sinister expressions in their eyes and big broad-brimmed hats that could speak volumes about the iniquitous conduct of the wearer," the Colo-rado Mormon was "an every-day sort of man." The only thing that distinguished Mormons from their neighbors, the *Post* said, was that the Mormons practiced what they preached.[136] The *Post's* assertion that Mormons did not "wear horns nor have two wives" was telling. As polygamy faded so too did Mormon physical peculiarities, although never completely.

In sum, government documents, newspapers, political cartoons, novels, Prot-estant tracts, diaries, journals, travel narratives, and editorials combined to create powerful physical descriptions of Mormons designed to undermine Mormon whiteness. The racialization process preceded the introduction of polygamy and included the growing theme that Mormons were "foreigners," "aliens," "de-graded," intellectually inferior, lazy, susceptible to superstition and fanaticism, and from the lowest stratum of European or American society. The introduc-tion of polygamy only confirmed such ideas and gave them new life. As some envisioned it, Mormonism threatened the progress of Western civilization by initiating a racial regression to barbarism and savagery. The combined message was clear: Mormons were a people apart, physically, not just religiously, and as such were unfit for the blessings of democracy. If this was true of Mormon Elder Berry's presumably "white" children, then it was even more the case with his red, black, and oriental children.

CHAPTER 2

Red, White, and Mormon:

"INGRATIATING THEMSELVES WITH
THE INDIANS"

In 1788, five years following the end of the American Revolution, the frontier was still a hotbed of hostility between Native Americans and colonizers. That year, in response to recent Cherokee raids, frontier settler John Sevier led a group of Euro-Americans in an attack against a series of Cherokee villages along the Hiwassee River on the North Carolina frontier. In the process of attacking, raiding, and killing the Cherokee, the settlers captured a young Native American boy and held him prisoner. Later in the campaign, a Cherokee ambush kept Sevier and his men at bay and allowed the fleeing Cherokee to reach safety. Perhaps out of spite, but certainly in a fit of anger, Thomas Christian, one of Sevier's men, murdered the captured Cherokee boy and then attempted to justify his brutality, reportedly stating that "nits make lice," as explanation for killing the child.[1]

This dehumanizing metaphor was not unique to the American-Indian context but had its first expression as early as 1675 in an English poem used to honor those who participated in Oliver Cromwell's subjugation of Ireland:

> For then, brave Sir Charles Coote
> . . . I honour, who in's Fathers stepps so trod
> As to the Rebells, was the Scourge, or Rod
> Of the Almighty: He (by good advise)
> Did kill the Nitts, that they might not growe Lice.[2]

Sir Charles Coote was the English military commander responsible for a massacre in Ireland in 1649.[3] As part of the conquest of Ireland, the English created a set of exaggerated characteristics associated with being Irish, variously described as lazy, barbarous, wicked, infidel, slothful, tribal, uncivilized, criminal, and beastly—in short, the Irish were "savages."[4]

With these Irish "savages" serving as powerful examples, the English colonizers traversed the Atlantic in the seventeenth century and quickly began constructing identities for Native Americans similar to those they had created to denigrate the Irish.[5] At some point the metaphor "nits make lice" also crossed the Atlantic and was employed at various times in North America "to justify military depredation and settlement" largely in the Native American context.[6] Over fifty years following the Sevier expedition, for example, an incident took place, in frontier Missouri in which the murderers used the same phrase to dehumanize their victims and justify the killing of children.

On 30 October 1838 over two hundred members of the Missouri state militia rode into Hawn's Mill, a small outpost along Shoal Creek in Caldwell County, and began firing indiscriminately. One villager "swung his hat and cried for peace." When the leader of the Missouri militia answered his gesture with gunfire, a slaughter began. Many in the village sought shelter in the blacksmith shop, but the militia simply poked their guns through the gaping holes between the log walls and fired at point-blank range. One elderly man who attempted to escape from the blacksmith shop was found alive and cut to pieces with a corn cutter. Another militiaman boasted of stealing the boots off of one victim "before [he] was done kicking!" Three boys, aged ten, nine, and six, hid behind the bellows in the blacksmith shop, trembling with fear. Upon discovery, members of the militia blew off the upper part of the ten-year-old boy's head, mortally wounded the nine-year-old boy, and wounded the six-year-old boy in the hip. As justification for shooting the boys, one militia member reportedly exclaimed, "Nits will make lice."[7]

Thirteen years later, in 1851, the phrase passed into popular culture and gained a wider audience. That year a book about the exploits of a historical frontiersman first appeared in print entitled *Tom Quick, the Indian Slayer*. Several different volumes and versions of Quick's life followed and, similar to the stories that surrounded Daniel Boone and Davy Crockett, Quick's life and adventures took on mythic proportions. As a young man he endured the horror of watching his father and relatives brutally murdered by Delaware Indians during the French and Indian War. In anger, Quick swore vengeance upon Native Americans; the legends that surrounded him were largely chronicles of his repeated successes at exacting revenge.[8]

One such story involved Quick on a hunting expedition when he noticed a family of Native Americans—a mother, father, and three children—paddling up the Delaware River in a canoe. Quick ordered them ashore at gunpoint and reminded them that their tribe had murdered members of his family. The Delaware father attempted to calm Quick, but to no avail; Quick shot him and he fell from the canoe into the river. Quick then waded into the river and tomahawked the mother and two older children to death. Overcome with compassion, however,

Quick spared the infant—at least temporarily. For a moment he envisioned giving the baby to a settler family to raise and redeem. He even anticipated the pleasantries of returning from hunting trips to play with and enjoy the companionship of the innocent child. Upon further reflection, however, Quick realized that within a few years the infant would grow to become an Indian, a thought that he could not countenance. He instantly dashed out the baby's brains and later justified the killing with the statement that "nits make lice."[9]

Fourteen years later, on 29 November 1864, the most infamous and perhaps well-known use of that expression came to be associated with the Sand Creek massacre in eastern Colorado Territory. Colonel John M. Chivington led a cavalry charge into a village of Arapaho and Cheyenne Indians, killing nearly 140 of them. Children were among the victims of that day's atrocities, as Chivington's men were reportedly spurred on by his command, "kill and scalp all, big and little; nits make lice."[10]

Each of these incidents shares the dehumanization of the people being massacred as unwelcome parasites infesting the American body. Using the phrase "nits make lice" as justification for murder goes beyond cultural difference to hint at the biological character of the victims. In the context of the English colonization of the Irish and later of the Native Americans, the phrase was employed as an imperial tool "purporting to preserve the health of the colonial state by removing from its midst those natives whose resistance might infect and enfeeble its rise to power."[11]

These conclusions are striking in their own right when applied to Native Americans, people for whom Euro-Americans created distinct racial identities to justify Indian removal and extermination.[12] They are even more striking when applied to the 1838 Missouri massacre at Hawn's Mill in which members of the Missouri militia killed and wounded the three boys hiding behind the bellows in the blacksmith shop, especially because it was a massacre of white Mormons who in appearance looked no different from the Missouri militiamen who shot them. As one survivor of the massacre later put it, "it was dreadfull to tell the awfulness of our Situation, & this abuse we received from men of our own coular & of our own nation."[13]

The Mormons and Missourians were all American citizens, with the Mormons as the newcomers attempting to settle in relative proximity to the established Missourians. The Missourians, then, justified the removal of the Mormons in ways that were partly religious but also included racial undertones that served to blur the distinction between Mormons and Native Americans. After putting a gun to the head of young Sardius Smith and pulling the trigger, Missouri militiaman William Reynolds declared, "Nits will make lice, and if he had lived he would have become a Mormon." A Mormon survivor recalled that the attackers spurred each other on with murderous yells, "Kill them, damn them. Kill them knits make lice."[14] In essence the Missourians appropriated the rhetoric of Indian hating in an effort to eliminate the moral compunction of exterminating and removing white people from their land in the same way that Americans had been exterminating and removing Native Americans for over two hundred years. Colonial overlords accused both the Irish and Indians "of being idle, lazy, dirty, and licentious," labels that outsiders employed against the Mormons as well.[15]

The founding era of Mormonism was a period wherein the broader nation conjured an identity for Indians filled with connotations of savagery and rebellion. But what did it mean when white Americans accused other white Americans of playing—and becoming—Indian? What did those accusations mean in the creation of Mormon, Indian, and American identities? Exploring the roots of the Indian child in Mormon Elder Berry's family offers potential answers.[16]

*   *   *

The Book of Mormon and Mormon doctrine more generally explicitly lent themselves to the conflation of Mormons with Indians. Unlike most of the other racial groups with whom Mormons were compared, the descriptions of Mormons as Indians carried at least some basis in truth. The special role that Indians played in Mormon theology and the elevated position Mormons reserved for Native Americans as descendants of ancient Israel set them apart from the broader view of Indians then permeating Jacksonian America. The idea that Indians were the remnants of the lost tribes of Israel did not originate with the Mormons but had existed in Puritan thought and found expression in a variety of publications from the seventeenth century onward. Even still, Mormons bolstered their claims with a new book of scripture that early saints frequently described as "a history of the Indians." Moreover, early Mormon leaders taught that Mormons had a divine obligation to bring the gospel message to the Indians, a group they sometimes viewed as a "chosen people fallen into decay."[17]

The Lamanites were peoples described in the Book of Mormon, descendants of ancient Israel led away from Jerusalem before its destruction in 586 BCE. God directed them and their generally more righteous sibling group, the Nephites, to the Americas as their promised land. The Lamanites eventually fell from grace and warred against the Nephites. At times, however, the Lamanites reversed roles with the Nephites and even preached the Christian message to them.[18] In the end the Lamanites triumphed over the Nephites and wiped them out in a series of bloody battles around 400 CE. Early Mormons believed that the Lamanites who survived were the ancestors of the American Indians and their descendants were waiting again for redemption.

The Book of Mormon described the Lamanite fall from grace in ways that Mormons read and understood racially. Because the Lamanites failed to follow God's commands, they were eventually "cut off from his presence." As a result of their "iniquity" the Lord cursed them with "a sore cursing." One Book of Mormon narrator, Nephi, described it this way: "Wherefore as they were white and exceeding fair and delightsome, that they might not be enticing unto my people, therefore the Lord God did cause a skin of blackness to come upon them." Bound up in the curse was an explicit prohibition aimed at the righteous Nephites against mixing with the Lamanites: "And cursed shall be the seed of him that mixeth with their seed, for they shall be cursed even with the same cursing." As a result of their unrighteous actions and the resultant curse, the Lamanites became "an idle people, full of mischief and subtlety" (2 Nephi 5:20–23).[19]

The Book of Mormon also prophesied a day of future redemption for the Lamanites, a time when they would be "restored" to the "knowledge of Jesus Christ." When that occurred, the "scales of darkness shall begin to fall from their eyes," and within a few generations they would become "a white and a delightsome people" (2 Nephi 30:4–6). These were verses that nineteenth- and twentieth-century Latter-day Saints tended to read literally. Some Mormons believed that the conversion and uplift of Native American peoples would be marked by a transformation into "a white and a delightsome people," an actual change in skin color and progression toward whiteness.

The Book of Mormon confirmed in their minds the long-standing Judeo-Christian notion that skin color was a curse; but the book added its own twist. Ironically, the curse in the Book of Mormon was "a skin of blackness" that Mormons applied to Native Americans, not to African Americans. Like other Euro-Americans, nineteenth-century Mormons sometimes described Indians as their "red brethren," "red neighbors," or "untutored red men."[20] The color they ascribed to Native Americans therefore did not fit the color of the Book of Mormon curse, a fact that Mormons failed to reconcile. There was a cultural assumption among Mormons that Native Americans were descendants of Book of Mormon Lamanites and that the curse was a skin color darker than white. The Native Americans who Mormons encountered conformed well enough, even if Mormons experienced them as red, not black. For an explanation of black skin among African Americans, Mormons turned to the Bible, not the Book of Mormon. Their view of blacks made them American, while their view of Indians marked them as Mormon.

The two curses in Mormon thought also significantly diverged in their practical applications. Mormons viewed themselves as God's agents in lifting Indians toward redemption and whiteness. As fellow lost Israelites they believed they had a providential role to play in Native American uplift and that they were on a mission to reclaim their fallen "red brethren." They had no corresponding role to play in removing the curse of Cain from blacks. That curse, in Mormon minds, was in God's hands only, a curse that marked blacks outside the bounds of a full covenant relationship with God and from Israelite lineage altogether. To Indians, they offered a new book of scripture containing a purported history of their ancestors. They also promised Native Americans spiritual if not physical redemption, as well as a prophesied part to play in ushering in the second coming of Jesus Christ.[21]

From its inception, then, Mormonism offered a message that conflicted with prevailing national ideas about Indians. Just two months after the publication of the Book of Mormon, President Andrew Jackson signed the Indian Removal Act into law, which called for the removal of eastern tribes from their traditional homelands to Indian Territory on the western edge of Missouri. It marked a transition away from the view of Indians as culturally inferior and in need of civilization and uplift to that of Indians as racially inferior, incapable of ever achieving the same level of civilization as white people.[22]

Lewis Cass, governor of Michigan Territory from 1813 to 1831 and a leading expert on US Indian policy in the era of removal, vigorously supported the Indian Removal Act. In a lengthy essay in the *North American Review,* in January 1830, he laid out his rationale. Cass declared earlier government efforts at civilizing and lifting Indians out of their degraded conditions failures and concluded that "barbarous people" could not live "in contact with a civilized community." Indians were in states of "helpless and hopeless poverty," they were of a "wretched race," "ignorant and barbarous," "uncivilized," and possessed of "inherent difficulty" in their "institutions, character, and condition." As Cass viewed it, there was "some insurmountable obstacle in the habits or temperament of the Indians" that prevented racial progression. "Truth and humanity" required their removal. In Cass's mind Indians were stuck on a lower rung than whites on America's racial ladder and were incapable of climbing higher.[23]

When outsiders attempted to position Mormons on that same racial ladder, they sometimes borrowed from the rhetoric of Indian removal. Outsiders did not necessarily argue that Mormons were incapable of upward racial mobility, but that Mormonism somehow produced racial decline. Even if Mormons were white at conversion, becoming Mormon, with its concomitant vision of Indian redemption, marked a deterioration toward redness. As some outsiders saw it, in choosing Mormonism a person chose redness, an automatic slippage from whiteness to levels of savagery and rebellion sometimes worse than the actual Indians.

As Indian removal played out nationally, Joseph Smith formally organized his new religion. He also announced several revelations that sent four early converts to spread the Mormon message in what became the fledgling church's first evangelizing mission. The mission was to deliver the Book of Mormon to the "Lamanites" and preach to them "the knowledge of their fathers." With that goal in mind, Smith sent Oliver Cowdery, Peter Whitmer Jr., Ziba Peterson, and Parley P. Pratt to preach "among the Lamanites" along the Missouri frontier.[24]

An equally important aspect of the mission was to locate a site for a "New Je-rusalem," which had been prophesied in the Bible and in the Book of Mormon. It was to serve as a gathering place for Latter-day Saints and as an important center that would function as a "New Jerusalem" during Jesus Christ's millennial reign.[25] Such grand ideas were thrilling for adherents to the new faith, but were troubling to outsiders. One newspaper reported that Mormon "fanatics" were headed "west of the Mississippi . . . to establish a New Jerusalem, into which will be gathered all the natives, who they say are descendants of Manasseh."[26]

The four missionaries first preached to Seneca Indians in New York and left two copies of the Book of Mormon for them to read. As they moved west they passed through northern Ohio and gained a significant number of converts from among former disciples of Alexander Campbell in the Kirtland region. Sidney Rigdon and around one hundred members of his congregation converted to Mormonism, and almost overnight Kirtland became an important stronghold for the upstart faith. The missionaries then continued west in search of Indian converts, this time taking Frederick Williams, a new proselyte, with them. When they arrived in Indian Territory, they preached to Shawnee Indians and then arranged to teach members of the Delaware nation. Their message focused on the Book of Mormon and its promise of peace. Pratt recalled teaching the Dela-ware that if they would receive the Book of Mormon as a record of their forefa-thers and abide by its teachings "they should cease to fight and kill one another; should become one people; cultivate the earth in peace, in common with the pale faces, who were willing to believe and obey the same Book, and be good men and live in peace." According to Pratt some of the Native Americans "began to rejoice exceedingly, and took great pains to tell the news to others, in their own language."[27]

The government Indian agent, however, felt differently. Pratt recalled that news of the Mormon missionary activities among the Indians "reached the fron-tier settlements in Missouri, and stirred up the jealousy and envy of the Indian agents and sectarian missionaries." The Mormons, in fact, did not have legal con-sent to preach in Indian Territory. The Indian agent, Richard Cummins, head of the Shawnee Agency, informed the missionaries of their need to first receive authorization from Superintendent of Indian Affairs General William Clark at St. Louis before they could preach to the Indians. Cummins ordered them to leave and then wrote Clark about the "very strange" men who claimed to be "sent by God" with "a new revelation" and "went among the Indians preaching to and instructing them in religious matters." Cummins informed Clark that the missionaries intended to apply to him for permission to return. If he refused, they said they would "go to the Rocky Mountains," so intent were they to "be with the Indians." Meanwhile the missionaries retreated to Missouri where they preached to white settlers and gained a few converts. Cowdery did write to

Clark seeking permission to return to Indian Territory and establish a school to teach the "Christian Religion." There is no record of a reply. Even though several whites joined the upstart faith, the missionaries had no Indian converts to show for their efforts. As Pratt later recalled, the missionaries were "ordered out of the Indian country as disturbers of the peace; and even threatened with the military in case of non-compliance." It marked the beginning of anxiety among outsiders regarding Mormon intentions with Indians.[28]

*   *   *

In October 1831 Ezra Booth, a Methodist minister who converted to Mormonism and then quickly became convinced that it was a delusion and a fraud, escalated that anxiety. Booth sent nine letters to the *Ohio Star* newspaper wherein he explained his reasons for leaving the church and pointed out the various flaws he found in his short-lived faith. The *Star* was printed in Revenna, Ohio, about forty miles from Kirtland, which was a site of growing Mormon strength. The attack hit close to home but also found a wider audience when some of Booth's letters were reprinted by newspapers elsewhere. In 1834 Ohio newspaper editor Eber D. Howe expanded on Booth's attack when he published an exposé on the new faith. Howe titled his book *Mormonism Unvailed*, the first in what became a growing tide of anti-Mormon works. As a part of his critique, Howe reprinted Booth's letters and thereby expanded their distribution.[29]

One theme in Booth's letters was the Mormon mission to the Indians and a growing desire among Mormons to "ingratiate" themselves into Indian society. In fact, four of Booth's nine letters either focused upon or mentioned Indian topics. Booth thereby established the three basic motifs to which later critics repeatedly returned throughout the nineteenth century: Mormons in their actions and characteristics assumed the identity of Indians, Mormons were intent upon forging Indian alliances to overthrow white America, and in order to bring about their nefarious purposes, Mormons entered into racially regressive marriages with Indians. Whether later observers and critics were aware of Booth's claims and mimicked them to their own ends, or they conflated Mormons with Indians of their own accord, the descriptions and denigrations that ensued largely remained within the confines that Booth created.[30]

In his third letter, Booth criticized the mode of worship practiced among the early converts to Mormonism at Kirtland, Ohio, especially the charismatic gifts of the spirit that Booth linked to an assumption of a Native American identity. The new proselytes at Kirtland had no established pattern of worship, so once the missionaries who baptized them departed, they were left to their own devices. As shocked observers viewed it, the manner of worship quickly veered toward the bizarre. One outsider recalled years later that Mormon worship in Ohio was orderly at first until some members of the congregation "got the power and began to talk in unknown tongues. Some called it talking Injun."[31] Another observer reported visions and revelations and speaking in tongues: "While in these visions they say they are carried away in the spirit to the Lamanites, the natives of this country, which are our Western Indians, which are the lost Jews, and which are now to be brought in with the fullness of the Gentiles." Some claimed to see in vision "the Indians on the banks of the streams at the West waiting to be baptized," while others talked "in Indian" and acted out "many Indian capers and motions."[32] John Corrill, a convert at Kirtland who later left Mormonism, recalled that some people in the congregation declared that the gift of tongues was manifest in "regular Indian dialects," languages that the persons who were speaking "had never learned." Corrill was left with the impression that the tongues he witnessed were "inspired by some supernatural agency."[33]

Booth, however, was not as sympathetic. He described the manifestations as "articulated sounds, which but few present professed to understand." Those who did understand declared it "to be the Indian language." Booth further elaborated that while they were thus "carried away in the spirit"—a type of "delirium" to him—they would sometimes "fancy themselves addressing a congregation of their red brethren." In such a state, a person might mount a stump or fence and "harangue their assembly, until they had convinced and converted them" and then lead them into the water for baptism. In the water, the Mormon "actors," as Booth called them, then "assumed the visage of the savage, and so nearly imitated him, not only in language, but in gestures and actions, that it seemed the soul and body were completely metamorphosed into the Indian." Among believers, Booth said, this was understood as a sign of the "extraordinary work of the Lord," and of the preparation of the young Mormon preachers "for the Indian mission." To Booth, it was evidence of the "work of the devil."[34]

As the charge of Mormons becoming Indians developed over the following decades, it took on a life of its own. By the 1850s it grew to include Mormons dressing as Indians to kill innocent whites, an accusation that predated the Mountain Meadows massacre by at least seven years. Mormons in these constructions actually transformed into Indians and became indistinguishable from them, both in look and in savage deed.

Booth's next allegation centered upon Mormons converting Indians for their own wicked and potentially bloody purposes. "It is well know[n] that the ostensible design of the Mormonites in settling in the western part of Missouri," Booth wrote, "is to convert the Indians to the faith of Mormonism." As Booth saw it, Mormons took as their model the sixteenth-century Jesuit priests who established a foothold in South America by first "gaining an entire ascendancy over the hearts and consciences of the natives, and thereby became their masters." When the Mormons selected Jackson County, Missouri, as the site for their future Zion, they did so because of its proximity to the "Indian Reserve" of the

United States. Even though Booth pointed out that "not an individual" Indian had yet embraced Mormonism—in his view there was no prospect that any Indians ever would—he nonetheless heightened fears of Mormon intentions with the Indians. He noted that Mormon preachers told the Indians that "the great Spirit designs, in this generation, to restore them to the possession of their lands, now occupied by the whites."[35]

It was not merely a reclamation of lands that Booth said was so crucial to the Mormon appeal to Indians but a bloody redemption: "and the Indians shall go forth among the white people, 'as a lion among the beasts of the forests, and as a young lion among the flocks of sheep, who, if he goeth through, both treadeth down and teareth to pieces, and no man can deliver. Thy hand shall be lifted up against thy adversaries, (the whites) and all their enemies (the whites) shall be cut off.'" This was the "method" that "Mormonite teachers" employed "for the purpose of enlisting the feelings, and ingratiating themselves with the Indians." Booth warned his readers that if the "minds of the Indians" became "inflamed with the enthusiastic spirit which Mormonism inspires," it may very well prompt them to shed blood in order to "expel white inhabitants, or reduce them to a state of servitude" and thereby "regain the possession of the lands occupied by their forefathers." In this construction, Booth explicitly placed Mormons and Native Americans together in contradistinction to "whites." The implied message was clear, that in associating with Indians, Mormons descended to their level.[36]

It was a view of Mormon-Indian relations deeply ingrained in Mormon theology. In fact, Booth quoted Mormon scripture (itself grounded in Old Testament prophecy) regarding the "lion among the beasts of the forests" to substantiate his claims. It was the Mormon vision of Indians as fallen descendants of ancient Israel, "Lamanites" in short, that most troubled outsiders and generated anxiety. Sometimes Mormon rhetoric slipped beyond notions of spiritual redemption to adopt a more militaristic tone. Those ideas in turn fueled a growing fire among outsiders that Mormons were in collusion with Indians in a bloody conspiracy to wipe out nonbelievers and prepare the earth for Jesus's imminent return.

In historian Richard Lyman Bushman's assessment, the Book of Mormon is more than merely "sympathetic to Indians; it grants them dominance—in history, in God's esteem, and in future ownership of the American continent."[37] It was an idea that energized early Mormons as they sought missionary opportunities among Native Americans, but it also engendered fear among outsiders. Increase and Maria van Deusen, two converts to the faith who later left Mormonism, wrote exposés about their experiences. They informed their readers that the "Golden Book, or Mormon Bible, claims to be the Indians' record." As they put it, the Book of Mormon taught that "the whites have an unlawful possession of this American land, and that the Indians are finally to drive them out and occupy the land." Mormons were only biding their time until they had "a sufficient increase of population." Then, when numerically strong enough, they would initiate "the Indians into the secret mysteries" of Mormonism and would "overthrow this nation by secret stratagem." The Book of Mormon after all "promised to the Indian the eternal possession of both North and South America."[38] As another alarmist put it, Joseph Smith's policy was "above all, to conciliate the Indians" and once that was accomplished, no power in America would be "capable of successfully opposing him."[39]

Rather than allay such concerns, some Mormons developed notions of Indians as "the battle ax of the Lord." Some Mormons became convinced that Indians had a special role to play in preparation for a great apocalypse ushering in Christ's return. This idea was reinforced by revelations Joseph Smith announced and shored up in Book of Mormon verses. The Book of Mormon foretold a future day when the "remnant of the house of Jacob," a metaphor Mormons interpreted to mean the Lamanites, would be "as a lion among the beasts of the forest, and as a young lion among the flocks of sheep, who, if he goeth through both treadeth down and teareth in pieces, and none can deliver" (3 Nephi 20:16; 3 Nephi 21:12). According to the Book of Mormon narrative, it was a sentiment that the resurrected Christ twice expressed to the Nephites and Lamanites whom he appeared among following his crucifixion. In doing so, the Book of Mormon Jesus merely quoted the Old Testament prophet Micah regarding the future redemption of a "remnant of Jacob" (Micah 5:8). Nineteenth-century Mormons came to associate this verse with Native Americans. As one outsider put it, a core tenet of Mormonism espoused teaching the Indians "that the Book of Mormon is a record of their Fathers" and that they were "the remnant of Jacob mentioned in Micah, chap. v. verse 8."[40]

One of Smith's revelations similarly predicted that "the remnant" of Jacob "shall become exceeding angry, & shall vex the gentiles with a sore vexation." In the same revelation Mormons were admonished to "stand . . . in holy places & be not moved untill [sic] the day of the Lord come," an indication that it was the Lord who might marshal the Lamanites for his own purposes, not the Mormons.[41]

The messages in Mormon scripture were simultaneously peaceful in forecasting a day when through the "seed" of the Lamanites "all the kindreds of the earth" would be blessed (3 Nephi 20:16, 19, 25–27). A revelation to Smith hoped for a day when "the Lamanites might come to the knowledge of their fathers" and "know the Promises of the Lord" and "believe the Gospel & rely upon the merits of Jesus Christ, & . . . be glorified through faith in his name." Another predicted a day when "the Lamanit[e]s shall blossom as the rose."[42]

Those more peaceful sentiments were lost on outsiders. As Booth's letter indicates, Mormon efforts to convert Indians and the theological vision Mormons promoted sometimes registered with alarm. Those ideas were enough of a departure from then current national attitudes toward Indians that they gave license, in the minds of Booth and others, to accusations of Mormon-Indian tampering and conspiracy to overthrow white America.

The final claim that Booth made was also grounded in Mormon theology. In his ninth letter to the *Ohio Star*, Booth asserted that Joseph Smith received a revelation instructing Mormon men to take Native American wives as one method of gaining access to Indian country. One way Mormons came to believe Indian redemption might occur, especially the transition from "red" to "white and delightsome," was through intermarriage. William Wines Phelps, an early convert to Mormonism and an editor, printer, songwriter, and scribe to Joseph Smith Jr., recalled, thirty years later, that Smith did in fact receive a revelation in July 1831 instructing Mormons to take Native American wives. "For it is my will, that in time, ye should take unto you wives of the Lamanites and Nephites, that their posterity may become white, delightsome, and Just, for even now their females are more virtuous than the gentiles." Phelps went on to suggest that three years later Joseph Smith told him that the revelation meant that Mormons should take Native American women as their plural wives "in th[e] same manner that Abraham took Hagar and Katurah [*sic*]." If Phelps's memory was correct, it was the earliest revelation to imply that Mormons should practice plural marriage. Nonetheless, this revelation was never canonized, nor was it widely known among Mormons. Phelps wrote it from memory in 1861, at a time when the LDS Church faced detractors over plural marriage and when some critics suggested that Brigham Young instigated the practice, not Joseph Smith Jr. Phelps's recollection was clearly designed to shore up the argument that God ordained plural marriage through Smith as early as 1831.[43]

Regardless of the circumstances of Phelps's belated recollection, Booth's ninth letter was chronologically close to the revelation, and it confirmed that Smith instructed some men to take Native American wives. The *Ohio Star* published Booth's letter less than six months after Smith received the alleged revelation. Booth reported that Smith made it "known by revelation, that it will be pleasing to the Lord, should they [Mormons] form a matrimonial alliance with the Natives." In Booth's mind, however, it was a "revelation" designed to facilitate Mormon efforts to "gain a residence in the Indian territory" in order to "disseminate the principles of Mormonism," rather than to turn Indians "white and delightsome." Booth made no claims about polygamy, and in fact the veracity of the revelation and its reported link to plural marriage was a moot point in his report. Booth's letter was intended to sway public opinion against Mormons, and it was designed to spark alarm among outsiders about Mormons tampering with Indians.[44]

Within the first two years of Mormonism's founding, members of the upstart religion sent missionaries to evangelize among the Indians and quickly earned public scorn in the process. Booth's three principal claims about Mormon-Indian relations—Mormons becoming Indians, conspiring with Indians, and marrying Indians—quickly took on lives of their own. The accusations shifted over the nineteenth century according to the personality of the teller and the circumstances surrounding the telling.

*   *   *

In every instance when Mormons faced growing animosity from outsiders and tension escalated between Mormons and their neighbors, accusations of a Mormon-Indian conspiracy were among the charges. The Mormon expulsions from Jackson County, Missouri; Clay County, Missouri; and from the state of Missouri altogether, along with their exodus from Nauvoo, Illinois, and the later Utah War were all accompanied by claims that Mormons were conspiring with Indians to wage war against white America. In between such episodes, the complaints did not entirely disappear.[45]

In November 1833, as the Mormons were driven from their homes in Jackson County, Missouri, a significant portion of the tension centered on the perception that Mormons had invited freed blacks to the county to incite a slave rebellion, but the construction of Mormons as Indians was also a motivating factor. The Indian Removal Act was then in process as Native American tribes relocated to Indian Territory just across the western border of Missouri. Ideas about removal were easily borrowed to justify similar policies toward Mormons. Some outsiders argued that Mormons were more like Indians than whites anyway. The Mormon removal from Jackson County in 1833, and the eventual creation of Caldwell County as a type of Mormon reservation in 1836, were mirrored by the broader Indian removal process playing out nationally.

During the Mormon expulsion from Jackson County, outsiders constructed a Mormon-Indian body that included the same character traits and physical attributes with which nineteenth-century Americans already denigrated Indians. In terms hauntingly similar to those that the English used in previous centuries to malign the Irish and Native Americans, the "citizens" of Jackson County complained that "from their appearance, from their manners, and from their conduct since their coming among us, we have every reason to fear that, with but very few exceptions, they [the Mormons] were of the very dregs of that society from which they came, lazy, idle, and vicious." Another petition pointed to the growing "swarms" of Mormons moving into Missouri as "characterized by the profoundest ignorance, the grossest superstition, and the most abject poverty."[46] Here the characterization mixed concerns over class with ideas about intellect and character that closely echoed the rhetoric used against Native Americans and Irish in previous centuries.[47]

Mormon leaders were sensitive to accusations of Indian tampering and took steps to curb enthusiasm among their followers in that regard. Mormon spiritual fervor sometimes amplified the anticipation of Indian conversions in conjunction with the second coming of Christ, especially ideas generated through speaking in tongues and the interpretation of tongues, New Testament "gifts" of the spirit practiced among Latter-day Saints, sometimes to their own detriment. Joseph Smith called on "ignorant & unstable Sisters & weak members" to temper their "zeal" and false prophecies which excited "many to believe that you are putting up the Indians to slay the Gentiles," a claim which he feared "exposes the lives of the Saints evry where."[48] Smith's counselor, Frederick G. Williams, also cautioned Missouri Saints against publicizing things spoken via the gift of tongues and the interpretation of tongues, especially claims that Mormons would go among the "Lamanites" and "'great things would be done by them.'" He asked them not to tell their neighbors that the time would come when the Lamanites "'should embrace the Gospel'" and that if the Mormons did not fight for themselves "'the Indians will fight for us.'" "Though all this may be true," Williams admonished, "it is not needful that it should be spoken for it is of no service to the saints and has a tendency to stir up the people to anger."[49]

Despite Smith and Williams's calls for moderation, fear of Mormon-Indian tampering did, as Williams predicted, "stir up the people to anger." As the Jackson County expulsion proceeded, one Protestant minister, the Reverend Isaac McCoy, published his view on the sources of the tension between the Mormons and other residents of Jackson County. As he saw it, one point of contention centered on Mormon expectations toward the Indians. "The Mormons," McCoy wrote, "came here so ignorant of laws, regulating intercourse with the Indian tribes, that they expected to pass on into Indian Territory, procure lands of the Indians, aid them in adopting habits of civilization, and attach them to their party." When those unrealistic expectations were dashed, they moved into Jackson County with similar passion and declared the village of Independence their "Zion," the "Nucleus of the New Jerusalem." As rumor had it, some among them "repeatedly declared that if the Almighty should not give it to them by any other miracle, it would be done by their sword." As tensions escalated, McCoy noted that some Jackson County residents "strongly suspected" that the Mormons were "secretly tampering with the neighboring Indians, to induce them to aid in the event of open hostility." For his part, McCoy admitted that he could not verify "legal evidence of the fact" but nonetheless "could not resist the belief that they had sought aid from the Indians."[50]

After expulsion from Jackson County, the Mormons migrated north into adjoining Clay County where they enjoyed relative peace for a few years. By 1836, however, Clay County residents began to clamor for their removal. In the summer of 1836 many of the leading men of that county met at the courthouse and adopted a resolution asking the Saints to voluntarily relocate in the hope that Clay County could avert "the horrors and desolations of a civil war." Among the reasons residents offered was that Mormons kept "a constant communication with our Indian tribes on our frontiers." Mormons even declared "from the pulpit, that the Indians are a part of God's chosen people, and are destined by heaven to inherit this land, in common with" the Mormons. It was an accusation that yet again paired Mormons with Indians against the "citizens" of Clay County and, by extension, against white America.[51]

Mormons responded with forceful denials. Their repudiations were calculated to position themselves as white people who were as fearful of Indians as any other Americans, especially those who lived on the frontier and were "acquainted with the barbarous cruelty of rude savages." "We deny holding any communications with the Indians," they insisted, "and mean to hold ourselves as ready to defend our country against . . . barbarous savages, as any other people." Far from being in collusion with Indians, Mormons themselves were afraid "for their own safety, in case the Indians should break out." Mormons, they announced, would be among "the first to repel any invasion and defend the frontier from all hostilities."[52]

As the accusations and denials mounted, Missouri Governor Daniel Dunklin responded that he could not determine who to believe, the Mormons or their neighbors. Rather than attempt to adjudicate between the opposing claims, he decided to favor majority rule. As he put it, in the American republic, "the *vox populi is the vox Dei*," which means the voice of the people is the voice of God. The people believed that the Mormons were guilty of "holding illicit communication with the Indians, and of being opposed to slavery," and unless the Mormons could convince them of their innocence, the people's belief was enough.[53]

A Mormon removal again appeared inevitable, especially as the residents of Clay County advised the Mormons to "seek some other abiding place." They suggested that the Mormons "explore the territory of Wisconsin" for possible relocation. It was "almost entirely unsettled" and offered space where Mormons could "procure large bodies of land," where there were "none to interfere with them." Another resolution suggested a location "where they will be, in a measure, the only occupants; and where none will be anxious to molest them."[54]

Political leaders made similar arguments in favor of the Indian Removal Act. President Andrew Jackson, in his 1830 State of the Union Address, argued that providing the Native Americans with land west of the Mississippi River, far removed from outside interference, was a humane option designed to save the Indians from extinction. "The waves of population and civilization are rolling to the westward," he proclaimed, and the Indian Removal Act would send the Indians "to a land where their existence may be prolonged and perhaps made perpetual." To save the Indian from "perhaps utter annihilation, the General Government kindly offers him a new home."[55]

After some Wisconsin residents strongly resisted the suggestion that Mormons look for refuge there, the Missouri state legislature carved a new county out of politically unorganized land north of Ray County and designated it as a Mormon county, a sort of land reserve for members of the suspect religious group. As envisioned by Missouri lawmakers, once relocated to Caldwell County, Mormons could elect their own officials, send a representative to the legislature, and live unmolested by outsiders. Some Missouri residents later claimed that the agreement included a promise that the Mormons would not settle beyond the bounds of Caldwell County. The understanding that Mormons should be content with this new land and should not settle beyond its borders was never formalized in writing; further, it was clearly unconstitutional and essentially consigned Mormons to a bounded land base like Native Americans in Indian Territory. When one Missourian wrote his version of events near the end of the century, he made that link explicit. He described Caldwell County as "a sort of Mormon reservation," a place "set apart for Mormon occupancy." In his memory there was an "implied" understanding that "their settlements should be confined within its limits." It was only after the Mormons' "willful non compliance" with that "understanding" that they were driven from the state.[56]

By 1838, as internal dissent and financial turmoil plagued Mormons at Kirtland, Ohio, Mormons fled to Missouri in increasing numbers and spread beyond the bounds of Caldwell County. As they did so, tensions over land and growing Mormon political and economic power boiled over. Some Missourians began the process of exclusion and expulsion all over again, harassing and plundering Mormon settlers. Some Mormons went on the offensive to attack the homes and property of Missouri vigilantes, and Missourians retaliated in kind. This time the violence did not end until Governor Lilburn W. Boggs issued an order of extermination and the Mormons were driven from the state. Among the accusations piling up in the governor's office and in circulation among Missourians was the recurring claim that Mormons were conspiring with Indians.[57]

On 1 September 1838, two months prior to the extermination order, Missourians Daniel Ashby, James Keyte, and Sterling Price wrote to Governor Boggs with a report of a rumored Mormon instigated Indian insurrection: "Our country is in a complete ferment, and our families are rendered daily unhappy in consequence of the reports which are constantly coming in concerning the hostile intentions of the Mormons and their allies, as it is currently reported and believed that they have ingratiated themselves with the Indians, and indeed they say so, to assist them in their diabolical career." Rumors of Mormon preaching about the role of the Indians in their cosmology were at the heart of their concerns. As they described it, the Mormons were "taught to believe and expect that immense numbers of Indians, of various tribes, are only waiting the signal for a general rise, when, as they state it, the 'Flying or Destroying Angel,' will go through the land,

and work the general destruction of all that are not Mormons." The petitioners then added direct testimony from a former Mormon who reportedly heard such teachings firsthand: "I distinctly recollect hearing Joseph Smith, the prophet, state in a public discourse that he had fourteen thousand men, not belonging to the church, ready at a moment's warning which was generally understood to be Indians." The witness further recounted Mormons teaching "[t]hat the time had arrived where all the wicked should be destroyed from the face of the earth, and that, the Indians should be the principal means by which this object should be accomplished."[58] In another petition to the governor, former Mormon John N. Sapp wrote of hearing Mormon leaders who claimed to have "twelve men of their church among the Indian" with an intent "to induce the Indians to join them . . . in making war upon the Missourians."[59]

The Mormons fought back with a narrative that again positioned them among other Americans as white and fearful. Joseph Smith and Sidney Rigdon called the allegations of Indian tampering "utterly false." "We have never had any communication with the Indians on any subject," they asserted, a disingenuous avowal given the 1830 mission to the Indians. "We, and all the Mormon church, as we believe, entertain the same feelings and fears towards the Indians that are entertained by other citizens of this state," they said. "We are friendly to the constitution and laws of this state and of the United States, and wish to see them enforced."[60]

Mormon apostle Parley P. Pratt also denied the allegations of Indian tampering and then attempted to shape a positive image of Mormons as true Americans, people who were devoted to law and order and who possessed peaceful spiritual visions of Indian redemption. He wrote that the accusations of Mormon-Indian collusions were "without foundation or truth." As Pratt saw it, members of the Missouri militia were the real savages, while the Mormons were patriots. "We are true Americans," he wrote, "we love our country and its institutions; we wish all war and bloodshed to come to an end. We are also friends to the red men, as human beings, and more especially as descendants of Israel." Rather than concoct plans to murder whites, Pratt maintained Mormons merely desired to teach Indians regarding their sacred ancestry "that they are descendants of Israel." Mormons sought to bring a "knowledge of Jesus Christ" to the Indians in the hope that "they may repent and obey the gospel, and become a peaceful and a blessed people." As Pratt characterized it, Mormon interaction with Indians was geared toward peaceful ends and had little to do with a "sore vexation" or a lion among sheep.[61]

In the minds of some Missourians, however, Mormon intentions were anything but peaceful. Missourians faced not merely a suspect religious group but, they feared, an impending Indian war. It was a war largely constructed out of rumors, false reports, and exaggerated fears of an innate Mormon ability to control Indians. It conflated Mormons with Indians in an attempt to strip Mormons of their whiteness and therefore their rights to life, liberty, and the pursuit of happiness, including a freedom to settle where they pleased. It simultaneously blurred the distinction between Mormons and the very people across the Missouri border whom the nation had removed from its midst. It also denigrated Indians as a people without agency and policies of their own. It claimed that Indians were easily controlled and inherently bloodthirsty, as well as people who waited anxiously for the signal from their Mormon overlords to unleash their fury on white America. As some Missourians' anxiety mounted, they invented a conflict that pitted red against white and savagery against civilization, with Mormons on the wrong side of both.

*   *   *

As relations between Mormons and some Missouri residents deteriorated, General H. G. Parks of the Missouri militia received orders to help keep the peace in Carroll County. After his arrival there, Parks wrote, "I hope to be able to prevent bloodshed. Nothing seems so much in demand here (to hear the Carroll county men talk,) as Mormon scalps—as yet they are scarce."[62] The rhetoric of expulsion continued to draw upon language more typically used in Indian conflicts especially as it culminated in an order of "extermination."

Although not a direct cause, the massacre at Hawn's Mill came just three days after Missouri Governor Lilburn W. Boggs's infamous extermination order. Boggs commanded the leader of the Missouri state militia that "[t]he Mormons must be treated as enemies, and must be exterminated or driven from the State if necessary for the public peace—their outrages are beyond all description."[63] This unprecedented order marked Mormons as the only religious people singled out in American history for state-sanctioned extermination.

The rhetoric of extermination in the Missouri conflict actually began with the Mormons. On 4 July 1838 Sidney Rigdon, Joseph Smith's right-hand man, thundered, "And that mob that comes on us to disturb us; it shall be between us and them a war of extermination, for we will follow them, till the last drop of their blood is spilled, or else they will have to exterminate us." This rhetoric, generally reserved for anger against Indians, would be used by Mormons for that very purpose after their arrival in Utah, but in Missouri they were the minority and clearly did not possess the will, the military capacity, nor the strength in numbers to enforce Rigdon's bluster. The state of Missouri, however, did.[64]

The language of extermination in American history was most frequently deployed in episodes of unequal power, a way to mark a minority group as both undesirable and expendable.[65] When the Mormons used it against Native Americans in Utah, they possessed the strength to enforce it. Like the Missourians before them, it marked them as white and superior and Indians as red and inferior. It was a difficult lesson for the Mormons to learn, a struggle for whiteness that stretched from Ohio to Missouri, and from Nauvoo to Utah, and lasted well into the next century.

After the murders of Joseph and Hyrum Smith at Nauvoo, at least two Mormon leaders acknowledged the reality of their minority status. They recognized Rigdon's speech as a turning point in Missouri. Jedediah M. Grant, a future counselor to Brigham Young, recalled in 1844 that Rigdon's speech "was the main auxiliary that fanned into a flame the burning wrath of the mobocratic portion of the Missourians."[66] Brigham Young agreed that "Elder Rigdon was the prime cause of trouble in Missouri, by his fourth of July oration."[67] It was difficult for the Mormons to accept their vulnerability in the face of a menacing majority.

Nonetheless, at least one historian has called Rigdon's extermination language more "a defensive ultimatum" than an act of aggression. By the time Rigdon gave his speech, Missourians had already indicated unwillingness for Mormon settlement to expand beyond a single county. Rigdon, in fact, specified that the Mormons would "never be the aggressors" and would "infringe on the rights of no people." They would not, however, passively tolerate aggression and were prepared to "stand for [their] own until death." Even if Rigdon's remarks were intended as defensive, Missourians' perception of them prevailed, especially after Mormons circulated Rigdon's speech in pamphlet form. Rigdon asserted Mormon "rights" and their intent to proclaim themselves "free." It was a quest for access to the fundamental American privileges that whiteness was supposed to guarantee. Missouri's extermination order rejected Rigdon's assertion with violence and expulsion. Rather than white, the order marked Mormons as "savages" in need of elimination.[68]

Extermination rhetoric also animated the Mormon removal from Illinois. In the events leading up to the murder of Joseph and Hyrum Smith, the editor of the *Warsaw Signal*, Thomas Sharp, employed the language of extermination to stir his readers to action. A leading anti-Mormon in Hancock County, Illinois, Sharp used his newspaper to inflame and galvanize sentiment against the Mormons. "War and extermination is inevitable!" he announced in June 1844, two weeks before the martyrdom of the Smith brothers. "Can you *stand* by, and suffer such INFERNAL DEVILS! To ROB men of their property RIGHTS, without avenging them? We have not time for comment, every man will make his own. LET IT BE WITH POWDER AND BALL!!" he urged.[69] A citizens' meeting followed Sharp's lead when it demanded that the Mormons surrender Joseph Smith and "his miscreant adherents" and, if they failed to comply, "a war of extermination should be waged to the entire destruction . . . of his adherents." The committee stood at the ready "to exterminate, utterly exterminate, the wicked and abominable Mormon Leaders, the authors of our troubles."[70]

After the Mormon expulsion to Utah, the *Christian Advocate and Journal* blustered in 1855 that if the Mormons ever attempted to return to the United States, "they would be swept away as chaff before the wind." Any action by an "invading force would be the signal for the extermination of the whole gang," the *Advocate* asserted, "they would be destroyed with as little compassion as a nest of hornets."[71] In each case, the extermination rhetoric was accompanied by dehumanizing metaphors designed to vindicate any violence that followed. Mormons thus were reduced to "infernal devils," "miscreants," "chaff," a "gang," a "nest of hornets," and "enemies" to public peace, all things that deserved elimination.

Accusations of Indian tampering offered additional justification for the Mormon removal from Illinois. In the summer of 1843, Pottawattamie Indians arrived at Nauvoo and sought an audience with Joseph Smith. At that meeting and in a subsequent exchange of letters, Smith was friendly, yet cautious. By that point he was sensitive to the accusations of Indian tampering and told the Pottawattamie that he was willing to help them with "instructions and advice," as well as "any other business" he could, as long as it was "not contrary to the laws of the United States." He told them he was willing to be their Indian agent but that he could do nothing unless appointed "by the authorities of our land." He noted that he was "interested in the welfare and prosperity of all my red children" and informed the Pottawattamie that the "Mormons are your friends." Wishing them "peace and prosperity," he advised them to "be at peace with each other and with all men for peace is what I seek for all my friends."[72]

Despite Smith's written affirmations of "peace," the local Indian agent, Henry King, saw the meeting as an ominous portent of things to come. In a report to the governor of Iowa Territory, King wrote that "a grand conspiracy" was afoot "between the *Mormons and Indians* to destroy all white settlements on the frontier." He acknowledged that word of the "nefarious plot" may have been mere rumor, but it was "too serious a rumor to be trifled with." His allegation again lumped Mormons with Indians as red and menacing and violently opposed to "white settlements."[73]

Even though the attacks never materialized, rumors persisted. In November 1844, five months following the murder of Joseph and Hyrum Smith, Hancock County residents grew uneasy when a group of Potawatomie Indians passed through the county about sixteen miles from Carthage, which was the county seat and site of the Smith murders. Rumors circulated that "the Mormons and Indians had assembled in great force, near Carthage . . . with hostile intentions towards some of the good citizens of the county."[74]

In 1848 Catherine Lewis, a disaffected Mormon, published an exposé in which she emphasized those earlier rumors as fact. The real peril at Nauvoo, she contended, was a Mormon-Indian cabal, two groups that were in secret collusion against innocent outsiders. At the time of the martyrdom of Joseph and Hyrum Smith, she said, "There were two or three tribes of Indians all ready to go through, avenge, and destroy the people of Carthage; they only waited for the word of command from the Church." For some unknown reason Mormon leaders "delayed" such an order "while they remained in Nauvoo, and the Indians were prevented from committing pillage, devastation, and bloodshed, for that time." Lewis also accused several Mormon leaders of boasting to have "large tribes of Indians" in waiting, warriors who "could be brought into the field against the U. States at a moment's warning." She insisted that "they intended to do so, as soon as the Church was strong enough to commence hostilities." She then prodded her fellow Americans, saying that "is it not time for us, in view of these things, to prevent the Mormons bringing upon us an Indian, and a civil, or uncivil war."[75] It was a dramatic revision of the Mormon expulsion from Illinois, a version of events that refashioned the victims as savage aggressors who were just as menacing as the Indians.

* * *

In February 1845 one minor political figure, William P. Richards from Macomb, Illinois, fifty miles east of Nauvoo, offered a potential solution to the mounting tension between the Mormons and Hancock County residents. In light of the continuing strain between Mormons and outsiders, a condition that Richards believed was "on the very eve of violent and bloody collision," he offered a plan for a land "*Reserve* to be set apart by Congress for the Mormon people exclusively," a place where they would be "safe from intrusion and molestation." He called for a twenty-four-square-mile section of land, north of Illinois and west of Wisconsin, bordering the western edge of the Mississippi River, to be "forever set apart and known and designated as the *Mormon Reserve*." With a design reminiscent of Indian reservations, Richards' proposal authorized the president to appoint and the Senate to ratify a "superintendent" to administer the reserve and ensure that only Mormons settled there. The residents would be allowed to draft a constitution for themselves, so long as it did not violate the US Constitution and thereby enjoy a measure of freedom and self-determination.[76]

As the proposal circulated locally, Richards met with Mormon leaders to cultivate their favor. The initial response from the Mormons was positive, although one leader believed that twenty-four square miles was inadequate space for the growing number of Mormons. Richards was not opposed to a larger reserve or to other potential locations in Oregon, Texas, or land west of Indian Territory.[77]

In making his case, Richards noted that the Indian Removal Act established a precedent for such a land reserve. It was a policy for the Indians that he deemed "at once enlightened and humane" since they would be "secure from future intrusion" and put in possession of homes that were "sure and permanent." Richards admitted that it was "not very complimentary to the Mormons to place them in the same category" as the Indians, but his focus was upon a peaceful solution to the Mormon problem. As he saw it, removing the Mormons to land "set apart for

their exclusive occupancy and use" would eliminate the threat of outside persecution. With persecution eliminated as a binding force among Mormons internally, Richards predicted "their present rampant religious zeal would evaporate
in a single generation and the Sect as such, become extinct." If they stayed at
Nauvoo, he feared "constant turmoil, collision, outrage and perchance, extensive
bloodshed." It was an echo from President Andrew Jackson's justifications for
the Indian Removal Act.[78]

Beyond a period of local discussion and debate, Richards's plan did not gen-
erate enough interest nationally to garner serious consideration. It did, however, indicate the persistent ways in which some outsiders linked Mormons to
Indians and demonstrated how dramatically Mormons were deemed to be so
different and so potentially hostile to American democracy that they required
physical separation. This was ostensibly to preserve them from the crush of civilization; but in reality Richards's plan was to preserve civilization from the threat
of Mormon savagery.

Rather than an organized "reserve," Illinois citizens banished the Mormons
to a new refuge in northern Mexico among "savage" bands of Great Basin Indians. As Brigham Young put it, Missourians had accused them of the "intention to tamper with the Indians" and so removed them from that state and their
relative proximity to the Indians. Then, ten years later, he said, "it was found
equally necessary . . . to drive us from Nauvoo into the very midst of the Indians,
as unworthy of any other society."[79] It was an ironic contradiction for the Mormons, one in which they recognized their own marginalization alongside Native
Americans, people whom they were supposed to simultaneously stay away from
for fear of conspiracy and live among for lack of whiteness.

Despite the Mormons' impoverished flight westward, some outsiders still
perceived them as a barbarous threat. Mormon Warren Foote experienced that
accusation firsthand. In 1846 after the Saints' removal from Illinois, some settlers in Iowa and what would become Nebraska exhibited apprehensions toward
the Saints spurred on by rumors: "The inhabitants are very much scared. They
are afraid that the 'Mormons' will soon be upon them and slay men, women, and
children," Foote wrote. In need of money and supplies, Foote stopped at a house
in the hope of selling something to the owner. As he recalled, "The man was not
at home. As I turned to go out the woman said 'You are a Mormon I suppose it
is a fair question.' Yes Madam I replied. She said 'There are a great many Indians
up there where you are camped.' I replied that I had not seen any. Said she, 'You
have not seen any! Why we hear that you are building forts and your women are
marrying in with the Indians, and that you are combining together [sic] and are
coming down here to kill us all off.'" The woman then added a bit of advice, telling Foote that "if the Mormons would scatter around amongst the white folks,
they could live in peace."[80] As Ezra Booth suggested in 1831, Mormons were

thought to be conspiring with Indians, marrying Indians, and descending to the level of Indians. If only they would scatter, they could blend and pass as white.

*   *   *

Mormonism's first two decades were fraught with concerns over mythic Mormon-Indian savagery as Mormons were equated with Indians and both groups seen as enemies to white civilization. Like their Native American counterparts, Mormons were confronted with treaties of removal, forced from their homes, faced an extermination order, endured additional extermination rhetoric, were dehumanized as nits that make lice, and relegated to a diminishing land base. By 1846 Mormons were driven again from their homes to land that no one else wanted, this time in northern Mexico.

Their only hope, according to one woman, was to "scatter around amongst the white folks." Rather than scatter, however, Mormons began to gather in ever-increasing numbers to their Zion in retreat, the Great Basin. Over the next sixty years they built settlements throughout the intermountain West, in the very heart of still "roaming" Indian tribes. Some Americans viewed these events as evidence that the Mormons had fled civilization and gone native. The Mormon withdrawal to the Great Basin was not only a withdrawal from refined society but also a withdrawal from American democracy. In their removal westward, Mormons descended the American racial ladder, away from white and closer to red.

In reality, the relationships between Mormons and Indians in the Great Basin were frequently messy. Mormons baptized, married, ordained, murdered, indentured, befriended, fought with, traded with, fed, employed, warred against, and ultimately aided in the displacement of Native Americans to reservations. Nonetheless, outsiders, government officials, overland migrants, authors, newspaper editors, politicians, and even the president of the United States continued to reduce those complex relationships to ones of conspiracy and control. They marked both groups as enemies of American progress and as national "problems" that needed solutions and pressing political "questions" that demanded answers.

CHAPTER 3

Red, White, and Mormon: White Indians

When the famed British explorer Sir Richard Burton visited Salt Lake City in 1860, he reported that one popular perception then in circulation about Mormons was that they were "white Indians." Mormons, acting as "white Indians," had allegedly killed government explorer Captain John W. Gunnison and seven of his men in 1853. Even though Gunnison's assistant commander, Lieutenant Edward G. Beckwith, determined that Pahvant Ute Indians from central Utah murdered Gunnison, the allegation against Mormons persisted. Beckwith called the claims of Mormon involvement "entirely false" and without "the slightest foundation," but seven years later Burton heard stories that Mormons were the real perpetrators. Burton described "the imminent peril of being scalped by white Indians" as one of several "stock accusations" against the Mormons, "copied from book to book and rendered somewhat harmless by want of novelty."[1]

In defining an Indian identity for Mormons, the broader American population tapped into a long-standing fear of racial "renegades" or "white Indians" that dated back to colonial times and persisted throughout the nineteenth century. These "white Indians," in the minds of the broader population, were people who for one reason or another transgressed cultural and racial boundaries to live with Indians and even to fight with them against their own people. Some of these renegades were captured by Indians and then chose to stay among their captors. Some were fur trappers who married Indian women and were then derisively labeled "squaw men"; others were the offspring of mixed parentage who adopted Indian culture and lived with Indian relatives. No matter the circumstances, in the minds of white society when a person joined forces with Indians it represented betrayal, treachery, and regression so much so that "white Indians" were frequently believed to degenerate beyond the limits of depravity of which real Indians were capable.[2]

Fear of "renegades" or "white Indians" permeated white society and created a readymade context within which "true" Americans could situate Mormons and justify their exclusion. The construction of Mormons as "white Indians," however, used the example of a few "renegades" to tar an entire people. In doing so, the "Mormon problem" was put on par with the "Indian problem," and the two were even sometimes conflated. In the minds of white society, Mormons, like Indians, threatened the very success of America's democratic experiment. White Americans sometimes painted Mormons red and repeatedly returned to Ezra Booth's three themes as "evidence." First, outsiders decried Mormons who married among Indians: this was an act that offered proof in their minds of racial decline inherent in the faith and one way Mormonism threatened America's racial purity. Second, especially during the Utah War of 1857–1858 and the related Mountain Meadows massacre, outsiders believed that Mormons dressed as Indians and, in effect, became Indians when they committed murder at the meadows. Finally, Mormon critics reinforced Mormon-Indian conspiracies throughout the century in an ongoing process that wedded the Mormon and Indian "questions" in the public mind.

Claims of Mormons marrying Indians and of Mormon-Indian alliances, especially those related to the Utah War, had some basis in reality. In the telling, however, outsiders grounded their denunciations in the assumption that Mormons somehow controlled the Indian tribes they settled among. Closely related and equally fallacious was the assumption that the Indians were mere dupes of Mormon control. Apart from the Gunnison and Mountain Meadows massacres, the charges lacked specificity. Mormons somehow, somewhere, at some point in time conspired with Indians to commit savage deeds. The disconnect between fiction and truth was especially stark considering the complex and multifaceted ways in which Mormons constructed an identity for Indians grounded in Book of Mormon theology. The gap is enlarged when the focus shifts away from Mormon religious ideas about Indians to the difficulties that Mormons encountered when they attempted to settle on Indian land. Interaction with the various Native American tribes among whom the Mormons built communities, the Shoshone, Ute, Goshute, Southern Paiute, and Navajo in particular, varied according to different circumstances and the various personalities involved.

In response to the realities of their new location, Mormon leaders developed a strategy in which messages about who Indians were varied according to audience, be it Mormon, Indian, or outsiders. Internally, Mormon leaders tended to reinforce messages of the potential for Indian redemption and encouraged their flock to view Indians as fallen descendants of ancient Israel in need of spiritual and temporal rescue. However, even those internal teachings sometimes devolved. When the audience shifted to the Indians, Mormon leaders attempted to cultivate friendships and bonds of trust, with intermarriage as one method toward those aims. Mormons also sought to cultivate a distinction in the minds of the Indians between the Mormonee and the Americans or Mericats, with the Mormons as the Indians' true friends.[3] Yet, Indians usually stymied Mormon efforts. Mormon-Indian interaction spawned warfare, atrocities, and death more than collusion, conspiracy, and control. When outsiders and government officials were the audience, Mormons asserted their role as agents of civilization and progress and as people who expanded the frontiers of American democracy in the face of hostile savages and a barren wilderness. Outsiders ignored or deliberately overlooked these complex interactions and competing relationships as they characterized Mormons as white savages in cahoots with their "red brethren."

*   *   *

After Mormons arrived in the Great Basin, their initial years of settlement were dominated by an approach to Native American groups that was sometimes more typically American than uniquely Mormon. In May 1849 Young himself expressed doubts about Indian redemption, especially among the older generation of Indians he encountered in Utah Territory. Mormon scripture referred to those who would be redeemed in the last days as a "remnant" of Jacob; Young began to ponder just how small that remnant might be. He questioned if any of the "old Indians now alive" would ever enter "the new and everlasting covenant." He concluded that it might take "many years" before Lamanite redemption was realized. In the meantime the older generation of Indians might just as well "die and be damned."[4]

Young authorized a limited extermination of Ute Indians in Utah Valley, and as early as 1850 Mormon leaders lobbied federal officials to establish a reservation for Great Basin tribes and remove them from areas where they interfered with Mormon settlement. By mid-1851, Young arrived at a long-term Indian policy that concluded it was "far cheaper for us as a people to feed them all than to defray the expense of an expedition against them." Still, Mormon interaction with actual Indians continued to vary. It was sometimes marked by compassion and charity and at other times by violence typical of the frontier.[5]

A letter from Brigham Young to Saints in southern Utah in 1851 perhaps best captured the tension between Mormon spiritual ideals and the practicality of settling among the Indians. "We are located in the midst of savage tribes who for generations untold have been taught to rob[,] plunder[,] and kill," Young wrote. "They are moreover ignorant and degraded[,] living in the lowest degree of filthiness[,] practicing extreme barbarity." However, the Indians had divine heritage, on par with that of the Saints: "They are of Israel, so are we," he said. "Our position among them furnishes abundant opportunities of doing good. We can here become saviours in very deed," he told the Mormons. "It is a privilege as well as a duty . . . to use our influence and exertion to bring them back to the Fold of

Christ for the promise is unto them of whom the Lord said, a remnant should be saved." Mormons should "seek to elevate" the Indians "in the scale of beings, seek to bring them to a knowledge of their Fathers and our Fathers[,] their God and our God." Nonetheless, their "savage nature" was a threat that could "at any moment become excited and arrayed against us," he warned. In short, Young counseled the Saints to "be mild, yet firm[,] generous yet economical and use diligence, patience and perseverance in inducing them to return to habits of Industry."[6] It was an idealistic spiritual vision tempered by the earthly realities of living with Indians as neighbors.

Even the idealistic spiritual vision sometimes suffered. The model of redeemable Lamanites occasionally devolved into unredeemable Gadianton Robbers, a nefarious band of thieves from the Book of Mormon whose depravity and insolence placed them beyond redemption. In 1851, for example, Brigham Young instructed settlers in southern Utah to be on guard against "the children of the Gadianton robbers who had infested the mountains for more than a thousand years and had lived by plundering all the time." Other Mormon leaders and lay members sometimes viewed Great Basin Indians in the same light. In 1858 a Mormon in southern Utah insisted that "these Indians in these mountains are the descendants of the Gadianton robbers, and that the curse of God is upon them, and we had better let them alone."[7]

Mormon ideas about Native American identity shifted as they interacted directly with Indians. In his communications with Native American leaders, Young sought harmony, yet the challenges of establishing Mormon settlements on Ute, Shoshone, Goshute, Navajo, and Southern Paiute hunting, gathering, and agricultural lands inevitably led to tension. In 1849 Young wrote Chief Wákara, a powerful Ute leader in the San Pete Valley, 130 miles south of Salt Lake City whom the Mormons called Chief Walker. "We want to be friends to you," he told Wákara, "and will not do you or your people any hurt." "We are the friends of the Indians," he continued, "and we want them to be at peace with us." The friendship was symbolically solidified in 1850 when Wákara entered the waters of baptism and joined the Mormons. Local leaders later ordained him an "Elder" in the Mormon lay priesthood, as they did other male Indian converts, including Tut-se-gav-its and Taú-gu among the Southern Paiute, Kanosh among the Pahvant, Sagwitch among the Shoshone, and Arapeen and Sowiette among the Ute. It is impossible to ascertain the level of real conversion among these Indian proselytes, but for some of them baptism was merely an outward symbol of peace toward their new neighbors, as well as an avenue of access to Mormon material goods.[8] Over the ensuing years Young continued to cultivate a friendship with Wákara and other Indian leaders. In an 1852 letter he reminded Wákara, "We are your brothers & you are our brothers," and as such we "must live in peace." He reassured him, "We hear some bad white men tell indians, mormons are their Enemies. This is false. We are friends to all good men, and to the indians."[9]

Within a year, however, Mormon efforts to end the Ute-Mexican slave trade and the growing displacement of Utes from their lands led the two groups into war. The Walker War lasted from July 1853 to May 1854 when Wákara signaled a desire for peace. It was a struggle in which raiding, killing, and atrocities were committed by Indians and Mormons alike.[10] Four years later Bannocks and their Shoshone allies attacked the Mormon mission at Fort Limhi (Lemhi), killed two missionaries, stole cattle, and led to the closure of the mission.[11] The Black Hawk War followed in 1865 with sporadic raiding and skirmishes dragging on over the next seven years. At least seventy whites and twice as many Native Americans died in that struggle, making it the worst Mormon-Indian conflict in Utah history.[12] In Utah as elsewhere across the West, the federal government responded by placing the Great Basin tribes on reservations. Outsiders failed to acknowledge these conflicts when they imagined Mormons and Indians in collusion with each other to the threat of true Americans.

Joseph Smith and Mormon leaders in Missouri had attempted to refute allegations of Indian tampering with assertions that Mormons were afraid of Indians just like other Americans were. Mormons, like other westward migrants, sometimes did fear Indians as well as complain of stolen cattle and remained vigilant against the perceived threat of attack. In Utah, however, Mormon leaders developed a triumphal account in which they were the agents of civilization, people who prevailed over the wilderness and its savage inhabitants to spread American ideals westward.[13]

In communications with outsiders, especially government officials, Mormon leaders emphasized their own civility and whiteness vis-à-vis Indian savagery and redness. In 1850 they wrote President Zachary Taylor requesting permission to raise a company of riflemen to protect "White Citizens" against "Indian depredations." In a correspondence with Abner Morton, editor of the *Detroit Free Press*, Brigham Young similarly described Indians as "the mountain savage" and noted that some tribes were "rather dangerous to travelers." In an 1852 letter to Mormon John M. Bernhisel, Utah's territorial delegate to Congress, Young noted the need of the Saints "to protect ourselves from the Indians." In a separate letter to President Millard Fillmore a few weeks later, Young stated that the Mormons had moved West, "far from the confines of civilization" to "seek, amid the wild and savage tribes of the Rocky mountains . . . peace, safety, quiet, and repose."[14]

Over time those sentiments developed into the standard story Mormons told, especially when addressing prominent politicians or government officials. "We dug our way into these mountains to free ourselves from oppression," Young said in 1852. Mormons settled "the wild and barren waste and inhospitable clime of the Deserts and mountains," and did so even as they defended themselves "against the savage tribes, and were still enabled to feed them and measurably clothe their nakedness." Mormons were agents of civilization and progress, in other words, the carriers of the agrarian dream into the driest region in the continental United States, and as such deserved respect.[15]

As governor of territorial Utah and ex officio superintendent of Indian affairs, Young expressed similar notions of white dominance. He instructed one Indian subagent in 1854 to visit the Indians and to "preserve and exercise an influence which shall be calculated to inspire them with the superiority of civilization and lead them from their savage acts, and wandering mode of life."[16] Indistinguishable from the sentiment of any number of Indian agents then supervising Indian districts across the American West, these words signaled Young's ability to blend in with his white neighbors and to conform to their approach to Native Americans.

In a letter that same year regarding Indian affairs in Utah Territory, Young wrote to Jefferson Davis, then serving as US secretary of war. In the letter he used similar language to characterize the Mormons as "a people struggling, amid surrounding hosts of savages, to keep to the breeze the stars and stripes of our common country in a region so isolated and dreary, but at the same time so central and important." The Mormons, in Young's mind, were agents of American empire. They served the vital interests of the United States, taming an inhospitable and undesirable desert in the face of hostile Indians. It was difficult frontier service which in the Mormon view should have garnered praise from a thankful nation rather than derision and scorn.[17]

Such Mormon narratives notwithstanding, outsiders continued to conflate Mormons with Indians in ways that often bore little resemblance to reality. The charge that Mormons married Indians was one such example. Mormon leaders did in fact openly encourage intermarriage with Indians, but there was still considerable discrepancy between the way that outsiders imagined the practice and the experience of Mormons who engaged in it.

In broader American society, fears of Indian-white mixing did not reach the same levels of anxiety as those generated by black-white mixing, at least if laws prohibiting such unions are an indication. From colonial times on, forty-two states, colonies, or territories passed some form of law aimed at preventing mixed-race marriages, mostly those between whites and blacks or whites and "mulattos." Some colonies, states, and territories also banned Indian-white marriages, and Louisiana and North Carolina barred Indians and "Negroes" from marrying. Of the thirteen original colonies, only Virginia, North Carolina, and New York prohibited Indian-white marriages, whereas fourteen states or territories passed laws against it, six of them (Arizona, Idaho, Nevada, Oklahoma, Oregon, and Washington) in the trans-Mississippi West. Utah, with a majority

Mormon population, never did. Mormons viewed marriage to Indians as one avenue to redemption, since such unions would produce a more "white and de-lightsome" mixed offspring.[18]

Of the various "racial groups" with whom outsiders accused Mormons of mixing, Native Americans were the only one that had a basis in actual church policy. In 1845 Brigham Young "sealed" Lewis Dana, an Oneida man, to Mary Gont, a white woman, in the first known mixed marriage of any type solemnized in a LDS temple.[19] As the Saints migrated westward in 1846 and 1847, however, Young forbade racial mixing with Indians, which was a position of expediency that lasted only as long as they were in transit.[20] Only four days after Young's arrival in the Salt Lake Valley, in July 1847, Mormon apostle Wilford Woodruff recorded Young's speech for the members of the pioneer vanguard party. In it Young announced his intent to have the Mormons "connected with every tribe of Indians throughout America." He envisioned a future in which Mormons "would yet take their squaws[,] wash & dress them up[,] teach them our language & learn them to labour & learn them the gospel of there forefathers." He also encouraged Mormons to "raise up children by them & teach the Children." As he saw it, "not many generations Hence they will become A white & delightsome people & in no other way will it be done." Young told his followers "that the time was nigh at hand" for such a vision of Indian redemption to unfold. Capturing this speech more succinctly, Young's secretary, Thomas Bullock, recorded that Young predicted that "the Elders would marry Wives of every tribe of Indians," and "the Lamanites would become a White & delightsome people."[21]

By the 1850s, as Young sent Mormons on missions to convert and "civilize" Indians in the intermountain West, he actively encouraged them to take Indian women as wives. James S. Brown was one missionary sent in 1853 to evangelize Shoshone Indians and establish Fort Supply in what was called the Green River Shoshone mission located in present-day Wyoming. Brown recalled that the missionaries were instructed to "build an outpost from which to operate as peace makers among the Indians, to preach civilization to them, to try and teach them how to cultivate the soil, to instruct them in the arts and sciences if possible, and by that means prevent trouble for our frontier settlements and emigrant companies." Brown then added that "we were to identify our interests with theirs, even to marrying among them." The missionaries were especially encouraged to "take the young daughters of the chief and leading men, and have them dressed like civilized people, and educated." The purpose for "forming that kind of alliance" was to "have more power to do them good, and keep peace among the adjacent tribes."[22]

Two years later, Brigham Young offered further advice regarding marriage to Indians. He informed Brown and the other missionaries that when they were ready to marry an Indian bride the ceremony should be "performed by some of the [Mormon] Elders." In deference to Shoshone traditions he noted that it was appropriate to comply with their marriage customs as well, if the Indians so desired. Young favored an "imposing ceremony" with "a kind of feast" and "general rejoicing with worshipping the Lord by prayer and singing" and anything else calculated to form "a lasting impression." His objective was for the Mormons to identify their interests with those of the Shoshone and for the Shoshone to do the same, "that you may become one and inseparable." Other Mormon leaders, including Young's counselor Jedediah M. Grant and apostle Orson Hyde, also encouraged Indian missionaries to take Native American wives.[23]

The response among the missionaries was mixed, as was the success of some of the resulting marriages. Hosea Stout recorded in his diary that when apostle Hyde visited the Green River missionaries in May 1854, he "recommended the marrying of squaws in the most positive and strong terms." Hyde suggested that one of the men should wed an Indian woman named Mary who had been among them "all winter." Although Stout described her as "an old haggard mummy looking" woman, one of the missionaries, Moses Martin Sanders, "already seemed to have some inklings that way." Sanders immediately commenced his courtship after Hyde's speech and through an interpreter asked Mary to marry him. According to Stout, she asked for time to consider the proposition, "he being a stranger & she dont like him much any how." Among the observers at Fort Supply, the incident "created an unusual amount of fun & jokes." The following day, Mary apparently consented to the marriage and Hyde performed the ceremony on the spot. The new union, however, was short lived as Mary "refused to have any thing to do with" Sanders within two days. As Stout put it, the "matrimonial alliance thus entered into has proved a signal failure."[24]

Other missionaries were much less enthusiastic than Sanders about taking Indian wives. Henry Weeks Sanderson, for example, recorded his reaction to Hyde's preaching this way: "Orson Hyde . . . paid us a visit & while preaching informed us that the way the Indians were to become a white & delightsome people was by our marrying their women." Sanderson thought that the idea "may well be all right" but felt that Hyde "as an Apostle Should set the example." Sanderson decided that when Hyde "took a Squaw to wife" perhaps he would but "the example from that Source was never Set."[25]

Elsewhere, as Mormons expanded and colonized Native American lands and peoples, the question of intermarriage or "amalgamation" was hardly a settled matter or a universally understood principle. In southern Utah, when one Latterday Saint preached in meeting on the "great and all absorbing question of amalgamation with the natives" other men in the congregation resisted. The bishop intervened to announce that "he had received no orders to instruct the brethren to take Indian wives."[26]

Nonetheless, Mormon leaders generally approved the practice, especially among Indian missionaries, as one avenue toward forging friendship, peace, racial uplift, and mutual interests with the Indians. Ira Hatch and Jacob Hamblin were the most notable southern Utah Indian missionaries to marry Indian women. Historian Richard Kitchen documented at least eighty such marriages or relationships over the course of the nineteenth century. Mormons in Wyoming, Idaho, Utah, Nevada, and Arizona entered into mixed marriages, some including white women and Indian men.[27]

In the minds of outsiders, the results of any race mixing between Mormons and other groups were bound to be sullied. Elizabeth Cornelia Woodcock Ferris, wife of former territorial secretary of Utah Benjamin G. Ferris, found little to like about the Mormons during her time among them. In 1854 she published a book about her experiences in which she repeated as fact a rumor she heard about Mormon apostle Parley P. Pratt. Pratt was in need of money and so arranged a trade with Wákara, one of his plural wives in exchange for ten of Wákara's horses. Women, after all, were "a species of property" in Utah with "a marketable value," as Ferris described it. "Martha, a good-natured English girl," was the wife selected for the bargain, and despite her desperate plea to be spared such a fate, Pratt remained resolute. In the days leading up to the swap Martha suffered considerable mental and physical anguish: "Her cheeks became sunken and pallid; her countenance exhibited the deep-drawn lines of unmistakable agony; and, finally, when she was brought face to face with Walker, with eyes red and swollen with weeping, the savage turned his back with disgust, saying, '*me no want old white squaw.*'"[28] Mormon polygamy debased women so thoroughly that even an Indian would not marry a Mormon "squaw."

Ferris's story was likely based on two factual but unrelated incidents. In 1851 Wákara did request a plural wife from among the Mormons with an expectation that Brigham Young would give him a wife to marry. Young replied that he did not assign wives in such a manner but that Wákara was welcome to marry any Mormon who accepted his proposal. Wákara found no takers. The other aspect of Ferris's story was grounded in an unhappy relationship between Pratt and his ninth wife Martha Monks, a convert to Mormonism from England whom he married in 1847. By July 1849 she had become disgruntled with Pratt, polygamy, and Mormonism and departed for California. Following her disappearance, rumors circulated that Pratt had sold her to the Indians. Ferris's invented retelling linked Mormons with Indians in a perverse version of polygamy based upon bartering horses for human flesh.[29]

A dime novel published in 1857 was another fictional account that emphasized Mormon-Indian mixing, with racial decline the result. The novel described rural Mormons as "coarse and rude in manner, impudent, staring and curious, miserably dressed in a costume half-way between that of the Indian and white man. You are surprised at the unmistakable marks of Indian descent that many of the younger ones exhibit. The straight, well-proportioned figure, long coarse hair, high cheek bones, and wary expression of eye and countenance betray to the most casual observer the mixture of the races."[30]

The following year during the Utah War a cartoon in *Harper's Weekly* also played to fears of racial mixing (see figure 3.1). Brigham Young in this scene was imagined as an Indian "Chief," too soft and rotund to lead his forces into battle but perfectly willing to stay back and watch over their plural wives. Young was content to send "Brigadier-General Bombshell, of the Mormon Army" into battle "to exterminate the ruthless Invaders from the States," rather than to fight himself. Yet the noticeable unease "Bombshell" felt over the situation was not the result of dread over going to war but concerns about leaving his wives in Young's care. The issue was not polygamy per se but racial mixing. "Bombshell" was worried over whether he could trust his white wives with an Indian chief, which was a fear that went back to the colonial era when white settlers feared the loss of wives and daughters to Indian raids and the loss of female virtue to

Figure 3.1 "Affairs at Salt Lake City. Brigadier-General Bombshell, of the Mormon Army, before leaving his home to exterminate the ruthless Invaders from the States, confides the care of his Twenty-seven Wives to his Chief—Brother Young." Reprinted from *Harper's Weekly*, 1 May 1858, 288. Library of Congress.

Indian men. The cartoon portrayed Young and the Mormons as immoral threats to womanhood, as well as racial threats to whiteness.[31]

In 1872 when Mark Twain published *Roughing It*, his tales of adventure in the American West, he included a story about Indian marriage and racial decline, implicating Brigham Young. The story had an accompanying illustration simply titled, "A Remarkable Resemblance" (see figure 3.2). Twain's account began with a woman showing up at Young's home one day with a child in tow. The little boy had "a curious lifeless sort of complexion" similar to his mother's. The woman proclaimed to Young that the child was his and that she was Young's wife. She told Young that she had married him some time ago but that she had forgotten which number wife she was. It did not matter, as Young could not recall her name anyway. The woman then called Young's attention to the child, a boy whom she declared looked like him. It was a fact that Young said he could not dispute. Young dutifully placed the child in his nursery, and the woman left. To Young's later astonishment, "When they came to wash the paint off that child

Figure 3.2 "A Remarkable Resemblance." Reprinted from Mark Twain, *Roughing It* (Hartford, CT: American Publishing Company, 1872), 103–104. L. Tom Perry Special Collections, Harold B. Lee Library, Brigham Young University, Provo, Utah.

it was an Injun!"[32] The illustration and the text both implied that Young was a father to racial decline and by implication furthered civilization's backward descent into savagery.

An account published in *Scribner's Monthly* in the 1870s tapped into Mormon beliefs concerning racial uplift but this time to theocratic ends. Mormon missionaries were to "marry Indian women as extensively as possible, and to form close alliances with the savages." They were to "multiply with a rapidity unknown to the barren Gentile" and thereby produce a "hardy race, uniting both the Nephite and Lamanite (Indian) seed of Israel." With this accomplished, the missionaries would go forth "singing the 'Battle Hymn' of the Mormon Theocracy."[33]

Most frequently it was racial decline, not interracial theocracy, that animated concern among outsiders. The Salt Lake City–based *Anti-Polygamy Standard*, a Protestant women's monthly newspaper, was especially adept at sensationalizing those concerns. Even though the stories frequently lacked specific details or verifiable information, they were written to carry an air of truth. In its opening issue, in April 1880, it described the living conditions of one particularly degraded plural family in rural Utah. Three women and their offspring were all crowded into a one-room "hut," wherein a "low, smoky, filthy room" served as living room and sleeping apartment for the numerous inhabitants. The writer was so shocked by the conditions she could hardly fathom "such dirt, rags and squalor existing in a Christian country." In fact, even "the digger Indians" were "models of cleanliness and modesty" and "quite civilized in comparison."[34]

Six months later the *Standard* similarly decried a rumored interracial marriage in southern Utah. With no identifying information or evidence to support its claims, it printed a "letter" from a "San Pete" who in turn learned from his "friends" that an unidentified Mormon man married a Native American woman in the St. George Temple. As "San Pete" put it, the "good brother" married the woman and in doing so added to "his kingdom an *Indian squaw*." "San Pete" then posed two questions to the *Standard's* more civilized readers, the so-called Eastern ladies. He wondered how they would like it if their husbands rotated their living quarters each week, staying with them one week and then "the next go and spend with an *Indian squaw?*" How would they like it if their own children pointed to "some naked half breeds" and proclaimed them to be "'father's children by the Indian woman.'" It was a degradation "San Pete" could hardly countenance. "Oh God," he exclaimed, "how long is this wickedness to be permitted to go on in the name of religion?"[35]

In the minds of outsiders, then, Mormon-Indian marriages were imagined in ways that were diametrically opposed to how Mormons imagined those same marriages. Rather than agents of progress and empire as the Mormon narrative suggested, the stories that outsiders told were ones of racial regression and civilization's decline. As one account suggested, rural Mormons lived at a level

lower than that witnessed among the most sullied "digger Indians." In marrying Indians, Mormons transgressed the boundaries between red and white, savagery and civilization, theocracy and democracy, wickedness and righteousness,
morality and depravity, monogamy and polygamy, and ultimately racial purity
and racial filth.

* * *

The Utah War, more than any other nineteenth-century event, raised fears of
Mormon-Indian tampering. The war emerged from tensions between Mormons
and the federal government over self-determination in Utah Territory, an issue
that caused problems between federal officials and settlers throughout the West.
Rootless and independently minded westerners resented the territorial system
with its federally appointed officials and its lack of local control. The Mormons
were no different.[36] However, their status as a cohesive religious group that practiced polygamy and conflated religious and political roles in Utah Territory created a context ripe for a high level of agitation between their way of life and what
Congress and the nation were willing to tolerate. By 1857 several federal officials
abandoned their posts in Utah and reported that the Mormons were in a state of
open rebellion against the United States. In response, President James Buchanan
opted to replace Brigham Young as territorial governor and send a 2,500-man
army to Utah to enforce federal rule.[37]

Buchanan neither clarified his intent nor did he inform Young that he was
being replaced and that federal troops were on their way to Utah. In the absence
of any official communication, Young reacted out of fear and determination, especially given the past expulsions of his people. He chose to treat the approach-
ing troops as an army of invasion, a decision that touched off war panic and the
dread of removal, yet again, among Mormon settlers. Young sent the Nauvoo
Legion, the official name for the Utah territorial militia, to harass army supply
trains, which led the army to spend the winter of 1857–1858 surviving on half-
rations outside the burned-out remains of Fort Bridger in what is now Wyoming.
Young eventually accepted Buchanan's appointment, Alfred Cumming, as the
new governor of Utah Territory, and the conflict played out without any pitched
battles between Mormons and federal forces. The army marched through a de-
serted Salt Lake City in June 1858 and established Camp Floyd roughly fifty
miles southwest of the capital city.[38]

The national press followed the conflict with zeal and could not resist res-
urrecting long-standing claims of Mormon-Indian alliances in opposition to
federal forces. In September 1857, in an outgrowth of the broader Utah War,
Mormons massacred 120 members of the Baker-Fancher party at Mountain
Meadows, a popular camping spot along the Old Spanish Trail in southern Utah.
The Baker-Fancher party, an overland migrant group from Arkansas, was passing

through Utah on its way to California as war hysteria gripped southern Utah. Mormon leaders instructed settlers throughout the territory to preserve grain and other supplies and not to trade with outsiders. As the overland migrants passed through Utah, their requests for trade and places to graze their livestock were rebuffed. Following an altercation with settlers at Cedar City, hotheaded leaders there set Mormon principles of forgiveness aside and determined to punish the migrants. They recruited Southern Paiute from local bands to aid in an initial attack on 7 September. When that went badly it led to a five-day siege of the wagon train, during which time the Mormons became convinced that the Baker-Fancher party was aware that whites were involved in the siege and not just Indians. Southern Utah Mormons decided to eliminate the entire company, sparing only seventeen children. Under a white flag of truce, Mormons, with a disputed number of their Southern Paiute allies, massacred men, women, and children at Mountain Meadows on 11 September 1857.[39] The bloodshed reinforced accusations of conspiracy, especially as the Mormons incited Southern Paiutes to join with them in the initial attack and then laid the blame for the actual massacre at the feet of the Paiutes.

There was a particular type of Mormon-Indian allegation that surrounded the Mountain Meadows massacre, however. In some versions it included the charge that Mormons dressed as Indians on the day of the initial attack and in other versions on the day of the massacre itself. Mormons in these stories committed the grisly deed in Indian costume, signaling their descent into savagery. This claim became embedded in the history of the massacre and has subsequently plagued efforts to separate fact from fiction and Mormons from Southern Paiutes on those fateful days in 1857.[40]

Some Mormons who participated in the massacre quickly shifted blame to cover their crime. They initially reported the massacre, even to church leaders and fellow Mormons, as an Indian atrocity and implicated the Southern Paiutes as the perpetrators.[41] A countervailing story circulated among outsiders that any Indians who were at the massacre were in reality Mormons dressed as Indians, part of an elaborate and orchestrated coverup that began before the massacre and culminated with Mormons donning red face and killing women and children at Mountain Meadows. In these stories, Mormons dressed, acted, and looked like Indians and committed savage deeds like them as well. Captain Albert Tracy, a soldier and member of the Utah Expedition stationed at Camp Floyd after the Utah War, concluded two years later, that Mormons killed the Baker-Fancher party "in the guise of Indians who, with a few exceptions for show, were painted and costumed for the purpose."[42] James H. Carleton of the US Army First Dragoons visited the massacre site in 1859 and reported to Congress that Jackson, a Southern Paiute leader, told him that the Mormons who conducted the initial attack on 7 September "were all painted and disguised as Indians."[43] US Secretary

of the Interior Jacob Thompson also reported to Congress that he had "sufficient evidence to justify the belief that the most atrocious cases of murder and
rapine charged to the account of the Indians, have, in reality, been committed by
white men wearing the disguise of Indians."[44] From the 1850s to the present, the
nature and extent of Southern Paiute involvement have been contested. On one
hand, Mormon accounts attempted to blame the entire episode on the Southern Paiute, a deliberate lie to cover the tracks of the Mormons who committed
murder. On the other hand, outsider accounts sometimes attempted to replace
stories of an Indian massacre with stories of a "Mormons as Indians" massacre,
further evidence of Mormon savagery.

It is possible that John D. Lee, an Indian missionary among the Southern
Paiute and the Mormon leader of the initial assault on 7 September did paint his
face. At least two southern Utah residents, Peter Shirts and Annie Elizabeth Hoag
(Shirts's wife at the time of the massacre) offered hearsay accounts of Lee painting his face for the first attack. Nephi Johnson, who arrived sometime during the
five-day siege, later said he may have noticed some paint around Lee's hairline
but also expressed doubt about the reliability of his memory.[45] If Lee did paint
his face, it is unlikely that he dressed in Indian attire. His own confessions and
testimonies from other participants recounted Lee showing them bullet holes in
his hat and coat. He certainly was not disguised as an Indian on the day of the
massacre, because he personally met with the Baker-Fancher party under the
ruse that the Mormons were there to protect the emigrants from the Indians.[46]

Further complicating matters, the accounts from government officials are
likely traceable to Jackson the Southern Paiute leader Carleton named as his
source. Carleton, Judge John Cradlebaugh, William H. Rogers, and James Lynch
each released reports of the massacre that included stories of Mormons dressed
as Indians. All of them were present in 1859 for the interview with Jackson, and
the consistency of their accounts makes it probable that Jackson was the sole
source.[47] Jackson was not at the initial attack on 7 September, and it is unclear if
he was there for the massacre on 11 September. Other reports implicated him
in the murder of two emigrants who escaped the siege midweek in an effort to
reach California for help.[48]

In reporting Mormons dressed as Indians, Jackson may have referred to Ellott
Willden a massacre participant who admitted to disguising himself as a Paiute
with Joseph Clewes and running across the meadows during the five-day siege,
dodging gunfire from the emigrant camp as they ran. Willden claimed that he
and Clewes did so at the insistence of the Paiutes who wanted "proof of an assertion made by Lee to the effect that the bullets of the emigrants would not
hurt the 'Mormons.'" Another Mormon, John M. Higbee, arrived at Lee's camp
during the siege and recounted that he saw "two or three [men] painted as Indians," likely Willden and Clewes.[49]

What these various conflicting accounts fail to acknowledge is that stories of Mormons dressing as Indians to commit violence appeared in print as early as 1850, at least seven years before the massacre took place. William Smith, the younger brother of Joseph and Hyrum Smith, originated the charge. William was one of the twelve apostles in his older brother's church but following the murder of Joseph and Hyrum, William's earlier sexual exploits and erratic behavior created strained relationships with the other apostles. After clashing with Brigham Young and other leaders, he was excommunicated in 1845 from the main body of Saints under Young and thereafter flirted with a variety of schismatic groups, some of which he personally led. By 1850 he had proclaimed himself leader of the authentic Church of Jesus Christ of LatterDay Saints and rightful heir to his brother's authority. It was in that role that he published allegations of Great Basin Mormons dressing as Indians and killing people.[50]

William's follower and associate Isaac Sheen published the short-lived *Melchisedek & Aaronic Herald* newspaper in Covington, Kentucky, in which William first disseminated his allegation: "I am in possession of evidence," he announced, "that bands of these Salt Lake Mormons, armed, dressed, and painted—having the appearance of Indians—are stationed on the way to California and Oregon, for the purpose of robbing the emigrants." He further contended that "[m]any murders and robberies have already been committed by these demons in human shape," atrocities that the Mormons "published to the world and attributed to the Indians."[51] Trenton, New Jersey's *State Gazette* picked up the story and reprinted it in slightly altered form in March 1850. Another reprint appeared in the *New York Herald*, a copy of which Utah's territorial delegate, John M. Bernhisel, forwarded to Brigham Young.[52]

Within a few years the allegation had taken on a life of its own. Either inspired by Smith or originating independently, the popular press, westward travelers, and government officials all made similar claims. The 1850s were replete with tales of Mormons and their murderous exploits as white Indians ("demons in human shape") who impeded westward migration and therefore American progress. Not all of the accounts included Mormons dressed as Indians, but the various versions shifted between that tale and oft-repeated stories of Mormons instigating Indians to commit bloody deeds. By the mid-1850s the stories entered official government correspondence and when President James Buchanan sent federal forces to Utah in 1857 he used the threat of a Mormon-Indian conspiracy as one justification.

When fifteen-year-old Pauline Wonderly left Galena, Illinois, with her family for the California gold fields in 1852, she recalled an encounter with Mormons on the overland trail. She was pleasantly surprised at the "reasonable" prices the Mormons charged for supplies, especially because "we had dreaded the Mormons as much as the Indians and did not expect fair treatment from them. The tales told of the Mormons in those days were worse than those of the Indians."[53] This revealing statement encapsulated the type of stories that circulated about Mormons and Indians leading up to the Utah War and the Mountain Meadows massacre.

In 1855 Afreda Eva Bell's sensationalized dime novel, *Boadicia, The Mormon Wife*, pushed the dread to new heights. Bell chronicled a bloody story of murder and corruption bound up in Mormonism. Her novel was replete with Mormon murders and mysterious disappearances, especially among those characters who refused to practice polygamy or comply with the dictatorial power of Mormon leaders. In one such instance, the narrative explained the vanishing of a male character in the following way: "It was stated that the Indians had killed him, but one of the peccadilloes of the Mormons consists in disguising themselves in Indian costume, and waylaying such persons as are obnoxious to them, and putting them to death. . . . Numbers were known to have disappeared in this manner: the blame then fell upon the Indians . . . . Even those poor savages were incapable of committing deeds so infamous, so bloodthirsty, and so cruel, as were common practices of the Mormon Elders, under the name of religion."[54]

The accompanying illustration gave visual "proof" to the allegations (see figure 3.3). It featured in the foreground two armed men skulking behind a tree, half dressed in what 1850s readers would readily recognize as Native American attire. Both men were shirtless with dark skin; one man wore feathers in his hair, and both were sketched to portray stereotypical images of Indians. The two "savages" concealed themselves along a worn path through the woods where they waited to ambush and murder an unsuspecting traveler who approached on horseback in the distance. The caption simply read "Mormons disguised as Indian spies," giving further evidence for William Smith's earlier accusation.[55]

That same year fears of Mormon-Indian tampering made their way into government reports, exacerbating the growing tension between Mormons and the nation. In May 1855 federally appointed Indian agent Garland Hurt wrote to his superior in Washington, DC, US Commissioner of Indian Affairs George W. Manypenny, to express his concern over the collusion that he felt dominated the relationship between Mormons and Indians in the Great Basin. Hurt feared that "either accidentally or purposely" Mormons had "created a distinction in the minds of the Indian tribes of this territory between the Mormons and the people of the United States" (something the Mormons did do), which he feared would work to the disadvantage of the government. He noted that Brigham Young had recently appointed missionaries to preach to the Indians, and Hurt feared that it would be a problem not confined to Utah Territory but that there would not be "a tribe on the continent" not visited by a Mormon missionary. "I suspect their first object," he wrote, "will be to teach these wretched savages that

Figure 3.3 "Mormons Disguised as Indian Spies." Reprinted from Alfreda Eva Bell, *Boadicea; The Mormon Wife. Life-Scenes in Utah* (Baltimore, Philadelphia, New York, and Buffalo: Arthur R. Orton, 1855), 81. Special Collections, Rare Books Division, J. Willard Marriott Library, University of Utah, Salt Lake City.

they are the rightful owners of the American soil, and that it has been wrongfully taken from them by the whites, and that the Great Spirit had sent the Mormons among them to help them recover their rights."[56]

Adding to Hurt's concern, he found the "character" of the missionaries sent to preach to the Indians degraded. "They embrace a class of rude and lawless young men, such as might be regarded as a curse to any civilized community," he complained. He hoped that his letter would be used to alert "all superintendents, agents, sub-agents, and all other loyal citizens residing or sojourning in the Indian country" that any Mormon missionaries working among Indians should be "subjected to the strictest scrutiny."[57]

In July, Hurt's letter was forwarded to US Secretary of the Interior Robert McClelland. A follow-up memo recommended that McClelland put superintendents "throughout the Indian country" on notice "to watch with an eye of vigilance the movements of the Mormons" and if their "efforts, under the guise of missionary labors, should tend to create a spirit of insorbordination [*sic*] among the Indians" the agents should immediately notify the Indian department.[58]

In June 1855, as Hurt's report circulated among federal officials in the nation's capital, a similar accusation appeared in a DC newspaper. *The National Era* printed a story claiming that Brigham Young had gone to "great pains and considerable expense to procure and retain the friendship of the Indian tribes. He has made them valuable presents, has invited them to his settlements, has educated their children, and loaded them with every favor which it was in his power to bestow."[59] In an 1856 follow-up letter to Manypenny, Hurt echoed the *National Era*'s claim that Young was "liberal" in "making presents" to the Indians. As a result, he reported that the Indians in the territory "made a distinction between *Mormons* and *Americans*" that was calculated to operate to the government's disadvantage.[60]

In 1855 Brigham Young did send additional men on missions to preach among Native American peoples, telling those he sent that "by and by they [the Lamanites] will be the Lord's battle ax in good earnest."[61] It was the only recorded incident where Young used the phrase. It did not figure prominently in the preaching of other Mormon leaders, and Hurt did not mention the phrase in his letter to Washington. Hurt's concern was that Mormon missionaries would teach Indians "that they are the rightful owners of the American soil."[62]

Nevertheless, a "battle ax" discourse percolated in the minds of some Mormons and found expression in local records. In the 1880s as Mormon settlers in Arizona faced opposition from outsiders, including the loss of land and cattle, some of them looked to the Indians as possible saviors. Jesse N. Smith, a local Arizona leader, urged Mormons there to renew their efforts to missionize among the Indians and reminded Saints of the Indians' promised role as the "battle ax of the Lord."[63] In similar fashion, John Henry Standifird, another Mormon, drew upon Joseph Smith's earlier revelation (Doctrine and Covenants 87:5, 8) to note in his journal a belief that "our own nation before long will be broken to pieces because of their unjust dealings with the saints. Ere long," he wrote, "the red men will sorely vex the United States." Mormons were commanded to "stand in Holy places while the indignation of the Lord passes over the wicked," a reference to Mormon temples as places of refuge for the Saints in times of trouble. It was an indication that Standifird viewed the Indians as potential weapons in the Lord's hands, not theirs, which was an important distinction frequently lost on outsiders.[64]

None of the reports to Washington, DC, or any of the stories of Mormon-Indian collusion in circulation in the 1850s considered the possibility that Mormons evangelized among Indians for the sake of converting them to the gospel of Jesus Christ, similar to Protestant missionaries working among Indians across the American West. In June 1855, at the same time that Hurt's accusations spread in Washington and the *National Era* reported on Mormon Indian tampering, Brigham Young wrote one Indian missionary to express his hopes for Indian redemption. Intermarriage was among Young's instructions but not to nefarious ends. "Seek unto the Lord, for counsel to guide you in all things[,] be patient, persevering, and faithful, and the Lord will bless your labors to the salvation of some of the outcasts of Israel, and the downtrodden race," Young wrote. "You will be instruments in saving a remnant, and have the proud satisfaction of redeeming some of the seed of Abraham from the curse." "The time has come to favor Zion," Young continued, "and the Lord has promised to turn away iniquity from Jacob.... It is our duty now to extend the knowledge of the gospel and its concomitant blessings unto them." Young reminded the missionary that the Latter-day Saints were "the happy recipients of true knowledge" and as such it was their obligation to share that knowledge with "the Children of him who was called Israel by the Great Jehovah." The missionary's charge was to "administer freely of the good word of life and salvation unto" the Indians and "by the spirit of gentleness, patience and wisdom lead them back unto a knowledge of their fathers and of their God." The "salvation and exaltation" of the Indians were the missionaries' ultimate objectives, and to those ends Young prayed for their success.[65]

Government officials and others looked beyond spiritual salvation to imagine the worst. In August 1856 an overland traveler recorded an episode along the Oregon-California trail that demonstrated how deeply suspicions of Mormon motives had permeated the minds of at least some Americans. Helen McCowen Carpenter recorded in her diary that somewhere east of the Raft River five armed and mounted Indians appeared and approached her wagon company single file on the trail. The men of the company quickly armed themselves, not sure of what to expect. The Indians passed by the wagons "peering" into them "in a very curious manner." According to Carpenter, the emigrants assumed that the Indians were "trying to learn our strength." After the Indians passed by the wagons and traveled an additional fifty yards, they stopped, dismounted their horses, and "in a line across the road, executed a dance." The emigrant company interpreted this as a "bad omen" and feared what might happen next. Carpenter and her associates perceived that one of the Indians "was so unlike the others in his every movement, that he was unhesitatingly pronounced a white man, and if so, a Mormon."[66]

Carpenter's sister, Emily McCowen Horton, recalled the same incident with slight differences. In her version the Indians traveled 300 yards past the wagon train before a single Indian dismounted to dance in the road. As she described it, "Some thought he acted like a white man. And as we had heard of Mormons joining with Indians to attack whites, the movement was anything but reassuring." The incident ended peacefully, but as Carpenter commented after a later encounter with Latter-day Saints, she and other members of her party were "suspicious of anything connected with Mormons."[67]

The following year, as events leading to the Utah War escalated, William Smith renewed his earlier accusations. This time the *New York Tribune* published the charges as a letter from Smith. Smith learned that territorial officials had recently abandoned Utah and leveled a series of allegations against the Saints. "I have no doubt whatever of the truth of the charges against the Mormon people of having committed the most wanton and cruel murders in the disguise of Indians," Smith wrote. He also claimed to have "heard Mormons talk openly" in the 1840s, during their sojourn in Illinois, of their thieving and murderous plans. It was their announced intention, Smith asserted, that "when they got among Indians, they would lead them on to the slaughter of the men, women and children of the American people." *The National Era* reprinted the *Tribune* story in truncated form on 11 June 1857, just three months before Mountain Meadows.[68]

Further complicating matters, Mormon leaders did attempt to forge Indian alliances in the face of an impending federal invasion. Brigham Young's Indian interpreter, Dimick Huntington, met with Shoshone Indians in August 1857, and Young and Huntington met with Southern Paiute in early September at Salt Lake City. They invited both groups to join the Mormons in what was taking shape as a potential war with federal troops. As inducement, Huntington and Young extended Shoshone and Southern Paiute leaders permission to steal the cattle of emigrants on the overland routes, constituting actual Mormon attempts to instigate Indian plundering of the property of overland migrants. The meetings also evidenced Mormon efforts to forge alliances with Native Americans to fight against federal forces should warfare break out. The accusations that had been leveled against Mormons for years were in these incidents actually true.[69]

Were it not for the complicating factor of Indian agency, the stories may have reflected an even stronger semblance of reality. When asked to forge an alliance, the Southern Paiute protested that in the past the Mormons had told them "not to steal." They told Young "the[y] was afraid to fight the American[s] & so would raise grain & we [the Mormons] might fight." Despite such protests in Salt Lake City, southern Utah Mormons did independently incite some Southern Paiute to join them at Mountain Meadows. Paiute also raided a subsequent emigrant train in response to Young's inducement at Salt Lake City. In these particular incidents the allegations of a Mormon Indian collusion proved true but not without Paiute agency. The proposed alliance with the Shoshone, in contrast, never came to fruition. When Huntington issued the invitation, the Shoshone "sayed it was some thing new[;] they wanted to council & think of it." In February 1858 some Bannock and Shoshone made their decision clear when they attacked the Mormon mission at Fort Limhi in Idaho and killed two Mormons. The accusations always included a seamless unity between Mormons and Indians, with Indians somehow under the iron grip of Mormon power. Huntington's and Young's efforts at forging alliances and the mixed responses from the Indians proved such accusations false.[70]

Nonetheless, claims of Mormon instigated alliances and murder continued unabated. As the Utah War played out over the winter of 1857 and 1858, the perception persisted that Mormons "were no better than so many savages."[71] One resident of Portland, Oregon, even feared that the Utah War would not be contained in the Great Basin. He worried that "the Mormons may stir up the Columbia Valley and other Indian tribes to wage another war upon Oregon and Washington territories." He had "no doubt but our Government will have to wage a war of extermination" against the Mormons in order to subdue them.[72]

In December the *National Era* alleged that Mormons were intent upon a campaign of extermination. The paper claimed that Mormons at Carson Valley, Nevada, and San Bernardino, California, had gathered in Salt Lake City to aid in the extermination of federal troops marching on Utah. Once that was accomplished, the Mormons promised to return westward, and "in predatory bands, allied with Indians," they would "rob, plunder and murder until they shall have replenished the Lord's treasury, and revenge insults put upon his chosen people."[73]

That same month President Buchanan finally entered the ongoing national dialogue on the unfolding Utah War. For the first time since ordering the formation of an army to march on Utah Territory in late May, he openly announced his rationale for that order in his annual message to Congress. Buchanan called it "a well grounded belief" that "the Mormons were instigating the Indians to hostilities against our citizens" and that they "were exciting amongst the Indian tribes a feeling of insubordination and discontent." If the Mormons did not occupy such a strategic location along the main transcontinental route across the nation, "forbearance might still be prolonged," but their location along the "great pathway" to the Pacific seaboard demanded action. "They stand a lion in the path," Buchanan claimed, "encouraging, if not exciting, the nomad savages who roam over the vast unoccupied regions of the continent to the pillage and massacre of peaceful and helpless emigrant families traversing the solitudes of the wilderness."[74]

Ironically, Buchanan declared that his intent was for the army to escort the newly appointed civil officers to the territory and to establish Utah as a "geographical military department." Once stationed in Utah the troops could then be deployed to hold "the Indians in check throughout the whole circumjacent region of country."[75] Alfred Cumming, Brigham Young's replacement as territorial governor, amplified this claim as the two sides moved toward a peaceful resolution to the war. As Cumming articulated it, the federal troops were sent to protect the Mormons from the Indians, not to protect the nation from a Mormon-Indian cabal. In April 1858 Cumming spoke to a Mormon congregation in Salt Lake City and confirmed that there were "a large number of armed men" on the "frontiers" of Utah Territory, but he announced that they were "not sent for any aggression upon the Mormon people, but for their protection." He asked the Mormons to "remember what I say, protection against the lawless savage that has been committing depredations upon you from time to time."[76]

It was a message that the Mormons remembered but refused to believe. Following Cumming, Mormon Gilbert Clements rose to speak to the same congregation. He called the troops an "invading army" and found the notion that they were sent "to protect us!" the "most miserable, mean and transparent subterfuge I ever heard in my life." Clements could not help but wonder that if the government was so interested in protecting the Mormons, why "did they not come when we were weak—when we were a mere handful in these wild and inhospitable regions, surrounded on every hand by a subtle and savage foe?" He informed Cumming that in the past Mormons had to leave their "homes and farms time and time again to go on Indian expeditions" in order to protect their "infant settlements from the depredations of the red skin." And in response, "The general government has winked at our difficulties, thinking perhaps we would be used up by the numerous savage tribes that surround us." Now that the Mormons had grown strong and capable of caring for themselves, "Behold! they are filled with compassion towards us, and come along with 'the Gospel according to gunpowder' to *protect us*," Clements continued. "What an overflowing of the 'Milk of human kindness'!! It is the tenderness of the crocodile which never sheds tears till it is about swallowing its victim!!!" The Mormon audience met Clements's rousing speech with "immense applause, loud cheers and other demonstrations of approval." Governor Cumming "cordially joined" the response.[77]

Brigham Young also found the idea of an army of protection absurd. In 1858 he wrote one settler in central Utah in a sarcastic tone regarding recent Indian depredations, "We must do the best we can with our savage neighbors, until we can dispose of our kind *civilized friends*, who have been so magnanimously sent to protect us from the Indians."[78] He saw the US Army as a hindrance in maintaining peace with the Indians because the troops only served as "a refuge and protection to thieves, liars, black legs, whoremasters and drunkards, and a nest egg to su[b]tlers, freighters, contractors and other speculators, exhibiting a most pitiful and shameful expenditure of the people's money."[79]

At the same time that Mormons and federal officials debated the intent of US troops in Utah, the popular press continued to conflate Mormons with Indians to the denigration of both. The idea found expression in a cartoon printed in *Yankee*

Notions in April 1858, as the Utah War moved toward resolution (see figure 3.4).
It depicted Brigham Young leading a charge of Indians, not Mormons, against
an ironic sea invasion of US troops. The illustration was captioned, "Defiant
attitude of Brigham Young and ye Indians towards ye Uncle Sam," a summary
that wed Mormons with Indians in rebellion against federal authority. Young
wildly led a charge of clearly savage forces against the nation. He ran out front,
dressed in proper Euro-American attire carrying a variety of guns and swords in
an attack against a peaceful yet wary soldier. A group of barbaric "Indians" followed him into battle. The depiction marked Young—and the Mormon people
as a whole—as white Indians, people whose withdrawal into the Great Basin was
really a withdrawal into barbarism.[80]

The most compelling evidence of those accusations focused upon the Mountain Meadows massacre specifically, not a generalized Indian-Mormon alliance.
Within a month of the massacre rumors and stories began to appear in print.
Some of the earliest stories refused to believe that it was solely an Indian massacre. At a mass meeting in Los Angeles a month following the massacre, concerned
citizens concluded that "the atrocious act was perpetrated by the Mormons, and
their allies the Indians."[81] Another early account blamed it on "Mormon traitors
and Indians," while a different report argued that Mormons "conspired with the
Indians to commit the depredations and outrages" at Mountain Meadows.[82] The
San Joaquin Republican ran an article titled "The Mormons in the Capacity of
Savages"and asserted that "the Mormons, and not the Indians, have robbed and
killed the people who have been robbed and killed on their way to California."
One 1870 account placed Indians at the massacre but argued that they "refused
to participate," so they "stood back amazed, without firing a gun or shooting an
arrow," for the "slaughter" of "an entire company of unoffending men, women
and children, was more than even savages could do."[83]

Figure 3.4 "Defiant Attitude of Brigham Young and ye Indians towards ye Uncle Sam."
Reprinted from *Yankee Notions*, April 1858.

Eight months after the fact, Los Angeles' *Southern Vineyard* concluded that "there were no Indians engaged in the affair." Rather, the Indians were actually "Mormons in disguise."[84] The following year at least three news reports made similar claims. The *San Francisco Daily Evening Bulletin* stated that one of the seventeen surviving children recalled seeing "the Bishop of Coal Creek washing the paint from his face, which he had used to disguise himself as an Indian." Philip Klingensmith was the bishop of Cedar City (also known as Coal Creek) who participated in the massacre but did not paint his face. He marched in single file next to one of the emigrants under the pretense of protection from the Indians, a fact that would have precluded him from donning red face at the massacre. Three months later the same newspaper gave an account that the massacre was not "perpetrated by Indians," but "really by Mormons disguised as Indians."[85] The *Christian Observer* meanwhile laid blame on "Mormons disguised as Indians" and on actual Indians.[86] At least four government reports, each likely derivative from the interview with Jackson, also included various versions of Mormons dressed as Indians either at the initial attack or at the massacre itself. [87]

These charges merely echoed an old theme made newly relevant after Mormons actually did savagely murder innocent victims at Mountain Meadows and incite Indians to join them. Mrs. C. V. Waite's book, *The Mormon Prophet*, published in 1866, helped to popularize the idea. Waite's account included a "revelation" from Brigham Young instructing Mormons to "follow those cursed gentiles . . . attack them, disguised as Indians, and with the arrows of the Almighty make a clean sweep of them, and leave none to tell the tale."[88] Mark Twain's *Roughing It* borrowed heavily from Waite's rendition of the massacre and reached a much larger audience. In addition to quoting from Waite, Twain wrote his own summary of the massacre wherein he described, "a large party of Mormons, painted and tricked out as Indians, [who] overtook the train of emigrant wagons some three hundred miles south of Salt Lake City, and made an attack."[89]

Survivor accounts and Southern Paiute oral tradition also include stories of Mormons dressed as Indians. Rebecca Dunlap Evins, age six at the time of the massacre, recounted forty years later that she "saw quite a number of white men washing the paint from their faces," and Martha Elizabeth Baker Terry, age five at the time of the massacre, recalled over eighty years after the fact that "there was not a real Indian in the group, for they went to the creek and washed the paint from their faces."[90] In 1998 Southern Paiute Clifford Jake, then eighty years old, repeated a story he heard from another Southern Paiute, Isaac Hunkup. It involved two unnamed Paiute brothers who were out hunting deer at the time of the massacre and who witnessed the event from the vantage point of their mountain location. Following the massacre, as Jake related it, "They clean themselves; they took off their Indian outfits off—clothes, Indian clothes. And they were white people. Them white people, they washed themselves up and cleaned themselves. They were white people that done it." The two brothers then hurried to warn various Southern Paiute bands: "We are going to get blamed, going to get blamed for what those white people did. There were no Indians in that massacre."[91]

For the Southern Paiute and Baker-Fancher survivors, repeating such stories served purposes all their own. For the survivors, the stories likely served to reinforce the Mormons' savage nature and to place the blame where it belonged. Their very personal and deeply violent encounters with Mormon settlers in southern Utah left them orphans on the overland trail. It was not the Southern Paiute who stripped them of their mothers, fathers, and siblings, but white Indians, men more savage than the savages. The stories suggested that when the Mormons washed the paint from their faces they revealed their true selves, duplicitous and murderous to the core.[92]

For the Southern Paiute the stories served to reject years of blame and scapegoating, a way to defend their reputation as largely peaceful people. The oral tradition that the Paiute were "going to get blamed for what those white people did" thus served a three-fold purpose in Paiute culture. It reinforced the reality that Mormons did, in fact, blame the Paiutes, even as it pushed that blame back in the direction of the Mormons. It also protected Paiute redness. When the Mormons "took off their Indian outfits" and revealed that "they were white people" it served to clarify the boundaries between red and white, Paiute and Mormon, honesty and dishonesty, savagery and civility. For Southern Paiutes it meant that being red and Paiute were equal to authentic pacifism, while being white and Mormon were tantamount to costumed savagery. For the Southern Paiutes, Mormon whiteness was far from "delightsome" and certainly could not be trusted.[93]

Although the full nature and extent of Mormons donning red faces at Mountain Meadows will never be known, it is clear that if any Mormons did so, they were acting out roles that William Smith and the popular press prescribed for them long before the massacre took place. The Mountain Meadows massacre, if nothing else, proved to outside observers that their fears were justified. In carrying out the attack, Mormons reified a long string of allegations against them. In perpetrating the massacre at Mountain Meadows, Mormons fulfilled their destiny—at least in popular perception.

*   *   *

The conflation of Mormons with Indians continued for the remainder of the nineteenth century. The allegations tended to erupt at times when outsiders perceived that either Mormons or Indians were a threat. Mormon conversion of Indians, especially several mass conversions in the mid-1870s, was one such indication that a supposed alliance was underway. So too were rumors of Indian uprisings in the intermountain West. At various times following the Utah War, the "Mormon problem" and the "Indian problem" were sometimes combined as two pressing national issues in need of congressional solutions.

In May 1858, as the Utah War reached a resolution, mining residents of western Utah Territory petitioned the US Congress for the creation of a new territory, to be named Nevada, out of the western third of Utah Territory. In it they explicitly conflated Mormons with Indians and offered a potential solution to the "Mormon problem": "It is believed that if a new Territory were formed, extending within convenient distance of Salt Lake City, that the dissatisfied Mormons would cheerfully escape from a dominion which they despise; and thus this dangerous and growing *tribe* would be repressed. . . . Some think that the most effective way of ending our Mormon difficulties would be by repealing the act organizing the Territory of Utah, and subjecting the Mormon population thereof to our Indian policy."[94] Nevada Territory was carved out of the western third of Utah Territory in 1861, but not before rumors caused additional alarm. As one Mormon put it, some Nevada silver miners "imagined two Indians and a Mormon behind every rock and sage bush in the Territory."[95]

One critic of Brigham Young accused him in 1870 of inculcating a division in the minds of Indians that "the Americans and Mormons were two distinct and separate peoples," a "damnable proposition" that Young expected "every bishop in Utah, and every elder, priest, teacher and deacon" to echo. Young was also charged with teaching the Indians "to prepare for hostilities against the United States," that they were "the 'battle-axe of the Lord'" and that their mission was to "lay waste the Eastern States," with "'none to deliver.'" It was a "treasonable teaching" that was "common throughout the Territory," the critic alleged.[96] Although Mormons did attempt to cultivate in the minds of Indians a distinction between themselves and other Americans, such allegations failed to acknowledge the complex reality of Mormon-Indian interactions, especially the possibility that religious ideals were the objective of missionary efforts among Native Americans.

In the mid-1870s hundreds of Southern Paiute, Goshute, and Shoshone converted to Mormonism in mass baptisms, events that the Mormons interpreted as proof that a "remnant" of Jacob was finally returning to the gospel fold. Outsiders saw the same events differently and sounded alarm bells. The non-Mormon community of Corrine in northern Utah even posted guards outside of town, and the governor requested that federal troops from Fort Douglas in Salt Lake City march to Corinne for protection.[97]

Rumors of a Mormon-inspired Indian invasion of the town made local and national news. One report warned that "Brigham Young and his emissaries have been tampering with the Indians" again and that "fifteen or twenty lodges of Shoshones or Snakes have been baptized." A story circulated that Brigham Young labeled the new converts "the battle axe of the Lord" and that the Mormons were "endeavoring to make allies of these savages, for the purposes of murder and assassination against outsiders." The same account called it "an old game" of the Mormons "to make cat's paws of the aborigines." Another report claimed that nearly a thousand Indians were baptized and then supplied "with ammunition and guns."[98]

The Southern Paiute Indian agent was not so alarmist in his concern over mass baptisms. Following the baptism of 166 members of the Shivwits band he did, however, complain that "every Indian who participated in this farce thinks he is a better Mormon to-day than Brigham Young himself, and that the ceremony alluded to has clothed him with a sort of armor against any responsibility which he may incur for such trifling matters as horse stealing, or other petty thefts. If he be caught in an overt act, he proudly exclaims, 'Me good Mormon Indian; me heap wash.'" Other Indian agents reported that Mormons made baptismal invitations throughout the territory. One agent called it a "corruption akin to the spirit actuating the famed Mountain Meadow massacre."[99]

In 1882 *Harper's Weekly* gave the overworked accusation pictorial expression. In this portrayal a "polygamous barbarian" is in cahoots with an Indian companion, a beastlike creature whose hands are already dripping with blood from the murdered US soldiers strewn across the battlefield (see figure 3.5). The Salt Lake Tabernacle, a recognizable symbol of Mormonism, sits in the background as the shell of religious corruption that the conspiracy unfolds against. The wily "barbarian" instructs his savage cohort that as soon as springtime arrived the Indian would get "much guns, much ammunition, much whiskey, and much kill paleface." Here Mormons became Indians in the very act of conspiring with them to carry out cruel deeds against "pale-faces." Mormons plied Indians with weapons, ammunition, and alcohol, as incentives to murder white people. Mormons and Indians were thus wedded as barbaric companions in a struggle that pitted red against white and situated Mormons on the wrong side of that racial divide.

Even if the accusation was not conspiracy, guilt by association was a common theme used in several political cartoons in the 1880s to marginalize Mormons alongside other undesirable groups. In 1881 the San Francisco *Wasp* brought the "Mormon Question," "Indian Question," and "China Question," together as the nation's "three troublesome children" (see figure 3.6). In this scene Lady Columbia is harassed by a Chinese immigrant pulling on her hair, a Mormon man spitting in her face, and a tomahawk-wielding Indian chopping US soldiers in half at her feet. Uncle Sam is meanwhile oblivious to the problems his "children" present. He is too preoccupied with "politics" to discipline his children with the whip of "law" that hangs unused on the back of his chair. Lady Columbia and Uncle Sam are parents to a trio of troublesome children, a white couple who somehow gave birth to a mixed-race family. The trouble was not simply that their children were unruly but that they were racially undesirable. Including Mormons in the mix implied that they did not match Uncle Sam's familial ideal either.

Figure 3.5 Thomas Nast, "'When the Spring-Time Comes, Gentle'—Indian!
Polygamous Barbarian, 'Much guns, much ammunition, much whiskey, and much kill
pale face.'" Reprinted from *Harper's Weekly*, 18 February 1882, 109. Library of Congress.

Allegations of Mormon-Indian conspiracies continued to dog the Mormons
up through the Ghost Dance "outbreak" in 1890. That year Major General Nelson
A. Miles, after investigating what he called the Ghost Dance "craze" among western tribes, concluded that "I cannot state positively, but it is my belief that the
Mormons are the prime movers in it." As Miles reasoned, "there are 200,000
Mormons and they themselves claim to believe in prophets and spiritual manifestations, and they even now claim to hold intercourse with the spirit of Joe
Smith. Besides, they have had missionaries at work among the Indians for many
years and have made many converts."[100]

The Ghost Dance religion and Mormonism shared prophetic traditions,
and both groups at various times benefited from the convergence. Especially
during the 1870s the religious excitement generated by the Ghost Dance religion coincided with Mormon missionary success among Shoshone- and

Figure 3.6 Keller, "The Three Troublesome Children." Reprinted from *Wasp*, 16 December 1881. Courtesy of the Bancroft Library, University of California, Berkeley.

Bannock-speaking groups. Both Mormons and Indians tended to interpret the same events as reinforcements of their respective worldviews. One theory also suggested that the purportedly bulletproof "ghost shirts" among the Lakotas were derived from Mormon temple clothing or protective "garments."[101]

Such parallels notwithstanding, the Mormons did not instigate the Ghost Dance. The 1890 manifestations of the dance centered upon Wovoka, a Northern Paiute, whose prophecies demonstrated a Christian influence, likely derived from his childhood affiliation with devout United Presbyterians. Although it is plausible that Mormon elements were absorbed into Ghost Dance doctrine, to suggest that the Mormons were "the prime movers" in the religion was a claim clearly beyond the evidence. It was the last in a string of nineteenth-century ac-cusations that paired Mormons and Indians in unholy alliances.[102]

The solution, some Americans argued, was to enact policies against Latter-day Saints similar to those enacted against Indians. To the *New York World*, Utah was "virtually a Mormon reservation" anyway.[103] "The Mormons must be kept on their reservation," another newspaper demanded, "and their reservation should be a rope."[104]

* * *

Government documents, novels, diaries, overland travel journals, politi-cal cartoons, and newspapers combined to form a chorus of voices convinced that Mormons conspired with Indians against whites. Some accounts pushed beyond the conspiracy to suggest that Mormons looked like Indians, dressed like Indians, acted like Indians, and should be treated and hated like Indians—or worse. The descriptions and accusations were slippery and inconsistent, but they generally conformed to the three themes Ezra Booth established in 1831: that Mormons conspired with Indians, married Indians, and became Indians.

In Utah, Mormons were sometimes viewed as "white Indians," racial rene-gades who fled civilized society in 1847 to join the savages. Outsiders reinforced this idea with persistent accusations of Mormon-Indian conspiracies, stories of Mormons baptizing and controlling whole tribes, thousands of armed Indians at the beck and call of Mormon leaders ready to overthrow civilization as soon as Mormon prophets gave the signal, Indian agency notwithstanding. In some versions, Mormons did not merely conspire with Indians, they became Indians. They intermarried among them, produced "half-breed" children with them, dressed in Indian disguise, and murdered innocent citizens. By these accounts Mormons sank below the level of Indians and revealed their true nature to a suspicious outside world. It naturally followed that Mormons would be treated as Indians, removed from their land, placed on "Mormon reservations," or "ex-terminated." At the very least they should be subjected to the "Indian solution" as an answer to the Mormon problem.

In coloring Mormons red, outsiders justified discriminatory policies against them. Mormons in turn used scriptural validations to racialize Native Americans as fallen Israelites in need of redemption. The "white and delightsome" ideal for Mor-mons was a vision of racial uplift not only for the Indians but also for themselves: it was a way to position themselves higher on the American racial ladder as agents of racial improvement. Outsiders, however, only saw racial decline. It was a struggle for whiteness with far-reaching implications. At the same time that Mormons con-tested their whiteness against allegations of redness, they also entered the fraught American racial nexus between black and white, a contest in which Mormons sought to burnish their whiteness at the expense of their own black converts.

CHAPTER 4

Black, White, and Mormon: Amalgamation

Q. Walker Lewis was a well-respected figure in the Lowell, Massachusetts, community. He ran successful barbershops in both Boston and Lowell and was particularly gifted at cutting children's hair. He was actively engaged in local and national movements, especially as a radical abolitionist who favored the immediate emancipation of slaves and full black equality. In 1826 he was a founding member of an abolitionist society in Lowell and actively pursued its agenda. In the 1820s he also rose to the rank of "most worshipful grand master" in a local Masonic lodge. Baptized into the First Congregational Church of Barre in 1815, he was worshipping at the Baptist church in Boston by 1830 and at St. Anne's Episcopal Church in Lowell by the late 1830s; however, sometime in the early 1840s he converted to Mormonism. Among a fledgling group of local Latter-day Saints, he earned a reputation as a "meek humble man" and dedicated follower of the new faith.[1] No surviving sources specify Lewis's reasons for embracing the Mormon message. The evidence that does survive indicates that in the summer of 1843, or perhaps the following summer, Mormon apostle William Smith, the younger brother of Mormon founder and prophet Joseph Smith Jr., ordained Lewis an elder in the Mormon lay priesthood.[2]

Lewis might be viewed historically as somewhat unremarkable, a barber by trade, a community activist, a leader in a fraternal order, and a member of the lay priesthood in a local Mormon congregation. None of those roles were striking enough in their own right to draw any undue attention—that is unless one understands that Walker Lewis was black. What set Lewis apart was that he was a radical black abolitionist, a founding member of the Massachusetts General Colored Association, a leader in Boston's African Grand Lodge of Masons, and a black elder in the Mormon priesthood.[3] Lewis's son, Enoch Lovejoy Lewis, followed his father into Mormonism and was no doubt poised in the 1840s to benefit from a multigenerational legacy of respectability. Enoch found a marriage partner within the small Mormon community in Lowell. On 18 September 1846, at age twenty, Enoch married Mary Matilda Webster. Seven months later she gave birth to their only child, Enoch R. Lovejoy Lewis.[4]

In the summer of 1847, however, the seemingly unremarkable nature of the Lewis family's presence in the Mormon community came to an end. Walker, Enoch, Mary, and the young couple's infant son came to the attention of William I. Appleby, a visiting Mormon authority. Appleby wrote to Brigham Young to seek clarification on matters of race, priesthood, and marriage, offering a unique lens into the position of blacks within Mormonism as the new faith approached its twenty-year anniversary. The letter would have far-reaching implications for Mormon ideas about race, and especially about interracial marriage. In it Appleby informed Young that Lewis was black and held the priesthood, but more troubling was that his son Enoch, a black man, had married Mary, a white woman, and they had a child together.[5]

Appleby had been a Latter-day Saint for only seven years when he was appointed to preside over and care for the small and scattered Mormon congregations, or "branches," in the northeastern United States. It was in that capacity that Appleby visited Lowell, at the same time that Brigham Young led a vanguard company of Saints into northern Mexico to seek refuge in the Great Basin. Appleby brought with him his own ideas about race and priesthood and especially about "amalgamation," the pre–Civil War term used to indicate the mixture of racial blood, something deemed increasingly unnatural in the popular American mind.[6]

By the end of 1847 Appleby's letter to Brigham Young prompted a meeting of a majority of Mormon apostles at Winter Quarters, in present-day Nebraska. More significantly, that meeting took place in the aftermath of the expulsion of another black Mormon, William (Warner) McCary, from the church for his interracial sexual excesses at Winter Quarters.[7]

A unique confluence of events in 1847 began the protracted and erratic process of black priesthood denial and ban on full temple participation for black Mormons. The William McCary case had already produced the first ideas on priesthood denial, ideas that would become so firmly entrenched in collective Mormon memory that by the early decades of the twentieth century Mormons believed that they had been a part of Mormonism from its beginnings. Those false memories ignored a significant racial history both within and without Mormonism that dramatically impacted the decisions Mormon leaders made about the place of blacks in LDS theology and in LDS society.

While Mormon leaders were making crucial decisions regarding black Mormons, Americans persistently painted Mormons black in one form or another. The Mormon struggle for whiteness in the church's initial two decades centered on the charge that Mormonism favored and facilitated interracial mixing. The paradox was that on the issue of amalgamation, Mormons were consistently and stridently like their white American neighbors. Those neighbors projected their own fears of a disappearing white race onto Mormonism and charged Mormons with "race treason."[8]

At least a part of the rhetoric deployed against Mormons tapped into long-standing white perceptions of black racial characteristics, especially aggressive sexuality. Particularly in the South where white slave masters sometimes sexually violated enslaved blacks, Southern whites turned the tables and stereotyped black men as the true aggressors. Anxiety over slave revolts in the South were accompanied by a corresponding unease that, once a slave rebellion began, the natural target of black aggression would be white women. Whites in general sometimes imagined black men as sexually wanton brutes who harbored secret desires for white women. In Ohio and Missouri, that fear manifested itself among outsiders when they accused both real and fictive black Mormons of transgressing racial boundaries. The irony was that while the Mormon position on black priesthood ordination and temple participation solidified across the course of the nineteenth century, its position on interracial sex and marriage remained remarkably firm, even as outsiders insisted otherwise.[9]

The 1830s were a violence-ridden decade with surges of mobs rioting across the North in backlash against radical abolitionists who were quickly denounced as amalgamationists in disguise. It was only natural for these pressing political issues to have an impact upon Mormonism. Converts from across the spectrum of political and racial positions responded to the Mormon message, including abolitionists, antiabolitionists, enslaved blacks, former slaves, slave holders, and free blacks. When they joined Mormonism they brought their understandings and sympathies with them, a fact made abundantly clear when Appleby met Lewis at Lowell.[10]

Lewis was a radical black abolitionist in favor of full black equality and obviously not concerned about interracial marriage. His wife, Elizabeth, was the product of an interracial union, and his son's marriage continued this trend in the Lewis family.[11] In contrast, Appleby was a white Northerner disgusted by amalgamation who held strong opinions about the proper position of blacks in society. The Mormon message brought both men into the gospel fold. Initially their political views existed independent of their faith, but it was Appleby who curried favor with LDS leaders and whose position ultimately held sway. By the end of the century, it became an inside position, shored up by theological explanations and justifications.

Appleby was born in 1811 in New Jersey and only received a formal education through the ninth grade. He nonetheless learned the skills of a carpenter and millwright and then became a justice of the peace, associate judge for the County of Burlington, New Jersey, and a township clerk. He additionally worked as a scrivener and taught school. Although Appleby's views on the antiabolitionist riots that rocked New York City in 1834 are not known, his proximity to the events and the prominence of the radical abolitionist cause and antiabolitionist backlash in the national press certainly came to his attention. Yet when he wrote Young in the summer of 1847, he was clearly unaware of Mormonism's difficult history navigating between slavery and immediate abolitionism.[12]

Appleby heard future apostle Erastus Snow preach the Mormon message in the fall of 1840. Snow baptized Appleby shortly thereafter, and the new convert quickly became a devoted follower of the faith, evangelizing in the evenings in the same house in which he held his day school. Within a short time he recruited over twenty new converts. He journeyed to Nauvoo to meet Joseph Smith in 1841 and thereafter solidified his commitment to Mormonism through various preaching tours.[13]

In his assignment over the scattered Mormon branches in the Northeast, Appleby traveled, according to his own calculation, nearly two thousand miles during the summer of 1847. As he described it, his tour took him "through the States of New York, Connecticut, Massachusetts, New Hampshire & Vermont, where I have been laboring, among the Branches of the Church, organizing, teaching, counceling [sic] and instructing them in the ways of their duty . . . restoring peace, where difficulty existed." For Appleby, "the situation and standing of the Churches, in general exceeded in some respects my most sanguine expectations. Some one or two I found unorganized, they had held no meetings for eighteen months past, yet they believed the work, and wanted organizing and instructing." He found the various congregations to be "in a Good and prosperous Condition," and described many Saints desirous "to emigrate, as soon as they can Command the means."[14]

It was what he found at the Lowell, Massachusetts, branch that prompted his most pointed queries to Brigham Young: "At Lowell there are some twenty members, rather in a cold state," Appleby began. "I endeavoured [sic] to stir up their mind to a remembrance of their covenants and duty which I trust they will adhere to." Yet it was not the spiritual coldness at Lowell that most concerned Appleby but the unabashed interracial warmth. "At this place I found a coloured brother, by name of 'Lewis,' a barber, an Elder in the Church, ordained some years ago by Wm Smith."[15]

Young was already fully aware of Walker Lewis and of his priesthood ordination. He favorably referred to Lewis himself as he dealt with the reputation of William McCary. Lewis's priesthood was not an issue but an accepted fact, not just by Young but by other apostles as well. In performing Lewis's ordination, William Smith merely followed the example set at Kirtland, Ohio, when a black man, Elijah Abel (sometimes Abels), was ordained there in 1836 with the sanction of Joseph Smith Jr. himself.[16]

For Appleby it was not merely a black man's ordination to the priesthood that caused him concern but the mixed-race nature of his family. "This Lewis I was informed has a bro- or son who is married to a white girl," Appleby wrote, "and both members of the Church there." This news prompted him to question church policy. "Now dear B^r I wish to know if this is the order of God or tolerated in this Church ie to ordain Negroes to the Priesthood, and allow amalgamation. If it is I desire to know it, as I have yet got to learn it." In Appleby's mind the question of priesthood ordination was immediately linked to "amalgamation." Even his use of the word signals his awareness of the ongoing national struggle over the issue and makes his query sound as much American as it does uniquely Mormon. Appleby wondered what interracial marriage meant for the Lowell branch specifically and for Mormonism in general. These were pressing questions that emerged from a broader national context wherein Americans were making very similar demands of each other.[17]

Maryland was the first colony in 1664 to prevent marriage between freeborn English women and enslaved black men. In 1691 Virginia expanded beyond slavery to prohibit marriage between any white man or woman and any black, mulatto, and Indian man or woman, slave or free. Other colonies followed, as did new states created after the formation of the republic. By the 1820s the vast majority of states, seventeen out of twenty-three, banned marriage between blacks and whites. At the outbreak of the Civil War in 1861, the number of states with laws against interracial marriage grew to twenty-eight out of thirty-four.[18]

Even as the majority of states adopted legal codes against the practice, Massachusetts abandoned its ban in 1843. The marriage about which Appleby questioned Brigham Young was solemnized in 1846, three years after Massachusetts made such unions legal. As Appleby's reaction indicates, this did not automatically mean social acceptance. Even those who advocated the repeal of the Massachusetts law did so only when they had sufficiently replaced legal prejudice with the notion that natural preference and good taste would prevent interracial unions.[19]

Appleby clearly had his own ideas about interracial unions, ideas he more freely expressed in his private journal once he visited the couple under question and witnessed their relationship for himself. Appleby recorded that "in looking for a B^r. in the Church, I called at a House,—a coloured man resided there; I set myself down for a few moments. presently in came quite a good looking White Woman, about 22 years old I should think, with blushing cheeks, and was introduced to me as the negro's wife, an infant in a cradle near by bore evidence of the fact." In recounting his visit, Appleby could hardly contain himself, "Oh! Woman, thought I, where is thy shame . . . Respect for thy family, thyself— for thy offspring and above all the law of God?" Even more disturbing for Appleby was the very fact that Enoch and Mary were Mormons, "for indeed I felt ashamed and not only ashamed, but disgusted, when I was informed they were both members of o[ur] Church!"[20]

It is a telling entry, and it situates Appleby firmly within a broader national context wherein many Americans declared themselves revolted by interracial mixing, so much so that respectable members of the middle-class North and slaveholding South were willing to riot and murder in defense of racial purity. Before Appleby joined Mormonism, its leaders attempted to navigate that difficult and violent national context, steering a course somewhere between radical abolitionism on the one hand and the harsh brutalities of chattel slavery on the other.

By the time that Appleby met with Young in late 1847, Mormon leaders had almost two decades of experience with the issue of racial amalgamation. Some of their predecessors, including Joseph Smith Jr., consistently sided with the white majority against amalgamation, especially in the face of charges that Mormons favored and even encouraged interracial mixing. It is impossible to understand Mormonism's evolving racial views about priesthood without understanding Mormonism's closely linked views on interracial marriage. It is equally impossible to understand these positions without first understanding Mormonism's racialization at the hands of outsiders. Those interrelated stories brought considerable historical weight to bear upon Brigham Young when he met with William Appleby in December 1847 at Winter Quarters. He joined with other Mormon leaders and discussed Appleby's visit to the Northeast. More pointedly he learned firsthand of interracial marriage at Lowell, a report that came in the wake of William McCary's sexualized "sealings" to white women earlier that year.

*   *   *

At least one African American joined Mormonism in 1830, the year of its founding, and others trickled in over the course of the nineteenth century. Their presence dramatically impacted the faith as a whole, especially as black converts forced LDS leaders to confront issues of priesthood ordination, interracial sex and marriage, and temple worship. It was both the actual presence of blacks inside the LDS fold and the racialization of white Mormons at the hands of those outside the fold that prompted statements regarding the place of blacks in the Mormon kingdom. Mormon leaders responded to their black converts within a broader national context that persistently suggested that Mormonism provided convenient cover and ready excuse for interracial sex and marriage. While a causal relationship is impossible to substantiate, LDS authorities nonetheless made public pronouncements, declarations, talks, and policy decisions designed to assert respectability. They simultaneously attempted to dispel popular notions that Mormonism was darkening the white race and making it unfit for democracy. Statements from Mormon leaders across the span of the nineteenth century affirmed Mormonism's growing stridency against interracial mixing even as outsiders branded Mormons as harbingers of racial contamination and decline.

One of the first African Americans to join the fledgling movement was a former slave known in the historical record as "Black Pete." Pete was a part of the enthusiastic reception that the first Mormon missionaries received in the Kirtland, Ohio, region in 1830. These were the same missionaries on their way to preach to Native Americans on the Missouri frontier. They were in search of Indian converts but found a black convert instead. They only passed through the Kirtland area but were warmly received among a group of former Campbellite restorationists, followers of Alexander Campbell who were looking for a return to primitive Christianity. The Mormon missionaries declared that a restoration had begun under the leadership of a new prophet, Joseph Smith Jr., and introduced the Book of Mormon as evidence of their claims.[21]

As many as two hundred adults at Kirtland converted to Mormonism in 1830, with Black Pete prominent among them. He may have been ordained to the priesthood although proof of an ordination is not conclusive. His presence as an early Mormon was nonetheless seen as newsworthy among outsiders. The New York *Albany Journal* reported in February 1831 that among the Mormons in Ohio was "a man of color, a chief man, who is sometimes seized with strange vagaries and odd conceits." In August of the same year *The Philadelphia Sun* announced that "The Mormonites have among them an African . . . who fancies he can fly."[22]

Black Pete received particular notice as a member of the new religion, likely because he was one of only six blacks in Geauga County, Ohio, but also because of the method of worship he engaged in. Once the missionaries departed, the newly converted were left to their own devices as to how to practice their new faith. In the absence of guidance, many drew upon the charismatic gifts of the spirit that they had encountered in some of the more enthusiastic traditions of the period. Black Pete may have relied upon traditions he learned as a slave. In any case, he actively preached and participated in the religious enthusiasm that drew the attention of outsiders and raised a few concerns regarding Mormon worship.[23]

Reuben P. Harmon, one observer of the new movement, remembered Black Pete as "a low cunning illiterate negro" who "used to get the power and writhe around in various contortions on the floor. At times he would run over the hills and say he saw holes of fire." Mormon leader George A. Smith later recalled that Black Pete received a written commission from heaven, carried to him "by a black angel." "He started after it, and ran off a steep wash bank twenty-five feet high, passed through a tree top into the Chagrin River beneath. He came out with a few scratches, and his ardor somewhat cooled." This episode became fodder for a story that circulated about a black "Mormonite" who thought he could fly. A different story reported that "Black Pete said . . . that fire would not burn him."[24]

Another observer, Jesse J. Moss, recalled one meeting in which three Mormons, "one a Negro, were impelled by the *Spirit* to go out and preach to the Indians. They left the meeting house on the run, went up a steep hillside, mounted stumps, and began holding forth in gibberish to an imaginary audience." Moss suggested "this was a common occurrence and night was frequently made hideous by their unearthly screams and yells."[25]

It was not just outsiders who found the ecstatic expressions troubling, but some within the new movement did too, particularly the older generation. Convert John Corrill attributed the extreme practices at Kirtland to "many young persons" and noted that "the more substantial minded looked upon it with astonishment, and were suspicious that it was from an evil source."[26]

When Joseph Smith learned of the number of conversions in the Kirtland region he announced Ohio as the new gathering place for the Saints and went there himself in early 1831. He moved quickly to rein in the religious excesses but also to deal with accusations of adultery and open marriages. "It was claimed all things were common, even to free love, among the Mormons in Kirtland," one observer recalled. These charges likely stemmed from the conversion of the Isaac Morley communal "family" at Kirtland. Prior to joining the Mormons, Morley established a collective family organization patterned after that of reformer Robert Owen. Eleven families joined his group, which was inspired by the New Testament ideal that the primitive saints had "all things common" (Acts 2:44). There is no clear indication as to the nature of marriage arrangements among Morley's "family," but as its members converted to Mormonism, outsiders perpetuated the charge of free love.[27]

In addition to the specter of free love, the possibility of that love crossing racial boundaries caused some outsiders to talk. Reuben P. Harmon remembered that "white women" chased Black Pete about, while others suggested that Black Pete did the chasing. Lovina Williams, a fourteen-year-old daughter of convert Frederick G. Williams, was reportedly the focus of his attention. W. R. Hine suggested that "Black Pete claimed to receive revelations to marry her," but Henry Carroll recalled that "Pete joined the Mormons and wanted to marry a white woman. Jo Smith said he could get no revelations for him to" do so. In response, Pete claimed to receive a revelation for himself. These charges all emerged from remembrances published in the 1880s and likely reflected the much more common accusation of that decade that Mormonism facilitated race mixing. In any event, Lovina never married Black Pete, but she later married his white friend Burr Riggs in 1834.[28] Although outsiders viewed Pete as a leader among the more radical element of the Kirtland converts and a violator of religious norms, more troubling were Black Pete's attempted violations of racial norms. In the minds of outsiders, he was a black man who pretended to receive revelations designed to legitimize his desires for white women. It was a part of a century-long process that imagined Mormons as religionists who pierced racial boundaries.[29]

Before long the charges against Black Pete in Ohio morphed into broader accusations against Mormons in Jackson County, Missouri. This time the concern was centered on the threat of a Mormon-slave conspiracy, an allegation which grew to include assertions that Mormons promoted black equality and interracial sex. The episodes in Jackson County came at a moment when the nation was experiencing a second wave of concern over interracial sex and marriage. In many regards, the Jackson County expulsion was an early salvo in a violent, riot-filled antiabolitionist backlash that swept the nation in the 1830s. Although the Mormon expulsion included decidedly religious overtones, fears of a Mormon-black conspiracy and race treason permeated the exchanges between the Mormons and long-term Jackson County residents and were a major impetus behind the resort to violence.[30]

The first national wave of concern over interracial mixing centered on rumors that Thomas Jefferson was having an affair with his black slave Sally Hemings. Jefferson was president of the United States when news broke in 1802, and his political opponents, the Federalists, used reports of an alleged relationship to their advantage. The Federalists particularly used the rumored relationship to make a false connection between Jefferson's political philosophy and his personal behavior. In their minds, Jefferson's vision of a liberal democracy as expressed in the Declaration of Independence, that "all men are created equal," meant that he and his ilk advocated social, economic, and political equality between blacks and whites, which automatically led to interracial mixing. The lyrics of a song published at the height of the scandal poked fun at Jefferson and Hemings and by extension derided their preference for people of a different color. Written in first person, as if Jefferson were the author, it intones:

"She's *black* you tell me—grant she be—
     Must colour always tally?
Black is love's proper hue for me—
     And white's the hue for Sally."

Here, the interracial nature of the relationship was "proper," a sentiment that, in the minds of Jefferson's opponents, was a natural outgrowth of black equality.[31]

The repercussions went well beyond Jefferson to strike at the heart of America's still-fledgling experiment in self-rule: if eighty thousand white men in Virginia followed Jefferson's example and fathered "five mulatto children" each, the product would be "FOUR HUNDRED THOUSAND MULATTOES in addition to the present swarm," one Jeffersonian opponent shuddered. The consequences would be grave: "The country would be no longer habitable, till after a civil war, and a series of massacres." It would take violence to restore order and eradicate from the nation the darker-hued offspring of interracial mixing. For those Americans with "proper" and "natural" sensibilities, Jefferson's racial transgression threatened "the ruin of his country."[32]

In the early decades of the nineteenth century some Americans appropriated the word "amalgamation" from the field of metallurgy as shorthand for "race mixing." By the time the second wave of concern over interracial relations hit America in the 1830s, "amalgamation" was in common usage and came to dominate the national debate. So deep was the American revulsion over race mixing that at least 165 antiabolitionist riots convulsed the North in the 1830s, with Ohio, a center of Mormonism, as the state with "more anti-abolitionist mobs than any other" in the nation. It was into this tumultuous period of racial unrest that Mormonism was born.[33]

A conservative version of abolitionism had long existed in America and predated the Mormon founding. The American Colonization Society, established in 1816, advocated gradual emancipation of slaves. Most importantly it organized a colonization effort to Liberia, on the western coast of Africa, for the freed slaves. The society's advocacy of colonization offered a built in solution to the problem that many whites perceived to accompany emancipation: that is, what to do with the former slaves once they were free? The colonizationists believed that America suffered under the strain of twin evils, which were slavery and an alien race. Colonization offered America its only hope to rid itself of both. Perhaps Jefferson articulated it best when he argued that once freed, a slave should be "removed beyond the reach of mixture." Colonization remained the majority Northern position up through the Civil War. Even Abraham Lincoln was a colonizationist and remained so through the early years of his presidency.[34]

The antislavery movement, however, changed dramatically in the 1830s with the growth of a minority group of radical abolitionists who began advocating for immediate emancipation and full black equality. William Lloyd Garrison, a prominent leader in this movement, founded a newspaper, *The Liberator*, and published his first issue on 1 January 1831, less than nine months after the official organization of what became the LDS Church. In the second edition of his paper Garrison struck not just at slavery but at Northern prejudice against blacks. He even advocated for the repeal of the Massachusetts law banning interracial marriage, which was the first time someone so publicly supported this stance. Garrison went on to launch an attack against the American Colonization Society, whose ideas he derided as evil and anti-Christian. Initially the colonizationists tolerated the rhetorical abuse, but as the immediate abolitionists gained momentum and members, the colonizationists struck back, calling them (among other things), "amalgamationists," "fanatics," "lunatics," and "firebrands."[35] The colonizationists used the charge of amalgamation to distance themselves from the immediate abolitionists. The argument was that if a person wanted to free the slaves and live among them rather than send them to Africa, then ultimately that person favored race mixing. Some accused Garrison of attempting to repeal the Massachusetts marriage ban out of a desire to marry a black woman himself. Similar charges were leveled against a variety of leaders in the immediate abolition movement.[36]

In 1833 the number of antislavery societies that advocated immediate emancipation expanded dramatically to include forty-seven local organizations in ten states. In the spring of that year an incident in Connecticut captured national attention. Prudence Crandall, a Quaker schoolmistress, first admitted a black student to her day school and then decided to open her boarding school exclusively to black girls. She was quickly denounced for promoting an influx of unwelcomed blacks and for promulgating amalgamation. The state legislature soon ruled against her. She was put on trial and found guilty even as antiabolitionist mobs stoned her schoolhouse, attempted to set it on fire, and finally destroyed her home. By the fall of 1834, Crandall capitulated and moved to Illinois.[37]

The violence in New York City was even worse. Following the organization of the American Anti-Slavery Society there, its leaders were smeared with amalgamation rhetoric, especially as their meetings included blacks and whites fully integrated in mixed audiences. The tension culminated in July 1834 in a series of antiabolitionist riots. The violence lasted for eleven days and included the sacking of homes and stores of abolitionist leaders and sympathizers. At the heart of these attacks was the rioters' persistent charge that support of abolitionism equaled support of amalgamation and was grounds for physical assault.[38]

Two years later in Missouri, an antiabolitionist mob smashed the printing press of Elijah Lovejoy, a Presbyterian minister, newspaper editor, and emerging critic of slavery. After Missourians drove Lovejoy from their state for his outspoken stance on black freedom, he relocated across the Mississippi River to Alton, Illinois, where he again opened a newspaper and advocated immediate abolitionism. Vigilantes in Illinois wrecked his press three times, and on one occasion they threatened to tar and feather him, but Lovejoy refused to relent. In 1837 a mob attacked the warehouse where Lovejoy's press was stored. In the ensuing violence, members of the mob fatally shot Lovejoy five times and then demolished his press. No one was ever convicted for Lovejoy's murder.[39]

Amidst these three incidents, a very similar episode played out among the Mormons in Jackson County, Missouri. The trouble began in July 1833 with a column titled "Free People of Color" published in the LDS newspaper *The Evening and the Morning Star* and written by editor William Wines Phelps. Phelps came to Mormonism with prior abolitionist sympathies but of the more conservative colonizationist stripe, which was a crucial distinction lost on the residents of Jackson County. Phelps was surprised by the backlash against his column, so much so that he rushed to print an "extra" broadsheet attempting to explain the earlier column and to simultaneously distance Mormonism from blacks, but especially from immediate abolitionism and the corresponding brush of amalgamation. This frantic attempt to claim whiteness for Missouri Mormons failed to convince the people who mattered most in Jackson County. Before the affair ended, a Jackson County vigilance committee destroyed Phelps's printing office and drove the Mormons from the county.[40]

"Free People of Color" was Phelps's effort to educate and even warn free black Mormons in other states about the potential pitfalls and difficulties that awaited them should they decide to move with their fellow Saints to Missouri. It is not clear, besides Black Pete, how many African Americans had joined the movement by 1833, but certainly the numbers were small. According to historian Mark Lyman Staker even Pete "disappeared" from the Mormon community at Kirtland sometime between 1831 and 1834. Elijah Abel, another early black convert, was baptized in 1832, and other blacks may have also joined. LDS apostle Parley P. Pratt defended Phelps's column in 1839, with the argument that the Missourians' fears of a black Mormon influx were unfounded, especially because "one dozen free negroes or mulattoes never belonged to our society in any part of the world, from its first organization to this day." If Pratt's estimate is even close to accurate it is uncertain why Phelps felt the column necessary in the first place, let alone who he had in mind as his target audience.[41]

In any case, the column indicates that Phelps had a vision of a universal Mormon message in 1833, open to blacks as well as whites, that reflected the generally expansive perspective early Mormons adopted throughout the 1830s and 1840s. Like many Christian believers of his day, Phelps understood racial categories through a biblical lens, especially the idea that the entire human family descended from the three sons of Noah following the great flood. In this view, Shem was the father of Asians, Ham gave rise to Africans, and Japheth to Europeans. Nevertheless, the gospel message in Phelps's mind transcended those divisions. Phelps wrote in 1835 that "all the families of the earth . . . should get redemption . . . in Christ Jesus," regardless of "whether they are descendants of Shem, Ham, or Japheth." Another publication declared that all people were "one in Christ Jesus . . . whether it was in Africa, Asia, or Europe." Apostle Parley P. Pratt similarly professed his intent to preach "to all people, kindred, tongues, and nations without any exception" and included "India's and Afric's sultry plains" in a poetic expression of his global dream for Mormonism. Even one outside observer noted that Ohio Saints honored "the natural equality of mankind, without excepting the native Indians or the African race." It was an open attitude that may have gone too far for its time and place. That same observer noted that the Mormon stance toward Indians and blacks was at least partially responsible for "the cruel persecution by which they have suffered." In his mind the Book of Mormon ideal that "all are alike unto God," including "black and white," made it unlikely that the Saints would "remain unmolested in the State of Missouri."[42]

Such inclusive ideals were incompatible with a growing national sentiment against race mixing. Phelps poorly gauged the depth of suspicion regarding Mormonism then percolating among some of his Missouri neighbors. In his own words, he wrote his July 1833 column "to prevent any misunderstanding among the churches abroad, respecting Free people of color, who may think of coming to the western boundaries of Missouri, as members of the church." He quoted two sections of Missouri legal code concerning freed blacks and the necessity of possessing proper paperwork to certify their status. If freed blacks violated Missouri law, the punishment was ten lashes on a bare back and expulsion from the state. Phelps no doubt hoped to prevent any black Mormons from enduring such a consequence. As he noted, "Slaves are real estate in this and other states, and wisdom would dictate great care among the branches of the church of Christ, on this subject." Phelps then made it clear that Mormonism was open to blacks, but urged wisdom if any black Mormons should desire to migrate to Missouri. "So long as we have no special rule in the church, as to people of color, let prudence guide," he counseled.

In another column in the same edition he further cautioned, "Great care should be taken on this point." He then elaborated on slavery and articulated a decidedly colonizationist sentiment regarding abolition: "As to slaves," he wrote, "we have nothing to say. In connection with the wonderful events of this age, much is doing towards abolishing slavery, and colonizing the blacks, in Africa." This message, a clear signal as to the brand of antislavery Phelps subscribed to, included in it the unstated but clearly understood notion that colonizationists were by their very nature opposed to amalgamation. The Jackson County crowd either missed or chose to ignore this second column. The perception that Mormons were inviting freed blacks to Missouri quickly riled residents. They accused Mormons of attempting to incite a slave revolt and more seriously of promoting interracial mixing.[43]

By 16 July Phelps had attempted to calm some of the fears that his original column heightened. In an "extra" edition of the *Star* he attempted to reposition Mormonism in relation to blacks: "Having learned with regret, that an article entitled FREE PEOPLE OF COLOR, in the last number of the Star, has been misunderstood, we feel it duty bound to state, in this Extra, that our intention was not only to stop free people of color from emigrating to this state, but to prevent them from being admitted as members of the church." It was his desperate attempt to suppress suspicions and was simply not true. There is no indication that Phelps was setting official church policy or that he consulted Joseph Smith before issuing his broadsheet.[44]

Phelps then quoted his other column from the July edition of the *Star* that included his sentiments about abolitionism and his support for "colonizing the blacks, in Africa."[45] Why would Phelps assert abolition sentiment in a broadsheet designed to quiet fears of a Mormon-led slave insurrection? It only makes sense when couched within the broader split within the antislavery movement itself. Phelps was deliberately attempting to align himself with the more prevalent Northern middle-class colonizationists and to simultaneously distance himself from the minority radical abolitionists who advocated immediate abolition and were already branded as supporters of amalgamation. It was a move by Phelps to quiet fears of insurrection.[46]

Phelps's broadsheet did little to alleviate suspicions among Jackson County residents. In response to the growing alarm, prominent citizens of Jackson County formed a vigilance committee. Its leaders described Phelps's initial column as "an indirect invitation to the free brethren of colour in Illinois, to come like the rest to the land of Zion." They dismissed the "extra" as a "weak attempt to quiet our apprehension" and called it "a poor compliment to our understandings." As they noted, Phelps's original column "contained all the necessary directions and cautions, to enable the free blacks, on their arrival there, to claim and exercise the rights of citizenship."[47]

Other accounts complained about the growing migration of white Mormons to Jackson County and the declining quality of character that some residents perceived to be evident among the newly arrived Saints. One critic reported that "the Mormonites number some 1200 souls in that county, and that each successive spring and autumn pours forth its swarms among them." So degraded were the white Mormons that they had "nearly reached the low condition of the black population." Another detractor said that the Mormons were "little above the condition of our blacks either in regard to property or education."[48]

Jackson County residents further accused Mormons of conspiring to incite a slave rebellion and ultimately to promote a racial assault on white women. The vigilance committee blamed the Mormons for "tampering with our slaves, and endeavoring to sow dissentions and raise seditions amongst them." It complained that Phelps's article in the *Star* was an open invitation to "free negroes and mulattoes from other States to become mormons and remove and settle among us." Some residents said that the Mormons had "opened an asylum for rogues and vagabonds and free blacks," while others were concerned that Mormons promoted black "ascendancy over the whites."[49] Their fear of slave revolt was akin to that which permeated Southern society, particularly in the wake of Nat Turner's 1831 slave revolt in Virginia that left around sixty whites dead. Southern state legislators passed laws designed to prevent slave revolts and to ensure white domination. They outlawed the education of blacks, the congregating of blacks, and the movement of blacks without proper papers, such as the Missouri codes that Phelps quoted in the *Star*. As slave masters viewed it, large populations of freed blacks represented an incentive for liberation to their slaves. For Jackson County residents, then, Phelps's article was nothing short of a Mormon attempt to "corrupt our blacks and instigate them to bloodsheds." As they saw it, an influx of black Mormons would produce a "stench, both physical and moral" that would be enough to make the situation in Jackson County "insupportable."[50]

As with Black Pete in Ohio, however, it was not simply the presence of blacks among Mormons that was a breach of societal norms, but the interracial threat that imagined throngs of black Mormons migrating to Missouri represented. Missourians declared themselves flatly unwilling "to receive into the bosom of our families, as fit companions for our wives and daughters the degraded and corrupted free negroes and mulattoes, that are now invited to settle among us." As was typical of antiabolitionists elsewhere, Jackson County residents raised the specter of amalgamation and projected it onto the Mormons.[51]

Only four days after Phelps's extra appeared in print, a throng of Jackson County residents, perhaps 300 to 500 strong, stormed the *Star* office and destroyed all remaining copies as well as the original July issue. Mob members scattered Phelps's type and the press itself along with Mormon sacred writings. They demolished Phelps's office and then used crowbars, hammers, and their bare hands to level the Phelps home. The mob seized Bishop Edward Partridge and Charles Allen, dragged them to the town square, and covered them in tar and feathers. Before the end of the year Jackson County residents expelled an estimated 1,200 Mormons from the county.[52]

The Evening and the Mormon Star did not publish another issue until December 1833, and then in Kirtland, Ohio, instead of Missouri. Oliver Cowdery, a close associate to Joseph Smith, served as the *Star's* new editor when it resumed publication, with Phelps occasionally submitting reports from Missouri. Cowdery initially focused on chronicling the Mormon version of events at Jackson County, responding to charges leveled against Missouri Saints, and painting the Missourians as the true violators of racial norms.

Cowdery asserted that Mormons, like all whites, understood Southern racial protocol and were very much aware of potential slave revolts: "All who are acquainted with the situation of slave States, know that amid a dense population of blacks, that the life of every white is in constant danger," he wrote. It was simply absurd to suggest that Missouri Mormons would undertake such a foolish project as to foment a slave rebellion because it would jeopardize "the life of every white inhabitant in the country. For the moment an insurrection should break out, no respect would be paid to age, sex, or religion; by an enraged, jealous, and ignorant black banditti." Mormons, in other words, were white and just as susceptible to death in the wake of a slave rebellion as their Missouri neighbors. "Any one who might be found influencing the minds of slaves with evil, would be beneath even the slave himself, and unworthy the privileges of a free Government," Cowdery asserted. "We deny the charge, that the slaves in that county were ever tampered with by us, or at any time persuaded to be refractory. . . . Any charge of that nature is wholly and entirely unfounded."[53]

For Cowdery, it was the Missourians who were truly "degraded," especially as they violated fundamental American rights when they forced "peaceable inhabitants from their own lands without a cause." It was not just the violation of property rights, however, that tarnished the Missourians but the violation of racial boundaries. Just as the Missourians complained that Mormons were attempting to debauch their wives and daughters, the Mormons leveled a similar charge. According to the *Star,* sometime before the Missourians demolished Phelps's printing press, "the mob sent their negroes to insult and abuse certain young women" among the Mormons. The plan was for enslaved black men to sneak into "a small cabin" where the girls slept and rape them. The Mormons, however, learned of the plot and were able to thwart it. The unfulfilled plan, nonetheless, illustrated in Cowdery's mind the bold hypocrisy bound up in the accusation that the Missourians made against the Mormons. In Cowdery's mind, Jackson County residents were "so far beneath every thing heretofore extant on earth in the form of wickedness, that they will set their Afric colored population to steal into the dwellings of peaceable neighbors and defile the virtuous!" In the end, the incident left Cowdery to wonder, "Is it color that constitutes a savage, or is it the acts of men that appear disgustful?"[54]

This rumination was designed to force Missourians to consider the ways in which the same brush used to paint the Mormons black could be turned on them. In 1835 Phelps even suggested that blackness was a divine punishment for gospel apostasy. He argued that "God causes the saints, or people that fall away from his church to be cursed in time, with a *black skin.*" "Can we not observe in the countenances of almost all nations, except the Gentile, a dark, sallow hue," he wondered, a sign which denoted "that they have fallen or changed from the original beauty and grace of father Ad-am."[55]

Similarly in the 1840s Mormons characterized members of the mob who murdered Joseph Smith Jr. as "artificial black men," especially because they blackened their faces before attacking Smith. They were "murderers who paint themselves black in order that they may not be known when they commit a crime." Even a non-Mormon observer suggested that mob members must have been ashamed of their "white skins" otherwise "they would not have painted themselves when they went to kill Joseph and Hyrum Smith." In his view "they wished to make their faces correspond with their hearts." Such sentiments, even though aimed at outside enemies, no doubt impacted how Mormons viewed their own black converts.[56]

The episode in Missouri also influenced the view of Mormon leaders toward immediate abolitionism and amalgamation. Mormons repeatedly distanced themselves from any notion that they intended to incite slave rebellion or even associate with abolitionist societies. They simultaneously expressed fear that wholesale and immediate abolishment of slavery would send an uneducated and jobless mass of blacks throughout the country who would automatically threaten white women. Mormons inserted themselves into the national debate in an effort to avoid the same type of antiabolitionist violence then impacting the North and a repeat of events that led to their expulsion from Jackson County.

In 1835 Mormons joined many other denominations that decade to declare themselves against immediate abolitionism. Methodists, Baptists, Catholics, Presbyterians, and even Quakers either adopted formal resolutions, spoke out against abolitionist movements, or took steps to distance themselves from radical abolitionists. The Quakers had long been opposed to slavery but emphasized gradual emancipation. In 1837 Orthodox Quakers in Philadelphia embraced a conservative stance and counseled against joining fanatical antislavery groups. Two years later a Baltimore faction of Quakers also cautioned its members against uniting with immediate abolitionists. In a similar fashion, between 1831 and 1835, almost all leading Congregational clergymen "lined up squarely against abolitionism." In fact, when forty theological students at one Congregational seminary failed to heed warnings not to attend an abolition rally, administrators dismissed them. The following year, a majority of delegates at a Methodist conference in Cincinnati called the abolitionist movement a danger to the union.[57]

The disruption to the American religious landscape did not end with abolitionism. In the 1840s and 1850s the Baptist, Methodist, and Presbyterian churches experienced schisms or split altogether along a North-South divide over slavery and questions about race.[58] The Mormon position avoided any such split. It did so in a way that created space within the fold for slave masters who converted to Mormonism and for enslaved blacks. There was no proscription against slaveholding as a barrier to membership, priesthood, or missionary service. Mormonism, in fact, honored the master-slave relationship when it made preaching to slaves and baptism of slaves contingent upon the permission of a slave's master. The LDS stance proclaimed, "We do not believe it right to interfere with bondservants neither preach the gospel to, nor baptize them, contrary to the will and wish of their masters." It was a sentiment that the Saints canonized as a declaration of beliefs, not as revelation, and included in the Book of Commandments and its successor the Doctrine and Covenants, books they accepted as scripture.[59]

While carving out this position in the mid-1830s was politically expedient and even perceived as necessary to prevent the same type of violence that led to the Mormon expulsion from Jackson County, it simultaneously helped to create the circumstances that would lead to Brigham Young's announcement of a priesthood ban in 1852. Young's announcement was made to the Utah territorial legislature as it considered how to deal with the issue of slavery, an issue that was relevant only because slaveholders from the South converted to Mormonism, as did some of their slaves, and then moved to the Great Basin with the rest of the Saints. The decision in the 1830s that attempted to maintain an open gospel message for slave masters and slaves alike, while simultaneously avoiding the perceived pitfalls of immediate abolitionism, had consequences that were perhaps unintended. It avoided the split or schism that tore the Methodists, Baptists, and Presbyterians apart, even as it created the circumstances—the inclusion of slaves and slave masters in the Mormon fold—that would later lead Brigham Young to split the lay priesthood along racial lines. It was a case of the universal Mormon message casting a net wide enough to incorporate "black and white, bond and free" (2 Nephi 26:33) and then sorting those who responded according to prevailing cultural notions of racial superiority, white and free over black and bound. The very universalism of the opening decades of Mormonism laid the groundwork for the later racial constriction.

In the meantime, Mormon antiabolitionist sentiment found its fullest expression in 1836 in a series of articles published in the *Messenger and Advocate*, a newspaper published out of Kirtland, Ohio, with Oliver Cowdery as editor. The immediate context for the articles was the visit of an abolitionist agitator, John Watson Alvord, who Mormon leaders wanted to distance themselves from. Alvord was a student at Oberlin College, sixty miles west of Kirtland, where in 1835 school administrators voted to admit African American students. Alvord embraced his school's progressive stance on race and became an organizer for the American Anti-Slavery Society. During a speaking tour of northern Ohio in the winter of 1835 and 1836, he preached abolitionism and organized local antislavery societies wherever he found receptive audiences. Sometimes antiabolitionists pelted him with snowballs and apples, as well as drowned out his lectures with ringing bells and blowing horns. At Kirtland, however, he was "well received." He organized an antislavery chapter there with eighty-six members, some of whom were Mormon.[60]

In the immediate aftermath of Alvord's visit to Kirtland, Joseph Smith Jr. moved to put as much distance between Alvord and the Mormons as possible. Smith wanted to be clear that simply because Alvord spoke at Kirtland, it did not follow that Mormons endorsed his ideas. Smith and two other Mormon leaders, Warren Parrish and Oliver Cowdery, published responses in the *Messenger and Advocate*. Smith noted that there were no "mobs or disturbances" that marked

Alvord's visit, which might have given outside observers a false impression that the Mormons "received as gospel and the word of salvation" all that Alvord said. While Smith was pleased that there was no violence, he wanted it known that there was no enthusiasm either. In fact, he reported that Alvord was nearly ignored, left "to hold forth his own arguments to nearly naked walls."[61] Warren Parrish went further in announcing that "we do not countenance the abolition system, nor fellowship those who advocate its principles." He asserted that any person who "would stir up rebellion among the blacks, is an enemy to the well being of society."[62]

Smith advised Mormon missionaries preaching in the South to exhort "all men . . . to repent" but stipulated that "we have no right to interfere with slaves contrary to the mind and will of their masters." It was a bit of universalism tempered by the social and political realities of preaching in the South. He suggested that "it would be much better and more prudent, not to preach at all to slaves, until after their masters are converted." He hoped that no Mormon missionaries would be "found stirring up strife and sedition against our brethren of the South." He suggested that one potential result of a wholesale abolition would be to "set loose upon the world a community of people who might peradventure, overrun our country and violate the most sacred principles of human society,— chastity and virtue." It was a message that signaled Smith's full understanding of the national context in which he was immersed. He followed his renunciation of immediate abolitionism with a rejection of interracial mixing.[63]

Oliver Cowdery editorialized in the same issue against abolitionism and further emphasized his fear of amalgamation. In his mind, abolishing slavery would set loose "paupers, and a reckless mass of human beings, uncultivated, untaught and unaccustomed to provide for themselves the necessaries of life—endangering the chastity of every female who might by chance be found in our streets." For Cowdery, "the notion of amalgamation is develish![sic]".[64]

In a follow-up unsigned article the *Advocate* decried the evils of the abolitionists' "glorious doctrine of AMALGAMATION!" The article flatly declared that Mormons "do not hold to any such doctrines—neither do we fellowship those who do." It then explained the politically expedient reason for so forcefully speaking out against it: "Being aware that our brethren are numerous in the South . . . it was thought advisable to come out decidedly in relation to this matter, that our brethren might not be subjected to persecution on this account—and the lives of our traveling elders put in jeopardy." Mormon leaders responded out of fear of the violence then permeating the nation which led even some of the nation's most radical abolitionists to distance themselves from accusations that they favored amalgamation. Mormons worried that "if madam rumor, with her thousand poisoned tongues, was once to set afloat the story that this society had come out in favor of the doctrines of Abolitionism, there would be no safety for one of us in the South." They could have just as well added "or in the North."[65]

At the same time that Mormon leaders entered the highly charged national debate over abolitionism, they also signaled their immersion in and inheritance of centuries-old religious understandings regarding the biblical origins of race-based slavery. Genesis chapter 9 contains the story of Ham discovering his father, Noah, naked and intoxicated in his tent. Ham announced Noah's condition to his brothers Shem and Japheth who then properly covered their father's naked-ness while diverting their eyes. Upon awakening and learning of Ham's appar-ent misdeed, Noah cursed Ham's son Canaan, "a servant of servants shall he be unto his brethren" (Genesis 9:18–25). It is one of the most widely interpreted, explained, and overtly stretched stories in the Bible, put to use most explicitly in the antebellum South to justify racial slavery and in postbellum America to shore up racial segregation.[66] Irrespective of the fact that these verses do not mention black skin and that Noah's curse was placed upon Canaan not Ham, the broader Judeo-Christian tradition consistently held that Ham was somehow black, married to a black woman, and/or the father of a black race. His posterity was cursed to become slaves, a divine injunction in which mortals should not interfere. It was an argument that long predated the founding of Mormonism and even of the United States; in the long course of Western civilization it took shape in a variety of forms and was used to different ends. In sum, the story of Ham's curse served as "the single greatest justification for Black slavery for more than a thousand years."[67]

It was not only Southern defenders of slavery who employed the curse of Ham; Northern theologians did so as well. Some Northern religious leaders based their resistance to the radical abolitionists upon the idea that the Bible was the literal word of God and that it sanctioned slavery. As some clergy articulated it, an attack on slavery amounted to an attack on the Bible itself. In the same vein, to accept immediate abolitionism was to reject God's word. The Irish-born Epis-copal bishop of Vermont, John Henry Hopkins, for example, defended slavery "on the grounds of the inescapable authority of scripture." Charles Hodge, an old school Presbyterian and the dominant figure at Princeton Theological Seminary for fifty years, likewise believed that "the Scriptures do sanction slaveholding." Hodge argued that to call slavery "a heinous crime" was tantamount to "a direct impeachment of the word of God."[68]

Joseph Smith, Warren Parrish, and Oliver Cowdery were fully immersed in this culture and not surprisingly used the same justification to argue against im-mediate abolition. Smith quoted from Genesis regarding the "sons of Ham" and asserted that he was ignorant as to "the design of the Almighty" in this event but was confident that "the curse is not yet taken off the sons of Canaan, neither will be until it is affected by as great power as caused it to come." In other words, immediate abolitionists were attempting to undo what God had put in place. Smith felt sure that "the people who interfere the least with the decrees and purposes of God in this matter, will come under the least condemnation before him." Parrish concurred and argued that "God's curse pronounced by his servant Noah will remain upon them; and Canaan must dwell in the tents of Shem and be his servant until He, who pronounced it shall order it otherwise." He added that "all the abolition societies that now are or ever will be, cannot cause one jot or tittle of the prophecy to fail." Mormon missionaries preaching in the South were directed not to teach slaves until after their masters were converted and to instruct converted masters to treat their slaves humanely.[69]

As Smith articulated it, however, the curse was slavery and not a ban against blacks holding the priesthood. The arguments for priesthood restriction developed later, following Smith's death. For the time being Mormons attempted to navigate a charged, violence-filled national context, one in which they claimed that their Zion was located in Jackson County, Missouri. Zion for Mormons in the 1830s was slave territory, land they had already been driven from, in part as a result of perceived infractions against Southern racial protocol. The simultaneous co-headquarter of Mormonism was in Ohio, the state with the most anti-abolitionist mob violence in the nation. Radical abolitionist James Alvord's visit to Kirtland in 1836 added a sense of immediacy to Mormon leaders' efforts to position themselves in a way that prevented vigilante action against Ohio Saints and that protected Missouri Mormons as well as missionaries then preaching in the South. In these circumstances, Smith, Parrish, and Cowdery attempted to honor the universalism of the Mormon message while simultaneously striking a balance between the extremes of slavery and a radical abolitionism linked to amalgamation. They also spoke at least partly out of a desire to protect female virtue from racial assault, which was a message clearly crafted to appeal to the sympathies of antiabolitionist mobs.

Even while Joseph Smith's views on slavery continued to evolve, his views on interracial mixing remained constant. The Mormon move to Illinois coincided with a national decline in antiabolitionist mob violence. It also followed on the heels of the Mormon abandonment of Ohio and expulsion from Missouri, which freed Smith from the need to be overly sympathetic toward slavery. In the 1840s Illinois residents increasingly supported antislavery sentiments and political positions, which created space for Mormons to speak out against slavery themselves.[70]

In 1843 a conversation with apostle Orson Hyde offered an opportunity for Smith to express his private feelings as to "the situation of the Negro." In Smith's view, notions of black inferiority were entirely created by environmental circumstances and not inherent racial characteristics: "They come into the world slaves mentally & phy[s]ically. change their situation with the white & they would be like them," Smith reasoned. "They have souls & are subjects of salvation," he added, a rejection of an idea expressed by some thinkers of his day. Smith even suggested that "slaves in Washington [were] more refin[e]d than the presidents" and that bootblack "boys will take the shine off those they brush & wait on." Smith concluded by saying that if he had "any thing to do with the negro—I would confine them to by strict Laws to their own Species [and] put them on a national Equalization." His earlier defense of Southern slavery was gone and in its place a more progressive vision of black equality took shape. Any perceived deficiencies in African Americans were purely byproducts of the lack of educational opportunities under slavery. Remove the barriers and blacks were capable of the same or higher levels of attainment as whites.[71]

Smith's views on racial mixture, however, remained fixed. "Strict laws," like those already in force in a majority of states, should maintain separation. It was a notion Smith himself enforced the following year when two "negroes" attempted "to marry white women" at Nauvoo. With no explanation for the distinction, Smith fined one man twenty-five dollars and the other five dollars.[72]

Smith enunciated his most strident antislavery views when he proposed a system for emancipation of slaves in his 1844 bid for the US presidency. Even still he maintained a stance in favor of colonization and, by implication, a stance against amalgamation. Smith envisioned the officers of the federal government as truly "the servants of the people," with a mission to "ameliorate the condition of all: black or white, bond or free." He drew upon the Bible to advocate a vision of a universal human family: "God hath made of one blood all nations of men, for to dwell on all the face of the earth." It was a paraphrase of Acts 17:26, a verse Brigham Young would also cite in 1847 in an interview with William McCary, a black Mormon. For the time being, Smith advocated granting "liberty to the captive" through federal intervention, a system whereby the government would pay "the southern gentleman a reasonable equivalent for his property, that the whole nation might be free indeed!" "Break off the shackles from the poor black man, and hire him to labor like other human beings," he insisted.[73]

But even as he spoke against slavery, he distanced himself from "abolition doctrine" and still had to confront the issue of what to do with the slaves once they were freed. In a March 1844 speech he demonstrated sympathy for colonizationist ideals when he proposed annexing Texas and then liberating the slaves in two or three states. He would financially compensate their former owners and then send the freed slaves to Mexico where interracial mixing was less of a concern ("where all colors are alike," or where "they are mixed blacks," as two different observers of the speech recorded it). It was a proposal that demonstrated the persistent fear of interracial mixing that continued to permeate American society.[74]

The following decade, in his famous debates with Stephen A. Douglas, even Abraham Lincoln was forced to refute the claim that because he advocated for black freedom that he did so out of a desire to "vote, and eat, and sleep, and marry with negroes!" Lincoln pointed to the illogic behind the view that "because I do not want a black woman for a *slave* I must necessarily want her for a *wife*." As Lincoln put it, "I need not have her for either, I can just leave her alone." Smith's proposal no doubt emerged from the same impulse. In taking a stance against slavery he was not automatically taking a stance in favor of amalgamation.[75]

*   *   *

When William Appleby wrote Brigham Young in June 1847 to inquire whether the Church of Jesus Christ of Latter-day Saints "tolerated" the ordination of "Negroes to the Priesthood" and whether it permitted "amalgamation," both questions carried considerable historical weight within and without the movement. It was not only the news of Enoch Lewis's marriage to Mary Webster that was on the minds of Mormon leaders when they convened a meeting at Winter Quarters to discuss the matter but the disturbing sexual exploits of another black Mormon, William McCary.

McCary claimed to be of mixed African American and Native American ancestry. He was certainly of African American descent, but his claims of Indian inheritance were likely calculated to position himself higher on the Mormon and American racial ladders than being black might allow. A runaway slave from Mississippi, he had invented a variety of identities and aliases for himself. He arrived in Nauvoo in late 1845 and converted to Mormonism in early 1846. He was baptized and possibly ordained to the priesthood at the hands of apostle Orson Hyde, although the evidence for a priesthood ordination is not conclusive. Around the same time, McCary married Lucy Stanton, a "white woman" who converted to Mormonism with her family as a teenager in the Kirtland region.[76]

McCary's relationship with Mormonism was tenuous at best and fraught with difficulties. It was not a particularly favorable time to join the Saints. The main body of Mormons were then fleeing their homes in Nauvoo in search of refuge in the West. McCary parted at least twice from the Mormons before his final expulsion in the summer of 1847. A temporary break may have taken place as early as the fall of 1846 when several newspapers picked up a story first printed in the *Cincinnati Commercial*, which suggested that McCary had already abandoned Mormonism and struck out on his own. The story referred to "a big burly half Indian, half negro, formerly a Mormon, who has proclaimed himself Jesus Christ!" It claimed that the savior figure had nearly sixty followers, about half of whom were women and that "he shewed his disciples . . . the scars of wounds in his hands and limbs received on the cross!" It is impossible to ascertain the reliability of such reports, but the *Commercial* was clearly premature in suggesting that McCary was no longer a Mormon.[77]

Sometime during the winter of 1846–1847, McCary arrived among the Saints at Winter Quarters, in present-day Nebraska, one temporary stopping place for Mormons on their westward migration. There McCary gained a reputation for his abilities as a flutist and his talents as a ventriloquist. In February 1847 he entertained Brigham Young, who remarked that his "skill on the flute cannot be surpassed," while another report called McCary "a natural musician" and noted "his ability as a mimic."[78]

Even though McCary's musical skills won Young's favor, his increasingly flamboyant claims and erratic behavior led to growing suspicions about his motives. Mormons at Winter Quarters variously referred to him as "a half blooded Indian," "the Coolurd man," "the Indian prophet," "a half breed Indian negro," "the Negro prophet," "a mulatto or quarterrun," "the Indian musician," and, most derisively, "the nigger prophet." Even in February, there was already concern over some of his camp activities. One Mormon, Nelson W. Whipple, recalled that McCary "understood the slight-of-hand, the black art or that he was a magician or something of the kind, and had fooled some of the ignorant in that way." Another Saint, Lorenzo Brown, said that McCary "styled himself a prophet[,] the ancient of days whose hair was as wool," while the official church record noted that McCary claimed to be "Adam, the ancient of days" and was said to "have an odd rib which he had discovered in his wife." Even still, Young was indulgent and concluded that McCary seemed "willing to go according to counsel and that he may be a useful man after he has acquired a[n] experimental knowledge." He counseled Mormons to "use the man with respect."[79]

Yet, Young's call for respect did little to quiet concern about some of McCary's more outlandish claims. In response, an assembly of Mormon leaders gathered on 26 March to interview McCary themselves. As president of the Quorum of Twelve Apostles, Brigham Young presided, with seven other apostles in attendance, including Heber C. Kimball, Willard Richards, Amasa Lyman, Orson Pratt, Ezra T. Benson, Wilford Woodruff, and George A. Smith. Several lower-level leaders rounded out the group, as did McCary's wife Lucy. The official summary of the meeting noted that McCary made "a rambling statement" and that he "exhibited himself in Indian costume." He also "played on his thirty six cent flute" and performed as a "mimic."[80]

The assessment of McCary's interview as "rambling" was certainly true. McCary offered a series of unrelated statements and a jumbled defense of his reputation among the Mormons. Although his interview wandered widely, it was primarily centered on his claim that he could assume the identity of Adam, based upon his belief that he was missing a rib. The Saints at Winter Quarters, in McCary's mind, were not treating him with the respect that such an important person deserved. His complaint was oddly merged with an unclear understanding of his own racial identity; however, he made a decided effort to assert an

Indian identity over a black identity. And when that failed, he claimed that he was Adam, supernaturally manifesting himself in a new prophetic role.[81]

As McCary began his interview, he complained that he was "hypocritically abused" among the Mormons and that some lower-level leaders had counseled their flocks not to let McCary into "their wig wams." When McCary and his wife passed by, some people in camp scornfully remarked "there go the old nigger & his White Wife." "I came in as a red man," McCary asserted, and "want to go out as a red man." "We were all white once," he insisted, "why am I the stain now"? "Don't these backbiters think that I [h]av[e] feeling[s] if I was a nigger?" he wondered. He declared himself thankful for his baptism, but in terms of his acceptance among the Saints, he said he would "as like to be as a nigger as an Indian as many think they are as one."[82]

With his racial identity so problematic, McCary then moved on to his unconvincing claim that he could assume the identity of Adam and was missing a rib. He claimed that "when Adam comes he will bring the lost rib with him," but he was most concerned why his missing rib caused "so much fuss" among the Saints. "One man confesses to be Adam—ano[the]r the Ancient of Days," he lamented, and in response others try and "get up a mob to drive me out of the city."[83]

McCary then offered the gathered Mormon leaders an opportunity to examine his body for themselves. With a brush off of "mock modesty" he disrobed in front of the gathering and put on an "Indian costume." Willard Richards, a Thomsonian physician and LDS apostle, then "felt his ribs," while Brigham Young questioned McCary as to the purpose behind the examination. McCary responded that he wanted to prove that he had "been here bef[ore]," presumably as Adam, although it is entirely unclear what McCary meant. He went on to suggest that he was intent upon laying himself before the apostles as their servant. In the meantime, Richards concluded his examination and announced that he did not "discover any thing novel" and that his ribs were all properly in place.[84]

The conversation then deteriorated into a confusing exchange regarding McCary's ribs until Young intervened. He told McCary, "Your body is not what is your mission." McCary returned to his plea for protection against the poor treatment he supposedly received at the hands of the Saints. "All I ask is, will you protect me—I've come here & given myself out to be your servant," McCary pleaded.[85]

With the missing rib story becoming a pointless pursuit, Young attempted to come up with a stronger answer to McCary's primary concern: his racial identity. He complained that the people sometimes called him Adam and sometimes "Old Nigger," and that he wanted to know "what is the diff[erence]"? Was he Adam, an "Indian prophet," or merely an "Old Nigger" as some Saints called him? "Its nothing to do with the blood," Young asserted, "for of one blood has God made all flesh."[86]

It was an echo of the same New Testament verse (Acts 17:26) that Smith quoted in his presidential platform three years earlier. Both drew upon the Bible to assert a broad commonality among humankind and were simultaneously acknowledging a wider racial debate then animating the scientific and Christian communities. In paraphrasing Acts 17:26, Young and Smith were referencing an important verse then commonly cited among nineteenth-century Christians. Believers used the verse to defend against a polygenesis theory then stirring scientific arguments about the origins of the various races. Scientists who promoted the polygenesis theory believed that there were multiple independent creations rather than just a single biblical creation. Each creation gave rise to a new race, which meant that whites and blacks were in fact from different species. Even though the two species could biologically reproduce, one argument was that an innate repugnance against interracial mixing was intended to preserve "species distinction." Those who violated the innate repugnance were really violating nature, which was a sure sign of their moral degradation. Physical degeneracy followed and within a few generations the offspring of such unions would be sterile.[87]

The debate between those who accepted the single creation of the Bible and those who explained racial distinctions through multiple creations naturally impacted Christianity and animated the ways Christian Americans viewed race in the nineteenth century. For many religious people, the scientists who advocated a polygenesis position were in essence challenging the biblical creation narrative, the story of Adam and Eve, the fall, and therefore the need for redemption. The very foundations of Christianity were at stake. Smith and Young sided with their Christian cohorts in favor of a single creation and the universal relatedness of the human family.[88]

In the absence of multiple creations, however, the question of the origins of the different races persisted. Young would later turn for an explanation to the Judeo-Christian tradition where he found long-held notions of divine curses against Ham, Canaan, and Cain as commonly accepted answers. For the time being, however, Young maintained an open vision of the commonality of the human family in an effort to calm McCary's worries. Not only did God create racial diversity out of "one blood," Young went on to assert that color did not matter to Mormons, using Q. Walker Lewis as his proof: "We have to repent & regain what we [h]av[e] lost," Young insisted, "we [h]av[e] one of the best Elders[,] an African in Lowell—a barber," he reported. Young offered Lewis as evidence that McCary's identity, whether it be as a black man, an Indian, or even a presumably white Adam, did not matter. Even black men were welcome and eligible for the priesthood.[89]

It was a satisfying answer for McCary. As he dressed again, he told the apostles that he hoped church members would "let me live in peace" and declared himself "satisfied." He announced that "if any one molests me I will come to bro. Brigham." He declared that even "if I am a donkey, I want to serve God." It was a sentiment to which Young proclaimed, "Amen."[90]

The tedious discussion did not end there but continued in other arbitrary directions. It eventually turned back to McCary's standing among the Saints and his color of skin. "I am not a Pres[iden]t, or a leader of the p[eo]pl[e]" McCary lamented, but merely a "common bro[the]r," a fact that he said was true "because I am a little shade darker." It may be an indication that McCary was not ordained to the priesthood, or at the very least that he held no positions of import within the lay Mormon structure. Young again asserted a colorblind ideal and responded that "we dont care about the color." Still skeptical, McCary wondered if it was only a sentiment that Young held or if the other Mormon leaders felt the same. "Do I hear that from all?" he asked. Those present immediately responded with a unified "aye."[91]

Apostle Heber C. Kimball then wondered "dont you feel a good spirit here bro William." "Yes—thank God," McCary replied. He still worried that "there r 2 or 3 men at the end of the camp who want to kill me," but he was nonetheless "satisfied" with his interview. Young finally counseled McCary to ignore "what the ppl say, shew by your actions that you dont care for what they say—all we do is to serve the Lord with all our hearts." McCary promised to "pick up the cross of Christ," and after some additional ramblings, including demonstrations as a mimic, the meeting ended.[92]

It was a truly remarkable event, a sustained interview with eight Mormon apostles over issues of race, identity, and prophetic claims. The outcome was amicable and included sincere statements of concern over McCary's welfare. More significantly it put Brigham Young on record as favorably aware of Walker Lewis's priesthood ordination, as an advocate of the broader relatedness of the entire human family, and as not concerned "about the color" of McCary's skin. It was perhaps an apex in Mormon universalist sentiment but it proved short lived.

William McCary, despite his promises otherwise, continued to promote his identity as an Indian prophet and to attract followers. Young and the vanguard pioneers, including all of the apostles who interviewed McCary, departed for the Great Basin in mid-April. Apostles Parley P. Pratt, John Taylor, and Orson Hyde arrived at Winter Quarters from their various missions after the meeting with McCary and therefore did not have a shared experience to base their interactions on. Before Pratt and Taylor departed later that year at the head of a large emigrant company, Pratt spoke out against McCary.[93]

Some of the roughly four thousand people who remained at Winter Quarters grew increasingly impatient over meager provisions, sickly conditions, and the protracted wait for a final destination. For his part, McCary moved away from the main body of Saints, back across the Missouri River to Mosquito Creek, and attracted followers to join him. He and others facilitated a general scattering of Saints that Pratt in particular felt it necessary to renounce. Less than a month after McCary's meeting with the departed apostles, Pratt censured him and his supporters. In doing so he made the first recorded statement of a race-based priesthood curse.[94]

On 25 April at a gathering at Winter Quarters, Pratt gave a speech designed to prevent a further diffusion of Saints. He castigated those who would "cross the River without Council" and then challenged those assembled: "Ye who want to scatter[,] go and scatter to the 4 winds[,] for the Lord can do without you and the church can do without you[,] for we want the pure in heart to go with us over the mountains." Pratt then specifically called out James Strang, one leader of a schismatic group, and William McCary, another person he deemed a detractor. "If people want to follow Strang," Pratt insisted, that was their prerogative. If they want "to follow this Black man who has got the blood of Ham in him which linege [*sic*] was cursed as regards the Priesthood," that was also their choice, but Pratt clearly did not approve.[95]

It was a bit of rhetorical bluster on Pratt's part, an effort to forestall further dissention and scattering, but it was clearly an about face from the color-blind sentiment expressed only a month earlier. McCary's actions no doubt facilitated the shift; he went from calling himself Young's "servant" and expressing a desire to follow council, to blatantly leading his own schismatic group. But Pratt was absent from the McCary meeting, and it is impossible to know what type of briefing he received, if any, regarding McCary and his conflicted status within the fold.

Pratt was striking out on his own in regard to notions of cursed priesthood but was nonetheless drawing upon sentiments expressed in the Book of Abraham, a text that Joseph Smith Jr. claimed to produce from Egyptian papyri. Smith himself never applied the same meaning as Pratt to any verses from Abraham, nor did he ever use any scriptural text to argue for a priesthood curse. While Pratt's statement was the first in regard to cursed lineage and priesthood, a single declaration did not make a policy. There is no indication that Pratt's statement played out immediately in any practical way, even in regard to William McCary, nor did any future leaders refer back to Pratt or remember the 1847 meeting as a precedent. Yet it does indicate the idea of a racial restriction in the mind of at least one apostle as early as 1847, three years after Joseph Smith's death and five years before Brigham Young's open announcement of a priesthood ban.[96]

It is not clear exactly when the full extent of McCary's activities became known among the Saints, but it was his sexualized violation of racial boundaries that raised the most ire among the Mormons and led to McCary's expulsion. The episode no doubt impacted Mormon attitudes regarding interracial sex and marriage and factored into the discussion Mormon leaders had in December regarding Enoch Lewis. According to Nelson Whipple, a local leader who was familiar with McCary's activities, McCary cultivated a small group of followers. "He was in favor of holding his meetings of the men and women separately, saying that his teaching to the men and to the women was entirely different." Whipple considered his "talk and pretentions" to be "of the most absurd character," and felt that "no rational being would adhere to it for a moment, but many did."[97]

It was not the gendered nature of McCary's instruction that was most disturbing but rather the sexualized rituals he conducted with his female followers. According to Whipple, McCary "had a number of women sealed to him" in a ceremony of his own invention, a corruption of plural marriage that Smith had instigated at Nauvoo. McCary's version included inviting prospective brides to his home where his wife Lucy Stanton was present. Then, with Lucy in the room, "the form of sealing was for the women to bed with him, in the daytime . . . three different times[,] by which they were sealed to the fullest extent."[98]

McCary apparently continued his exploits for "a considerable length of time" before one potential initiate "revolted and ran," despite Lucy's best efforts to prevent her escape. Word soon spread, especially among the husbands whose wives attended McCary's ceremonies. One of these husbands, Sessions A. Chase, refused to believe the accusations against his wife until she admitted that they were true. The news left him "very much astonished," so much so that he did not speak for three weeks. He eventually recovered and remained with his wife, and they both stayed Mormon. In total, Whipple detailed at least eight women who were "sealed" to McCary, including one who was "upwards of 60 years of age." Whipple recalled that church authorities excommunicated most of McCary's followers for being "sealed in that way to the old darkey," but the break was not permanent; most chose to be rebaptized and to migrate to Utah with the rest of the Saints.[99]

As for McCary, one account said that he "made his way to Missouri on a fast trot" and later sent for his wife to join him. Another report said that apostle Orson Hyde denounced McCary after which McCary and his wife left the Saints and went "south to his own tribe." In either case, he left a variety of angry Mormons in his wake. A brother Hamon Cutler even announced his intent to track McCary down and shoot him "for having tried to kiss his girls." In June one Mormon wrote that "the Negroo prophet has made his exit, and is defunct." This time McCary's departure from Mormonism was final.[100]

McCary was thus already gone from Winter Quarters when Brigham Young returned from his initial foray to the Great Basin. Young arrived in the fall of 1847, about a month before William Appleby. It is not clear when Young received Appleby's summer letter, but upon Appleby's arrival on 2 December Young and the other apostles were anxious to learn of his trip and to hear of conditions among the various branches of the church in the East. The leading authorities, the same group of apostles who met with McCary in March, absent Orson Pratt, but including Orson Hyde, met with Appleby the following day.

The meeting began at six thirty in the evening and did not break up until ten thirty when Heber C. Kimball "retired to bed," leaving Young, Hyde, and Willard Richards "chatting until one oclock." Despite what must have been a protracted discussion on perhaps wide-ranging topics, the official notes capture less than thirteen handwritten lines of the conversation. Most of them deal with the issue of interracial mixing and offer only a glimpse into the thoughts of those present. They are nonetheless drenched with ideas then in circulation about amalgamation and the biological condition of those who mixed racial blood.[101]

Appleby informed the apostles that "Wm Smith ordained a black man Elder at Lowell & he has married a White girl & they have a child." Appleby (or Thomas Bullock, the taker of the minutes) here seems to conflate Walker Lewis, whom William Smith ordained to the priesthood, with his son Enoch who married Mary Webster. No matter, the real issue was interracial marriage and Appleby felt it important enough to bring before Mormonism's governing council.[102]

Brigham Young responded with force: "If they [Enoch and Mary] were far away from the Gentiles," he insisted, "they wo[u]ld all [h]av[e] to be killed— when they mingle seed it is death to all." It was an extreme stance, even in the context of the times, but not devoid of precedent. As early as the eighteenth century American colonies and then states stipulated death in cases of black men raping white women. In New York a black man convicted of two attempted rapes was burned alive. In North Carolina murder and rape by black men were capital crimes, and in Maryland the death penalty was prescribed for black men who raped white women. After the Civil War, one black legislator in Arkansas advocated the death penalty for any white man "found cohabiting with a negro woman," a turnabout designed to highlight the sexual exploitation of female slaves by their masters when slavery was in force. Following Reconstruction, the lynching of black men in the South sometimes stemmed from the mere hint that racial boundaries were violated. In that sense, the death penalty became a de facto law in the South against race mixing, with over 2,400 African Americans lynched between 1877 and 1930.[103]

Young, however, was not speaking of rape but merely interracial marriage. His statement in this case was made to an intimate gathering of apostles and William Appleby, but it was a position he would return to in more public venues in Utah Territory. His stance was never encoded into Utah law but was a part of Young's sometimes bombastic preaching from the pulpit, which no doubt helped to shape attitudes among Mormons regarding interracial marriage and black people in general.

Young went on to explore a hypothetical scenario, perhaps to distinguish if baptism were permissible for interracial couples. "If a black man & white woman come to you & demand baptism can you deny them?" he asked. "The law is their seed shall not be amalgamated," he answered. "Mulattoes r like mules[,] they cant have the children, but if they will be Eunuchs for the Kingdom of ~~Gods~~ Heaven's sake they may have a place in the Temple." Apostle Orson Hyde insisted that "if girls marry the half breeds they r throwing themselves away & becoming as one of them," something which Brigham Young declared was "wrong for them to do."[104]

Young then distinguished between Indians and blacks to assert that "the Lamanites r purely of the house of Israel & it is a curse that is to be removed when the fulness [sic] of the Gospel comes." It was an important distinction that served to inform Mormon interactions with both Indians and blacks for the remainder of the century. Indians were redeemable descendants of fallen Israel, a curse that was to be removed with the very gospel restoration then underway. Blacks, on the other hand, were cursed with a "mark" that placed them outside of a clear plan for redemption.[105]

To further distinguish between the two, Young then noted that even some Native Americans distanced themselves from blacks. It was a clear indication that he was aware of the broader clamoring for position then prevalent among marginalized groups: "The Pottawatamies [sic] will not own a man who has the negro blood in him," he specified, "that is the reason why the Indians disown the negro Prophet." Even Native Americans rejected McCary due to his "negro blood," Young insisted, a claim designed to bolster the Mormon stance against intermarriage and to affirm a position for Mormons above blacks and Indians on America's contested racial ladder.[106]

Young may have not been aware, but several Native American groups positioned themselves against intermarriage with blacks. Before 1825 the Creek Nation declared it a "disgrace to our Nation for our people to marry a Negro." In 1839 the Cherokee Nation adopted a provision against its citizens marrying "any person of color," and the Chickasaw Nation did likewise in 1858.[107] Like Mormons, some Indians were seeking acceptability in a national culture that so thoroughly deplored interracial mixing. In this and other ways McCary's specter haunted the meeting and was used to firmly and completely dismiss amalgamation among Mormons.

In some regards, Young and Hyde were only confirming the ideas that Smith, Cowdery, and Parrish articulated in 1836, which amounted to a position against "amalgamation." In other ways, however, they expanded on the older ideas and pushed them in new directions. Even still, Young and Hyde were speaking more out of certain strands of then-current ideology about race than out of any uniquely Mormon position.

The ideas of Dr. Josiah Clark Nott seem most prominently at play at the meeting. Nott was best known as a founder of the so-called American school of anthropology but it was his ideas about race that most dramatically impacted America. Nott was firmly against amalgamation, the offspring of which he referred to as "hybrids." In 1843 he published an influential article titled "The Mulatto a Hybrid—Probable Extermination of Two Races If the Whites and Blacks are Allowed to Intermarry." He also gave two public speeches that were later published.[108]

Nott posited a variety of positions, all of which centered on the notion that blacks and whites were from separate species and that their mixing produced degraded offspring. He claimed that "mulattoes" were "the shortest lived of any class of the human race," that they were "intermediate in intelligence," and that "mulatto women" were "delicate" and "subject to a variety of chronic diseases." He argued that they were "bad breeders and bad nurses," by which he meant that "many" of them did not conceive, "most" were "subject to abortions," and "a large portion" of their children died young. Referencing the mule as a prime example of hybrids that "do not breed," he suggested that the consequences of interracial mixing among humans would produce the same results. He submitted that if "a hundred white men and one hundred black women were put together on an Island, and cut off from all intercourse with the rest of the world, they would in time become extinct." He concluded that "the mulatto is a degenerate, unnatural offspring, doomed by nature to work out its own destruction."[109]

Young's and Hyde's ideas seem too similar to Nott's to be mere coincidence. At the very least, Hyde and Young demonstrated an awareness of certain strands of racial thought then percolating in American society. They introduced them into Mormonism, where they impacted the racial trajectory of the faith over the course of the nineteenth century. Even still, the discussion centered on race mixing, not priesthood. The sparse surviving minutes do not mention a priesthood ban or curse. If such a matter was discussed, Bullock failed to capture it in his notes.

Appleby may have left that meeting, nonetheless, with the belief that ordaining black men to the priesthood was wrong. In 1848 and 1849, as he created a "compilation" of his journals, he may have inserted a priesthood ban into his recollection of his initial meeting with Q. Walker Lewis in the Lowell Branch, on 19 May 1847: "In this Branch there is a Coloured Brother, (An Elder ordained by Elder Wm. Smith while he was a member of the Church, contrary though to the order of the Church or the Law of the Priesthood, as the Descendants of Ham are not entitled to that privilege)." Even still Appleby recorded a favorable impression of Lewis and described him as "an example for his more whiter brethren to follow."[110]

It is impossible to know if Appleby arrived at his conclusions regarding Lewis's priesthood of his own accord or if he inserted the "Law of the Priesthood" clause anachronistically back into his entry for 19 May. Appleby encountered the Book of Abraham in 1841 in Nauvoo and copied the verses regarding a cursed priesthood lineage into his journal without commentary. His assessment of Lewis's ordination could have been his own inference based upon his reading of the Book of Abraham. After meeting Walker Lewis in May, and learning that his son Enoch was married to a white woman, he may have mulled over the matter. Then, on 2 June he decided to ask Brigham Young if black priesthood ordination and "amalgamation" were acceptable in the church.[111]

Alternatively, evidence within Appleby's "autobiography and journal" indicates that he compiled that record in 1848 and 1849. He thus could have included a new understanding of "the order of the Church" regarding race and priesthood as a result of his discussion with the apostles in December 1847. It is possible, in other words, that racial priesthood restriction was a topic of that meeting and Appleby decided from that conversation that Lewis's priesthood ordination was done in error. In this scenario, he inserted that idea back into his entry for 19 May 1847, based upon his discussion with the apostles on 3 December.[112]

The problem with such a supposition is that the scant minutes for the four-hour meeting do not mention any such conversation. In fact, Appleby's own journal entry for that meeting is equally silent on the matter. If a decision was made on race and priesthood in December 1847 the logical place for Appleby to include such news would have been in his entry for that very meeting. Instead, he only recorded that he "had the pleasure of being in company with the Council of the twelve" and that he "esteemed it a privilege to hear the words of wisdom that flowed from their lips." He was pleased "to obtain knowledge and understanding in regard to the Kingdom of God." He gave an account of his "stewardship" and reported on "the situation of the Churches" in the Eastern states. He did not mention a discussion of mixed marriages, let alone a priesthood ban.[113]

If a decision was made regarding race and priesthood at that meeting, there is no evidence to date to corroborate it (other than Appleby's problematic entry for 19 May 1847). It would be another five years before Brigham Young publicly and forcefully announced a ban. When he did so, he linked it to a curse upon Cain and drew his rationale from the Bible, not the Book of Abraham as Pratt and Appleby appeared to do in 1847.

* * *

When William Appleby wrote Brigham Young in June 1847, his short letter captured the crux of a long and complicated racial history that situated Mormons firmly at the center of a national struggle over the meaning of whiteness. From its beginning, Mormonism found itself on the wrong side of white, a racially suspect religion that outsiders feared not only for its new doctrines but also for its reported violation of racial boundaries.

After the Mormons openly announced their practice of polygamy in 1852, outsiders looked at them with renewed fear of amalgamation. Charges of inter-racial mixing, however, clearly predated the consternation over polygamy. Polygamy offered additional proof that the earlier accusations were true and gave new life to a racialization already underway. Before the Saints acknowledged polygamy, Brigham Young declared a racial priesthood ban, a move away from blackness that did little to stem the tide of outside racial contempt.

CHAPTER 5

Black, White, and Mormon: Black and White Slavery

In May 1849 overland migrant John Burt Colton stopped at Council Bluffs, Iowa, just across the Missouri River from Winter Quarters, to prepare for the difficult portion of his journey ahead. Colton paused to write a note to his friends before crossing the inhospitable and unsettled "plains." He described Council Bluffs as "the jumping off place from civilization into eternal uncivilization"; in his view it was "the last place inhabited by civilized people." Even then, he was not quite sure. "Iowa is full of nothing but Mormons," he wrote, "and all going to the Salt Lake[;] they are perfect slaves," he continued, "you have to look out for them or they will clean the cash out of you in a hurry."[1]

It was a brief comment, and a seemingly offhanded assessment of the people he encountered. This was probably not a racial comparison: Colton likely meant that the Mormons were the ecclesiastically enslaved dupes of an oppressive priesthood. Nonetheless, Colton's characterization of Mormons as "slaves" became a shared theme among outsiders that accumulated meaning over time and grew to frequently include comparisons to race-based slavery. Especially after Mormons openly announced the practice of plural marriage in 1852, outsiders suggested that polygamy was in fact "white slavery." Political cartoons, news reports, government documents, dime novels, exposés, journals, and books all conflated black slavery in the South with "white slavery" in Utah.

As outsiders viewed it "white slavery" in Utah sank below the chattel slavery practiced in the South simply because it transgressed accepted racial norms. Blackness equaled slavery and whiteness equaled freedom, a fundamental American definition that Mormonism violated. Slavery meant degradation, exploitation, the abandonment of liberty, and a "connection with blackness." As "white slaves" Mormon women became the "counterpart of the negro" and therefore racially tarnished. The paradox was in the combination of the terms "white" and "slave," two words that by their very definitions should have never been paired. In

Mormon polygamy, however, those words came together to blur the distinction between black and white.[2] "One thing is certain," the *Chicago Daily Tribune* suggested in 1873, "Mormonism is the most dreadful tyranny ever exercised over any white people on this Continent, and is . . . as degrading as old-fashioned negro slavery."[3] At least southern whites enslaved racially inferior and divinely cursed blacks; white slavery was worse because it involved whites enslaving whites.

Stories of white slavery in broader American society existed independent of those that came to be told about Mormons. In antebellum America, white slaves became popular fodder in the abolitionist press, a ploy designed to prick the conscience of Northern whites and prod them into opposing black slavery. The abolitionists believed that if they could convince Northerners to imagine themselves or their white relatives in bondage, it might prompt sympathy for enslaved blacks and convince people to join their cause. To that end, abolitionists sometimes told stories of white slavery that usually involved orphan girls who through various tragic scenarios were ensnared in slavery's grasp and brutalized alongside racially inferior blacks. Northerners used such stories to evoke horror at the thought of white people mistakenly enslaved in the South.[4] The stories created a readymade national consternation over white slavery within which Mormon polygamy was rapidly subsumed. In the American mind, an occasional mistaken white slave in the South paled in comparison to an organized system of white slavery in the West. Especially during and after the Civil War, the allegation grew in urgency.

Mormon leaders were clearly aware of the ways in which politicians and the press described them. "It is marvellous [*sic*] what foolish, preposterous things are spread about the state of things in Utah," one missionary in England wrote to Brigham Young in 1861. He could not imagine "the absurdities believed." He was particularly pleased that he had brought his wife with him on his mission, simply because it allowed him to refute the charge of white slavery so prevalent in England. "There are such ludicrous and ridiculous stories afloat here and in print about the cruelty to women in Utah, that they are all slaves, dare not write, are whipped, sold, . . . and none ever get away or return to England," he wrote. Fortunately, his wife offered "living refutation to such base fabrications." He noted that "many strangers, men and women, have called on purpose to see her and converse, in order that they may give the lie to such foul reports."[5]

In America, during and after the Civil War, correspondence to Brigham Young routinely described similar perceptions. In 1856 two Mormon apostles, John Taylor and George A. Smith, then lobbying in Washington, DC, described for Young the "howlings" and "groans" of Republicans over polygamy, charges which Taylor and Smith summarily dismissed as "nonsense & hypocrisy." Other letters mentioned a "pledged hostility to Polygamy" dominating the public consciousness and a "popular prejudice against Mormonism" pervading the nation. One writer noted that lyceums around the country sometimes debated whether slavery or polygamy was worse. He then complained that polygamy "always gains the ground" in such debates.[6]

The irony was that in 1852 Utah's territorial legislature legalized black "servitude" when it crafted a law clearly designed to elevate white Mormons above their black counterparts. It was an internal move that increasingly complicated the ways in which outsiders imagined racial degradation taking place among Mormons. Mormons legalized their own version of black servitude in an effort to distinguish between black and white, bound and free. At the same time, Brigham Young announced a race-based priesthood restriction partly intended to substantiate Mormon racial purity. These internal moves highlight the ways in which race was an aspiration for Mormons and not merely something outsiders ascribed. The price of Mormon whiteness was thus partially calculated in the LDS Church's effort to distance itself from blackness.

* * *

In 1851 an overland traveler passed through Utah Territory and stopped in Salt Lake City on his way west. He filed an anonymous account of his visit with the African American newspaper the *National Era*, published in Washington, DC. The report offers a unique lens into both the ways outsiders viewed Mormons as slaves and into the nascent slavery in the territory. The news account described the Mormons in Salt Lake City as "a singular community" where "consistency and inconsistency, light and darkness, bigotry and toleration, are strangely blended." The traveler was somewhat perplexed that the Mormons he met reasoned "clearly and logically" and respected "man's natural rights and duties," and yet he found them to be "the *veriest slaves* of the priesthood."[7]

On the subject of racial slavery, however, he was more favorably impressed. He noted that the Mormons had not passed any slavery legislation to date and found the people expressing a belief in the equality of "all men." As he put it, the Mormons "very sensibly conclude that slavery can have no legal existence where it has never been legalized." Even still, he observed "a few black persons, perhaps a hundred, in the valley, who have been sent in by, and who still live with, their former masters, but they are not considered as *slaves*." He claimed to have learned from Brigham Young himself that "the idea of property in men would not be entertained a moment by any court" in the territory. It was a fairly accurate summation of the status of blacks among the Mormons in 1851.[8]

The US Congress created Utah as a territory in 1850, as a part of a broader compromise that year that admitted California into the Union as a free state and allowed popular sovereignty to determine the issue of slavery in New Mexico and Utah territories. Legislators in both Utah and New Mexico opted for systems of unfree labor, although Utah's law was best characterized as a form of gradual emancipation and "involuntary servitude" patterned after similar laws in Indiana and Illinois. New Mexico, in contrast, legalized chattel slavery modeled after slave codes in the South.[9]

Before the Civil War, rumors and speculation about the presence of enslaved blacks among Mormons sometimes appeared in news reports and even surfaced in Congress. In 1852 Mormons settled the question when they passed "An Act in Relation to Service," legalizing the ownership of the relatively few enslaved blacks in the territory who came west with their masters. Some of the slaves themselves joined Mormonism, but none were known to have been ordained to the priesthood. There were even three black men, Green Flake, Hark Lay, and Oscar Crosby, among Young's 1847 vanguard pioneer company. In total, roughly eighty enslaved blacks and thirty free blacks migrated to the territory by 1850. It was their presence more than any outside pressure that prompted the first Utah territorial legislature to legalize "servitude" in 1852.[10]

The all-Mormon body of lawmakers comprised thirty-nine members: twenty-nine from Northern states, three of foreign birth, and seven from the South, one of whom owned slaves. Those men met over the winter of 1851 and 1852 to address pressing legislative matters in the new territory. They were loyal and devoted followers of Young and Smith before him. William W. Phelps, who had published the controversial article in Jackson County, Missouri, on "Free People of Color," was a legislator as were several LDS apostles, including Wilford Woodruff, Heber C. Kimball, George A. Smith, Orson Pratt, and Willard Richards. The representatives presided over a territory that brought Southerners, Northerners, foreigners, abolitionists, antiabolitionists, free blacks, and enslaved blacks together. Such a diverse gathering highlighted the universalism of the Mormon message and its appeal across racial, political, and ideological boundaries.[11]

Yet legislators met in 1852 in an effort to create order out of that diversity and reassert racial, political, and ideological boundaries in a way that positioned white over black and free over bound. Brigham Young was at the forefront of that effort. He laid out his views regarding slavery while articulating a firm and forceful position concerning a race-based priesthood restriction grounded in biblical curses. Underlying all of it was a percolating anxiety, both within and without Mormonism, over interracial mixing.

When the first territorial legislature convened over the fall and winter of 1851 and 1852, among the difficult challenges it faced was dealing with the centuries-old Indian slave trade that Mormons unwittingly found themselves drawn into. On occasion Ute traders presented captive children to Mormons and insisted that Mormons purchase them. For the Indians it was a familiar interaction with Euro-Americans that dated back to the 1600s and their trade relations with settlers on the northern Spanish frontier. With the arrival of the Mormons, Native peoples saw the potential economic benefit of permanent trading partners living in close proximity. No longer would they have to take captive women and children to Mexican settlements or wait for traders along the Old Spanish Trail.[12]

For their part, the Mormons were caught off guard by the trade and clamored for appropriate ways to respond. Mormon sources described Ute traders arriving at Mormon settlements with captive children to sell. If the Mormons refused to buy them, a captor might kill one child in an effort to motivate the Mormons to save the remaining captives. In this way the Mormons found themselves enmeshed in a preexisting slave trade, with no laws to govern it.[13]

When the territorial legislature met, one priority was to outlaw the Indian slave trade while simultaneously legalizing the purchase of captive children into a form of indentured servitude. Legislators also addressed black slavery during the same lawmaking session. Some Mormon converts from the South brought enslaved blacks with them to Utah and as a result de facto slavery already existed.[14]

Utah legislators tackled these two challenges in a way that further demonstrated a diverging theological vision among Mormons regarding Indians and blacks. The system of indentured servitude required any Mormon purchasing an Indian captive to register with a local probate judge to ensure court supervision. The law also required Mormons with Indian children to provide at least three months of education annually to any child between the ages of seven and sixteen and to properly clothe them. The law further limited the term of servitude to twenty years or less, with liberation and integration into white society as the ultimate objectives. Brigham Young called it "purchasing them into freedom," an idealistic and overly simplistic vision of the new law that rarely worked well in practice. It nonetheless demonstrated the Mormon ideal of Native Americans as redeemable descendants of ancient Israel and of their own role as agents in that redemption.[15]

Blacks, on the other hand, were divinely cursed and their future redemption was in God's hands only, something in which no mortal could or should intervene. The "Act in Relation to Service" passed by the territorial legislature in 1852 did not include the word slave or slavery, but rather "service" and "servants." As Joseph Smith had done before him, Young attempted to strike a middle ground, somewhere between what he viewed as the harsh brutalities of Southern slavery and the full racial equality advocated by abolitionists. Young and Smith both felt bound to honor and compensate masters for the labor obligations their slaves represented. Smith envisioned a government-funded gradual emancipation program, whereas Young advocated contractual servitude for the life of a slave. Young most stridently differed from Smith over the potential for black equality. While Smith viewed the general low condition of blacks as purely a byproduct of environmental circumstances—most notably the lack of opportunity for education and self-improvement embedded in the slave system—Young asserted divine curses, a race-based priesthood ban, and the inherent incapacity of blacks to govern whites. For Young it was a divinely appointed inequality, something that God put in place as a result of Cain killing his brother Abel, and a matter in which mortals had no right to interfere, especially not "ignorant" abolitionists. It was a view more akin to Smith's 1836 antiabolitionist statement than to the position Smith adopted before his murder. In sum, it marked a new direction for Young and the Church, a stance not traceable to Smith in principle or in practice.[16]

As early as January 1845, less than six months following Smith's murder, Young laid the groundwork for his 1852 position in a sermon he preached at Nauvoo. Young tapped into ideas Smith first articulated regarding spiritual adoption into God's family but developed them in new ways. As Smith and Young envisioned it, conversion and baptism into the Mormon fold signaled adoption as a son or daughter of God. This idea evolved and expanded after Smith introduced the "sealing" power, a spiritual authority that he said bound or "sealed" human relationships on earth and in heaven. Adoption also came to signify being fused into a long covenant chain of interlinked human relationships, with a first generation convert at one end and a "sealed" or welded link stretching back through human genealogy to father Adam.[17]

In his 1845 sermon Young promised his Nauvoo audience that their posterity would "rise up" in "tens, hundreds, thousands, and millions," ultimately to "join with Adam who will be the King of all." While Young's vision of future posterity and of heavenly glory was inspiring, it also came with a warning. A person's place in the great chain of being, and therefore in the eternities, could be jeopardized through pollution of priesthood lineage. It was a lesson that Young hoped his followers might learn from the poor example of God's prior covenant people: the children of Israel. Rather than keeping their lineages pure, ancient Israelites brought a curse upon themselves "for mixing their seed with the Gentile races about them." As Young explained, "The nations have wandered in darkness for centuries. If they had not mixed their blood, the Priesthood would never have been taken from them." Young told his Nauvoo audience that the same conditions applied to them. If they mixed their blood "with others" it would bring a curse upon them "in relation to the Priesthood." The "children, in such mixed unions, would be high-minded and stiff necked," conditions that made them prone to apostasy. Apostasy, in turn, would break the great chain of being and disrupt the ordered fashion of the Kingdom of Heaven. Significantly, the cursed nature of priesthood that Young articulated in 1845 centered on Mormons mixing with "gentiles," not black-white mixing. Within four years, however, Young's concern shifted to mixing with the "seed of Cain."[18]

On 13 February 1849, in a council meeting with many of the highest leaders of Mormonism present, Young first articulated this position, although without mentioning priesthood—at least in the surviving minutes. Lorenzo Snow, a newly ordained apostle at the time of the meeting, introduced the topic. The official minutes of the meeting only indicate that Snow "presented the case of the African Race for a chance of redemption & unlock the door to them." What rationale he used, what evidence he cited, what position he articulated to make his "case" is unfortunately absent from the record. The brief notes only indicate that Young responded to Snow's presentation by establishing the basic argument that he would more fully express to the territorial legislature three years later. Young explained his stance "very lucidly," according to Thomas Bullock, his private secretary, "that the curse remains on them bec[ause] Cain cut off the lives of Abel to hedge up his way & take the lead but the L[or]d has given them blackness, so as to give the children of Abel an opportunity to keep his place with his desc[endan]ts in the et[erna]l worlds." It was the core of the argument Mormons used to ban black men from the priesthood and black men and women from temple worship. Blackness was a curse from God, a consequence for Cain's murder of his brother Abel. By killing a competing patriarch in Adam's family line and attempting to usurp Abel's position in the "Kingdom of God," Cain fractured the eternal human network and broke the great chain of being. Rather than allow Cain and his posterity to ascend above Abel in the eternities, the curse assured an inferior "place" for blacks outside of the great chain of being altogether. In Young's mind, when God placed a mark upon Cain, it excluded Cain from God's family and the Kingdom of Heaven. By 1852 Young added his own mark when he argued that black people, the assumed descendants of Cain, were also cursed from holding priesthood authority.[19]

Even still, the minutes of the 1849 meeting do not mention a priesthood curse, only "blackness." Some historians, nonetheless, have traced Brigham Young's first enunciation of a priesthood restriction to the 1849 meeting, relying upon the journal history or the manuscript history of the church as evidence. Those two records are compilations of sources used to construct daily catalogues of important events in Latter-day Saint history. They are not necessarily original sources themselves. They were sometimes constructed over a decade after the fact by a group of clerks assigned the task of creating a daily "history" for the church. Crafting such a retrospective record opened the process to the potential of inserting the present into the past.[20]

John Jaques, a clerk in the Church Historian's Office, crafted the entry for the 1849 meeting in 1861. In "gathering," "copying," "compiling," "inserting," and "enlarging," the 1849 history from the vantage point of 1861, Jaques likely introduced a priesthood restriction into his history that was not in the original minutes.[21] It was a way of reaching backward in time to make an enunciation of the ban retroactive to an earlier date than the historical record substantiates. The entry that Jaques created included a priesthood restriction not found in the original Bullock minutes: "But the Lord had cursed Cain's seed with blackness, *and prohibited them the priesthood*, that Abel and his progeny might yet come forward, and have their dominion, place, and blessings in their proper relationship with Cain and his race in the world to come."[22] Jaques added five crucial words to the minutes of the meeting. As it stands, there is no contemporary 1849 source to indicate a priesthood restriction. Brigham Young's openly articulated position was still three years in the future.

Nonetheless there is compelling evidence that a ban was in place before 1852. The substantiation comes from government explorer John W. Gunnison's book *The Mormons.* Gunnison spent the winter of 1849–1850 in Salt Lake City as a member of the Howard Stansbury surveying expedition. Mormon Albert Carrington was hired as an assistant for that expedition, and he and Gunnison struck a close friendship that lasted until Gunnison's untimely death in 1853. Carrington and Gunnison directed two crews in surveying the Jordan River and Utah Lake, and Carrington then aided Gunnison in writing the official report for the expedition. He also became Gunnison's principal consultant for his book about the Mormons.[23]

It was in that book that Gunnison revealed his knowledge about a race-based priesthood restriction as a tenet of Mormonism. The "Negro is cursed as to the priesthood and must always be a servant wherever his lot is cast," Gunnison wrote of Mormon beliefs. He further noted that a system of black "involuntary labor" was used in Utah but that it took place in the absence of "any law on the subject." Gunnison's description was therefore written before the territorial legislature passed its law on black servitude in February 1852. "Negro caste springs naturally from their doctrine of blacks being ineligible to the priesthood," Gunnison also reported. His book was published in Philadelphia in 1852, with the manuscript delivered to the printer sometime before 19 March, which was the day he wrote Carrington informing him of that fact. Thus, sometime between the fall of 1849 and early 1852, Gunnison learned of a race-based priesthood "doctrine" in operation among the Mormons. The language Gunnison used— "cursed as to the priesthood"—echoed that of the Book of Abraham. In 1852 Brigham Young would draw upon the Bible for his justification; this was another indication that Gunnison did not base his knowledge of the ban upon Young's position to the legislature. A priesthood restriction was certainly in operation before Young gave it public life, leaving its exact origins uncertain. On 23 January 1852 Young offered the first recorded articulation of a doctrine that he would use for the rest of his life to justify a ban that was already in place.[24]

In the meantime, Young continued to lay the groundwork for his views. In June 1851 he spoke of the "great excitement in the world about slavery." He suggested that "the abolitionists are very fearful that we shall have the Negro or Indian as slaves here," and went on to acknowledge that "we have a few

[Indians] that were prisoners that we have bought to save their lives." As for black slavery, he insisted that "the master of slaves will be damned if they abuse their slaves. Yet the seed of Ham will be servants until God takes the curse off from them." "Shall we lay a foundation for Negro slavery?" Young demanded. "No! God forbid! And I forbid. I say let us be free."[25]

* * *

With those earlier ideas as foundations, Young laid out his vision for the place of blacks in Utah Territory, but also in Mormon theology, in at least three speeches to the territorial legislature in 1852. Legislators that session contemplated several bills that attempted to define a variety of "unfree labor" relationships for people of all races. This included apprenticeship for minors, forced servitude for vagrancy or other crimes, indentured servitude for white immigrants, and various forms of servitude for Native Americans and African Americans. They also debated a voting rights bill and several municipal bills that included local voting rights provisions.[26]

The Indian and black servitude bills were hotly contested. In fact, the bill on black "service" witnessed Brigham Young squaring off against apostle and legislator Orson Pratt. University of Deseret chancellor and legislator, Orson Spencer, spoke in favor of the bill even as he described slavery as evil. Legislative debates thus produced the first known public articulation of a race-based priesthood restriction by a Mormon prophet.

In Young's mind there was a distinction between "Negro slavery" as practiced in the South and what he had in mind for Utah Territory. Young first weighed in on the matter in a prepared speech that his personal secretary, Thomas Bullock, read to a joint session of the legislature on 5 January. Only a small portion of his prepared remarks addressed Indian and black slavery. Young next spoke extemporaneously on 23 January, the day apostle and legislator George A. Smith introduced "An Act in Relation to African Slavery," with legislative scribe George D. Watt capturing the speech in Pitman shorthand. Young's final and most fully elaborated speech came on 5 February, the day after Young signed the black "servitude" bill into law and the legislature passed a voting rights bill. Watt again recorded Young's speech in shorthand while legislator and apostle Wilford Woodruff wrote a condensed summation in his journal. Of the three talks, only the prepared version read by Bullock was printed and distributed in both the legislative journal and the *Deseret News*. The two extemporaneous speeches contained full rationales for a priesthood restriction but were never published.[27]

The three discourses offer solid insight into Young's attitude regarding black slavery, a race-based biblical curse centered upon Cain's murder of his brother Abel, and of his views on interracial sex and marriage. Those views shaped Mormon belief and behavior well into the twentieth century and placed Mormons squarely

in the broader American racial mainstream. That same mainstream seemed unaware of Mormonism's internal positions on priesthood and intermarriage and
persistently charged Mormons with contaminating the white race.

Young was considerably more circumspect in his 5 January prepared remarks
than in his follow-up speeches. In the written version that Bullock read, Young
touched on many items then under consideration among lawmakers: from taxes
and Indian relations to slavery and colonization. His views on black slavery occupied only a small portion of the overall message. "My own feelings are, that
no property can or should be recognized as existing in slaves, either Indian or
African" he asserted. "No person can purchase them, without their becoming
as free, so far as natural rights are concerned, as persons of any other color." Yet
he was equally insistent that "service is necessary; it is honorable; it exists in all
countries, and has existed in all ages; it probably will exist in some form, in all
time to come."[28]

In Young's mind there was a distinction between the harsh brutality of slavery as practiced in the South and the type of "service" he had in mind for Utah
Territory. Blacks were "naturally designed" for service and he believed that "the
seed of Canaan will inevitably carry the curse which was placed upon them, until
the same authority which placed it there, shall see proper to have it removed."
"Service," in other words, was divinely sanctioned, and humankind should not
interfere with God's purposes. It was a step back to Joseph Smith's 1836 views,
and like Smith's earlier stance, Young drew upon Noah's curse upon Canaan as
"servant of servants." Even still, the curse was no excuse for brutality. "We should
not make them as beasts of the field, regarding not the humanity which attaches
to the colored race," Young asserted. He was not in favor of the opposite extreme
either. He did not want blacks elevated "as some seem disposed, to an equality
with those whom Nature and Nature's God has indicated to be their masters,
their superiors." As a corollary he also advocated against amalgamation in an
oblique reference to "the law of natural affection for our kind." He was striking
a moderate stance between the extremes of chattel slavery and full equality. It
was a middle ground he called "service." It was a restrained position that Young
seemed unwilling to let speak for itself.[29]

Young first addressed the proposed slave code on 23 January, the day the
bill was introduced to the legislature. "I am a firm believer in slavery," he announced. Yet his vision of the institution was different than the chattel slavery
practiced in the South. To emphasize that point, he altered the title of the proposed bill from "An Act in Relation to African Slavery" to "An Act in Relation
to Manual Service," a change that was more than mere semantics: "I would like
masters to treat well their servants," Young said. "When a master has a Negro
and uses him well, [he is] better off than [if] he was free," a sentiment that
reflected the prevailing white paternalism of his day. What Young envisioned

was "good wholesome servitude" without the degradation of physical abuse, a point he emphasized in his follow-up speech over a week later. Masters, he advised, should treat their "servants" the same as they would "their own children." "Their compassion should reach over them and round about them."[30]

Nonetheless, slaves also had an obligation to their masters. Young worried about converts in the South whose "means" were "vested in slaves." Their "servants want to come here with their masters," he claimed, but when they arrived "the devil is raised" through "a strong Abolitionist feeling," with fellow Saints whispering their disapproval. In consequence, Young said, "There should be a law made to have the slaves serve their masters because they are not capable of ruling themselves." Young was "firm in the belief" that enslaved blacks "ought to dwell in servitude." At the same time, he advocated for white servitude as well, a way to pay off immigration debts and honor labor contracts. The law that legislators passed included provisions to regulate both white and black servitude in the territory.[31]

As for the position of blacks in the church, Young noted that they "enjoy the rights of receiving the first principles of [the] gospel, which is liberty to all." Black Latter-day Saints "enjoy the privilege of being baptized," the gift of the Holy Ghost, and the "comforts [of] salvation, light, truth, [and] enjoyment." On those grounds Young believed that blacks "have the same privilege [as] white[s]." The difference was that blacks "can't hold the priesthood." As Young put it, "When the Lord God cursed old Cain, He said, 'Until the last drop of Abel's blood receives the priesthood, and enjoys the blessings of the same, Cain shall bear the curse.'"[32] It was the first open articulation of a priesthood curse by a Mormon prophet-president, a position Young expanded upon in a follow-up speech less than two weeks later.

In the meantime, not everyone agreed with Young's views. Orson Pratt spoke strongly against the proposed "servant code" several days later. Pratt found little to distinguish between servitude and slavery and called the latter "a great evil"; he moved that the "bill be rejected" in its entirety. Pratt argued that God alone dictated and administered divine "curses" and that they were particular to a time and place and did not automatically touch all future generations. "Shall we take then the innocent African that has committed no sin and damn him to slavery and bondage without receiving any authority from heaven to do [so]?" He found the idea "preposterous." It made Pratt feel "indignant" to think that the Mormons, after being themselves "damned" to what he considered a version of "slavery in [the] states," would then turn and "bind the African because he is different from us in color." It was "enough to cause the angels in heaven to blush." As Pratt believed, individuals should not "execute the curse of Almighty upon that race without being commanded to do [so]." Pratt predicted that even slaveholders would "blush for shame" if the legislature "voluntarily" introduced slavery "into a territory where it doesn't exist." He also feared that legalizing slavery in Utah would dampen missionary prospects abroad, meaning that "every enlightened nation" that had already abolished slavery "will never hear the gospel of Jesus Christ if we make a law upon this subject."[33] Pratt believed legislators were not acting under heaven's command in crafting a servant code. He did not accept Young's rationale that servitude was divinely sanctioned and did not consider curses to be multigenerational, a singular position in the unfolding theology of race in Mormonism and one that Young persistently rejected.

Orson Spencer followed Pratt with his own denunciation of the evils of slavery, but he nonetheless supported the proposed bill. Spencer agreed that slavery as practiced in the South "riveted chains of darkness" on the feet of the slave and was evil. In contrast, the "servitude" Utah lawmakers contemplated was an enlightened and humane alternative that honored the contractual right of a master to the labor of a servant. Spencer believed this was a necessary measure in order to convince converted masters to bring their slaves to Utah and thereby offer those slaves an opportunity to embrace the gospel. The Mormon message was for "every nation, bond and free," he declared. "Shall we put up the bar and say, bond men wait, none gospel for you?" He was especially concerned about what such a barrier might mean to spreading the gospel to the African continent. "I have thought how can the gospel be carried to Africa? We can't give them the priesthood. How are they going to have it? Must we go and live there?" he wondered. Spencer hoped that the light of the gospel might attract blacks to Utah where they could be "brought under the pale of righteous influence," receive instruction, and "be saved."[34]

Despite Pratt's opposition, "An Act in Relation to Service" passed the legislature just over one week later.[35] As Spencer and Young insisted, it was much different than the chattel slavery practiced in the South. In its final form, the act legalized white and black indentured servitude. For black servants it implemented a version of gradual emancipation modeled after similar laws in Illinois and Indiana. It was primarily designed to regulate masters, not their "servants." It required that masters register any servant with a probate court but stipulated that the servants had to enter the territory "of their own free will and choice." In practice, it is impossible to know how this provision played out, but the law nonetheless deferred to a servant's right to contract his or her labor. More importantly the law prevented the children of servants from being held in servitude for life and therefore mirrored the gradual emancipation codes of some Northern states. The statute further provided for the transfer of servants from "one master or mistress to another" but only if the servant gave consent privately to a probate judge. Masters could not take servants from the territory against their will and were required to provide "comfortable habitations, clothing, bedding, sufficient food, and recreation." They could "correct and punish" their servants but only "in a reasonable manner" and only if "guided by prudence and humanity." They were also required to send their servants to school for at least eighteen months when they were between the ages of six and twenty years.[36] The provisions for education and recreation especially stand in stark contrast to slave codes in the South, some of which prohibited masters from educating their slaves or even teaching them to read. The bill nonetheless legalized Utah's own version of "involuntary servitude."

The one issue on which Utah aligned itself with prevailing sentiment was on the persistent national concern over amalgamation. Lawmakers included a provision that outlawed sex between "any master or mistress" and "his or her servant or servants of the African race." They went one step further to prohibit sexual intercourse between "any white person" and "any of the African race," subject to a fine between $500 and $1000 and up to three years' imprisonment.[37]

Utah's new legal code registered only a mild reaction nationally. In Congress, which had final say on legislation passed in the territory, there was no reaction. Black abolitionist Frederick Douglass's newspaper did publish a brief note in 1854 stating that "the Mormons are carrying slavery into their territory." It claimed that "A Mormon elder passed through Iowa with six [slaves] in his possession" and predicted that "when Utah comes in as a State, it will be, it is said, a slave State." In 1859 when *New York Tribune* newspaper editor Horace Greeley interviewed Brigham Young he asked Young that very question. "No; she will be a free State. Slavery here would prove useless and unprofitable," Young replied. "I regard it generally as a curse to the masters." He further explained, "Utah is not adapted to slave labor." Even still, he acknowledged that servitude existed in the territory and called it a "divine institution," something that would not be "abolished until the curse pronounced on Ham" was removed from his descendants.[38]

*   *   *

On 4 February, the same day that Young signed An Act in Relation to Service into law, the legislature passed An Act in Relation to Elections, a multifaceted bill designed to establish and regulate the territory's voting system. Legislators amended several sections of the bill before the final vote, but the section that stipulated that "all free white male citizens" over twenty-one could vote remained unchanged. It was a standard definition of voter eligibility that should have attracted no special attention. If Orson Pratt or any other legislator spoke against the provision or protested it in any way, it does not appear in the legislative minutes.[39] Yet it was the election bill, not An Act in Relation to Service, that produced Young's most forceful speech on the position of blacks in Utah Territory and Mormon theology, and it emerged from a showdown with Orson Pratt.

When lawmakers met in joint session on 5 February, they asked Young to share "his views on slavery." It was a curious request considering that Young signed the "servant" code into law the previous day. Although Young did reiterate his views on slavery, he did so in a way that suggested he was responding to points made the previous day in a debate over the election bill, as well as reaffirming his stance on the servant code. A close reading of the speech suggests that Young was arguing against a previously articulated position. Perhaps Pratt's speech from the previous week was on his mind or, more likely, unrecorded sentiments from the passage of the election bill the day before. Young, for example, decried eastern abolitionists whose arguments were "calculated to darken counsel[,] *same as here yesterday*," an opaque reference to events from the day before. Young had, in fact, censured Pratt the previous day: "No man got up to talk until I got up," Young said. "Then Brother Pratt got up and motioned that the rules be suspended and the bill put right through. Why did he do this? It was to stick his thumb into me," Young insisted. Although the details of Pratt's views on 4 February do not survive, Young's vigorous response does.[40]

Following Young's speech on 5 February, the legislature took up two seemingly innocuous bills authorizing the incorporation of Cedar City, Utah, and the city of Fillmore. Both municipal bills included sections stipulating that "all free white male inhabitants" of those cities could vote. It was the same basic language from the territorial election bill, but the municipal bills became a way for Pratt to push back against Young, to again poke the prophet-governor with his thumb and indicate that at least one apostle-legislator did not agree with Young's vision of white superiority. Legislator Hosea Stout recorded that Pratt opposed all acts that day that denied blacks the right to vote. The legislative minutes show Pratt's "no" votes on both incorporation bills. For the Fillmore bill the minutes specify that "Councilor Pratt opposed the bill on the ground that colored people were there prohibited from voting."[41] It was an extraordinary stance for Pratt to take. It is possible that he arrived at the legislature determined to make a point regarding the rights of black residents in Utah Territory, and Young's speech only strengthened his resolve. He and Young were repeatedly at odds, and perhaps Pratt's position was one that spilled over from debate over passage of the territorial election bill. At the very least it was a stinging rejection of Young's speech. Pratt's votes were politically progressive, well ahead of Young, his fellow Saints, and the rest of the nation.[42]

Young's speech that day represented the most complete enunciation of a rationale for a race-based priesthood restriction within Mormonism. Its emergence from a legislative debate was hardly a conducive setting for receiving and declaring revelation, which was a claim Young did not make. Nonetheless, his position to the legislature became his position for the church.

Young admitted that he did not understand many of the items lawmakers then had under consideration, but "the principle of slavery I understand, at least I have self-confidence enough in God to believe I do." He went on to make his views clear. It was an odd moment in both the history of Utah Territory and in Mormon history, mostly because those histories so tightly converged when Young rose to speak. He was both territorial governor and president of the LDS Church, the latter of which made him "prophet, seer, and revelator" to the faithful. He was speaking on matters of territorial law to a group of devoted Mormon lawmakers. It was a speech drenched in biblical exegesis and theological justifications for racial curses and black inferiority, and equally designed to shore up legislation already passed that session. It was a speech that inherently bled into Mormon doctrine and significantly impacted the place of blacks in Mormonism long after the US Congress nullified Utah's territorial servant code just ten years later. It was a moment that points to the inherent challenges for Mormons, at that time and in the future, of ferreting out which hat Young wore when he spoke and whether his racialized views were prophetic, political, or personal. For Young, there was no conflict; he was comfortable mingling roles, a posture that outsiders labeled theocratic and un-American.[43]

Young's unrehearsed comments focused upon the biblical roots of black slavery. Rather than elaborating on what he meant when he distinguished between "slavery" and "service," Young focused more upon a biblical justification for a race-based priesthood curse. He also outlined a strident stance against interracial mixing, much more emphatic than the staid advice in his prepared message one month earlier.[44] This time, rather than emphasizing Noah's curse upon Ham, Young firmly grounded his notion of a cursed race in Cain's murder of Abel. He began his remarks metaphorically asserting that when Eve partook of the forbidden fruit in the Garden of Eden, humankind fell and as a result all people were slaves, as it were, to sin. As Young put it, "There has not been a son or daughter of Adam from that day to this but what were slaves in the true sense of the word." It was "the starting point of slavery" but certainly not its end.[45]

Young developed the biblical creation story and then focused upon Adam and Eve's sons, Abel and Cain. In response to Cain killing Abel, Young asserted that God told Cain, "I will not kill you nor suffer anyone else to kill you, but I will put a mark upon you." That mark, he said, "you will see . . . on the countenance of every African you ever did see upon the face of the earth or ever will see." In another sermon seven years later he was more specific, calling the mark "the flat nose and black skin." Young invoked his prophetic mantle and even asserted that he was striking out on his own in making his declaration: "If there never was a prophet or apostle of Jesus Christ spoke it before, I tell you, this people that are commonly called Negroes are the children of old Cain. I know they are, I know they cannot bear rule in the priesthood."[46]

It was a portentous moment for Mormonism, the fullest enunciation to date of a constructed identity for blacks that marked them as physically different. What started with Young's speech grew into a policy that was subsequently preached, applied (however inconsistently), and understood as doctrine, so much so that it took a revelation in 1978 to overturn it. Young was using the very same method outsiders used to racialize Mormons but now he applied it to blacks. In doing so, he set white Mormons apart from their black co-religionists and from potential black converts in the future. In constructing a cursed identity for blacks, he was simultaneously asserting an elevated and privileged identity for whites. Young was not simply negatively situating blacks within Mormon theology, he was attempting to situate whites more positively within American society.

Most importantly for events on the inside, Young evoked his prophetic role to make his assertion and further suggested that he was the first prophet of the Mormon restoration to do so. It was a new direction for Mormonism and a decided turn away from the universalist tone he had struck in the 1847 meeting with McCary when he insisted that "we dont care about the color." Color now clearly mattered to Young, and he went on to insist that it should matter in priesthood ordination. In Young's mind, blacks should only "receive the spirit of God by baptism, and that is the end of their privilege; and there is not power on earth to give them any more power."[47]

Even as Young separated himself from Smith and the other apostles and prophets of the Mormon restoration, he was not inventing new ideas about Cain to do so. Christians in America and Europe had been constructing similar identities for blacks for several centuries before Young vowed that "Negroes are the children of old Cain." Various Christian sources described blacks as "the cursed descendant[s] of Cain and the devil," and black skin originating "with Cain, the murderer of his brother, whose family were destined to have the black colour as punishment." It was an idea that infused American culture and permeated racialized understandings of who black people were. In 1829 African American David Walker fully recognized the degree to which the curse was employed in American society when he wrote that "some ignorant creatures hesitate not to tell us that we, (the blacks) are the seed of Cain . . . and that God put a dark stain upon us, that we might be known as their slaves!!!" In 1852 Young tapped into these ideas to both justify Utah Territory's law legalizing "servitude" and to argue for a race-based priesthood curse.[48]

Young suggested that "the Lord told Cain that he should not receive the blessings of the Priesthood, nor his seed, until the last of the posterity of Abel had received the Priesthood." It was an ambiguous declaration that he and other Mormon leaders returned to time and again. It suggested a future period of redemption for blacks but only after the "last" of Abel's posterity received the priesthood. Young and other leaders failed to clarify what that meant, how one might know when the "last" of Abel's posterity was ordained, or even who Abel's posterity were. For Young it was some future event; blacks would not receive the priesthood "until the times of the restitution shall come," another opaque reference that left the curse in place indefinitely and the conditions for its removal obscure. Young did, nonetheless, foresee a future time when blacks would "have all the privilege" that white Latter-day Saints then enjoyed, "and more." Young was, however, unambiguous about another matter. The curse was nothing humankind could influence or remove; it was so because "the Lord Almighty" ordained it so. "Men cannot, the angels cannot, and all the powers of earth and hell cannot take it off."⁴⁹

Young's remarks were clearly calculated as rejections of various aspects of abolitionist sentiments, especially the view of full black political equality. They were perhaps aimed specifically at Orson Pratt and designed to reinforce the voting rights bill from the day before. Young argued that "not one of the children of old Cain have one particle of right to bear rule in government affairs from first to last; they have no business there. This privilege was taken from them by their own transgressions, and I cannot help it." It was a return to his earlier notions regarding the ordered chain of being and Cain's attempt to disrupt that order. In the Kingdom of God in heaven, Cain and his posterity could not rule over Abel and his posterity, a condition Young argued also applied to political and religious positions on earth: "In the Kingdom of God on the earth, a man who has the African blood in him cannot hold one jot nor tittle of Priesthood," Young said. "I will not consent for a moment to have the children of Cain rule me nor my brethren." The legislature just as well make a "bill here for mules to vote as Negroes [or] Indians," Young insisted. He refused to countenance blacks governing whites in Utah Territory or in Mormon congregations.⁵⁰

It was a forceful tone, insistent and demanding. Young was clearly setting his own agenda on race, and it was a departure from Smith's earlier positions and from aspects of other foundational Mormon principles. The Book of Mormon unambiguously posited that "all are alike unto God," "male and female, black and white, bond and free" and that all were invited to come unto Christ (2 Nephi 26:33). Young was also departing from his own earlier position on Q. Walker Lewis's ordination to the priesthood. And when he suggested that the priesthood was taken from blacks "by their own transgressions," he was further creating a race-based division to cloud black redemption and make each generation after Cain responsible anew for the consequences of Cain's murder of Abel. Although Joseph Smith rejected long-standing Christian notions of original sin to argue that "men will be punished for their own sins and not for Adam's transgression," Young held millions of blacks responsible for the consequences of Cain's murder, something they took no part in. By insinuation Young's position removed the role of individual agency from the lives of blacks, a fundamental Mormon tenet. It instead gave Cain's poor exercise of agency immitigable power over millions of his supposed descendants. To make matters worse, Young's position failed to distinguish exactly what it was that made Cain's murder of Abel worthy of a

multigenerational curse when other biblical figures who also committed homi-
cidal acts did not experience the same fate. Moses killed an Egyptian and later
spoke to God face to face, while Elijah killed four hundred priests of Baal and
continued to serve as God's prophet. King David orchestrated the death of Uriah
and still provided the lineage through which Jesus was born. The key distinction in Young's mind could be traced back to his vision of an ordered Kingdom
of God in heaven. Moses, Elijah, and David did not kill a competing patriarch
in an effort to usurp his position in the great chain of being, as Cain did. It was
the fractured human network that resulted from Abel's murder that appeared
to most animate Young's articulation of a priesthood curse for Cain and his assumed descendants.[51]

The logical inconsistencies notwithstanding, Young maintained his stance
throughout his life. It became the de facto position for the LDS Church, especially as it hardened in practice and preaching across the course of the nineteenth
century. Other Mormon leaders echoed Young and shored up the race-based
priesthood ban. In 1853 apostle Parley P. Pratt asserted that "no man can hold
the keys of Priesthood or of Apostleship, to bless or administer salvation to the
nations, unless he is a literal descendant of Abraham, Isaac, and Jacob." Two
years later apostle George A. Smith elaborated upon the same principle when
he contended that some races "had the Priesthood taken from them" because of
"their corruptions, their murders, their wickedness, or the wickedness of their
fathers." In his estimation it was "useless for any man or set of men, to undertake
to put them in a position to rule."[52]

Young reinforced his ideas in later speeches. By 1859 he reconciled his prior
statement to William McCary—that all nations descended from "one blood"—
with his belief in a priesthood curse. Again drawing upon Acts 17:26, Young
reaffirmed that "God has created of one blood all the nations and kingdoms of
men that dwell upon all the face of the earth: black, white, copper-colored, or
whatever their color, customs, or religion, they have all sprung from the same
origin." Young insisted that "the blood of all is from the same element. Adam and
Eve are the parents of all pertaining to the flesh." Like Smith before him, Young
stressed a single creation, which amounted to a strong rejection of polygenesis
theories then in circulation.

In rejecting the idea of multiple creations, however, it left the question of
black skin unanswered. Young again tapped into the broader Judeo-Christian
tradition to fill the gap. The biblical curses of Cain and Ham explained the existence of black and white races while also justifying a priesthood restriction.
"You see some classes of the human family that are black, uncouth, uncomely,
disagreeable and low in their habits, wild, and seemingly deprived of nearly
all the blessings of the intelligence that is generally bestowed upon mankind,"
he said, immediately following his declaration that the entire human family

derived from "one blood." Black skin was a result of the "mark" God put upon Cain for killing Abel. Then, following the flood, God pronounced "another curse . . . upon the same race . . . that they should be the 'servant of servants.'" Here Young drew upon an idea that William W. Phelps articulated as early as 1835, that black people inherited "three curses; one from Cain for killing Abel; one from Ham for marrying a black wife, and one from Noah for ridiculing what God had respect for." In 1881 John Taylor as church president added his own take, confirming that the curse pronounced upon Cain "was continued through Ham's wife." For Taylor, blacks were allowed to "pass through the flood" out of necessity, so that "the devil should have a representation upon the earth as well as God."[53]

Although Phelps used biblical curses to explain black skin, and Taylor used these curses to explain evil, Young used them to justify black "servitude" and white rule in Utah Territory and a priesthood ban in the LDS Church. The common thread connecting all three men's views was their firm stance against the violation of racial boundaries through interracial marriage. All three men held that at least one aspect of the curses against blacks resulted from Ham's assumed mixed-race marriage.

At the legislature in 1852 Young saved his most pointed comments for that very topic. "Let my seed mingle with the seed of Cain," he posited, and it will bring "the curse upon me and upon my generations; we will reap the same rewards with Cain." It was a matter that in Young's mind directly impacted priesthood and the future vitality of Mormonism. He imagined a grave hypothetical scenario wherein he called upon the entire governing body of the LDS Church, the first presidency, the twelve apostles, the high counsel, the bishopric and even "all the Elders of Israel" and declared to them that "it is right to mingle our seed with the Black race of Cain, that they shall come in with us and be partakers with us of all the blessings God has given to us." The consequences of such recklessness would be swift and severe. "On that very day, and hour . . . the priesthood is taken from this church and kingdom and God leaves us to our fate. The moment we consent to mingle with the seed of Cain, the Church must go to destruction." Young then returned to his earlier notion of capital punishment for such an offense, an idea that he repeated again in 1863 to a Mormon audience: "If the white man who belongs to the chosen seed mixes his blood with the seed of Cain, the penalty, under the law of God, is death on the spot."[54]

Young's pronounced penalty for race mixing was extreme. His advocacy against it was not. The latter placed Young in the mainstream of racial thought for his day. Henry Hughes, a Southern lawyer and intellectual, wrote a treatise in 1854 in which he gave expression to a common American fear. "The preservation and progress of a race, is a moral duty of the races," he wrote, while "degeneration is evil" and an "extreme" sin. Race mixing was at the heart of the evil of which he spoke: "Hybridism is heinous. Impurity of races is against the law of nature. Mulattoes are monsters," he insisted and "The law of nature is the law of God." In his mind it was "the duty of the State" to prohibit "the sovereignty of the black race" and to keep blacks and whites "segregated." It was also "a hygienic ethnical necessity," he felt, "to prevent amalgamation" and thereby preserve "the purity of races." It was a sentiment with which Brigham Young signaled his agreement on more than one occasion.[55]

Despite Young's vigorous stance to the legislature in 1852, by the end of his speech he moderated his tone. He backed away from his more forceful assertions of prophetic authority to suggest that his views were personal and that there was room to disagree. Even still, he maintained that he was correct. "I may vary in my view from others, and they may think I am foolish in the things I have spoken," he conceded, perhaps in a nod to Pratt, but "I know more than they do." His speech represented a fully enunciated position on race. It was clearly designed to construct a cursed racial identity for blacks, justify their existence as "servants," argue against their right to vote, diminish the space for black participation in Mormonism to one of baptism into membership only, and to confirm a position against race mixing.[56]

Significantly, apostle Wilford Woodruff, a member of the legislative assembly, recorded his account of the talk in his journal. Woodruff's dramatically condensed, paraphrased, and reconstructed version encapsulated Young's assertion of prophetic authority in declaring a racial priesthood curse: "Any man having one drop of the seed of Cain in him cannot hold the Priesthood, and if no other prophet ever spake it before, I will say it now, in the name of Jesus Christ, I know it is true, and others know it!" Woodruff's summation of Young's speech is remarkably accurate in capturing Young's sentiment, but this crucial and oft-quoted sentence added key ideas that are not present in the verbatim version recorded by legislative scribe, George D. Watt: "If there never was a prophet or apostle of Jesus Christ [that] spoke it before, I tell you, this people that are commonly called Negroes are the children of old Cain. I know they are; I know that they cannot bear rule in the Priesthood." Woodruff's version had Young making his pronouncement "in the name of Jesus Christ," something Young did not do. Woodruff also inserted a crucial aspect of American racial understanding into the Mormon record, which was an idea that future Mormon leaders would struggle to implement.[57]

Woodruff's account introduced the "one drop rule" into Mormon discourse. It was a rule that played out especially in the South as a legal cover for white slave owners who fathered children with enslaved mistresses. Rather than slavery following the status of a father, some Southern states stipulated that a person's legal status followed his or her mother. In this way, children born of interracial relationships between white masters and slaves were still legally slaves. In 1855 the

Arkansas Supreme Court ruled that Abby Guy, a woman who appeared white and sued for her freedom, was nonetheless legally a slave even if she had only a tiny fraction of African ancestry, as long as it passed through her maternal line.[58]

In general, states were more liberal than the Arkansas Supreme Court in defining "black" and "white" rather than slave and free, but most laws still defined a person as black who had predominantly white ancestry. In many states a person was considered black if she or he had at least one-fourth "negro blood," or sometimes one-eighth, meaning that a person had one black great-grandparent. In other words, seven out of eight ancestors could be white, and a person was nonetheless considered black. Especially after the Civil War, as Southerners attempted to shore up white racial superiority, some states tightened their standards. Although Young did not refer to a "one drop" rule in any known later speech, those who cite Woodruff's account falsely imply that a "one drop" policy was in operation as early as 1852. At the beginning of the twentieth century, Mormon leaders did put their own "one drop" policy in place, a rule that emerged from its own context, not from Young.[59]

As for the priesthood ban, the LDS-owned *Deseret News* announced the policy in April 1852. It declared that only after "Abel's race is satisfied with his blessings" could "the race of Cain receive a fullness of the priesthood." In the meantime "Cain and his posterity must wear the mark which God put upon them." Even if white people washed "the race of Cain with fuller's soap every day, they cannot wash away God's mark." Other Mormon publications followed suit with similar notices regarding the policy. Outside of Mormon circles, however, the rule did not seem to capture much attention apart from Gunnison's book.[60]

It was Q. Walker Lewis's reaction to the new legislation and priesthood restriction that is most sorely missing from the historical record. Lewis was in Salt Lake City over the winter of 1851 and 1852. As a black Mormon elder and a radical abolitionist, he must have found these events chilling. Lewis left Massachusetts in the spring of 1851 and arrived in Utah sometime that fall. On 4 October he received a patriarchal blessing at the hands of John Smith. His trip to Utah and his seeking out a blessing, a spiritual pronouncement of gifts, promises, and status in relationship to God, signaled his continued devotion to Mormonism. Yet, by the fall of 1852, Lewis was back in Lowell cutting hair at his barbershop. His stay in Salt Lake City was brief and likely colored by the legislative session that winter.[61]

It is unclear if Lewis left Mormonism when he left Salt Lake City, or if he remained true to the faith in which he was an ordained elder. When he died in 1856 his wife had his body interred at the Episcopal Church in Lowell, representing the religion she belonged to. In any case, Lewis's death in Massachusetts, geographically removed from the heart of Mormonism, facilitated Mormon forgetfulness of the man Brigham Young called "one of the best Elders." Mormonism was moving in a decidedly different direction, away from an integrated black past toward a white future. Elijah Abel, the sole remaining black elder, made that transition messy—a process that was not complete until the first decade of the twentieth century. In the meantime, Utah's new law governing black "servitude" and Mormonism's strident stance against priesthood ordination for blacks were quickly eclipsed by a doctrine much more disconcerting to nineteenth-century Americans.[62]

* * *

Mormon apostle Orson Pratt's announcement in August 1852 captured national attention and overshadowed any concern over black bondage with a vigorous alarm over "white slavery." Pratt publicly acknowledged that Mormons were practicing polygamy and openly defended it as a religious principle protected under the free exercise clause of the US Constitution. It was an initial salvo in a contentious battle over polygamy that dragged on over the next fifty years.[63]

Outsiders soon seized upon the news to compare, contrast, and generally conflate polygamy with slavery. As outsiders portrayed it, it was a more sinister type of slavery than that practiced in the South. Mormon polygamy, when imagined as white slavery, disrupted prevailing racial conventions and threatened American democracy in the process. The idea of enslaved whites unified people in the North and South in disgust.

In 1855 Alfreda Eva Bell's dime novel *Boadicea the Mormon Wife* made the connection between slavery and polygamy explicit. Mormon "women are treated as but little better than slaves," she wrote; "they are in fact white slaves; are required to do all the most servile drudgery; are painfully impressed with their nothingness and utter inferiority, in divers ways and at all seasons; and are frequently . . . subjected to personal violence and various modes of corporeal punishment." Polygamy was slavery, in other words, for its degradation of women, its inherent violence toward them, and its revocation of personal freedom.[64]

This conflation seeped into the national political discourse of the 1850s and made polygamy fodder in the Union's growing sectional divide. Senator Stephen Douglas's controversial solution to the expansion of slavery, the idea of popular sovereignty, quickly caught polygamy in its crosshairs. Popular sovereignty allowed potential new states to decide by vote whether they would be slave or free states. But when it was applied to polygamy, it was deemed in the minds of some Americans a freedom too far. One newspaper headlined the problem as the "Freaks of Popular Sovereignty in Utah," and even Douglas himself recognized Mormonism as a fly in his popular sovereignty ointment. In response, he advocated a harsh solution before the end of the decade. Meanwhile, editorials and political commentaries roundly condemned polygamy, frequently using conflations with black slavery to do so. Some agitators worried that popular sovereignty gave settlers in the territories too much autonomy, a concern that prompted reformers to argue for congressional supremacy over the territories. It was a cause the Republican Party championed with zeal.[65]

In 1855 the *Transcript*, a newspaper in Portland, Maine, made its concern public. Speaking of Utah it announced, "It seems that in addition to polygamy both Negro and Indian slavery exist in the territory." Worried that Utah's population more than met the requirement of sixty thousand people for admission as a state, the *Transcript* warned that "we may expect to see the Saints, with all their delectable 'institutions,' soon knocking at the doors of Congress. We suppose, according to the doctrine of Squatter Sovereignty, they are entitled to come in with all their pollution!" In order to prevent this it asserted that Congress had the right to act as gatekeeper for the Union. It was Congress's duty to ensure that "Mormons can have no right to smuggle their licentiousness into our national system under the cover of religion." A commentator in the *New York Daily Tribune* expressed similar concern. If the Mormons were asking for admission as a slave state, with African slaves intact, it would be one thing; but it was "White Slavery, of deeper dye and more degraded form" that troubled him most. He too worried that Congress was willing to admit Utah as a state, which was an act he feared "would dim the luster of our national greatness," "bring with it present disgrace and future infamy," and create "the blackest page in our history."[66]

These anxieties did not fall on deaf ears. In 1856 the Republican Party made the link between slavery and polygamy integral to its very founding. Its circular for a national convention that year highlighted Mormonism as a prevailing issue for the new party to address. It drew attention to the "direct enslavement of the white race" in Utah Territory and decried any system "where a man hold a multitude of women as slaves, calling them his wives." It worried that the Democrat doctrine of popular sovereignty was being used to authorize "the Mormon State to come into the Union with the Turkish system full blown, which makes slaves of all colors, and wives without number." It was a fear that Republican delegates took with them to their convention and enacted as a plank in their first presidential platform. The newly formed party, with John C. Fremont as its presidential candidate, asserted that it was "the right and the imperative duty of Congress to prohibit in the Territories those twin relics of barbarism—Polygamy and slavery."[67]

Not to be outdone, the Democrats in the 1850s also adopted a firm stance against Mormonism, especially as reports of alleged Mormon abuses—"treason and crime, debauchery and infamy"—piled up in Washington, DC. President James Buchanan, a Democrat, ordered a 2,500-man army to Utah in 1857 to suppress a reported Mormon rebellion and to replace Brigham Young as governor. That same year Democrat Stephen A. Douglas proposed salvaging his doctrine of popular sovereignty by striking down the "freaks" who stood in its way. For Douglas it was a doctrine that was legitimate if exercised to legalize slavery, but not if used by Mormons to approve polygamy. In a speech delivered in Springfield, Illinois, Douglas described the Mormons as a community of "outlaws and alien enemies, unfit to exercise the right of self-government . . . and unworthy to be admitted into the Union as a State." His solution was for "Congress to apply the knife and cut out this loathsome, disgusting ulcer." He proposed repealing the Utah organic act that authorized the creation of Utah Territory in the first place and then dividing its land and people between two new territories. Douglas argued that the federal government was well within its authority to take such action.[68]

It was a point that at least some northern Democrats and Republicans agreed on. Republican US Representative John L. Thompson from New York sided with Douglas. In a speech before the US House, he argued that popular sovereignty met its limits in Utah. "I would pass a law making polygamy a crime in the Territories, and then send a force sufficient to scatter every harem to the four winds," he thundered. For him polygamy was evil because it was a practice that "the accursed race of Cain had introduced." It was most especially vile for its effects upon women. It was a "licentious system" that turned women "into a plaything of idle dalliance, or a breeding animal for children." It stripped the plural wife of "her sense of equality, her queenly pride as wife and mother, her sacred place at the board and the hearthstone," and instead placed her "beneath the roof of a creature who regards her as at once menial, mistress, and slave." In essence, Thompson argued, polygamy was slavery.[69]

Even still, in the decade before the Civil War, Mormons were not without sympathizers. During the Utah War, when federal troops marched against the Mormons, one Southerner could not help but see the parallels and predicted that federal troops would be marching on the South before long: "My sympathies as a State Rights man are with the Mormons. I do not approve of their domestic institutions," he said, but that did not matter. Polygamy was "their business, not mine," a sin for which he was not answerable. "Let the Mormons be crushed for their religion," he warned, "and it may not be long before our negro masters" are "crushed" for slavery.[70]

Others in the antislavery camp decried how fervently some in the Christian community denounced polygamy but tolerated black slavery. One writer noted the hypocrisy of those who condemned "with ecclesiastical precision, the Mormon idea of a *community* of wives," while countenancing slavery, "which embraces more glaringly than Mormonism the idea of a community of wives." To him they were "narrow souls" who were willing "to strain at a gnat, and swallow a *camel*, hoofs, hump and all!" A Northern paper, the *Portland Maine Pleasure Boat*, asserted a similar position. It pointed to the "religious papers" that were "croaking about legal Mormon polygamy" and wondered why the same type of outcry was not expressed over the de facto polygamy that it argued was bound up in slavery. "Females are raised in the south and sold to men who buy them for the purposes of prostitution," he wrote. "It is not an uncommon thing for slave holders and their sons to violate female slaves and sell their own children as they do sheep or pigs." Why such alarm over Mormon polygamy, he wondered, and "not a word . . . about such rascality as this." Congressman James M. Ashley, a radical Republican from Toledo, Ohio, agreed. In a speech before the US House he denounced interracial liaisons between white masters and enslaved blacks, an "amalgamation" of the races worse "than Mormon polygamy" because it was "an involuntary, forced, and revolting concubinage, from which there is no escape."[71]

The comparisons continued for political purpose but took on new relevancy when the Civil War began. By 1862, with Southern representatives gone, Republicans could pursue their plank against both slavery and polygamy in earnest. Ashley as chairman of the House Committee on Territories played a role in the passage of two bills, both of which demonstrated congressional authority to legislate for the territories. One of the bills outlawed slavery in the territories, while the other (the Morrill Antibigamy Act) was designed to "punish and prevent the practice of polygamy" there too. Abraham Lincoln signed them both into law. Republicans thereby made good on their 1856 pledge and simultaneously more firmly wedded the two barbarisms in the public consciousness.[72]

During the Civil War, at least one Southerner noted the similarities between the two "institutions" but resented the lack of attention federal authorities paid to polygamy. Mary Chestnut, a Southern belle and famous Civil War diarist, nursed a grudge against Mormons because in her view slavery was attacked so violently while polygamy went unpunished. She was particularly troubled that "there are no negro marital relations . . . half so shocking as Mormonism. And yet U.S.A. makes no bones of receiving Mormons into her sacred heart." She complained that Mormons "marry their slaves" but the Yankees still "hug the Mormons to their Puritan bosoms." It was a disconcerting hypocrisy to her. As she put it, "Yankees recoil in horror at the passion negroes have for marrying or doing without it," yet "they tolerate Mormons." She could not help but anticipate the time when the "Yankees" would "attack Mormonism" like they were then attacking the South.[73]

Following the Civil War others joined Chestnut's cry for decisive action against the remaining relic of barbarism. Polygamy became a lone target, as overland travelers, politicians, Protestant ministers, news editorials, and political cartoonists alike compared polygamy to slavery and advocated a solution to the former as violent as that which finally eradicated the latter. In 1866, when a freighter on the Bozeman Trail encountered a group of Mormons, he could hardly contain his disgust. "They are all filthy and dirty especially the females," he wrote. "May that curse (Mormonism) soon be treated as slavery, and die as hard a death to teach them a lasting lesson." It was a sentiment that echoed across the nation for the remainder of the century.[74]

One Christian minister visited Salt Lake City in 1870 and found Mormon men comprising "a kind of aristocracy" just like "the slaveholders constituted an aristocracy in the Southern States." He suggested that "it would be hard to find a tribe of savages in the interior of Africa who are more completely subject to despotic power than the Mormons of Utah." He worried that if Congress persisted to treat Mormons with "false tenderness" it would "sooner or later lead to scenes of violence and bloodshed."[75]

A composite picture of a tainted Mormon slave family emerged, a corruption equal to or worse than the debauched antebellum plantation. Outsiders depicted Mormon men identical to "the old slave-owners of the South," a morally corrupt band of lascivious patriarchs who denigrated their wives just like "southern slave lords used to speak of their 'likely young niggers.'" Polygamy destroyed "all that is manly, honest, and chivalrous in man, degrading him to the level of a brute." Mormon women, in contrast, were subjected to the "most abject slavery of soul and body"; they were "mothers, daughters and sisters" who languished "in a hated, loathsome, lecherous slavery." They were "as much of a slave as any negro that ever lived," women who were beaten and abused to the point that they "weep as bitter tears as slaves ever shed in the Negro quarters of an old-time plantation." So thorough was their bondage that when "the chains" of polygamy are finally broken, "these women will be found as jubilant and grateful as were the black slaves of the South when the War converted them into freemen."[76]

Outsiders were equally insistent upon the solution. One claimed that polygamy "must be firmly dealt with, and, if necessary, the whole diseased and corrupt mass must be cut off." Another argued that "a country that could free four millions of negro slaves and raise them to the dignity of citizenship, ought to be able to abolish pologamy [*sic*] in one of its territories." One writer feared that the government "will have to make the same resort that it did in 1861," and another prodded that polygamy "receive its death-blow" "by the sword," like "slavery in the great Rebellion." A report to Congress was just as demanding. It expressed "great faith in the moral power of bayonets," a solution employed "against slavery when nothing else would suffice." It was an answer that might be necessary "against polygamy, the other 'twin relic,' before we are well quit of that diabolism."[77]

Americans were not alone in expressing such animosity. One observer from across the Atlantic grew increasingly impatient with America's perceived tolerance of polygamy. In 1884 Englishman and former Mormon William Jarman complained that his Yankee brothers fell "*fast asleep* since the *Blacks* were freed." While they slept, "Utah's white slaves pitifully cry, 'Wake up and free us!' America *talks in her sleep,* and answers: 'N-o! W-h-i-t-e T-r-a-s-h a-i-n-t s-o i-m-p-o-r-t-a-n-t a-s N-i-g-g-e-r-s.'" "Oh! Americans, chop your Liberty Poles into kindling wood!" he stressed, "or wake up and free your white slaves in the west, held *now* in slavery of body and soul, worse than ever existed in the South, and *far more filthy.*"[78]

These descriptions found pictorial expression in at least a dozen political cartoons published in various magazines in the 1880s. Following President Chester A. Arthur's annual message to Congress in December 1881, wherein he called polygamy an "odious crime" and urged the "destruction" of "this barbarous system," *Judge* magazine pressed Congress to take action (see figure 5.1). "Arthur's Message" had already struck a verbal blow to polygamy, but congressmen only milled about in the background debating what to do. The *Judge* wondered who among them would "come boldly out and attack this evil of Mormonism." Who was willing to wield Arthur's axe and strike at polygamy with blows strong enough to topple it?[79]

The indecisive congressmen, however, were not the focal point of the cartoon. The "unsightly" white slavery in the foreground emphasized a defiant Mormon patriarch atop a polygamy tree. He shakes a rebellious fist at the capitol building and by extension the entire nation. The tree itself is posted with additional signs of insolence: HANDS OFF and LEAVE US ALONE. It is the women who attract the most attention, however. Bent, kneeling, and cowering with diverted eyes and chained necks, they are resigned to their fates. Polygamy stripped them of their worth, their beauty, their freedom, and their very identities. They were only numbers corresponding to the order in which they wed: wife number one, two, three, and so forth. It was a construction clearly designed to equate polygamy with slavery and to reinforce long-standing gendered stereotypes, especially that of the ruthless slave master and his ruined white slaves.

Whether prompted by this cartoon or not, Congress accepted Arthur's challenge with zeal. During the forty-seventh Congress, lawmakers introduced no fewer than twenty-three bills or constitutional amendments aimed at solving the Mormon problem. The only bill to make it into law was the Edmunds Act, sponsored by Senator George Franklin Edmunds of Vermont, who was the robust lawman featured prominently to the right side of the polygamy tree in the *Judge* cartoon. The heart of the Edmunds Act defined a new crime, "unlawful cohabitation," a measure designed to facilitate criminal convictions of polygamists because it eliminated the need to prove a plural marriage had taken place. Under the new law, federal marshals needed only to prove that a man cohabited with more than one woman. It was an effective bill that sent Mormons across Utah Territory into hiding and over one thousand men and some women to prison.[80]

When the Edmunds Act failed to bring Mormon leaders to their knees, Congress passed a more stringent Edmunds-Tucker Act in 1887. This bill

Figure 5.1 "An Unsightly Object—Who Will Take the Axe and Hew it Down?"
Reprinted from *Judge*, 28 January 1882. Library of Congress.

disfranchised all women in Utah Territory, disincorporated the LDS Church, and began taking LDS property valued at over $50,000 into federal receivership. As Congress contemplated this bill, the popular magazine *Puck* ran a cover image in March 1887 that again drew upon comparisons with slavery (see figure 5.2). In this depiction the male is lazy and uncaring, sitting in the foreground resting under a tree with the Book of Mormon in his hand. Meanwhile in a scene reminiscent of an antebellum Southern plantation, his many wives toil in the sun, nondescript and devoid of humanity. They are but farm animals, no better than property in a "system of Woman-Slavery": this was a system that clearly violated racial norms for not only enslaving one's own race but also Northern middle-class sensibilities centered on the ideals of hard work, merit, and masculinity. In this depiction, white slavery corrupted the men even as it ruined the women. The lounging man does not fulfill his expected role as provider but forces his

Figure 5.2 "An Interrupted Idyll. Danger Impending to the System of Woman-Slavery in Utah." Reprinted from *Puck*, 30 March 1887. L. Tom Perry Special Collections, Harold B. Lee Library, Brigham Young University, Provo, Utah.

wives to violate both gender and racial norms in performing manual labor. The Mormon male does not get ahead in life through his own hard work but through the subjugated work of others.[81]

This depiction of white slavery operated on a deeper level as well. In recreating a Southern slave aristocracy out of Mormon polygamy, the image from *Puck* implied that race was mutable, especially as Mormon women performed blackness. As white slaves in the field, Mormon women turned metaphorically black. Even though outsiders consistently referred to polygamy as "white slavery," the images and metaphors described Mormon men as slave masters and Mormon women as slaves. There were no enslaved Mormon men. It was a gendered definition of slavery that carried implied racial corollaries. Mormon men were on par with corrupt Southern slave holders who sexually violated their female slaves, and in turn Mormon women became black female slaves and thus the victims of white male racial transgression. Here the polygamous Mormon family produced the same indolence, gender, and racial corruption that Northerners hated about the Southern slave aristocracy before the Civil War, a hatred now redirected toward the Mormons. Hope, nonetheless, loomed on the horizon in the form of Senator Edmunds: a cloud moving toward Utah labeled "Edmunds' Law." It startled the indolent man out of his "idyll" and promised impending "danger" to the system of white slavery practiced in Utah.[82]

*   *   *

In words and pictures, in newspapers and dime novels, in government reports and Protestant tracts, a prevailing American fear centered upon Mormon polygamy as a thinly veiled system of white slavery. The irony here was that Brigham Young also believed in white superiority. He and other Mormon leaders brought significant theological weight to bear, especially as they embraced biblical curses and employed them to their own ends. In 1852 the all-Mormon territorial legislature signaled its understanding of the prevailing American racial order when it passed a "servant" code to govern the enslaved blacks then in Utah Territory and a voting rights bill that privileged white men. At the same time, Brigham Young laid out his vision of a segregated priesthood based upon the biblical "curse" of Cain. During the course of the nineteenth century the racial priesthood restriction would expand to include a temple restriction and curtailment of missionary activity among blacks.

Mormon efforts on the inside were designed to segregate and organize those peoples who responded to the LDS message "black and white, bond and free," according to prevailing American standards. Mormon speeches and the corresponding racial policies they prompted made little difference to those on the outside who only saw what they wanted to see: a racial corruption bound up in polygamy. White slavery, as outsiders constructed it, destroyed gender and race. Polygamy was on par with—or "far more filthy than"—black slavery and demanded an equally violent solution.

White slavery was not the only way outsiders imagined Mormon polygamy. Detractors simultaneously fabricated an even more racially charged identity for the Saints, an identity that turned overwhelmingly white Mormons into interracial families and placed them at the nexus of America's fears over racial deterioration.

CHAPTER 6

Black, White, and Mormon: Miscegenation

On 7 February 1859 the *New York Times* ran a front-page story from its corre-spondent in Salt Lake City. It included a string of accusations about the miscar-riage of justice in Utah Territory and the LDS Church's "complete control" over "the souls and bodies of its followers." Amid the charges against the Saints, one stood out simply because it was so different. It was a secondhand story passed on to the *Times* correspondent by so-called eyewitnesses, a rumor designed to amplify fear of race mixing as a natural occurrence among the Mormons. Two "negro balls" were purportedly held in Salt Lake City during the same week in January 1859: "Some ten or a dozen white women attended and danced with the negroes with perfect freedom and familiarity. White men were also 'mixed in,' and were dancing with the negro wenches." The entire affair "presented the most disgusting of spectacles—negro men and women, and Mormon men and women, all dancing on terms of perfect equality."[1]

The *Deseret News* made no mention of a dance or dances during the time in question and the anti-Mormon paper, *The Valley Tan*, also failed to report any such "negro balls." Yet it was an allegation that had a much broader context all its own. "Negro balls" as hotbeds of race mixing first gained relevancy in the national antiabolitionist backlash of the 1830s. Antiabolitionists used imag-ined interracial dances to their political advantage; it was one way in which they hoped to expose abolitionists as amalgamationists in disguise. Such accusations took pictorial form in two antiabolitionist lithographs, both by artist E. W. Clay. Clay's 1839 picture *The Amalgamation Waltz* and 1845's *An Amalgamation Polka*, both implied that "abolitionism" was a slippery slope that would first free the blacks and then invite them as social equals at interracial dances. The end result of course would be interracial sex and marriage. Democrats used a similar tactic against President Abraham Lincoln during his reelection campaign in 1864. They claimed that Lincoln's campaign headquarters in New York City played

171

host to a "Miscegenation Ball." The *New York Times* report of "negro balls" in Salt Lake City grew out of the same context and demonstrated the way in which outsiders tarred Mormonism with the same brush.[2]

When Lincoln's Emancipation Proclamation went into effect on 1 January 1863, it touched off a third wave of national concern over interracial sex and marriage. This time, opponents of race mixing branded Lincoln as a promoter of interracial marriage and even coined the term "miscegenation" to add an air of scientific legitimacy to the charge. David Goodman Croly, editor at the *New York World* (a widely influential Democratic organ) and George Wakeman, a reporter at the same paper, created the word in 1863 as part of their effort to oppose Lincoln's reelection. "Miscegenation" combined the Latin word *miscere* (meaning "to mix"), with *genus* (meaning "race") to indicate "the mixture of two or more races." "Miscegenation" quickly replaced "amalgamation" as the word of choice in the national discourse about race. At the same time, fear of race mixing became a key issue in the presidential election of 1864.[3]

Lincoln's Democratic opponents moved swiftly to denigrate him as a supporter of miscegenation. In fact, Croly and Wakeman anonymously wrote a political pamphlet, *Miscegenation: The Theory of the Blending of the Races, Applied to the American White Man and Negro*, which gained national attention and set the tone for ensuing debates. Croly and Wakeman's central question was, "What will you do with the negro when he is free?" It was the same question that animated the abolitionist debates of the 1830s, and in the wake of emancipation it took on a new sense of urgency. As Croly and Wakeman put it, "When the President proclaimed Emancipation he proclaimed also the mingling of the races. The one follows the other as surely as noonday follows sunrise." Democrats quickly took to calling the Emancipation Proclamation the "Miscegenation Proclamation" and painted Lincoln and his fellow Republicans black.[4]

Croly and Wakeman's pamphlet touched off a firestorm of controversy. Like the antiabolitionists of the 1830s, Democrats argued that because Lincoln sought to free the slaves, he favored race mixing. Samuel Sullivan Cox, a Democrat and congressman from Ohio, denounced the Republican Party's alleged embrace of race mixing and feared that the Republicans were moving the nation "steadily forward to perfect social equality of black and white," which was a digression that could "only end in this detestable doctrine of Miscegenation!"[5]

Another Northerner, Dr. J. H. Van Evrie, published his own pamphlet in 1864 in an effort to denounce the ideas promulgated in *Miscegenation*. To Van Evrie, "the inferior races are intended by the Creator for the lower and ruder kinds of labor," and therefore "no one has a right to try to make those equal whom God has made unequal." For him the foundations of America's democratic experiment were at stake. "Never can we have a true democracy, never can humanity be elevated and ennobled, or freed from poverty and its attendant crimes, until the laws of God are respected and obeyed." In this sense he viewed *"the equality of all whom God has created equal (white men), and the inequality of those He has made unequal (negroes and other inferior races), as the corner-stone of American democracy, and the vital principle of American civilization and of human progress."* Miscegenation and the Republican Party threatened to undermine this foundation.[6]

Despite such efforts at harming Lincoln's reelection bid, he won the presidency, and slavery was ultimately eradicated with the 13th Amendment to the Constitution. The 14th and 15th Amendments followed, granting civil rights and voting rights to blacks. Fear of race mixing escalated in the aftermath of these wrenching social changes and quickly caught Mormonism in its crosshairs.

Outside observers frequently suggested that Mormon blackness was not necessarily a matter of "Negro blood" but a matter of behavior. Because Mormons were so thoroughly white, the conflation with blacks tended to center on the notion that in practicing polygamy Mormons were performing race: they were acting in ways that peoples of African descent acted, therefore they were racially different. As legal scholar Martha Ertman sees it, outsiders charged Mormons with "race treason" when their actions violated general understandings of what it meant to be white. In some constructions Mormons acted black in marrying more than one wife; in others it was the sexual excesses outsiders believed were bound up in polygamy that made them black. These arguments found particular potency in a nation that was undergoing a fundamental racial fight of its own.[7]

The national contest, in fact, created essential context for outsiders to look at Mormon polygamy and see it as a racial menace. Brigham Young's forceful stance against race mixing, the 1852 territorial law banning black-white sex, and Mormon preaching of racial curses simply did not matter. Lack of information and misinformation regarding Mormons and blacks prevailed, so much so that outsiders simply filled the gaps with rumor, falsehood, and innuendo. Race, in these characterizations, was something ascribed from the outside. No matter how much Mormons aspired to whiteness from within, it would never be enough.

After the Mormons arrived in the Great Basin, accusations of race mixing took on a life of their own and were manifested in a variety of ways. The discourse developed around two interrelated themes. The first centered on the ongoing fear of amalgamation or miscegenation. Because Mormons advocated, practiced, and defended polygamy with all of its perceived sexual excesses, the assumption among outsiders was that they must therefore advocate interracial mixing. Free love in the minds of outsiders knew no sexual or racial bounds. In these descriptions Mormons pushed America rapidly toward the perils of "race suicide" and facilitated the darkening of the collective American body. Mormonism was miscegenation and embodied all of its most degraded results: a mongrel religious race that threatened the very foundations of American democracy.

Mormons here were not merely committing race treason but were guilty of racial contamination.

The second construction denigrated both Mormons and blacks and grew into a national discourse understood in brief as the "Mormon coon." Blacks who engaged in extramarital affairs or interracial relationships or who were deemed too overtly promiscuous were sometimes labeled "colored Mormons," or "Mormon coons." In these cases outsiders went beyond racializing Mormons to "Mormonize" race. African Americans sometimes even pushed back with their own efforts to assert a black identity separate from that of the pariah Mormons.

*   *   *

In 1856 the newly organized Republican Party began the process of constructing a mythical interracial family for Mormonism when it targeted Brigham Young's family for ridicule. Party members staged a grand parade that year in Indianapolis, Indiana, to highlight the Republican Party's position on key social and political issues of the day. In a story picked up by the *New York Times,* the parade was described as a "ludicrous" procession consisting of "400 young Republicans of Indianapolis" who marched in front of the state house. A person dressed as "his Satanic majesty" carried a banner that read "MY WORKS DO FOLLOW ME." It included "border ruffians" who charged on "Free-State men," in a mock reenactment of the troubles that popular sovereignty had introduced to Kansas when pro- and antislavery forces crossed its border to stuff ballot boxes in favor of their respective agendas. Another banner called slavery "A DIVINE INSTITUTION" and was followed by a wagon filled with a mock version of Brigham Young's family. The person representing Young held a banner announcing "HURRAH FOR THE KANSAS-NEBRASKA BILL—IT INTRODUCES POLYGAMY AND SLAVERY" and was surrounded by six wives holding six babies. A person dressed as Stephen Douglas followed with a placard that promised "WE WILL SUBDUE YOU."[8]

The procession was clearly designed to make light of the problems that Douglas's doctrine of popular sovereignty unleashed, especially the threat of slavery expanding into the West alongside polygamy. Its commentary on the Mormons, however, went beyond that. The Mormon wagon was carefully crafted as an interracial warning. Not only was Young's mock family polygamist, it was also interracial and therefore a threat to whiteness. Young's six wives seated in the wagon with him included "white, black and piebald better-halves," a group of women unmistakably costumed to heighten national fears of race mixing and project them onto Mormonism. The "piebald" or spotted wife no doubt added a comic element to the family group but also exaggerated concern over the "hybrid" offspring of interracial mixing.[9]

Brigham Young's family was again racialized following Young's arrest on charges of "lascivious cohabitation" in the fall of 1871. The case dragged on through the spring of 1872 and was eventually dismissed, but not before it provided fodder for the national press. *Frank Leslie's Budget of Fun*, a pictorial magazine published in New York City, capitalized on the story to imagine what the scene must have looked like when federal marshals hauled Young off to court (see figure 6.1). Young's "interesting little family" is noticeably distraught over the removal of their husband and father. It is the degraded and interracial nature of Young's family that most dramatically catches the eye. The lead wife who reaches toward Young with partially outstretched arms is a stereotypical black mammy from the South, a common caricature used by Southern whites to counter Northern charges that slavery was inherently brutal. For Southerners the black mammy was living, albeit fictionalized, evidence that slaveholders cared for their slaves and welcomed them into their families. The black mammy stereotype was a fat, happy, contented woman who was so well cared for and devoted to her owners and their children that she had no desire for freedom. She was also so overweight and ugly that no white man could possibly desire her sexually.[10]

When the black mammy was integrated into Brigham Young's family, however, the messages were reversed. Polygamy was so corrupt that Brigham Young was willing to do what no self-respecting Southerner would do: that is, have sex with a black mammy and marry her. The third wife to the left of Young is also black. The children were also interracial, with at least two black girls among them—evidence of the "hybrid" and darkened offspring of polygamy.

Even some of the white children and women were racialized. The second wife to the left of Young and several of the children are more apelike than human, sharing several key markings of racial deterioration. Irish-born immigrants were commonly depicted with simian or apelike features, a way to mark them as primitive and beastly, a construction aimed at the Mormons in this cartoon. The heavy brow and forehead, the flat nose, and the angle of the upper face were all key elements meant to evoke primate characteristics. The message was clear: polygamy despoiled the white race and marked a backward evolutionary descent into blackness and species decline.[11]

Fear of polygamy as a facilitator of racial regression became especially pronounced following the Civil War. In the wake of black emancipation the *New York World* in 1865 predicted that freed blacks would convert to Mormonism en masse. Given what the paper termed "the ungovernable propensity of the negroes to miscellaneous sexual indulgence," it was natural to expect freed blacks to flock to Mormonism to fulfill their sexual and religious desires. Black hypersexuality, the paper predicted, would combine with "the powerful instinct of their race toward unreasoning superstition" to make the four million newly freed slaves "the most promising field in the world for the propagation of the Mormon faith." The results of such conversions would be a threefold racial, moral, and

Figure 6.1 "Affecting Party of Brigham Young from his Interesting Little Family."
Reprinted from *Frank Leslie's Budget of Fun*, January 1872. Library of Congress.

political decline. The "corruption of morals progresses with greater admixture of races," the paper suggested, and the blending of Mormon polygamy with black equality were sure to produce such moral and racial decay.[12]

It was political decay that most animated the paper's alarm. The *World* explicitly rejected Republican proposals to extend voting rights to blacks simply because it believed that once blacks converted en masse to Mormonism they "will look to the Mormon priests and missionaries as their political guides." Suddenly the Mormons in the West and the newly converted and controlled black Mormons in the South "will hold the political balance of power in our presidential elections." Racial purity and democracy were at stake. "The institution of polygamy will hold the balance of power in our politics," the *World* warned, and "it may require as great a war to extirpate it as it has to overthrow the institution of slavery."[13]

Other postwar reports and cartoons pushed the *World*'s anxiety forward and made the interracial nature of Mormon polygamy real in the minds of Americans. The earliest illustration to visually heighten the fear of black-white race mixing as a natural condition in Mormon polygamy appeared in 1870. John D. Sherwood's *The Comic History of the United States* was a satirical take on American politics and peoples that enjoyed at least two editions in print and included a visual depiction of "A Mormon Family Out for a Walk" (see figure 6.2). The intended humor is readily apparent in the enfeebled Mormon patriarch who led

Figure 6.2 "A Mormon Family Out for a Walk." Reprinted from John D. Sherwood, *The Comic History of the United States, from a Period Prior to the Discovery of America to Times long Subsequent to the Present* (Boston: Fields, Osgood, 1870), 451. Special Collections, J. Willard Marriott Library, University of Utah, Salt Lake City.

a long line of wives, who in turn were followed by an endless stream of children. It is not the number of wives and children that make the depiction so striking but rather the matter-of-fact interracial nature of the Mormon family. The wives in the family come in not only a variety of shapes, sizes, and attractiveness but also, most jarringly, in a variety of races. The third wife is a stereotypical black mammy, large with tight curly hair and no shoes. The fifth is dressed in Asian attire and is meant to orientalize the Mormon family, while the eighth wife is Native American or Pacific Islander. Here Mormon polygamy represented the very racial degeneration that so many Americans feared when races mixed.[14]

The description of Mormonism in Sherwood's *Comic History* also plays off then-current ideas about race and "species" to call Mormonism "a new shrub" in America's "flowering ecclesiastial [*sic*] garden." It was a plant that "bore the female variety in alarming disproportion" and was identified as the *genus polygamous*. In Sherwood's words, it was "a very rank weed, smelling earthily to heaven," and its "numerous Young off-shoots," he suggested, "require severe cutting, if not distinct sub-soil treatment." In short, Mormonism was a weed of its own genetic classification, the offspring of which deserved to be eradicated.[15]

In 1881 *Chic* magazine also racialized the Mormon family (see figure 6.3). It ran a two-page pictorial entitled "The Elders' Happy Home," designed to poke fun at the imagined difficulty of polygamist wives getting along as bed partners. The cartoon depicted at least ten women fighting with each other in and around

Figure 6.3 "The Elders' Happy Home." Reprinted from *Chic*, 19 April 1881, 8–9. Library of Congress.

an oversized bed. The husband, meanwhile, detaches himself from the chaos; he is depicted as a helpless witness atop the boudoir and clearly not in charge of his wives (let alone his marital bed). In the foreground nine infants cry or lie otherwise neglected in an elongated crib. At first glance it is yet another jab at polygamy's perversion of gender and family, this time with strong and combative women dominating the home while a timid husband is relegated to the margins. Yet there is also an overt interracial statement embedded in the scene as well. The second baby from the left is the lone black person in the "happy home," a power-ful marker of interracial ruin. The fact that there are no black women among the fighting wives suggests that either a black wife is absent from the room or that the tainted nature of polygamous relationships produced cursed offspring inde-pendent of any black parentage. In either case, the wailing black baby offers clear evidence of racial deterioration inherent in Mormon polygamy.[16]

The vast majority of the interracial depictions, in pictures and in text, portray white males marrying black women, a familiar charge that paralleled Northern condemnation of interracial sex in the South between slave masters and their slaves. Yet it was ultimately the fear of black men stealing, raping, or otherwise soiling white women that generated the most fear and repulsion in the North before the Civil War and the most antiblack violence in the South afterward. This was especially the case in the post-Reconstruction South, where Southern whites violently reasserted supremacy, in part by shoring up old stereotypes of the wanton black brute and his passion for white women. It was an anxiety that outsiders projected onto Mormons as well.[17]

Especially in the postbellum South, Southerners sometimes viewed Mormon missionaries as threats to Southern womanhood. They suggested that the mis-sionary effort was merely a guise to steal ignorant and unsuspecting women and transport them back to Utah in order to feed the sexual desires of the waiting patriarchs. In a qualified sense, Mormon missionaries became "the white coun-terparts to the mythical black rapist." Southerners resorted to violence out of a strong sense of Southern honor that demanded the defense of women against sexual deviance. Southern violence against Mormons was nowhere near the same level as lynchings of blacks, but it did far exceed "the combined number of attacks against all other religious outsiders in the South." Historian Patrick Q. Mason documents over three hundred cases, including beatings, whippings, kidnappings, arson, church burnings, and outright murder. In 1879 a mob killed Joseph Standing, who was a Mormon missionary from Utah then preaching in Georgia. One account explained the resort to violence as a defense against the violation of home and family. As the newspaper put it, the Mormons "did not scruple to break up families, and take young women from their homes." In other justifications Standing was reduced "to a caricature of the lecherous Mormon polygamist" who "destroyed family bonds with sex." It was no wonder that the missionaries provoked the same type of anxiety that Southern white men manifested toward the mythical black rapist.[18]

But it was not merely a fear of white missionaries seducing Southern women that prompted concern. In some cases the threat morphed from white missionaries into mythical black Mormon men as the real violators of womanhood and whiteness. Most significantly at least two rumors of black men marrying white women in Utah came from black Protestant ministers, which was perhaps an effort on the part of the black community to portray the Mormons as the true transgressors of racial boundaries. In 1873 Alexander Walker Wayman, the long-time bishop of the African Methodist Episcopal Church, stayed overnight in Salt Lake City on a return trip from California to Maryland. An acquaintance gave him a tour of the downtown area and an appraisal of the city's African American community. Wayman reported that there were "some twenty or thirty of our people in Salt Lake City, a few of them are members of the A. M. E. Church, and others belong to the Mormon Church." He then repeated a story his guide must have shared with him. It was about "one colored Mormon brother" who desired to take a second wife in order to adhere to the doctrine of polygamy. He actually did so, only to have his first wife object and the second wife leave him in response. There is no indication as to the race of the two women, but the story nonetheless places the blame for the violation of traditional marriage on Mormonism, not on black hypersexuality. The story included a presumably black first wife who possesses the good sense to object. Mormons in this story were responsible for destroying the American family, not blacks.[19]

Ten years later another AME bishop, Henry McNeal Turner, also visited the city. His report, published in the African American *Christian Recorder*, again noted boundary transgressions inherent in Mormonism. Turner described polygamy as being on the wane in Utah, but he nonetheless congratulated the Mormons because "they are just as willing for their daughters to marry colored men as to marry white men." "As there are no colored young ladies here all the colored young men marry white Mormon girls," he noted, "nor are they driven from white society for it." Polygamy, however, was a different matter. Turner suggested that black Mormons were banned from participating. A "colored Mormon appealed to Brigham Young . . . for permission to take another wife," he said, but Young rejected the request. Young explained that "the negro race was under a curse" but that Jesus would return "soon" and remove the curse, thus making it possible for "the negro Mormons" to "marry as many wives as they desired."[20]

In this telling, interracial monogamy was approved, but black polygamy was not. Like Wayman before him, Turner repeated stories likely in circulation among Salt Lake City's black population. In this case it was an account that would have been at least six years old by the time he heard it, given that Young died in 1877. Considering Young's strong stance against race mixing, the story is highly suspect. Nonetheless, Turner's report places responsibility for interracial marriage with the Mormons, people who in his account did not care that their white daughters married black men.

Although it is difficult to be definitive, there were only a few black Mormon men who married white women in the nineteenth century, with Enoch Lewis and William McCary being the most prominent examples. McCary was the only black man to have practiced polygamy, although he was outside the bounds of official Mormon sanction and disciplined when discovered. Young's extreme speeches against black-white marriage hung heavily in the air, as did the brutal 1866 murder of Thomas Coleman, a black Mormon. Coleman's unknown murderers left his butchered body on Capitol Hill in Salt Lake City with a note affixed: "Notice to all niggers. Take warning. Leave white women alone." Yet, perception rarely conforms to reality, and the two AME bishops helped to shape a perception that Mormons allowed black men to marry white women.[21]

By the 1880s other Southern blacks joined a growing chorus of antipolygamy voices. Black members of the Methodist Episcopal (ME) Church in particular confirmed the similarities between polygamy and slavery but entered the anti-Mormon campaign for purposes all their own. If Mormon polygamy were allowed to expand, black women would again be victimized as unwilling sexual partners to white masters, which would be an unacceptable exacerbation of "the coercive sexual behaviors that already had widespread acceptance in the South." Black anti-Mormonism offered an opportunity for black ME members to assert a position alongside their white coreligionists as the true protectors of home and the monogamist family. The real threat of sexual excess and racial contamination came not from the mythical black beast rapist but from his white counterpart: the lecherous Mormon polygamist. Black men feared an expanding Mormon polygamy for the peril in which it placed their ability to protect their wives and daughters from white violators. Just as slavery had denied them their idealized role within the family, an encroaching polygamy presided over by lustful white patriarchs represented a menace too closely related to the slave system. In joining the antipolygamy crusade, blacks in part asserted their superiority over the pariah Mormons. Polygamy offered black ME members an opportunity to situate themselves as the preservers of family values and sexual purity. In America's highly contested racial milieu, black ME members asserted their acceptability over the Mormons, a group of religious outsiders who were looked upon as the true violators of family and race.[22]

In 1882 the *National Police Gazette* took that perception to its most explicit expression when it published Alfred Trumble's sensationalized burlesque *The Mysteries of Mormonism*. Replete with depictions of ritualized sexual violence reportedly conducted in Mormon temples, the book appealed to American voyeurism. It also heightened the nation's fears that interracial mixing was inherent in Mormonism. One illustration, simply titled "A 'Cullud' Mormon," captured the shock of an indignant nation at a pictorial "reality" that blacks and whites were allowed to marry in Mormonism (see figure 6.4). It was a shock that was compounded in this depiction by the fact that the relationship consisted of a black man and a white woman. The scene may in fact depict a polygamous relationship if the older woman to the left of the black man was intended to be his first wife. There is no text in *The Mysteries of Mormonism* to explain the illustration, but certainly it suggests a blatant violation of racial boundaries and a sexually charged racial attack on whiteness intrinsic to the faith.[23]

It was only one small step from the "cullud Mormon" to the "Mormon coon," which was the final caricature that outsiders invented to paint Mormons black. This time the target was mythical black lasciviousness more than Mormonism, but outsiders so firmly combined the two into a derogatory cultural discourse that by the 1880s "colored Mormon," "negro Mormon," and "Mormon coon" all came to signify black men who married more than one woman or who habitually slept around, frequently with white women.

The word "coon" came into popular usage in America in the 1880s as a designation for "Afro-American." It derived from two sources, the common perception

Figure 6.4   "A 'Cullud' Mormon." Reprinted from Alfred Trumble, *The Mysteries of Mormonism* New York *Police Gazette*, 1882. Special Collections, Rare Books Division, J. Willard Marriott Library, University of Utah, Salt Lake City.

that blacks loved to hunt, trap, and eat raccoons, and from a popular blackface minstrel figure named "Zip Coon" who, like another minstrel character, "Jim Crow," came to be identified with blacks. The first "coon songs" in a new genre also appeared in the 1880s. They soon grew into a full blown music "craze" that stretched across a twenty-year time span, from the 1890s to the 1910s. Not coincidentally, the federal crackdown on polygamy in Utah also brought increased public attention to Mormonism at the same time, making the wedding of the two marginalized groups, blacks and Mormons, an easy pairing.[24]

When Henry Thornton died in Macon County, Georgia, in 1879, news accounts noted that he left "a brace of wives to mourn his loss." One report claimed that "polygamy is openly and generally practiced by the negroes of that county, some of whom have as many as five wives under the same roof." Even though there was no evidence that Thornton was a Mormon, his blackness and alleged marital relationships earned him a description as "an avowed colored Mormon" in the press. Another story in Minnesota described a police raid on a prostitution ring in St. Paul. It included the arrest of a black man and his companion, a white "Norwegian girl" who had a "penchant for coons." The St. Paul *Daily Globe* described the affair as "evident colored Mormon doings."[25]

A similar pattern of merging blacks and Mormons continued throughout the 1880s always in relationship to a black man's reported sexual and/or racial transgressions. In Nashville, when "a married colored coon" ran off with "a black Tennessee tulip" the incident was headlined as "COLORED MORMONISM." In Lynchburg, Virginia, an officer arrested a black man on charges of bigamy for marrying two wives. The headline read, "SAID TO BE A COLORED MORMON." A similar headline, "COLORED MORMON," topped a story from New York that detailed the tangled marriages of a recently deceased black man, Richard Johnson. His two wives, one black and one white, experienced quite the shock when they learned for the first time of each other's existence at the coroner's inquest into their husband's death.[26]

By the early twentieth century "Negro Mormon," "Colored Mormon," and "Mormon Coon" had become common shorthands for a carousing black man. It was a well-developed theme that was also a central component of "coon songs," a wildly popular music genre of the period with over six hundred titles published in sheet music form during the 1890s alone. One popular example, "If the Man in the Moon were a Coon," sold over three million copies of sheet music, not an uncommon feat for "coon songs" of the period. The songs appealed to and reinforced white stereotypes of blacks already in circulation through minstrel shows and blackface performances. In coon songs blacks were stereotyped as "ignorant and indolent," "devoid of honesty or personal honor, given to drunkenness and gambling, utterly without ambition, sensuous, libidinous, even lascivious." The songs additionally served to reinforce white ideas about the necessity for segregation. Some coon songs suggested that blacks really "wanted to be white—to break down the most important barrier of all—the boundary separating 'us' from 'them.'" Race and sex were at the heart of the threats whites projected onto blacks in the coon songs, especially the lurking suspicions about "their sensuous nature and the unrestrained quality of their sexuality."[27]

All of these elements came together when Broadway performer Elphye Snowden took to the stage for a concert at the New York Theater on Sunday, 29 January 1905 and performed "The Mormon Coon" (see figure 6.5). The *Music Trade Review* called "The Mormon Coon" a "great coon novelty hit" published

Figure 6.5   Reprinted from Raymond A. Browne and Henry Clay Smith, *The Mormon Coon* (New York: Sol Bloom, 1905). Church History Library, The Church of Jesus Christ of Latter-day Saints, Salt Lake City, Utah.

by New York music executive Sol Bloom. It was one of several songs Bloom promoted that year that attracted the attention of trade magazines and was "featured by head-liners" in their performances. A trade listing called it one of "two very good coon songs" Bloom published in 1905 and another promotion listed it among the Bloom songs for which sales were "great."[28]

The cover illustration to the sheet music featured a somewhat debonair bald black man, "a black dandy" character from the minstrel shows of the era. This dandy sported a flowing white beard and was seated in a high-armed chair surrounded by the faces of a multiracial group of black, white, and Asian women. The black man's impressive beard was no doubt meant to conjure images of the then-current leader of Mormonism, Joseph F. Smith, a man whose own long beard became popular fodder in political cartoons across the nation. Although the cover image was meant to raise fears about perceived black and Mormon sexual excess and interracial mixing, the song's chorus made them explicit, even as it poked fun at black polygamy: "I've got a big brunette. And a blonde to pet," the Mormon coon began, "I've got 'em short, fat, thin and tall . . . I've got a Cuban gal, And a Zulu pal. They come in bunches when I call: And that's not all—I've got 'em pretty too, Got a homely few, I've got 'em black to octoroon. I can spare six or eight. Shall I ship 'em by freight? For I am the Mormon coon."[29]

Rather than an anomaly, "The Mormon Coon" fit into a broad, complex, and changing pattern of racialization that focused intently upon Mormons and constructed them as physically—not just religiously—different. By the early twentieth century Mormons were metaphorically black in these constructions, and blacks were metaphorically Mormon. As the *New York Age* suggested in 1891, "The Mormon and Negro questions are alike." The consequences would be dire if those two undesirable groups merged: "The days of the white race are numbered in this country," one news account predicted. "North America will be another African continent inside of two centuries." At the crux of this fearful deterioration was the "American of the future"— "a black Mormon."[30]

The perceived sexual excesses of both groups marked them as "other" and as people best segregated from white Protestant America. Blackness was easily identifiable, though slippery at the margins where blacks passed as white. Mormons, on the other hand, could not be identified by physical characteristics, which produced considerable anxiety in the white Protestant mind. In order to compensate, outsiders worked very hard to see blackness in Mormons, to project fears of racial contamination and deterioration upon them and ultimately to smear them with blackface.

Ever concerned about Mormonism's public image, LDS leaders did their part to combat such unfavorable press and especially to assert their whiteness against accusations of racial contamination. The *Deseret News* regularly carried news accounts regarding interracial mixing and sometimes took the opportunity to denounce it. During the Civil War, the *News* suggested that it was the abolitionists, not the Mormons, who favored "miscegenation without hesitation." When the war ended, the newspaper countered the allegation that Mormons were somehow in cahoots with freed blacks and planned to convert them en masse. There was no plan to unite the West and the South in a voting bloc based upon interracial polygamy. "Opposite races do not produce a superior race by amalgamating," it noted, while warning Southerners that "it is better for colored ladies not to admit the promiscuous attention of gentlemen of a lighter hue!" In another column in 1869 the *Deseret News* denounced race mixing and warned of its consequences. It claimed that miscegenation would weaken America because it would produce "a piebald race." It would "prove the ruin of any people who indulge" in it, and the nation as a whole would "speedily fall . . . prey to internal dissensions and the first aggressive white race that chose to assail it." In short, the *Deseret News* suggested that interracial mixing threatened America's political stability and led to national decline, which were claims remarkably similar to those leveled against the Mormons.[31]

At the height of the antipolygamy crackdown in the 1880s, the *Deseret News* printed a report from a Mormon missionary serving in the South. It was a letter designed to position Mormons higher on the racial ladder than Southern whites and turn the charge of racial contamination against them. The missionary's report made it clear that Mormons knew better than to engage in interracial mixing but Southern whites did not. In the missionary's mind, those in the South failed to "comprehend the awful consequences" of their actions. "A ride through the Southern States tells a fearful tale of the moral degradation which is rapidly setting its seal upon the entire community," he wrote. At every train station at which he stopped, "The sight of hordes of mongrels of all shades [caught his gaze], from the sickly white to the seven-eighths black, flocking around with no covering but dirt and rags." He feared that "in two or three generations the entire people will be tainted." He recommended that Southerners who favored "a pure and virtuous posterity," should "flee from the spreading curse." "The whole country is groaning under the curse of bastardy and prostitution!" he declared. Meanwhile the Latter-day Saints "realize the true nature of the curse of Cain, and [are] so far removed from its damning influence that any thing like an inter-marriage with the colored race is looked upon with aversion." Filled with the same language of racial decay that outsiders so frequently leveled against the Mormons, the report marked an effort to present Latter-day Saints as preservers of racial purity and those in the South as the real harbingers of racial decline.[32]

In the broader national context, however, Mormon efforts to speak out against race mixing simply did not matter. As outsiders described it, Mormonism was a spiritual pursuit run amok with very physical consequences. It ruined "the *souls and bodies* of thousands of men and women," destroyed their well-being and cursed them with blackness. As one antipolygamy activist viewed it, plural marriage was at the heart of the ruin. It weighed down Mormon women with "the signs of care and sorrow" and placed "a mark of Cain" upon them, "which separates them from the rest of their kind." It was a sign of physical deterioration "perceptible to even the most transient visitors, and those who tarry for any length of time can readily distinguish a Mormon woman from an outsider, though they have no personal acquaintance with either." The solution advocated by some commentators was violent: "Judge Lynch threatens to divide the white and black Mormon with a rope," one paper wrote, while another urged a similar fate upon Mormon missionaries preaching in the South, as soon as "the black men are all lynched."[33]

Clearly, Mormonism's racial history is best understood within a national context that placed considerable value upon whiteness and found Mormons wanting. Mormons, like other marginalized groups, experienced pressure to perform whiteness, to abandon the aspects of their culture—and in this case, their religion—that marked them too easily black. For Mormons this meant abandoning polygamy and all of the perceived racial violations it embodied, but it also meant claiming whiteness. In Jim Crow America whiteness as a function of citizenship was "measured in distance from blackness."[34] In order to distance themselves from fellow black Mormons, white Mormons spent considerable effort measuring their own whiteness through a racially segregated priesthood and temples.

CHAPTER 7

Black, White, and Mormon: "One Drop"

Scipio A. Kenner was in love. For about a year he had been "paying addresses to Miss Isabel Park," and their relationship was progressing rather nicely. When the romance began sometime in late 1869, Kenner consulted with Isabel's parents about his intentions with their daughter. As he recounted it, he received permission from Isabel's mother, Agnes Steel Park, to pursue the relationship. He then wrote a letter to Isabel's father, Hamilton G. Park, who was on a proselyting mission for the Church of Jesus Christ of Latter-day Saints in Scotland. Kenner acquainted the senior Park with the circumstances of his interest in Isabel and later recounted that Park gave his consent "freely and without reserve" for Kenner to continue courting his daughter. Isabel, for her part, was also in love and enjoyed the attention Kenner paid her.[1]

However, Isabel's parents soured on Kenner rather abruptly sometime in mid-1870. According to Kenner, the altered mood began with Isabel's mother, a woman he referred to in typical Mormon parlance as "Sister Park." As Kenner put it, "Sister Park has changed very materially and strangely from her former conduct toward me. After a succession of petty annoyances, she finally requested me not to visit her house again." In response Kenner kept himself "rigidly aloof from her and her house," but he did not keep himself aloof from Isabel. Agnes soon shifted her hostility toward her own daughter. "As if not satisfied with my expulsion," Kenner explained, "she then inaugurated a most heartless persecution against Isabel herself, whose regard for me remained, and is yet, unabated. Not contented with abusive language and threats, she finally resorted to *blows*." That was the last straw for Isabel; she "left her home, and," as Kenner declared, "will never return of her own accord."[2]

In some ways this may be a typical nineteenth-century romance, complete with parents upset over the less-than-desirable young man who stole the affections of their daughter. But it is also a story about what it meant to be black, white, and Mormon in the highly racialized national culture of the late nineteenth century. Scipio Kenner's love for Isabel Park offers a unique lens into racial attitudes among rank-and-file Latter-day Saints as Mormonism's racial policy toward blacks in general, and toward interracial marriage more specifically, continued to solidify following the Civil War. Beyond that, the Kenner and Park romance is a microcosm of broader forces then animating the Mormon struggle for whiteness in the face of a national effort to racialize Mormons as black.

Kenner and Park enter the historical record in November 1870 because Agnes Park somehow came to believe that Kenner *"had negro blood in [his] veins."* When Isabel pressed her mother about her change in attitude, Agnes admitted that "she knew nothing whatever against" Kenner and that he "had always acted the gentleman as far as she knew." For some unknown reason she came to believe that Kenner was tainted with "negro blood" somewhere along his ancestral line. He looked white, and even acted white in his gentlemanly behavior toward her daughter, but for Agnes even the suspicion of black blood was enough to justify banishing Kenner from her home and abusing Isabel for her continued devotion to him (see figure 7.1). He was a man who could only bring Isabel shame, dishonor, and second-class status within Mormonism's lay priesthood and within social, political, and cultural circles. For Agnes the possibility of "negro blood" transformed the well-behaved Kenner into someone she deemed "not . . . proper . . . for her daughter [to] marry." She wrote her husband concerning the matter while he was still in Great Britain. Unfortunately that correspondence is not extant, so it is impossible to know how Agnes arrived at her conclusion and what exactly she said. Nonetheless, Agnes conveyed a strong message to Kenner and her daughter from her husband who reportedly declared that if Isabel continued to pursue a relationship with Kenner and ultimately married him, "and thereby *mixed the blood of [Hamilton's] family,*" Hamilton "would follow [Kenner] to the ends of the earth but he would be revenged."[3]

It is difficult to know what caused Agnes to conclude that Kenner was tainted with "negro blood." It may have been something as simple as Agnes learning that Kenner's middle initial *A* stood for "Africanus." Kenner's parents must have had their minds fixed on ancient Rome when they chose the name of a famous Roman general, Scipio Africanus, best remembered for his defeat of Hannibal in the Second Punic War, for their son. Agnes, however, may have concluded that Kenner's middle name signaled African ancestry.[4]

Whatever it was that prompted Agnes's concern, her suspicion put Kenner in a difficult position. He sought a personal audience with Brigham Young in an appeal to a higher authority and in the hope of a reasonable solution. He called at Young's office on several occasions. But failing to find the Mormon leader available, he resorted to writing to him with the details of the ongoing struggle.

Figure 7.1 Scipio A. Kenner. Special Collections, J. Willard Marriott Library, University of Utah, Salt Lake City.

Kenner expressed his disgust with Agnes over her willingness to "give utterance to such an unqualified falsehood," especially because Kenner believed that she knew it to be false. He concluded that Agnes "must surely be in possession of the spirit of satan, and her pretensions to Mormonism excite in me naught but contempt."[5]

The real issue for Kenner, however, was his love for Isabel. He was not terribly concerned by Hamilton's "strange threat," because he believed it was "influenced by his wife's letters and his vengefulness is inspired only by a gross fabrication." The real point of writing to Young was Kenner's desire to marry Isabel. "Isabel has no home which she can call her own," he wrote. "I wish to marry her and she prefers me to all others. Would you advise us to marry, and trust to Bro. Park's personal investigation, on his return home, to vindicate us in his estimation? Or whatever other course you think best for us we will pursue."[6]

Unfortunately, there is no surviving reply from Brigham Young. It was a matter that Young likely addressed in person. It is not clear if Kenner was able to persuade Young, who then convinced Agnes that she was wrong about Kenner's tainted blood, or if Kenner convinced only Young. In any case, Kenner and Park were married in a Mormon "sealing" ceremony in Salt Lake City less than a month later, on 12 December 1870.[7]

Kenner successfully claimed whiteness for himself in the face of an unsubstantiated charge of "negro blood." This was an act that held the potential to drastically modify the course of his life. Had the decision gone the other way, deeming him polluted with "negro blood," it could have substantially altered his standing in the Mormon community and affected his familial ties, his marriage, and his status in American society.

Following the Civil War, Americans everywhere grappled with the question of what to do with newly freed black people. What political, economic, and social positions would they occupy, and what positions would whites allow them to occupy? While blacks in some instances did enjoy newfound equality, the freedoms guaranteed by the 14th and 15th Amendments to the Constitution eroded over time, especially after 1877 when federal troops were withdrawn from the South, and Southern whites began the process of reasserting white supremacy. Within a decade of the troop withdrawal, Southerners answered the "negro question" with segregation; blacks would occupy a separate space in schools, churches, employment, and many public places. New Jim Crow laws enshrined this separation into the Southern legal code, and the Supreme Court in 1896 placed its stamp of approval on it in *Plessy v. Ferguson*. Among Mormons, separation expanded to include priesthood and temples.[8]

States across the nation also modified marriage laws according to changing racial understandings. In the aftermath of the Civil War there was a period of uncertainty about the constitutionality of laws that prohibited interracial marriage, especially after passage of the 14th Amendment. That amendment guaranteed all citizens "equal protection of the laws" and caused at least some states to repeal their bans on interracial marriage. The reprieve, however, was short lived, especially as white Americans moved to reassert racial supremacy. As Reconstruction waned, Southern whites argued that antimiscegenation laws were constitutional, and before long the courts began to agree. The argument was that antimiscegenation laws applied equally to whites and blacks, as well as to a variety of other "races," and therefore were not violations of the 14th Amendment. In the 1870s and 1880s, Southern states that had repealed their earlier bans moved to reinstate them. Five Southern states even added bans on interracial marriage to their state constitutions. Other states increased penalties for violating antimiscegenation laws, with Missouri making it punishable by up to two years in prison and Virginia for two to five years in prison.[9]

Utah passed its own law in 1888, a piece of legislation that grew as much out of national concern over polygamy as it did over race mixing. Despite federal legislation outlawing polygamy then in force in Utah, one avowed critic of Mormonism in the territorial legislature, Representative E. D. Hoge, crafted his own marriage bill that prohibited polygamy. Before it was passed into law, territorial legislators added a provision that also outlawed mixed marriages between whites and blacks, as well as whites and "Mongolians," a common term of the era designed to include people of Asian descent. Mormon legislators joined with their non-Mormon counterparts to vote Utah's marriage bill into law, a clear signal that regardless of their differences over religion, sentiment against interracial mixing united whites.[10]

During the same time period, some states also refined and tightened their definitions of what qualified a person as black, especially in relation to their marriage laws. Before the Civil War some states had used "one drop" policies to define who qualified as a slave; then, during segregation, states implemented similar rules to delineate blackness. The same year that Kenner wrote to Young in an effort to assert his whiteness, the state of Indiana passed an antimiscegenation law that quantified what percentage of "Negro blood" qualified a person for penalty under the law. The Indiana statute prevented any person "having one eighth part or more of negro blood" from marrying a white person, by penalty of one to ten years in prison and a $1,000 to $5,000 fine. As early as 1853 Virginia lawmakers debated a "one drop" policy, but it was not until the twentieth century that they acted. In 1910 Virginia stipulated that one-sixteenth black ancestry qualified a person as "colored," and then in 1924 Virginia legally embraced the "one drop rule." It stipulated that *any* black ancestry meant a person was legally black. In 1939 the Utah state legislature moved in the same direction when it specified that "a mulatto, quadroon, or octoroon," were prohibited from marrying a white person. However, Utah stopped short of adopting a "one drop" rule.[11]

Nonetheless those ideas informed racial understanding in American society throughout the nineteenth century and seeped into Mormonism to impact Mormon views of priesthood and race. The "one drop" rule explains why Scipio A. Kenner, a person who by all outward appearances was white, had to appeal to Brigham Young in 1870 to substantiate his race. Even the rumor of black ancestry, however remote, was enough to infuriate his future mother-in-law and potentially bar him from the Mormon priesthood. By 1907, as legal segregation came to dominate the South, Mormon leaders began to apply their own "one drop" standard in decisions about ordination to the priesthood and admittance to temples.

Meanwhile, some members of the American scientific community did their part to push racism forward and to justify feelings of white superiority. In 1870

Edward Drinker Cope, a respected zoologist, paleontologist, and professor of geology at the University of Pennsylvania, published an essay in *Lippincott's* magazine that assessed the current state of racial thinking in America. "We all admit the existence of higher and lower races," Cope declared, an indication of the hierarchical racial vision that dominated the nineteenth-century mind. Cope went on to compare "the negro" to apes and described striking similarities in doing so. He found "the flattening of the nose and prolongation of the jaws" evidence of "resemblance" to apes, as was the "obliquity of the pelvis, which approaches more the horizontal position than it does in the Caucasian." He also believed that "the arms of the negro are from one to two inches longer than those of the whites," something he considered "another approximation to the ape." By way of comparison, he found "the Greek nose, with its elevated bridge," to coincide with both "aesthetic beauty" and "developmental perfection." Cope concluded that the "negro" race was "a species . . . as distinct in character from the Caucasian as those we are accustomed to recognize in other departments of the animal kingdom."[12]

With such ideas percolating, it is easier to understand Agnes Park's concern over the potential impurity of her future son-in-law's blood, as well as Kenner's desire to assert his whiteness. Their concerns were legitimized by the nation's ongoing contest over race. Nonetheless, the fact that Kenner and the Park family were Mormons added another layer of complexity to the episode. Despite Young's forceful statements against black-white marriages and sex, Mormons were imagined as living in interracial families and producing dark offspring. After Young's death, Mormon leaders again aspired to whiteness in ways that made them more American than uniquely Mormon and signaled a clear desire to reinforce their acceptability.

As the nation moved to legally segregate blacks, Mormon leaders segregated temple worship and the highest ordinances of salvation in the Mormon gospel. However, Elijah Abel retained his priesthood for life even as Mormon leaders used Abel and another faithful black Latter-day Saint, Jane Manning James, to formulate and solidify a temple restriction. If whiteness was "measured in distance from blackness," then during the course of the nineteenth century Mormon leaders moved further and further away from their own black members toward a collective passage to whiteness.[13]

* * *

For all of the rhetorical back and forth over Mormonism's contested whiteness, the Mormon stance on race was more complicated than either side could possibly capture in a public relations contest. It was in the lives of black Latter-day Saints that America's racial concern over Mormonism had its most dramatic impact. Mormon speeches on race no doubt influenced LDS attitudes toward black people, but it was when Mormon leaders enforced the messages from the pulpit in the lives of Saints in the pew that the racial policy began to accrue meaning and establish precedent.

A new pattern slowly replaced the older standard first established when Elijah Abel and Q. Walker Lewis were ordained to the priesthood. By the beginning of the twentieth century the memory of Lewis and Abel had sufficiently faded so that the next generation of Mormon leaders falsely remembered a ban that had always been in place. At the same time, a considerable number of judgments regarding race, complicated and inconsistent though they were, accrued meaning and lent historical legitimacy to each new decision.

In 1856 Samuel A. Woolley served as branch president or leader of a small Mormon congregation in Centerville, Delaware. While he was away visiting branches in Ohio he received a letter from a Latter-day Saint at Centerville informing him that one member of the congregation, a Brother William Knopp, had recently taken "a collored girl" as a plural wife. Knopp was a convert from England, sixty-two years old and married to fifty-eight-year-old Jane Vale Knopp, his first wife. Woolley sought advice from his ecclesiastical superior on how to handle the situation. He recorded in his diary that his personal inclination was to "take his priesthood from him & let him remain in the church."[14]

When Woolley arrived at the Delaware branch, however, the event did not play out as he had imagined. Woolley convened a church disciplinary council to consider Knopp's case, but Knopp notified the council that he was unable to attend the meeting. Council members deemed Knopp's reason for nonattendance unsatisfactory and proceeded in his absence. They concluded that he "had forfeited his right to the priesthood" when he married "the seed of Cain" and then opted for excommunication on two counts, "for contempt of council" and for "mingling with the Seed of Cain." Before the end of the year Knopp was rebaptized, presumably after divorcing his black wife, although branch records offer no details. In 1860 he moved with his first wife to Utah with no indication as to the fate of his former black wife.[15]

Knopp's case offers evidence of ways in which the speeches given at Salt Lake City played out in remote locations and small branches. Woolley's diary entries and his request for advice from higher authority indicate that there was not a clearly outlined policy or generally understood rule. As decided, the case indicated that a person's priesthood was in jeopardy for marrying a black woman, not just for being a black man. Even still, Knopp's hearing was compounded by his failure to appear before the church council, making it impossible to know how the case might have played out otherwise. The incident also demonstrates that despite Young's bombast regarding capital punishment for interracial marriage, it was not even contemplated in this situation. There was no threat of "death on the spot," nor any discussion of it. Knopp lost his membership, which was a disciplinary action that automatically stripped a man of his priesthood, but his excommunication was reversible. His return to the fold signaled full redemption in the eyes of the LDS community: this sort of redemption was possible for a white Mormon who married a black woman but impossible for black Mormons regardless of whom they married.[16]

The experience of Elijah Abel as a black priesthood holder made this point perfectly clear. The latter years of Abel's life marked an important transition taking place within Mormonism in real and personal ways. Abel and his descendants were the exceptions that proved the rule—a rule that hardened in response to Abel himself. LDS Church President Joseph F. Smith in 1908 recalled that Abel appealed to Brigham Young "for the privilege of receiving his [temple] endowments and to have his wife and children sealed to him, a privilege President Young could not grant." If Smith's memory was accurate, that appeal does not survive in Young's correspondence, but it may have taken place in person.[17]

In 1879, two years following Young's death, a request to Young's successor, John Taylor, does enter the historical record. By that date Abel was the only known black priesthood holder, and he desired to receive his full temple blessings. In Kirtland, Ohio, he received his washing and anointing, a temple ceremony designed to ritually wash the initiate clean from the sins and cares of the world. It was the only part of the temple ritual introduced in the 1830s and Abel participated. Abel was not at Nauvoo when the Saints received their "endowments," and he was not "sealed" to his wife and children, both ordinances that Joseph Smith Jr. presented in the 1840s. In 1879 Abel desired those higher ordinances for himself, especially because Mormon leaders taught that temple rituals were necessary for exaltation in the highest level of heaven.

Abel's request prompted an investigation into the status of blacks in Mormonism. This was an internal inquest that demonstrates the lack of a firm and universally understood policy as late as 1879. If a priesthood ban was unambiguously in place, why did Abel still hold the priesthood? If a race-based temple ban was standard, why the need for an inquest carried out under the direction of the church's top official? Although it is true that LDS leaders were not actively ordaining black men to the priesthood, even the highest officers in Mormonism were unsure of how to proceed in the case of Elijah Abel's desire to participate in the crowning rituals available to Mormons and to realize his faith's most sublime blessings.

During the investigation that ensued, poor or tainted memories began to slowly replace verifiable evidence. The first meeting took place on 31 May 1879 at the home of Abram O. Smoot in Provo, Utah. Smoot, a Mormon convert from Kentucky and former slaveholder, had served several church missions in the South in the 1830s and early 1840s. John Taylor headed the inquiry and

Zebedee Coltrin, who had ordained Abel to his office in the priesthood, was also present at the meeting.[18]

Taylor began his interview with Coltrin out of an attempt to confirm a story then in circulation that Joseph Smith Jr. had told Coltrin that blacks were entitled to the priesthood. As scriptural justification, Smith supposedly repeated the experience of Peter from the New Testament when he was instructed to take the gospel to the gentiles. Coltrin denied that Joseph Smith ever made such a statement to him. Instead, he claimed that in 1834 Smith told him that "the negro has no right nor cannot hold the Priesthood." He also asserted that he heard Smith "say in public, that no person having the least particle of Negro blood can hold the Priesthood."[19]

Coltrin went on to suggest that the only reason Abel was ordained a Seventy was "because he had labored on the Temple." He said that "when the Prophet Joseph learned of his lineage he was dropped from the quorum and another was put in his place." Coltrin then recalled anointing Abel at Kirtland during his "washing and anointing." It was an encounter that Coltrin recounted with disgust: "While I had my hands upon his head, I never had such unpleasant feelings in my life" he recalled. "I said I never would again Anoint another person who had Negro blood in him. Unless I was commanded by the Prophet to do so."[20]

Taylor questioned Abram O. Smoot next. Their conversation centered on Smoot's experiences as a missionary in the South in the 1830s. Smoot recalled Joseph Smith telling him that he could baptize slaves "by the consent of their Masters. but not to confer the priesthood upon them." It was a recollection consistent with the policies put in place during the 1830s regarding black slaves. It grew out of the tense years wherein Smith attempted to prevent further charges against the Saints of inciting a slave rebellion like those that led to their expulsion from Jackson County, Missouri. It applied to slaves specifically, not blacks in general. It was a moot point by 1879, since slavery no longer existed.[21]

Taylor convened a follow-up meeting a few days later. In the meantime, Joseph F. Smith, then an apostle, interviewed Elijah Abel himself. Those gathered on 5 June read Abel's patriarchal blessing and entered it into the minutes of their meeting, a document that confirmed Abel's ordination as an elder. Joseph F. Smith then asserted that "Coltrin's memory was incorrect as to Brother Abel being dropped from the quorum of Seventies, to which he belonged." He recounted that Abel showed him "his certificate as a Seventy, given to him in 1841, and signed by Elder Joseph Young, Sen., and A. P. Rockwood," two presidents of the Seventies. Abel produced a second certificate given to him after his arrival in Salt Lake City reconfirming his standing as a Seventy. Smith said that "Brother Abel's account of the persons who washed and annointed him in the Kirtland Temple also disagreed with the statement of Brother Coltrin." Abel said it was Coltrin who "ordained him a Seventy," a fact borne out by the Seventies record book for 1836. Finally, Abel asserted that "the Prophet Joseph told him he was entitled to the priesthood."[22]

As Joseph F. Smith demonstrated, Coltrin's memory was faulty on several key points. It was also likely clouded by his own racial attitude. He claimed that Joseph Smith Jr. announced a priesthood ban in 1834, which was a flawed assertion given that Abel was ordained an elder in March 1836 and then ordained a Seventy in December of that year by Coltrin himself. He incorrectly recalled taking part in Abel's washing and anointing ritual in the Kirtland Temple. Coltrin's discomfort at placing his hands upon a black man's head, therefore, likely took place when Coltrin ordained Abel a Seventy. Coltrin further suggested that Abel was dropped from the Seventy's quorum when Joseph Smith "learned of his lineage," a curious contention that suggested Abel somehow was light enough to pass as white. It was a claim that was simply not true. Abel was consistently identified in census records as "mulatto," a legal and societal designation that equaled black. The Saints also clearly recognized his race. Coltrin himself recalled his discomfort at placing his hands on Abel's head because of Abel's "Negro blood."[23]

In addition, a church conference in 1843 when Abel lived in Cincinnati affirms that the Saints fully understood him to be black. The visiting authorities called upon Abel to make "a few remarks" at that conference. Following Abel, apostle John E. Page remarked that "he respects a coloured Bro, as such but wisdom forbids that we should introduce [him] before the public." Abel replied that he "had no disposition to force himself upon an equality with white people." Later at the same conference, Abel's race was again made a point of concern. Page and apostle Orson Pratt expressed their views that the duty of the twelve apostles was to ordain and send men to their own country and kin. They therefore instructed Abel "to visit the coloured population," advice that was then "sanctioned by the conference."[24]

Clearly LDS leaders were aware of Abel's race and of his status as a priesthood holder, a Seventy, and as a missionary. Joseph Smith Jr. was still alive in 1843 when the conference took place. There is no indication that Abel was ever dropped from his standing in the Seventies or that his priesthood was revoked. In fact all indications are that he remained a faithful member of the third quorum of Seventies throughout his life. On 5 March 1879, three months before Taylor began his investigation into Abel's priesthood, Abel attended a "general meeting of the Presidents and Members of the Seventies" at the Council House in Salt Lake City. The roll call at that meeting indicated that seventy-one members and presidents from thirty-three quorums were present.[25]

Elijah Abel was among the speakers that day. He used his talk as a chance to reflect on his years of service as a Latter-day Saint and "gave an outline of his history and experience during a period of forty years." In doing so, he went back to his associations with Joseph Smith Jr. and Sr. and especially to a promise of

eternal life if he remained faithful to his priesthood. He recalled his days in Kirtland and his "ordination as a Seventy, and a member of the 3rd Quorum." He
fondly recalled that "the prophet Joseph . . . told him that those who were called
to the Melshizadec [sic] Priesthood and had magnified that calling would be
sealed up unto eternal life." He remembered "opportunities and conversations"
with Joseph Smith Sr., "while watching at his bedside during his last sickness." It
was a sweet opportunity for Abel to recount the meaningful highlights of his life
in the church.[26]

The investigation into Abel's priesthood less than three months later likely
came as a surprise to Abel. He was no doubt aware of the priesthood ban, but
he also held firm to his conviction that his priesthood was sanctioned by the
"Prophet Joseph" himself. Abel's application to receive his endowment and to
be sealed to his wife and family prompted the investigation in the first place.
Because of the incontrovertible evidence substantiating his priesthood and his
active participation as a priesthood holder, LDS leaders allowed that priesthood
to stand. However, they refused Abel's request to receive his remaining temple
ordinances. He became the living exception to the priesthood restriction even as
he was used to formulate a temple ban.[27]

Perhaps Abel's memory of the promise Joseph Smith made him regarding his
priesthood duties influenced his decision to accept a call to serve a third mission
for the church. At age seventy-five, he traveled east to preach the gospel, a proselyting stint that physically drained him. He died within two weeks of his return.
His obituary, published in the *Deseret News*, was more a substantiation of his
status as a faithful priesthood holder than it was a typical eulogy. It noted that he
was "ordained an Elder as appears by certificate dated March 3rd, 1836" and that
he was "subsequently ordained a Seventy, as appears by certificate dated April
4, 1841." That latter certificate was actually a renewal of his status as a Seventy,
an office initially bestowed on 20 December 1836, less than a year after he was
ordained an Elder, and reconfirmed twice thereafter. Following his death, Abel's
obituary served as a third witness to his status as a black priesthood holder in
Mormonism: this was a celebration of his race and his priesthood rank in the face
of a shrinking space for black Mormons within their chosen faith. Abel's obituary reads as if its unknown writer were speaking to the ages, challenging not only
those of Abel's day but also future Mormons to dare to refute his priesthood and
his devotion to Mormonism. The obituary writer seems desperately self-aware
of the transition then taking place within the faith, while hoping beyond hope
that the newspaper carrying news of Abel's death to Mormon homes throughout
the Great Basin might create a bulwark against the pressing racism then threatening to erase everything Abel represented.[28]

It was a barrier too thin to hold back the crush of a nation bent upon rees-
tablishing white supremacy in the wake of black liberty and a faith too tightly

wedded to those same ideas. The challenge of Abel's obituary went unheeded. In 1908 Joseph F. Smith, by then church president and the same man who defended Abel's priesthood in 1879, inexplicably reversed himself and falsely reported to Mormon leaders that Abel's priesthood at some point had been declared "null and void by the Prophet himself." It was a move that placed a final brick in the wall of a race-based priesthood policy and dishonored Abel's commitment to the gospel in the process. Abel's obituary noted that he passed of "old age and debility, consequent upon exposure while laboring in the ministry in Ohio" and concluded that "he died in full faith of the Gospel." In Joseph F. Smith's moment of historical forgetfulness, however, race trumped righteousness and rendered Abel's blackness an insurmountable obstacle, a condition that "full faith" could not overcome.[29]

*   *   *

The 1879 meeting and Abel's death in 1884 hardly settled the matter. There was no official repository of institutional memory that carried authorized decisions on matters such as race, and so each new generation of LDS leaders continued to decide the issue based upon memories of prior precedent and previous statements, sometimes reaching back to Joseph Smith in their minds and other times to Brigham Young. Between Abel's death in 1884 and the meeting in 1908 in which Joseph F. Smith errantly called Abel's priesthood invalid, LDS leaders met on several occasions to discuss racial matters, usually in response to incoming questions. The papers of George Albert Smith, eighth president of the LDS Church and an LDS apostle from 1903 to 1945, contain records of several top-level council meetings in which LDS leaders grappled with issues of race. Those meetings offer insight into the process by which the curse of Cain doctrine was used to justify race based priesthood and temple bans.[30]

With Abel dead, the priesthood ban as an a priori assumption hardened even more into something real and tangible in the minds of its creators, shaped and molded by men, baked in the desert sun of accumulated precedent and the heat of distant memories, and then laid at God's feet as if no human hands had touched it. John Taylor began that process in 1879, and Joseph F. Smith finished it in 1908. Other LDS leaders participated along the way, with each succeeding generation becoming increasingly locked into the previous generation's precedent, especially as they grew to believe that it was a pattern established by Joseph Smith himself.

John Taylor laid the groundwork and rationale that created room to both acknowledge Elijah Abel's priesthood and simultaneously to begin forgetting it. For Taylor that process began as he deliberated over what to do about Abel's appeal for temple blessings. On that occasion Taylor wondered if Abel's priesthood was not like "many other things done in the early days of the Church," they were sometimes done without proper knowledge, but "as the Lord gave further light and revelation things were done with greater order." In Taylor's mind, then, the Mormon principle of continuing revelation offered an explanation. It was Joseph Smith who erred in allowing Abel the priesthood and Brigham Young who revealed God's will when he declared blacks were cursed descendants of Cain. Taylor failed to consider a reverse scenario, as did subsequent leaders. He concluded that "what had been done through lack of knowledge, that was not altogether correct in detail, was allowed to remain." Taylor "thought that probably it was so in Brother Abel's case; that he, having been ordained before the word of the Lord was fully understood, it was allowed to remain." Abel's priesthood was a mistake, in other words, committed by Mormonism's founder but permitted to endure nonetheless. In Taylor's version of things, God failed to reveal his will to Smith but did so to Young. Abel's death in this scenario erased the mistake and allowed for the construction of a more ordered (i.e., whiter) memory to replace it.[31]

Jane Manning James, a black convert to Mormonism in the early 1840s and an 1847 pioneer to the Salt Lake Valley, complicated that process even as she provided a continuing impetus for it. James began a series of petitions to LDS leaders the day that Elijah Abel died. She, like Abel, desired her temple blessings. Priesthood was never an issue for her because Mormons have never ordained women to the priesthood. In James's case, the curse of Cain and its corresponding priesthood ban stretched across the gender divide to enfold black women within its racialized restrictions and bar them from temple blessings. "I realize my race & color & cant expect my Endowments as others who are white," Jane wrote John Taylor in 1884. "My race was handed down through the flood & God promised Abraham that in his seed all the nations of the earth should be blest & as this is the fullness of all dispensations is there no blessing for me?"[32]

It was a haunting question, grounded in LDS universalistic ideals and drawn from sacred texts. James likely derived her inspiration from the apostle Paul's teachings to the Galatians that through Abraham "all nations" would be "blessed" (Galatians 3:8). The Book of Abraham, a sacred text produced by Joseph Smith from Egyptian papyrus and canonized as scripture among Latter-day Saints in 1880, contained a similar message. It was the same book from which apostle Parley P. Pratt paraphrased in 1847, when he said that William McCary's lineage "was cursed as regards the Priesthood." James instead tapped into universalistic ideals to make her appeal for a color-blind gospel, one that harkened back to the standards that governed temple worship at the faith's first two temples: at Kirtland, Ohio, where Abel received his washing and anointing ceremony, and the temple built at Nauvoo, Illinois, before the Mormon expulsion. The view of temple admission at both places was expansive. The house rules at Kirtland allowed for the presence of "old or young rich or poor male or female bond or free black or white believer or unbeliever." At Nauvoo the Saints envisioned "people from every land and from every nation, the polished European, the degraded Hottentot, and the shivering Laplander" flowing to that city. They anticipated "persons of all languages, and of every tongue, and of every color; who shall with us worship the Lord of Hosts in his holy temple, and offer up their orisons in his sanctuary."[33]

The Book of Abraham also signaled an open priesthood and a universal gospel. In it the Lord promised Abraham that his seed would "bear this ministry and Priesthood unto all nations," and further stipulated that in Abraham's seed "shall all the families of the earth be blessed" (Abraham 2: 9, 11). James took such sentiments at face value and wondered "is there no blessing for me?" Her question was not rhetorical. Bound up in it was an implicit appeal to God to keep his promise to Abraham and a more explicit challenge to the men she sustained as God's prophets to honor that promise in her life. She knew her race and repeated the common understanding then in circulation that blackness was "handed down through the flood," but in her mind she was still a part of Abraham's family and desired the blessings such a heritage entailed.[34]

Even though no written reply from Taylor survives, James continued her quest. She wrote at least four additional letters to subsequent LDS leaders and pursued other avenues as well. James desired her temple blessings however she could receive them. She proposed various options to Mormon leaders, none of which they were willing to accept. "Be a Brother," she wrote to Joseph F. Smith, "I am anxious for My Welfare for the future." She asked to be sealed posthumously to Q. Walker Lewis even as she reminded LDS leaders that Lewis was black and ordained an elder. She claimed that he "wished me to Be Sealed to Him," an invitation, which if true, must have occurred when Lewis visited Salt Lake City in 1851 and 1852. In other petitions she asked to be adopted into Joseph Smith Jr.'s family "as a child," something she claimed Emma Smith offered her in Nauvoo. Not fully understanding the implications of Smith's offer at the time, she declined. Better still, she yearned to receive her own endowments and to "also finish the work I have begun for My dead." These were all aspects of the gospel in which her white brothers and sisters freely engaged, based only on their worthiness. In that light, she reminded LDS leaders of her righteousness but also of her race. "You know my history & according to the best of my ability I have lived to all the requairments [*sic*] of the Gospel," she wrote John Taylor. "Your Sister In the Gospel, Jane E James . . . I am Couloured [*sic*]," she ended a different letter to Joseph F. Smith. As was true for Abel, righteousness could not overcome race. After one meeting with James, LDS President Wilford Woodruff recorded in his journal, "Black Jane wanted to know if I would not let her have her Endowments in the Temple. This I Could not do as it was against the Law of God." Woodruff told her that because "Cain killed Abel," all of Cain's seed would have to wait for redemption until after Abel's seed was redeemed. This was an ambiguous condition with no clear timeframe.[35]

LDS leaders did make concessions for James. In 1875 she and seven other black Mormons served as proxy in baptisms for a variety of deceased ancestors and friends in the Endowment House, a temporary structure used for sacred rituals while the Salt Lake Temple was under construction. In 1888 leaders granted her a limited use recommend, which allowed her "to enter the Temple to be babtized [sic] and confirmed for your dead kindred." It was a ritual in which Elijah Abel participated at Nauvoo for a deceased friend and two deceased relatives, with no apparent concern on the part of leaders or record of special permission necessary. Forty years later, it was a privilege James was told that she "must be content with," while leaders awaited "further instructions from the Lord." James, however, was not content. She longed for the rest of her temple blessings, both for herself and for her ancestors. In another concession to her persistent appeals, in 1894 she was "adopted" as a servant to Joseph Smith Jr. by proxy, with Joseph F. Smith standing in for the murdered prophet and Zina Diantha Huntington Jacobs Smith Young, a prominent white LDS leader, standing in for James.[36]

It was an unprecedented ceremony on two grounds. It adopted someone as a servant to Joseph Smith, suggesting an eternal unequal relationship grounded in Noah's curse of Canaan as "servant of servants," and it included a white proxy standing in for a living black person, not for someone who was dead as was typical in LDS proxy work. While the ceremony was designed to appease James, it served to verify her cursed status. That status was reinforced in the interactions LDS leaders had with James and reified in the temple ritual they invented for her. A white body stood in place of her black body so that she could be vicariously "attached" to a white man as a servant.[37]

Still not content, James pressed her case. In 1895, following another appeal, James's request became the subject of a council meeting of LDS leaders. The meeting again hardened the rationale for the temple restriction but curiously did so through priesthood justifications. The church president on this occasion was Wilford Woodruff. He informed the small gathering of leaders that "Sister Jane James, a negress of long standing in the Church, had asked him for permission to receive her endowments." He informed the brethren that "he and his counselors had told her that they could see no way by which they could accede to her wishes," but still they wanted advice from those present, "if they had any ideas on the subject favorable to her race." Joseph F. Smith spoke first and confirmed his position from 1879 when the prior council met regarding Elijah Abel. Smith reminded LDS leaders that Abel was ordained to the priesthood "at Kirtland under the direction of the Prophet Joseph Smith." It was a statement made with no elaboration in the minutes nor any suggested link to the case under review.

It was the only position expressed in favor of an open policy toward James. Smith gave no indication why he felt Abel's priesthood was a relevant matter in James's appeal for temple privileges, but his statement framed the ensuing discussion around priesthood rather than temples.[38]

George Q. Cannon, then a member of the LDS First Presidency, spoke next. He countered that Joseph Smith Jr. taught that "the seed of Cain could not receive the Priesthood nor act in any of the offices of the priesthood." It was an idea he wrongly attributed to Smith, and in doing so he helped to shape a false memory that the restriction began with Smith, not Young. Continuing the misattribution he recalled Smith stating that "any white man who mingled his seed with that of Cain should be killed," another of Young's teachings, not Smith's.[39]

George F. Gibbs, secretary to Woodruff, then further complicated the discussion. He cited an example of a woman who had married a man known to have "negro blood in him." She was now divorced and remarried to a white man. She sought temple privileges just like Jane Manning James. She was denied temple access, however, by her local leader because "she had married a man with negro blood in him and borne him children." George Q. Cannon responded to this situation with a sense of concern over the woman's two daughters. What problems might it create if leaders allowed the woman temple privileges but barred her daughters? "It would be unfair to admit the mother and deny them this privilege," he argued. In order to be consistent, the ban that leaders enforced against James since 1885 required that they refuse the woman's daughters temple access on the grounds that the daughters inherited "negro blood" from their father.[40]

In light of these complex factors, Cannon argued that "to let down the bars in the least on this question would only tend to complications." The council decided "it is perhaps better to let all such cases alone, believing, of course that the Lord would deal fairly with them all." Woodruff acquiesced and the priesthood ban, despite Abel's memory being evoked to the contrary, was used in this case to deny James full temple privileges. The ban was also used to do the same to a white woman who had married and bore children with a black man, even though she was now divorced and married to a white man. Priesthood was not an issue in either situation; rather, gender and race were conflated in curious ways to shore up a growing precedent for banning black people—and white people married to black people—from the temple. A growing precedent regarding race and interracial marriage created barriers against temple attendance LDS leaders were unwilling to breach.[41]

Mormon leaders dealt with a smattering of similar cases during the last decade of the nineteenth century and the first decade of the twentieth. An 1897 letter wondered, "Can a man (white) be permitted to receive the priesthood, who has a wife who is either black or is tainted with negro blood?" Another inquiry in 1900 questioned if a man could hold the priesthood if he inherited "some negro blood . . . through his mother," "provided the white blood predominates." Yet another letter recounted a case in South Carolina where two black men were ordained to the priesthood by the missionary who baptized them, a situation that left local leaders desirous "to know what should be done about this." (George Q. Cannon argued that "negroes were debarred from the priesthood," but the council did not arrive at a conclusion regarding the two black men). In 1902 a report arrived of a man who had married a woman who was "one-quarter negro," and now the son of this couple was about to get married. The son's future wife worried that "inherited negro blood would be a bar to his receiving the priesthood and endowments."[42]

The very existence of these inquiries offers compelling evidence that despite speeches from LDS leaders (especially Brigham Young), and even persistent decisions against temple access for Elijah Abel and Jane Manning James, the increasingly firm doctrine of a cursed black race and exactly what that meant in the lives of black, white, and mixed ancestry Latter-day Saints was far from universally understood or applied. Leaders struck a persistently conservative stance in response to the questions that arrived at headquarters; it was a stance that mirrored the growing strident segregation of American society around them. By the 1890s Jim Crow laws in the South effectively stripped blacks of their constitutional rights, and the US Supreme Court approved. Rather than challenging this growing tide of segregation and racial prejudice, Mormonism swept it along. Unlike Southern whites, Mormons were not struggling to reclaim white superiority but were struggling to claim whiteness in the first place. In this light, their decisions regarding race, priesthood, and temples at the turn of the century are best viewed as efforts by Mormon leaders to facilitate Mormonism's transition from charges of racial contamination to exemplars of white purity. Mormon leaders refused to allow blacks to marry whites in their temples, let alone blacks to marry blacks. The other sacred rituals of the faith (apart from baptisms for the dead) were protected by a color line as well, which kept blacks out even as it attempted to usher whites into the temple as well as the white race.

The responses of LDS leaders to the questions they received were consistent and conservative, especially as they moved toward a "one drop" rule for priesthood ordination and temple admittance. Their deliberations included concern over black-white marriages and over how much of a person's ancestry or "blood" qualified him or her as black. The justification for their decisions largely centered on the rationale Young elaborated in 1852 regarding a curse of Cain and Cain's attempted usurpation of Abel's position in the kinship network leading back to Adam. In 1890, as president of the Quorum of Twelve Apostles, Lorenzo Snow articulated his recollection of the curse as taught by Brigham Young. Snow used the occasion of a private meeting of the apostles held in the Salt Lake Temple to recall Young's teaching on the priesthood restriction. As Snow remembered it,

"The reason negroes could not receive the Priesthood was through the exercise of their own agency before they came to this earth." Snow further explained that "Cain and Abel were princes in the first estate [their premortal existence] and stood at the head of a vast body of spirits for whom they were to beget bodies. Cain knew this and in slaying Abel he realized he was doing injury to all who acknowledged him as prince." The curse that God placed upon Cain then impacted all of his future posterity. In the premortal council, however, the "vast body of spirits" over which Cain presided were offered "the privilege of selecting some other medium through which to be born, but rather than select another prince they decided to be born of Cain and become partakers of his curse." As Snow put it, it would not be "until all of Abel's royal family have received bodies" that the curse would be "raised from Cain's posterity." It was a full articulation of Young's position, replete with the connection Young made to the great chain of being and Cain's sin of attempting to displace Abel in the chain. The curse, as Young and Snow described it, ensured that Cain's plan was thwarted and that "Abel's royal family" would enjoy its rightful position in Adam's expansive family network.[43]

The curse of Cain thus remained central to the decisions LDS leaders made regarding race, priesthood, and temples in the last decade of the nineteenth century and the first decade of the twentieth. It was bolstered by the sharing of lore about Ham's marriage to Egyptus and by scriptures in the Book of Abraham. Historical precedent, however, played the most important role in justifying the bans. Leaders attributed some teachings to Joseph Smith and others to Brigham Young, but in all cases they were unwilling to move against a historical precedent that banned blacks from the priesthood even though the ban itself was a violation of the precedent Joseph Smith established when he sanctioned the ordination of black men to the priesthood. By 1908 Abel's priesthood was falsely remembered as invalid. Forgetfulness replaced evidence to solidify the ban in Mormon collective memory.

At a meeting in 1900, church president Lorenzo Snow again recalled hearing from Brigham Young the curse of Cain idea, but this time he could not state definitively "whether the President had had this revealed to him or not . . . or whether he was giving his own personal views of what had been told him by the Prophet Joseph." At the same meeting, Snow's councilor, George Q. Cannon, "understood" that the teaching originated with Joseph Smith. Later that same year Cannon attributed the curse doctrine to Young and John Taylor who he said were "taught it by the Prophet Joseph Smith."[44]

Also in 1900 Cannon added scriptural weight to the idea. He "read from the Pearl of Great Price showing that negroes were debarred from the priesthood," drawing from the Book of Abraham. Over time the Book of Abraham became a standard scriptural justification to reinforce the ban and give it divine legitimacy, even though Joseph Smith never interpreted it that way. By the second decade of the new century "this relatively new argument had become a foundation of Church policy." A reading of the Book of Abraham to substantiate a ban was based upon faulty reasoning and a misapplication of biblical genealogy. In essence, the misreading of Abraham "elevated extracanonical theories to the status of church doctrine."[45]

The Book of Abraham speaks of an Egyptian Pharaoh, a descendent of Ham who was "cursed . . . as pertaining to the Priesthood." He was described as descending from a "lineage by which he could not have the right of Priesthood" (Abraham 1:26–27). George Q. Cannon and other LDS leaders read those verses as scriptural justification for a race-based priesthood ban that applied to all blacks of African descent (a lineage problem in itself in that black African ancestry is not traceable through Egypt). A careful look at the same verses renders a scripturally consistent reading that "the ability to hold the priesthood was not the issue; it was the ability to preside in a patriarchal order that allowed only one lineage," such as Isaac's bestowal of a birthright upon Jacob, not Esau. The Pharaohs feigned a claim to preside over the priesthood through Noah even though the "right of priesthood" or "the right of the firstborn" had passed to Shem and his posterity. As Abraham declared, God preserved "the right of priesthood" in Abraham's "own hands" (Abraham 1:31). Only one lineage could preside in the priesthood, or hold the "right of Priesthood," much like Joseph Smith declared when he ordained his father as presiding patriarch to the church, a lineage-based calling for several generations in Mormonism. Nonetheless a "basic belief" existed in Mormonism independent of the verses in Abraham that black people descended from Cain through Ham. It was therefore easy to read that belief into the Book of Abraham while simultaneously ignoring the universalistic verses in that same book, let alone the Bible, Book of Mormon, and Pearl of Great Price.[46]

It was not just the Book of Abraham that Mormon leaders turned to as they contemplated questions of race at the turn of the century. On two different occasions Joseph F. Smith added a bit of cultural lore to reinforce their determination. Smith repeated a story that he was told "originated with the Prophet Joseph," but admitted "he could not vouch for it." The lore explained how "the full blooded negro came through the flood." If Ham carried the curse through the flood due to his mixed marriage with a black woman, the children of such a union were obviously mixed. It begged the question, how did full blacks survive the flood? Smith's story offered an answer: "The woman named Egyptus was in the family way by a man of her own race before Ham took her to wife." A full black child named "Cainan was the result of that illicit intercourse." When Smith returned to this story in 1908, he again admitted that he "could not vouch" for its truthfulness but recounted that "it had come to him through the late President Jesse N. Smith, [a stake president and cousin of Joseph Smith Jr.] who claimed that it had come to him indirectly from the Prophet [Joseph Smith]." The story was thus at least fourthhand when Joseph F. Smith shared it. Even if it did originate with Joseph Smith Jr., it was mere lore with no validity, and yet it became a part of the racial deliberations that leaders engaged in. Joseph F. Smith told them that "Ham's wife was an adulteress, and that she went into the ark pregnant from the seed of Cain." It was from her that "the early inhabitants of Egypt" originated. It was a cultural story that supported Cannon's reading of the Book of Abraham and further justified a priesthood restriction.[47]

In 1902, as president of the church, Joseph F. Smith presided over a council that again addressed the issue of race and this time considered what percentage of African ancestry qualified a person as cursed. Smith cited the precedent established in the cases of Elijah Abel and Jane Manning James as justifications for a racial ban. Their repeated appeals for temple blessings ended "of course in vain," Smith told the council. Apostle John Henry Smith countered that "persons in whose veins the white blood predominated should not be barred from the temple," an argument for a more liberal standard than was then being applied. Joseph F. Smith replied with an idea that he attributed to Brigham Young. The belief was that racial blood was not passed proportionately to each child but that one child might inherit all of his or her racial blood from a black ancestor, no matter how remote, while the rest of the children might all be white. In Smith's "opinion" then, "in all cases where the blood of Cain showed itself, however slight, the line should be drawn there; but where children of tainted parents were found to be pure Ephraimites, they might be admitted to the temple." He then clarified, "This was only an opinion" and suggested that "the subject would no doubt be considered later." As finally articulated sometime before early 1907, leaders put a firm "one drop" rule in place: "The descendants of Ham may receive baptism and confirmation but no one known to have in his veins negro blood, (it matters not how remote a degree) can either have the Priesthood in any degree or the blessings of the Temple of God; no matter how otherwise worthy he may be."[48]

LDS leaders also contemplated black-white marriages and what such unions meant for a couple so married. In 1897 George Q. Cannon remembered that John Taylor argued for capital punishment against a priesthood holder "who would marry a woman of the accursed seed." Apostle Lorenzo Snow suggested that if a man divorced his black wife and married a white woman, "he would then be entitled to the priesthood." LDS leaders concluded that being black or marrying a black person might prevent one from holding the priesthood and entering an LDS temple.[49]

Noticeably missing from the justifications used in these counsel deliberations to reinforce racial restrictions was any mention of black people as less valiant in their premortal existence. This unique teaching grew out of a Mormon belief that all people existed as spirits before they were born on earth. In their premortal condition spirit beings engaged in a battle that pitted Satan against Jesus for control of the redemption of humankind. It was an idea grounded in the Book of Revelation: "And there was war in heaven: Michael and his angels fought against the dragon; and the dragon fought and his angels . . . And the great dragon was cast out, that old serpent, called the Devil, and Satan" (Revelation 12:7–9). Those who followed Satan were banished from heaven, never to receive physical bodies, while those who followed Jesus were born on earth. It was a belief that lent itself to theories about why some people were born into a cursed lineage. Mormon apostle Orson Hyde first posited an answer in pamphlet form in 1845. Hyde claimed that "those spirits in heaven" that did not "take a very active part" in the war between Satan and Jesus "were required to come into the world and take bodies in the accursed lineage of Canaan; and hence the negro or African race." In Hyde's version it was a curse that accounted for the "African race" but not a priesthood ban. That notion emerged later.[50]

Brigham Young denounced the idea of black neutrality in 1869. He taught that "there was No Nutral spirits in Heaven at the time of the Rebelion. All took sides. . . . All spirits are pure that Come from the presence of God." He then reasserted his standard explanation for black skin: "The posterity of Cane are Black Because He Commit Murder. He killed Abel & God set a Mark upon his posterity." The idea of black neutrality, however, did not die out in Mormonism, but was kept alive in various publications. Apostle Orson Pratt hinted at it, while Mormon intellectual Brigham H. Roberts gave it full expression. It found new life in the twentieth century with a subtle shift. As some leaders articulated it, blacks were not neutral, but "less valiant" in the premortal realm, a revision that made space for Brigham Young's stance against neutrality but that still attributed the ban to presumed choices that black people made as spirits in a pre-earth life. Even though such ideas existed in Mormon thought, they did not inform the decision making process in the same way that the curse of Cain did.[51]

In 1908, when leaders again met to consider racial matters, they did so following yet another inquiry regarding the church's policy. This time it was a letter from the recently returned leader of the church's mission in South Africa, Ralph A. Badger. "What shall be done where people tainted with negro blood embrace the Gospel" Badger questioned. He further wondered if the gospel should be preached at all "to the native tribes" of South Africa. By this point, LDS leaders had a long record of decisions dating back to 1879 when they denied Elijah Abel temple privileges. At the meeting in 1908 they completed the slow process of historical forgetfulness even as they constructed a revised memory regarding Abel's priesthood.[52]

In response to Badger's inquiry, Joseph F. Smith recited for the gathered council the stories of Elijah Abel and Jane Manning James, and specifically their appeals for temple blessings. In telling their stories, Smith used them to shore up segregated priesthood and temples. Q. Walker Lewis was forgotten altogether by any of the current generation of leaders. When the council met it was only four months after James's death, an event that Joseph F. Smith personally commemorated when he spoke at her funeral. With the two main black agitators for reform now gone, their memories and the weight that their lives might carry in Mormon history were raw material yet to be shaped for future generations. Smith used the 1908 meeting to craft a memory of Abel and James that firmly cemented the temple and priesthood restrictions in place and ensured that the lives of these two Saints were effectively erased from Mormon history.[53]

In the retelling, Abel's priesthood became a mistake made and corrected by the founding prophet himself, Joseph Smith Jr. In refashioning this memory, Joseph F. Smith relied heavily upon historical precedent. He argued that there was nothing more current leaders could do other than "refer to the rulings of Presidents Young, Taylor, Woodruff, and other presidencies," all of whom maintained that "people tainted with negro blood may be admitted to Church membership only."[54]

Smith recited Abel's story as precedent but remembered it differently than when he personally interviewed Abel in 1879 and witnessed Abel's priesthood certificates firsthand. It was now nearly thirty years later, Abel had been dead for over twenty years, and racial attitudes in America and in the LDS Church had hardened in favor of segregation. This time Smith's recollection centered on Abel's priesthood as invalid and declared so by Joseph Smith Jr., the very man who Abel maintained sanctioned that priesthood in the first place. Smith falsely projected then-current policy onto the past and argued that the policy had always been in place. In doing so, he effectively erased Abel's priesthood from Mormon collective memory and solidified a segregated racial future. In the new memory, priesthood was white, temples were white, and the Mormon future would be white too—a passage into acceptance and respectability in America.[55]

Smith recalled that Abel was ordained to the priesthood "in the days of the Prophet Joseph" but then suggested that his "ordination was declared null and void by the Prophet himself." Four years earlier Smith had implied that Abel's ordination was a mistake that "was never corrected," but now he claimed that Mormonism's founder had in fact corrected the mistake although he offered no evidence to substantiate his claim. Smith then recalled that Abel applied for his endowments and asked to be sealed to his wife and children, but "notwithstanding the fact that he was a staunch member of the Church, Presidents Young, Taylor, and Woodruff all denied him the blessings of the House of the Lord." His inclusion of Woodruff as "President" in his recollection was a mistake, since Abel died three years before Woodruff became president of the LDS Church. Smith also recounted the persistent appeals from "Aunt Jane" for her temple blessings but noted that they were rejected. In light of those two precedents Smith argued for a "position without any reserve" toward black Latter-day Saints, "giving them to understand that they are descendants of Cainan, that the curse has not been removed, and that all of his race are deprived of the rights of the priesthood because of the decree of the Almighty." Smith insisted that "until the Lord sees fit to remove that curse," black Mormons should "content themselves with the privilege of receiving the First Principles of the Gospel" and nothing else. He emphasized that in all cases where the priesthood was bestowed upon men with "tainted" blood, "their ordinations must be regarded as invalid."[56]

As for preaching among blacks, the council decided that missionaries "should not take the initiative in proselyting among the negro people, but if negroes or people tainted with negro blood apply for baptism themselves they might be admitted to Church membership in the understanding that nothing further can be done for them." These decisions ensured that black conversions remained low in the twentieth century and that Mormonism was branded a white church.[57]

Even as Mormon racial ideas froze into a firm set of policies supported by a doctrine of cursed lineage, exceptions slipped through the "one drop" wall of exclusion. It was a standard impossible to police, especially as Mormonism grew in international locations such as Brazil with long histories of mixed marriages. Even in the United States, Elijah Abel's son and grandson were both ordained to the priesthood. Although the circumstances for those ordinations are unclear, the LDS leadership obviously could not monitor all aspects of race, priesthood, and temples in all cases in a growing church. They reinforced the ban when circumstances came to their attention, but exceptions, inconsistencies, and paradoxes still dot the historical record and underscore the difficulty of regulating racial boundaries.[58]

*   *   *

Scipio A. Kenner's letter to Brigham Young in 1870 highlights the challenges Mormon leaders faced. Secure in his whiteness Kenner married Isabel Park in 1870 and then went on to enjoy a successful career. He worked as editor for several small newspapers before taking a position as associate editor at the *Deseret News*, Mormonism's premier news organ. He also filled prominent positions in politics and public service. He was elected a Justice of the Peace in Beaver County in the 1870s and went on to serve as a Democrat in the Utah House of Representatives. He worked as a Deseret telegraph operator and was admitted to the bar of the Utah Supreme Court. He was known as a "peacemaker," a "good speaker," a powerful writer, and a person "well known in state." In sum, Kenner's brief brush with "Negro blood in [his] veins" had no lasting impact upon his career or political ambitions. By all counts he was a respected public servant, a person who figured "conspicuously" in the political life of the state, and a faithful Latter-day Saint. LDS Church president Joseph F. Smith spoke at his funeral in 1913, as did two other church officials: Brigham H. Roberts and Seymour B. Young. William M. McCarty, a justice of the Utah Supreme Court, also addressed the crowd of mourners who "occupied every available seat" at Kenner's "impressive funeral services."[59]

When Jane Manning James died in 1908, she was also remembered as a well-respected person within the Mormon community. The *Deseret News* printed her obituary on its front page and included a picture of James standing next to her brother Isaac. "Few persons were more noted for faith and faithfulness than was Jane Manning James," the story read, "and though of the humble of earth she numbered friends and acquaintances by the hundreds." She was recalled as "hale and hearty," "kind and generous," and "loved and respected." James's friends and acquaintances contributed "flowers in profusion" to commemorate her "undaunted faith and goodness of heart." She was an original pioneer of 1847, the year the Mormons arrived in the Salt Lake Valley, but was best remembered as a "servant" in the family of Joseph Smith Jr. She was lauded as a person who "remained loyal and true to his memory."[60]

By all counts James, like Kenner, was a prominent western pioneer and a devoted Latter-day Saint. She was an esteemed member of her community and a person who earned the admiration of then Mormon Prophet Joseph F. Smith, so much so that he blessed her memory with a talk at her funeral. It was a singular honor not extended to the average Latter-day Saint, a fact that denoted James's place of prominence within the Mormon fold. On that count, James was on par with the more economically and politically prominent Kenner, but that was as far as the similarities went. Gender and race were their two chief differences, but it was race that created the greatest barriers in James's life. As a woman, she could not hold the priesthood, but being black barred her from the saving rituals performed in Mormon temples—a key aspect of her belief system that she had no access to. Meanwhile, Kenner's whiteness presented no such obstacles. By the time he died, Kenner's friends and family failed to mention his whiteness at all in their commemorations of his life; they simply took it for granted. Kenner likely did too, despite his brush with blackness in 1870.

James's remembrances, in contrast, were laced with reminders of her race. The first sentence of her obituary on the front page of the *Deseret Evening News* defined her as "an aged colored woman familiarly known as 'Aunt Jane.'" The *Salt Lake Herald* likewise told its readers that James was "colored" and that she was "one of the servants in the household of Joseph Smith" before his martyrdom in Illinois. The report of her funeral again called James an "Aged Colored Woman" and noted that the chapel was "crowded" with mourners, many of whom were "of her own race." While Kenner was able to escape accusations about his blackness, Jane could not escape her skin.[61]

The contrast with Kenner is even more striking when Kenner's avocation as an actor is considered. Kenner and his future wife Isabel Park first met when she performed in a play in Ogden, Utah, at the same theater at which Kenner made his acting debut. The theater sparked their romance and remained a source of mutual fondness after they wed. At some point following a move to southern Utah, Kenner joined a comedy troupe known locally as the "Negro Minstrelsy." Kenner played the role of "Sambo" and his partner, Joseph W. McAllister, was "Bones." Other actors, all in blackface, added to the performance, which according to one remembrance "burlesqued everything and everybody." LDS authorities sometimes attended the shows and were known to "roll back in their seats and roar with laughter at the doings and saying of the Negro Minstrels."[62]

Blackface theater was a part of the entertainment scene in Utah as early as the 1850s. National touring groups as well as local performers played to audiences throughout the Great Basin and performed in a variety of venues, including the Mormon-operated Salt Lake Theater. At the heart of the performances were white actors (and sometimes black) with burnt cork smeared on their faces as makeup designed to exaggerate racial stereotypes, especially big lips and raccoon eyes. The shows parodied what it meant to be black in the minds of white Americans and reinforced negative stereotypes. The characters in the shows were outlandish in their behaviors, especially as they embellished mythic elements of blackness including speech, mannerisms, and behavior. The stock roles in the minstrels were most often deliberately ignorant although sometimes wily and sage; they were frequently carefree, especially as they danced, sang, and cracked jokes and generally played the buffoon. Blackface characters were at once humorous and pathetic, caricatures not worthy of being taken seriously and clearly not equal with whites. They were a curious mixture of uncivilized and yet endearing distortions of who black people were, meant to evoke feelings of pity while simultaneously reinforcing the correctness of white domination.[63]

When Scipio A. Kenner donned blackface, then, he did so as a parody of black people. He was secure enough in his whiteness to put on blackness with no fear of lingering suspicions over his own tainted blood. His performances in blackface, sometimes with LDS leaders in the audience, signaled in a very real way that his body and his blood were no longer in question; he was white enough to dress in blackface and thereby blend in. His blackface role indicated a full acceptance within the Mormon community, temples, and priesthood.

For Mormonism as a whole, the process was more complicated. By the early twentieth century, professional minstrels largely disappeared from Utah. In their place, Mormon publications, magazines, and newspapers sometimes picked up minstrel themes in jokes, stories, and advertisements, all of which reinforced negative stereotypes in the minds of Mormon readers. The minstrels themselves also continued to provide amateur entertainment in Mormon congregations or wards throughout the intermountain West. Church socials on a local level sometimes included blackface shows as fundraisers for missionaries or other causes. In 1948 one Salt Lake City unit took its performance of "Sambo's Minstrel Show" on tour throughout the valley where the actors entertained "thousands of members of the Church" (see figure 7.2). The show included a cast of over thirty participants, all of whom donned blackface for charitable purposes. The proceeds were used to sustain at least two missionaries who were then spreading the gospel message outside of the Mormon corridor. Any additional profits went into a general "mission fund" used to aid Mormonism's "great missionary work."[64]

The minstrel shows continued through the first half of the twentieth century. In 1951 a different Mormon congregation, this time one in the American South, put on its own show. A report of this act noted that it included "a stage full of 'darkies' all bubbling over with rhythm." The show featured "Sambo" and "Bones" as lead characters. Ten years later another Mormon congregation, this

Figure 7.2 "Sambo's Minstrel Show—Presented by 196th Quorum of Seventy." Reprinted from *Church News/Deseret News*, 15 August 1948. Church History Library, the Church of Jesus Christ of Latter-day Saints, Salt Lake City, Utah.

time a unit in Idaho, staged its own minstrel, a production that featured "more than a hundred boys, girls and adults" who "used a little black makeup and a lot of talent" to help boost the congregation's "lagging missionary fund." The irony was that by the mid-twentieth century the church's missionary effort was significantly hampered and deliberately curtailed among black peoples due to the church's entrenched priesthood and temple restrictions.[65]

Like Kenner in the nineteenth century, Mormons in various US congregations unintentionally signaled to outsiders that Mormonism as a whole was confident enough in its whiteness that it could join other white Americans in painting their faces black. Mormons had secured a white identity for themselves at the expense of their black brothers and sisters. Black Pete, Q. Walker Lewis, Elijah Abel, Jane Manning James, William McCary, and various other black Mormons became forgotten pioneers, replaced in collective Mormon memory by a white priesthood, white temples, and a segregated theology that insisted that God implemented Mormonism's bans and that they had been there from the start.

From the time of the LDS founding in 1830, when Black Pete joined the new movement, to the turn of the twentieth century, Mormons were persistently charged with racial degradation. In effect, outsiders collectively smeared Mormons in blackface and turned them into caricatures of themselves—they were painted as religious buffoons in racial disguise not worthy of being taken seriously—yet a serious threat to the Protestant vision of American democracy based upon racial purity. As outsiders imagined it, Mormon polygamy was white slavery, which created a conduit to racial contamination and moral decline. Mormon leaders' forceful efforts to create racial boundaries within the fold could never fully satisfy the allegations from without.

As second-class Saints, black Mormons such as Elijah Abel and Jane Manning James witnessed the space for full black participation shrink over the course of their lives. By the 1950s Mormon minstrel actors could return home from their racial burlesques, wash the burnt cork from their faces, and join the American mainstream. Jane Manning James, Elijah Abel, and other black Mormons, however, could not wash their faces white. In the lives of its own members—both black and white—Mormonism's passage to whiteness was secured at a high price.

CHAPTER 8

Oriental, White, and Mormon

When Reverend Thomas DeWitt Talmage of the Central Presbyterian Church in New York City rose to speak at the Brooklyn Tabernacle on 19 September 1880, he had recently returned from a trip to the Pacific Coast and various points in between. His journey and the people that he met during his travels were on his mind that Sunday, as they were the following week when he spoke again from the same pulpit. Talmage took as subjects for his two sermons prevalent political and social issues then dominating the US West: the Chinese question first, and then Mormonism.[1]

Talmage was by no means the first preacher to juxtapose the Mormon and Chinese "problems" in nineteenth-century America. In fact, politicians, cartoonists, intellectuals, news editors, and social commentators perceived Mormonism as an oriental problem on American soil very early in its existence. The parallels, comparisons, conflations, and contrasts continued across the course of the nineteenth century. Talmage was somewhat unique in his position toward the two undesirable groups simply because he advocated assimilating the Chinese and excluding the Mormons. Most other commentators advocated harsh solutions designed to preserve Western democracy against these two oriental threats.[2]

In the chorus of national voices weighing in on the Mormon and Chinese questions, Talmage was one of the most prominent and influential. The *New York Times* suggested that with the possible exception of Henry Ward Beecher, Talmage enjoyed "a more widespread reputation than any other American preacher of the gospel." "For over forty years he has been a conspicuous figure in the religious life of America," the *Times* wrote in 1902. Throngs gathered each week to hear him speak at the spacious Brooklyn Tabernacle. When a fire in 1872 destroyed the original structure, Talmage had it rebuilt on a much grander scale. The new building boasted a "seating capacity of five thousand," and included "wide and spacious aisles and foyer" that offered standing room for an additional one thousand worshippers. The heart of the church was its "vast cathedral-like amphitheater, elegant in design and finish, and quite impressive, both interior and exterior." Talmage captivated audiences with his forceful style and spirited sermons, so much so that his followers reported that on some Sundays they had to turn people away for want of room. Talmage's weekly sermons were widely distributed through thousands of newspapers and journals nationally and internationally. Although impossible to verify, Talmage's print audience was said to reach into the millions. So popular were his orations that in 1884 New York publishing house Funk and Wagnalls printed a collection of his sermons, a grouping that included the September 1880 speeches about the Chinese and Mormons.[3]

On Talmage's trip west he visited Utah Territory and met both Mormons and their opponents, including "many of the prominent Gentiles of Salt Lake City." He then traveled to San Francisco where he was given a tour of that city's Chinatown and encountered Chinese immigrants firsthand. He also listened to community leaders who resisted the Chinese presence in America and argued for their exclusion. Upon his return to New York City Talmage took opportunity to educate his East Coast audience on both of the undesirable groups.[4]

When Talmage preached about the Chinese question that Sunday in September his recent trip added an air of legitimacy and import to his comments. The title for his sermon was the simple question then "raging" on the West Coast: "Must the Chinese Go?" Talmage spent the bulk of his talk answering his own question with a resounding "no," which was a progressive Christian attitude designed to counter the growing exhortations for the federal government to exclude Chinese people from coming to America as immigrants. Just one week later, however, Talmage replaced his progressive stance toward the Chinese with a decidedly conservative and even dogmatic answer to the Mormon question. "Unless we destroy Mormonism, Mormonism will destroy us," he insisted. Arbitration or "peaceful proclamation" were his preferred methods of dealing with the Mormons, but if those two approaches failed, Talmage called for "howitzer and bombshell and bullets and cannon-ball" to do the job. "*Mormonism will never be destroyed* until it is destroyed by the guns of the United States Government," Talmage demanded.[5]

The two speeches, coming as they did on successive Sundays, offer an intriguing juxtaposition of ideas and approaches: one called for compassion and neighborliness, the other demanded a resort to force and destruction. The contrast departs dramatically from the ways in which nineteenth-century Americans thoroughly conflated the two groups to construct the Mormons as an American-born oriental threat. Unlike Talmage, other Americans looked eastward, beyond the Native Americans and blacks, to find Muslims, Turks, and Chinese as the most undesirable and un-American peoples with whom to compare Mormons. Polygamy and a susceptibility to authoritarian systems were the most common ways in which outsiders argued that Mormons performed orientalism and assumed Asian racial characteristics.

As was typical for Talmage, he built his sermon around a biblical passage. For his homily on the Chinese he chose Luke 10:29 as a scriptural departure, specifically the question from a "certain lawyer" to Jesus, "Who is my neighbor?" To answer that question in a modern industrialized setting, Talmage pointed to the shrinking nature of the global community. Steamships linked Southampton to New York and China to San Francisco, even as railroads stretched across "all the continents" and cables snaked "under all the seas" to "literally [make] the whole earth one neighborhood." In this global context, Talmage pressed his audience to consider the following questions: "Is the Chinaman a neighbor? Does he belong to the race of which God is the Father? Is he a brute, or an immoral? Will he help us, or will he hurt us? Must he be welcomed, or driven back?"[6]

To answer those questions Talmage drew upon his recent experiences. Of his tour of Chinatown, he admitted that he "saw the worst." "It is bad enough and filthy enough and dreadful enough," he said, but maintained that the seamy side of New York City was worse. "The white iniquity of our Atlantic coast cities is more brazen than the yellow iniquity of San Francisco," he claimed. In the Chinese he found not a threat but a promise. "Of all the foreign populations which have come to the United States during the last forty years," Talmage declared, "none are more industrious, more sober, more harmless, more honest, more genial, more courteous, more obliging than the Chinese." He praised the integrity, "love of order" and industry of the Chinese people. They were unequaled "as laundrymen" and "house help" and their work ethic was superior to that of other races. Talmage then systematically dismissed the standard objections against Chinese immigrants, that they took jobs from Americans, sent their earnings back to China, and were pagans who wore "peculiar dress" and sported queues.[7]

It was Talmage's argument on religious liberty, however, that offered the most striking comparison to his commentary a week later on the Mormons. "Do you think the Huguenots and the Pilgrim Fathers and the patriots of the Revolution would have contended as they did for civil and religious liberty in this country, if they had known that their descendants would make religious belief a test of residence and citizenship?" he wondered. "If this Government continues to stand, it will be because alike defended are the joss-houses of the Chinese, the cathedrals of the Roman Catholics, the meeting-houses of the Quakers, and the churches of the Presbyterians." It was an open stance on religious pluralism and its purported link to the founding generation of Americans who crossed the Atlantic in search of the very freedom of worship that Talmage insisted should be expanded to include the Chinese.[8]

For Talmage, if the choice was between paganism and "a religion which insults and stones a man because of the color of his skin or the length of his hair or the economy of his habits," then Talmage vowed, "Give me paganism." What he really wanted his audience to envision was the Chinese as potential Christian converts. "If you have a superior civilization, a superior Christianity, present them to these people in a courteous and Christian way," he admonished. "These Chinese make good Christians," he declared and then suggested that it was "the God of the Bible" who was ultimately responsible for Chinese immigrants in America. Talmage preached that the mass Chinese migration came with a higher purpose: "to have them Christianized, and multitudes of them sent home again for the redemption of China." It was an optimistic assessment of the Chinese and a bright vision of a Christian future.[9]

Talmage, however, was much less sanguine about the Mormons. Talmage framed his sermon on Mormonism with the Old Testament story of God's destruction of the wicked city of Sodom. "Then the Lord rained upon Sodom brimstone and fire from the Lord out of heaven," Talmage began (Genesis 19:24). He flatly declared, "Sodom and Salt Lake City are synonymous. You can hardly think of the one without thinking of the other." The comparison was especially true because both cities were "the famous capitals of [a] most accursed impurity" and both were "doomed." Mormon polygamy was on par with the culturally understood sexual deviance of ancient Sodom, and the consequences would be similar in Talmage's mind.[10]

Although Talmage did not attempt to reconcile the two sermons, the implication was clear. Mormonism fell so far outside the bounds of an acceptable religion that it did not deserve the same type of respect as that which he advocated for the Chinese. For him, Mormonism was filled with "hideous deformities," a long list of which he leveled against the faith. It was *"one great and prolonged cruelty," "a great blasphemy," "an organized filth,"* "one great surge of licentiousness," a "stupendous indecency," a "beastly outlaw," and an "incestuous abomination." Most troubling for him was that Mormonism was moving forth unchecked "to debauch this nation." In Talmage's mind there was no grave deep enough to bury it. The "stout, thousand-armed, thousand-footed, thousand-headed, thousand-horned, thousand-fanged corpse" called Mormonism was simply too monstrous to contain. As a solution Talmage advocated a presidential proclamation that demanded Mormons abandon their plural wives "or go to jail, or quit the country" altogether. Failing those options "only extinction and death" would do.[11]

Lest his followers object to such harsh measures against a religion, Talmage attempted to set their minds at ease. His problem was not with Mormon beliefs but with their evil practices. This was a distinction that the Supreme Court made the previous year in its landmark polygamy decision, *Reynolds v. U.S.*, in which it argued that the Constitution protected religious belief but not religious practice. As Talmage put it, "If these Mormons want to believe that Joseph Smith was God, or that Brigham Young is the second person of the

Trinity, the law has no right to interfere with them." As it stood, however, Mormonism not only antagonized Christianity but also "good morals," so much so that "the infidel and the Christian stand side by side in denouncing Mormonism as foe to free institutions." The consequences would be dire if Americans did not unite in opposition to the Mormon threat. "If God be good and pure and just," Talmage warned, "He will not let this nation go unwhipped much longer. . . . Every day as a nation we consent to Mormonism we are defying the hail and the lightning and the tempest, and the drought and the mildew, and the epidemic and the plague, and the hurricane, and the earthquake of an incensed God."[12]

The irony of Talmage's contrasting views on the Mormons and the Chinese was not lost on a political cartoonist for the New York–based *Judge* magazine, who captured the divergent views in pictorial form (see figure 8.1). The depiction featured Talmage dressed in medieval armor atop a metal horse, the Bible hanging from his shoulder with the Brooklyn Tabernacle in the background. In one arm Talmage carefully protected a small Chinese person who looked to be safe, happy, and in no apparent danger. In the other hand Talmage clutched his "sermons on Mormonism" in the shape of a lance, a weapon intended to attack

Figure 8.1 "'The Chinese may stay, but the Mormons must go.'—DeWitt Talmage." Reprinted from *Judge*, 27 October 1883. L. Tom Perry Special Collections, Harold B. Lee Library, Brigham Young University, Provo, Utah.

the Salt Lake Tabernacle, mislabeled in this picture as the "Mormon Temple." The caption concisely conveyed the meaning behind Talmage's two orations: "The Chinese May Stay but the Mormons Must Go."[13]

It was a perfect summation of Talmage's sermons but also a clear indication as to how thoroughly the Mormons were imagined as foreign enemies on American soil. The conflation of Mormons with Indians and blacks drew upon domestic marginalized groups and peoples who were a part of America's "racial" history almost from the beginning. The white majority held both groups at bay in part because they comprised local and immediate sources of anxiety. As such they offered convenient wellsprings from which Protestant white America could drink racial understanding and then spew it back at the Mormons.

In conflating Mormons with Asians, however, outsiders turned the Mormon question into a foreign problem, making Mormons so thoroughly "other" that they were no longer domestic threats. In these constructions the nation's premier American-born—even frontier—religion was transformed into an exotic Eastern sect of a different race, a way for outsiders to distinguish between East and West, authoritarianism and democracy, morality and debauchery. It was the product of undesirable hybrid mixing and a bastardized faith that might have originated in America but because its fruits were so thoroughly alien and its practices so Asiatic, it did not qualify as a religion at all and need to be eliminated.[14]

As outsiders imagined it, the conflation between Mormons and Asians centered on three variations of the same theme. First, Mormons were very early compared with Muslims, and the faith was labeled the "Islam of America." This construction was rife with religious comparisons that morphed into racial conflations, especially as outsiders concluded that Mormons were predisposed to blind obedience and oppressive theocracies, two conditions that marked them as more Asian than American. Second, Americans sometimes projected unbridled sexuality onto Muslims (and especially Turks) and then used comparisons with Mormon polygamy to justify their antipathy toward all three groups. Finally, beginning in the 1850s and assuming more import as the "Chinese problem" increasingly occupied America's attention, Mormons were frequently depicted alongside Chinese as one of the nation's pressing foreign dilemmas. Politicians, ministers, news editors, and even the US Supreme Court conflated the two Asiatic questions as they cast about for solutions.

For their part, the Mormons early on adopted open attitudes toward peoples of Asian descent. That open stance gave way when Chinese immigrants began to move to Utah. By the turn of the twentieth century, Mormon publications participated in the same type of orientalization that had been so thoroughly deployed against them. It was one way Mormons marked themselves as emerging monogamists: people who were white and Western and willing to assimilate.

* * *

In 1841, when the city council of Nauvoo, Illinois, drafted a provision on religious liberty for the predominantly Mormon city, it was expansive in its vision
of a pluralistic society. The council listed a variety of Christian denominations
welcomed in Nauvoo: Catholics, Presbyterians, Methodists, Baptists, Latter-day
Saints, Quakers, Episcopalians, Universalists, and Unitarians, and "all other religious sects, and denominations, whatever" as groups who were granted "free
toleration, and equal privileges, in this city." The only non-Christian religion specifically mentioned in the code was "Mohammedans," which was a striking inclusion, especially considering that Joseph Smith was derisively labeled an "American
Mohamet" very early in his religious journey. At Nauvoo the city council signaled
a welcoming attitude toward "Mohammedans" should they desire to settle among
the Latter-day Saints. It was an unlikely scenario simply because there were so few
Muslims in Illinois and elsewhere in the United States.[15]

The open attitude persisted in Utah as well. In 1855, for example, LDS
apostle George A. Smith defended Mohammed to a Mormon audience in Salt
Lake City. "There was nothing in his religion to license iniquity or corruption,"
Smith said, "he preached the moral doctrines which the Savior taught," including the worship of one God, to treat others as you want to be treated, and not
to "render evil for evil." In fact, Smith found Mohammed to be an instrument in
God's hands, a man "raised up by God on purpose to scourge the world for their
idolatry."[16]

In a follow-up speech on the same day, fellow apostle Parley P. Pratt was more
direct. He found Islam preferable to Catholicism, a religion he derided for its
idol worship, religious iconography, and veneration of saints. For Pratt, "Mahometan doctrine" was a standard raised against such corruption. Three years later,
fellow apostle John Taylor was not so complimentary toward Islam when he
linked Mohammed to the "power, prowess, and bloodshed" of his day. Even still,
the Mormon position was remarkably accepting within a national culture that
tended to view Islam as a religious corruption and its founder as an imposter.[17]

The conflations between Mormonism and Islam were part of a larger patch-
work of Mormon orientalization permeating the nineteenth century. From the
1850s through the 1880s, especially in the decade surrounding the Chinese
Exclusion Act (1882), the rhetoric slipped easily into blurred metaphors with
Asians in general and Chinese more specifically, even as Muslims and Turks remained standard foils. The national discourse also frequently seeped beyond the
religious to the racial. This was an effective way to further heighten American
fears of Mormons by fomenting suspicions about their whiteness, as well as a
way to color them yellow, Eastern, and Asian and thereby racialize religion.[18]

The comparisons with Islam and Mohammed began early and persisted
through the first decades of the twenty-first century. They included the creation

of a "domestic orient" out of Mormon places, domestic Mohammeds out of Mormon leaders, and a domestic sultanate in the American West. In the minds of outsiders Mormon settlements were rendered despotic regimes filled with subjects predisposed to blind obedience and oppressive theocracy.[19]

Similar to Talmage's description of Salt Lake City as a modern Sodom, other nineteenth-century observers found such comparisons irresistible. As they imagined it, Mormon geography transformed into oriental geography, Mormon towns into Middle Eastern villages, and Saints into blindly devout Muslims or "lustful Turks." Joseph Smith's younger brother William, for example, bemoaned the "many faint and incorrect descriptions" of Nauvoo, Illinois, which circulated in the 1840s among "travelers, passers by, and others." William complained that their reports created an image of a barbaric city "stuck into the nethermost corner of the universe where none but Indians, Hottentots, Arabs, Turks, Wolverines and Mormons dwell." Ironically, William resorted to similar orientalization himself after he broke from the Saints under Brigham Young. In 1849 he petitioned the US House of Representatives to not admit Utah into the Union as a state, in part because he insisted that the Mormon settlement at Salt Lake City was too much "like Sodom and Gomorrah."[20]

Popular author and travel writer Sarah Jane Lippincott (using the penname Grace Greenwood), was reminded of Palestine, not Sodom and Gomorrah, when she visited Utah. She found that the entire region had "a singularly foreign aspect" to it, something she described as "strange and ancient and solemn." Another traveler called the Salt Lake Valley "one of the most beautiful of any on the globe," and said "no wonder that the Mormon leaders selected it for their Mecca—their Jerusalem—their Holy City." It was their "Canaan" and Salt Lake City was their "Tadmor of the Desert," a reference to a Syrian oasis city at the intersection of caravan roads. In this traveler's mind the only elements lacking to turn Salt Lake City into the "Asiatic Orient" was "the crescent-crowned dome and the minaret." Sir Richard Burton likewise called Utah "the Holy Land of the West." He found Salt Lake City to be "somewhat Oriental," more similar to an "Asiatic rather than to an American settlement." Another observer was more succinct: "Turkey is in our midst. Modern Mohammedanism has its Mecca at Salt Lake."[21]

An 1879 dime novel claimed that Salt Lake City "wears a distinctly Oriental appearance" and offered a vision to Americans of how Damascus might look. "White houses shining amid rich masses of green foliage. A dome, a tower, a spire, that may answer for a minaret, deep gardens, buildings with flat roofs, a faint mist of dust marking the line of a travelled street." Even the sky evoked "Oriental softness," so much so that it cast an Eastern hue on such "a strange city, a new city, born within the last half century; a city of its own kind." Salt Lake City created a scene "as striking, as novel, as interesting, as unprecedented" and, in essence, as foreign, as to make it an Asian outpost in the American West. In short it was "Orientalism in the extreme Occident."[22]

Not all nineteenth-century observers agreed. One dime novelist noted that it was the Mormons who were "fond of comparing [Salt Lake City] to the ancient capital of Judea," but to him "any resemblance" required "a great stretch of imagination." The valid comparison was with the Mormon people, not with the land. Mormons behaved in oriental ways and in the process became oriental themselves: "When the saints from the United States, or other parts of the world, arrive within sight of the city, they prostrate themselves to the earth like the Mohammedans when they discover the sacred edifices of Mecca," he wrote. In their shrewd and greedy business dealings, they also resembled "the Jews of old, who while affecting to despise the Gentiles, were at the same time strongly enamored of Gentile gold." One former Mormon tended to agree. In her mind Mormons had supplanted "the teachings of Christianity" with "the barbarism of Oriental nations in a long past age." In Mormon hands, "the sweet influences of the religion of Jesus were superseded by the most objectionable practices of the ancient Jews."[23]

In other accounts Mormons simply blended with Asians; they became Eastern and foreign with nothing to distinguish them as Western and American. A noted Frenchwoman and world traveler boasted that she had visited "the Mormons, Chinese, Japanese and Cingalese" in her journeys around the globe and "ridden side by side with Bedouins and climbed the Himalayas." In her mind the Mormons fit naturally in her list of exotic peoples and were oriental with the rest. Sarah Jane Lippincott described Mormonism as a "new, old faith," a "strange conglomerate of Christianity, Judism, and Mohammedanism." Others were less sure how to categorize Mormons or their religion, but in selecting groupings some observers situated them among Eastern peoples and faiths. One list placed "idolaters, Parsees, Brahmins, Buddhists, Mohammedans, [and] Mormons" together in contradistinction to "Christians," while other lists clustered "Jews, Chinese and Mormons" or linked Mormonism with Paganism and Buddhism. One congressman placed Mormons alongside "Persians, Hindoos, and Musselmen," while a Protestant minister classified them with "Mohammedans, Hindoos, Fuegians, Caribs and Hottentots." A different critic equated the "Mormon woman in polygamy" with "the Turkish woman in the harem," and "the Hindoo woman on the funeral pyre of her husband." The *New York Daily Tribune* bridged the East/West divide when it described Mormonism as "the new Mohammedanism in England and America." A French journalist who visited Utah in 1904 likewise defined Mormons as "Christians with Mohammedan instincts."[24]

Similar to the ways in which polygamy provoked fears of Mormon men as hypersexual black rapists, orientalism generated myriad comparisons to and conflations with Turkish harems and their imagined sexual excesses. Polygamy in the minds of some Americans was an ancient oriental practice, one that Western civilization and proper Christianity had triumphed over in its enlightened march toward liberty and democracy. "The modern nations of Europe are free from this scourge," Utah's former territorial secretary, Benjamin G. Ferris, wrote in 1854. President Millard Fillmore appointed Ferris, a lawyer from New York, to his post; however, he was so shocked by Mormon practices that he resigned after only six months in office. He later wrote a scathing critique titled *Utah and the Mormons,* a tome that Parley P. Pratt described as "the meanest Book ever yet published against the saints." Pratt deemed it "not decent to be read in a Brothel."[25]

Ferris called the Mormons in Utah a "strange and eccentric community" and referred to Salt Lake City as the "valley of Sodom." Polygamy to him was a decided regression in evolutionary progress and a step eastward toward racial decline: "No nation of ancient or modern times, in which polygamy has existed as a part of its political or religious institutions, has exhibited a permanent degree of vigor or prosperity," he asserted. "It belongs now to the indolent and opium-eating Turks and Asiatics, the miserable Africans, the North American savages, and the Latter-day Saints." In his mind, polygamy was "the offspring of lust, and its legitimate results are soon manifest in the rapid degeneracy of races."[26]

The strength, vitality, and racial purity of America were again at stake. Dr. George Napheys, an influential American physician, likewise feared that oriental racial regression was at work among the polygamists in Utah. If "left to themselves" he argued, they would "soon sink into a state of Asiatic effeminancy." Other commentators believed that Mormons represented both racial and political decline, especially as they refused to conform to "the spirit of progress and improvement and enlightened humanity." As critic Mrs. C. V. Waite put it, Mormonism was "an antagonism to our Government" and a threat to American exceptionalism. In her mind, it could "scarcely fail to result in national trouble." Congressman Caleb Lyon from New York told the US House of Representatives, "Point me to a nation where polygamy is practiced, and I will point you to heathens and barbarians. It seriously affects the prosperity of States, it retards civilization, it uproots Christianity." In the words of one district judge, polygamy was "incompatible with civilization, refinement and domestic felicity."[27]

At least a few Mormon leaders took exception to such characterizations and fought back with arguments that attempted to turn the tables on the West and to elevate Eastern and Asian morals as enduring, ancient, and stable—clearly superior to Western decline. They argued that Asian civilizations were longer lived and exhibited higher standards than those in the West. Apostle Parley P. Pratt suggested that a significant "portion of the oriental country has been preserved from the grossest idolatry, wickedness, confusion, bloodshed, murders, cruelty, and errors in religion that have overspread the rest of the world, under the name of Christianity." He conceded that "Mahometan institutions are corrupt enough," especially among "men in high places" but nonetheless found them to "have better morals and better institutions than many Christian nations."[28]

Apostle George Q. Cannon was most emphatic about the superiority of "polygamic races" over those that practiced monogamy. In 1869 he asserted that world history offered proof that the practice of polygamy "resulted in greater good" than "the practice of monogamy or the one-wife system in the so-called Christian nations." Cannon signaled his awareness of the accusations made against Mormon polygamy when he flatly rejected the claim that "no great nations ever practiced plural marriage." As he put it, "They who make such an assertion are utterly ignorant of history. What nations have left the deepest impress on the history of our race? Those which have practiced plurality of marriage," he answered.[29]

Cannon acknowledged that people of the United States and Europe boast that their political and social institutions are "the most permanent, indestructible and progressive of any institutions existing upon the earth," but he disagreed. He claimed that "the Christian nations of Europe are the youngest nations on the globe," whereas "the nations that have existed from time immemorial" were in Asia. The key difference between the two was racial polygamy. Enduring civilizations were "not to be found in Christian monogamic Europe, but in Asia, among the polygamic races—China, Japan, Hindostan and the various races of that vast continent."[30]

Even though Western society looked upon Asian peoples as "semi-civilized," Cannon viewed them as superior, especially in their treatment of women. It was a key distinction that the fate of nations revolved around. Polygamy allowed for the expression of sexual desires within marriage and prevented men from going outside the bonds of matrimony to find comfort in the arms of "multitudes of courtesans," a sign of a given civilization's corruption and decay. In his estimation "the shortest-lived nations of which we have record have been monogamic." Ancient Rome served as his prime example. Even though it was "once the mistress of the world," its "glory faded" as "the numerous evils" of extramarital excess "laid the foundation" for its ruin.[31]

Cannon countered those critics who pointed to the "Turks and other Oriental nations" as evidence of "how women are degraded and debased" in polygamy. Even if women in Turkey or other locations were deprived, it did not automatically follow that women in Utah were treated similarly. The difference in his mind was "the Gospel of the Lord Jesus, the principles of which elevate all who honor them." Rather than debased, the LDS gospel made women "noble and good in the presence of God and man."[32]

Cannon's and Pratt's speeches were delivered to Latter-day Saints, with no real indication that outsiders were remotely aware of their defenses. The two sides talked past each other, both wielding the sword of orientalism against the "other." The arguments on both sides were reductionist positions suggesting that the fate of nations hung in the balance, somewhere between polygamy and monogamy with women caught in the middle.

It was not merely women's roles in polygamous societies that were contested but also the treatment of women at the hands of men. Outsiders saw despotic Turks presiding over oppressed harems with polygamous wives no better than prostitutes. Mormons turned the same argument around and saw monogamist men wandering lustfully outside the bounds of marriage to fulfill their sexual desires, as if men were incapable of controlling themselves and polygamy were the only "civilized" solution. As Cannon viewed it, the search for sex outside of marriage was a sure sign of a nation's moral decay. Mormon detractors were equally convinced that, if left unchecked, the sexual excesses that they believed polygamy promoted would end in America's demise.

Neither side considered the voices of women themselves in making their claims. At least some elite plural wives defended polygamy with strong feminist arguments about the freedom and independence it provided and how it was an avenue to self-determination outside the purview of men. While the exposés of some former plural wives became fodder for antipolygamy crusaders, the majority of women who remained Mormon were rarely considered by the men on either side of the debate. In 1870 a group of Mormon women declared their opposition to the Cullom antipolygamy bill then under consideration in Congress. It was a piece of legislation that promised to free them from their reported oppression: "We . . . are believers in the principle of plural marriage or polygamy," they responded. To them it was "an elevating social relationship and a preventative of many terrible evils which afflict our race." To its critics, however, polygamy thwarted divinely sanctioned marriage between one man and one woman; it also denied Protestant values of hearth and home. It was "Asiatic," a condition that made its adherents more susceptible to despotic rule and less capable of democracy.[33]

*   *   *

A common element in the orientalization of Mormons was the depiction of Mormon households as exotic Turkish "harems," with the women secluded in seraglios(the part of a Muslim house or palace set aside for concubines or plural wives). Such descriptions were popular throughout the nineteenth century. Politicians, news editors, Protestant clergy, and social commentators alike interlaced Muslim and Turkish references into their criticisms in deliberate efforts to orientalize Mormons. The oppressive slave drivers of white slavery morphed into equally oppressive Turkish sultans, Muslim patriarchs, or violent "Bluebeards." In these depictions mythic Arabs stole women and carried them back to what one politician called an "American Harem, a Mormon Seraglio." The inherent sexual excesses bound up in these constructions gave way in some instances to a more politically based concern over a Near Eastern sultanate entrenched in America's western desert, a priestly dominion of corruption erected in defiance of federal authority and republican principles. So thorough were these various orientalizations that by the 1870s the pairing of "Mormons and Turks" grew into its own cultural discourse, the butt of jokes and a shorthand for polygamy and philandering, much like the Mormon coon.[34]

When a reporter for *Harper's Weekly* visited Salt Lake City in 1857, the news magazine published the story under the title "Scenes from an American Harem." Upon arrival in the Great Basin the reporter noted, "Of course our first anxiety was to see the Prophet and his seraglio; for our curiosity felt much piqued to gaze at the twenty-five American women who could approve of polygamy." It described Brigham Young as a "horrid old sensualist" and noted that among his wives were "the black-eyed and raven-haired houris of the old Mohammedan dreams of Paradise," a reference to the beautiful virgins allegedly provided to faithful Muslims in the afterlife. An 1867 exposé took a similar title: *The Mormon Prophet and His Harem.* It described Brigham Young in his advancing years as "rich," "haughty," and "proud," and reported that his wives "fear and reverence him as their God." It was a system of female oppression governed in every regard by "Brigham as Lord of the harem."[35]

Benjamin Ferris likewise drew upon Eastern imagery in his description of Mormon polygamy. He compared it unfavorably to that which was practiced in Turkey and styled Mormon women "concubines" and "sultanas." In Utah it was a system that involved the regular exchange of women; plural wives in his view were no better than "thorough-paced strumpets," used by Mormon men until rejected for younger wives. "Elder Wilford Woodruff, one of the twelve apostles, has a regular system of changing his harem," Ferris wrote. "The girls discarded by one become sealed to others, and so travel the entire rounds," he explained. The first wife "most severely felt" the effects of "the plurality system." Upon marriage she became "the reigning sultana for a time," but when the husband tired of her she was cast off in favor of "a fresh one."[36]

In its effects Ferris believed polygamy destroyed female virtue and turned men into brutish lechers. It was a system of "degrading licentiousness" filled with "brutality and wretchedness" that shattered the traditional family. "Polygamy introduces an element of disorder into families, and saps the foundations of social order." "In Turkey," he reasoned, "where polygamy has long existed" it created women "too much degraded to be the companion of man" and turned them into "so many slaves." He perceived a similar deterioration of the wife in Utah. "There is a sad, complaining, suffering look, obvious to the most ordinary observer." It produced "premature old age," or caused some to sink "into an early grave under an intolerable weight of affliction." They were confined as "inmates of a priestly harem" and a "domestic hell."[37]

The men, too, demonstrated polygamy's debilitating effects. "A Man living in common with a dozen dirty Arabs, whether he calls them wives or concubines, can not have a very nice sense of propriety," Ferris wrote. "From the moment he makes up his mind to bring one or more concubines into the family," he "becomes always neglectful, and in most cases abusive to his wife." Under the "double influence of domestic discord and gross indulgence" the husband "loses his energy, becomes discouraged, [and] sinks into the bloated, vulgar debauchee."[38]

The mythic Mormon seraglio found its fullest expression in the 1880s during the height of the federal crackdown on polygamy. *Puck* magazine, published in New York, ran a pictorial depiction of a Mormon harem under the caption, "I imagine it must be a perfect Paradise" (see figure 8.2). The depraved Mormon sultan is sucking on a hookah tube surrounded by his concubines in a scene of hedonism. The women are present only for the pleasure of the man, fulfilling his every desire: food, drink, music, dance, smoking, and presumably sex. The scene is thoroughly oriental, something unimaginable in America, and certainly not Christian. In every regard it represented the ways in which outsiders fantasized about the Mormon Turk with all of his propensities to lead Western civilization into decay.[39]

It was political decay that formed a parallel avenue of concern among outsiders. The idea of an alternate, oriental system of government in the American

Figure 8.2 "I imagine it must be a perfect paradise." Reprinted from *Puck*, 13 February 1884. Library of Congress.

West created deep-seated national fears. Mormons in these variations became weak and servile even as they were simultaneously portrayed as fanatical and violent dupes to priestly rule. Joseph Smith and Brigham Young were the corrupt authoritarians who governed with iron fists. Outsiders reasoned that people of Asian descent did not participate in republican forms of government but rather gave their political wills over to despotic leaders. Mormons proved their orientalism in the same way; in their willingness to follow "Sultan 'Brigham'" and Joseph Smith, "the vicegerent of Almighty God—the modern Mohammed of Mormon Allah," Mormons also performed race and demonstrated their otherness.[40]

Francis Lieber, a German-born political philosopher and professor of history and political science at South Carolina College (University of South Carolina today) addressed those ideas in an article in *Putnam's Monthly* in 1855. Lieber's article anticipated that the Mormons in Utah Territory would soon apply for statehood, and Lieber urged Congress to deny this application. As he saw it, Utah would introduce a "foreign and disturbing element" into the sisterhood of states, an element that violated "sound morality" and republican government. Monogamy and republicanism were both racial to him and the preserves of European civilization. "Monogamy goes beyond our religion," he wrote. "It is 'a law written in the heart' of our race," the special domain of the "western Caucasian." As Lieber saw it, monogamy was "one of the pre-existing conditions of our existence as civilized white men" and "together with the endeavor to establish political liberty" it constituted two of "the main distinctions between Asiatic and European mankind."[41]

With those guiding principles, Lieber found Mormon politics and marriage more Asiatic than European. "The Mormon polity is no republic," he announced. "The Mormons themselves call it a theocratic government, and a theocracy is not a republic." To Lieber the Mormon system was "revolting" because Brigham Young claimed "to be daily and hourly inspired by direct infusion of the Divine Spirit." It was a system without historical rival, even in the Orient. "The most absolute chalif [caliph] has never claimed any similar authority; no such authority even in Mohammed was acknowledged by any of his followers."[42]

In case his readers were sympathetic to Mormon claims that polygamy was a religious principle protected by the Constitution, Lieber argued that religious liberty had its bounds and that the Mormons had transgressed them. He was concerned that the growing tide of immigration from China would produce "a large influx of Asiatic paganism, coupled with a distinct race." Were there no limits to the free exercise clause of the Constitution? To make his point, he drew upon a variety of Eastern religious practices that might come under the cover of religion, similar to Mormon polygamy. What about a Brahmin in India who in an act of suttee recommended that a widow perform self-immolation upon the funeral pyre of her husband? What of infanticide or religiously inspired murder?

"There is not a crime or vice, however mean or frightful, in the long catalogue of sin and shame, that has not at some time or other formed an avowed element of religious systems," Lieber declared. Mormonism was no exception. "To speak of all the immoralities and obscenities sanctioned by the Mormon Law, would be impossible," he wrote. Polygamy alone was enough to provide evidence of Mormon "poisonous fruits." Its "vulgarity and knavery" and its "foulness and cheating jugglery" made "Eastern polygamy" appear like "a state of refinement compared to this brutality." In both their political system and their marital practices, Mormons performed orientalism, which made them more Asian than American.[43]

Other nineteenth-century observers emphasized similar themes, especially a fear of Mormon political power in the guise of a Sultanate. As early as 1831 one report compared the Mormon creed "to that of the Mahometans: 'God is great, and Jo Smith is his Prophet.'" Joseph Smith's detractors sometimes referred to him as an "American Mahomet," a characterization that grew over time to play on fears of violence and political power lurking behind Mohammad's, and therefore Smith's, religious mission. Thomas B. Marsh, a high-ranking Mormon who was in the processes of a bitter break from the faith, asserted that Smith himself made a comparison to Mohammed, but in a threatening way. As Marsh reported it, in 1838 Smith said "he would yet tread down his enemies, and walk over their dead bodies; and if he was not let alone, he would be a second Mohammed to this generation." With Smith in the lead, "it would be one gore of blood from the Rocky Mountains to the Atlantic Ocean." Like Mohammed's motto "'the Al-coran or the Sword,'" so it would be with the Mormons, "'Joseph Smith or the Sword.'" Another dissenter, John Corrill, recalled Smith stating that if outsiders left the Mormons alone, they "would preach the gospel to them in peace; but if they came on us to molest us, we would establish our religion by the sword, and that he would become to this generation a second Mahomet." Even though scholars debate whether Smith actually made such statements, the allegations left a public impression of Mormonism as a violent theocracy in the heart of the American republic.[44]

In 1856 the New York Daily Tribune added its own twist to the growing theme. Speaking of the Mormons in Utah, it complained of clannishness and a perceived blind devotion to authority: "It would be a matter of the greatest surprise and astonishment to the people of the States, could they only peep into this our Mecca, and see where the confidence and patronage of the Government is placed." It decried the unanimous votes of the Utah territorial legislature and the "harmony and unanimity" of which its members boasted. Even "Egypt's be-nighted conclaves are divided in feeling, sentiment and policy," while the "Mormons speak, act and think as one man." The other "Oriental feature" to which it also objected was the perception that "the edicts of their Prophet be implicitly obeyed." It feared that the Mormons were "absolutely governed by *one* will," a condition that had the potential to degrade the entire nation "to the level of an Asiatic slave."[45]

Two years later the *Tribune* again weighed in on the issue, this time with particular alarm over the potential for Mormonism to spread to poor whites and blacks in the South. It referred to Brigham Young as "his supreme highness, Sultan 'Brigham,'" a leader whom his followers regarded as "great, holy and *powerful*." In contrast, the *Tribune* found him to be "ignorant, beastly and cruel, but confident and cunning." Most disturbing however, was Young's reported intent to return to Missouri to reclaim the lost Mormon Zion. In doing so, the *Tribune* feared that he might attract "thousands of vicious, ignorant, imbruted 'poor whites'" to increase his "corps of janizaries." He would then "raise the crescent" as a banner and "call upon the blacks" to join his army. Before long "three millions of fanatics, beastly and cruel beings, will follow him as the Arabs followed Mohammed." The end result, the paper predicted, will be "an empire (of the same kind) in the West as Mohammed [founded] in the East; an empire of blood."[46]

Other commentators were alarmed over Mormonism's frightful propensity to win converts and spread its influence outside of Utah. In 1881 the *Chicago Advance* pointed to the "rapidly growing" number of Mormons and predicted that before long they "will control the other Territories around them by their great resources of colonization." As a result, "interior America will be given up to the worst phase of Asiatic barbarism." The *Advance* hoped that "patriotism, and firmness, and fearlessness" could "avert this direful consummation." Another newspaper worried that Mormonism's "leprous hands are already stretching out into other fields. In a few years it would become powerful and arrogant, and assume to defy the national authority."[47]

Fears of Mormon despotism dressed in oriental garb persisted to the end of the nineteenth century. One 1889 report called Brigham Young "the sainted Turk of 36 wives and concubines" and complained of the lack of self-rule in Mormonism. "They teach a Government of the priests, by the priests, and for the priests," it noted, and every Mormon "is sworn to obey all the orders of the priesthood." Another account, published in 1899, three years after Utah statehood and nine years after Mormon leaders disavowed polygamy, still highlighted Mormon "harems" and announced that "In Utah there are twelve Sultans. They are called the First Presidency of the Church, and are sometimes known as the Twelve Apostles."[48]

*   *   *

By the 1880s a new twist on the oriental theme had emerged. The fears of a Mormon sultanate in America's western desert merged with the simultaneous fears of Turkish harems to create the "Mormon bluebeard," a mythic Arab brute who abused captive women as well as defied federal authority. The term

"Bluebeard" came from a French folktale first published in 1697. It told of a young woman who married a wealthy aristocrat with an ugly blue beard. The aristocrat had married several times before, but the whereabouts of his earlier wives remained a mystery. Shortly after they wed, Bluebeard left his young bride alone at his large castle as he departed on a journey. Before leaving, he entrusted his wife with keys to the various rooms in the castle but forbid her to open one particular small chamber. Overcome with curiosity, she opened the forbidden room as soon as her husband was gone and to her horror found a scene of unimaginable gore. The mutilated bodies of her husband's former wives hung from the walls while the floor was slick with blood. Bluebeard returned shortly thereafter and recognized his wife's discovery. Fortunately, her brothers arrived just in time to rescue her from sure death; they killed Bluebeard as he tried to escape.[49]

This well-known folktale was rewritten as poetry and stage plays as well as retold in various forms, including a 1798 version set in Turkey. It shared similarities with at least one of the folktales in *Arabian Nights* and in some versions adopted a decidedly oriental flare. As it came to be applied to Mormons, "bluebeard" served as a universally understood cultural discourse that equated Mormons with domineering male power, the subjugation of women, secret acts behind closed doors, and murderous defiance of federal authority.[50]

One Protestant minister, Joseph Cook, was particularly fond of the "Mormon Bluebeard" as a symbol of corruption inherent in the LDS faith and a cause for alarm. He announced in 1879 that "it is literally true that the opening of the gates of the Rocky Mountains has revealed in Utah a Blue Beard's chamber full of headless women and dead men's bones, and all uncleanness." He recommended "the only safe course to pursue in regard to Utah is to keep her out of the Union and under the control of Congress." On another occasion Cook warned that the Mormon Bluebeard "stands with one hand locking the door of his chamber of horrors, and with the other he knocks for admission" to the Union.[51]

The Mormon Bluebeard found its fullest expression after Congress passed the Edmunds Act in 1882, a law that defined the new crime of "unlawful cohabitation" and marked a decided federal crackdown on polygamy. The New York–based *Daily Graphic* published three political cartoons in 1883 with Bluebeard as the central theme. The picture in the 21 August edition is typical of all three (see figure 8.3). It featured a defiant "Modern Bluebeard" striding out from Salt Lake City to confront lady liberty. She stood resolute with the shield of the US Congress in one hand and a drawn sword in the other. Bluebeard clutched in his teeth the knife of "Mormonism," a weapon with which he had no doubt murdered his prior wives. He dragged in his hands a cluster of women, some of whom begged lady liberty for relief. Bluebeard brazenly stepped on the Edmunds Bill as he approached, a clear signal of the Mormon rejection of congressional law and federal authority. The encounter took place outside of the city with the Salt

Figure 8.3 "The Modern Bluebeard." Reprinted from *Daily Graphic*, 21 August 1883, 1. L. Tom Perry Special Collections, Harold B. Lee Library, Brigham Young University, Provo, Utah.

Lake Tabernacle in the background. It was a confrontation that played out in the space between Washington, DC, and the Great Basin and between federal power and western defiance. In the twisted orientalism of the metaphor, however, the cartoon turned the geographic representation around so that it simultaneously symbolized the space between the Asiatic Mormons—Eastern, Turkish, and racially unfit for self-rule—and Western civilization, the white preserve of liberty and the rule of law.[52]

Three years later, as federal marshals scoured the Great Basin for Mormon lawbreakers, *The Judge* ran a cartoon that depicted Senator George F. Edmunds of Vermont as a medieval Christian crusader towering over a "Mormon Blue-beard" (see figure 8.4). Bluebeard this time is dressed in Middle Eastern attire and wields the barbaric club of "polygamy." Edmunds brandished the sword of his own bill, a weapon with which he was prepared to strike a death blow to Mormonism. In the background a "Mormon Castle" represented the thick walls of oriental defiance that was bound up in Mormon resistance to federal author-ity. The castle no doubt was filled with locked chambers of gore, the secrets of Mormonism that Bluebeard defended. Edmunds confidently raised the sword of Christian righteousness and the sharpened edge of Western democracy against a weakened and cowering sultan.[53]

Figure 8.4   D. Mac, "Hit 'Em Again." Reprinted from *Judge*, 9 January 1886, 1.
L. Tom Perry Special Collections, Harold B. Lee Library, Brigham Young University, Provo, Utah.

Even as these images of Mormon defiance were designed to heighten alarm and solidify national resolve, the comparison between Mormons and Turks became a universally understood metaphor; it was a signal of sexual excess, polygamy, and the denigration of women. In 1869 the *New York Sun* reported on the exploits of a dictator in Paraguay, a man whom the paper described as "cruel and sensual." He kept a "French woman" as "concubine" while he subjected "to his passions" "the young girls of any beauty in his dominion." In short, the paper said, "He is Mormon and Turk combined."[54]

By the 1880s, the Mormon-Turk grouping morphed into lighthearted humor as a way for outsiders to laugh off the perceived hypersexuality of both groups and their inherent violations of Victorian morality. In these versions the Mormons were still oriental, but the alarm of oppression was replaced by the relief of laughter. The pairing of "Mormon and Turk" became a nationally understood shorthand that needed no explanation. A poem published in the *New York Sun* in 1880 rhymed, "The Mormon and the Turk/Unchided for their shameful lives/ Still flaunt their plural wives." A joke that depended upon wordplay went the rounds in several newspapers; it varied in form but generally included a man playing golf or cards with his spouse. Afterward the man told a friend about his game with his wife. His friend responded, "Which won?" The first man, somewhat annoyed by the question, replied "Which one?" "What do you think I am, a Turk or a Mormon?" Another joke featured a teacher asking her class, "Who are the greatest money-makers in the world?" One student replied, "The Turks and the Mormons." When asked to explain, the student responded that the Mormons and Turks had to be: "Look at the number of wives they have!" By 1903, several newspapers picked up a column of "Cynic's Definitions" that demonstrated how thoroughly the two terms were wedded in the American mind: in the column's long list of humorous meanings, a "Mormon" was simply defined as "An American Turk."[55]

* * *

The same themes that animated conflations of Mormons with Muslims and Turks were used in the racialization of Mormons as Chinese. In the case of the Chinese, however, concern sometimes grew to include fear of race mixing. Muslims, Turks, and Arabs primarily existed in the minds of Americans, but the Chinese were a visible presence in America. Alarmists sometimes perceived the Chinese as a growing oriental threat invading the West Coast, an undesireable immigrant group far too close to America's other oriental problem: the Mormons in the Great Basin.

Benjamin Morgan Palmer pastored the First Presbyterian Church in Columbia, South Carolina, in January 1853, when he delivered a lecture simply titled "Mormonism" to the Mercantile Library Association in Charleston. While best remembered as a proslavery supporter of secession, on this occasion he focused on the trouble brewing in the American West, not the South. "We cannot cast our gaze beyond the Rocky Mountains, and scrutinize the face of society collecting upon our extreme western coast, without a measure of anxiety for the unfolding future," he announced. "Our country is certainly entering upon one of the grandest experiments it has ever been called to undertake, and is passing through the severest crisis it has ever been made to know."[56]

The crisis he referred to was not the impending sectional rift but the Mormons and the Chinese. As Palmer saw it, Mormonism represented "a bold attempt . . . by Anglo-Saxons themselves to reproduce the old civilization of Asia." If that were not bad enough, "a strong and copious tide of really Asiatic population has been pouring into our California territory." He estimated that 17,000 Chinese arrived on the West Coast within a three-month period during the prior year. It was an alarming number, especially when considered in light of the growing Mormon presence in the Rocky Mountains. The Chinese and Mormons were two Asiatic groups who were in Palmer's mind destined to mix. "What is to be the issue of this commingling of races on this continent?" he wondered.[57]

It was a question that "time alone" could answer. Americans nonetheless could not afford to "be insensible to the momentous crisis" looming ahead. It would surely subject "the elasticity of our government" to "severer tests than its framers ever dreamed." For his part, Palmer certainly hoped that "republicanism" would triumph over "that stubborn civilization of past centuries" then taking root in California and Utah.[58]

The depth of the Mormon Asiatic "crisis" in Palmer's mind and its potential impact upon American government were ironic given his later stance on secession. Even though his position on the Mormons and Chinese was not unique, he did arrive at it comparatively early. As the tide of Chinese immigration grew from the 1850s to the 1880s American fears of an Asiatic invasion seemed to grow with it. Mormons, with their Asiatic "sensualism" and subjection to authoritarian regimes, were natural allies for the Chinese at least in the imaginations of some Americans.[59]

The conflation of the two groups occurred against a backdrop of growing American consternation over what was frequently described as the "yellow peril" of Asian immigration. The Chinese in particular were targets of this fear. Prompted by overcrowding and poor economic opportunities at home and a desire for a better life in America, particularly the allure of the California gold fields, Chinese immigrants moved to the West Coast in droves beginning in the mid-1850s. By 1860 almost 35,000 Chinese lived in mainland United States, most in California and other western states and territories. By 1880 their numbers swelled to over 100,000. In 1882, more than 39,000 entered the United States, the same year that Congress passed the Chinese Exclusion Act barring all Chinese laborers from immigrating to the United States. Two years later the number of Chinese immigrants fell to less than three hundred. Activists, newspaper editors, clergy, and especially politicians decried Chinese immigrants as un-American pagans, licentious, filthy, diseased, imbecilic opium-smoking heathens, people who were inherently incapable of progress; they were lewd polygamists with low morals, proponents of a new form of slavery and adherents to despotic systems of government. In short, they were racially inferior and incapable of assimilation. With the exception of opium smoking, Mormons were described by outsiders in the same ways.[60]

As with blacks, at least a part of the fear of Chinese centered on the deterioration of the white "race" through interracial mixing. In 1854 a Portland, Maine, newspaper reported a rumor that Mormon and Chinese mingling was already underway. "A company of Chinese have gone from San Francisco to Utah, having been converted to Mormonism," it stated. The paper then wondered how much the Chinese were "likely to improve by their change in religion," an indication that the newspaper held the faith of both groups in equally low regard.[61]

By the 1860s, as the level of Chinese immigration increased, so too did the alarm. The *Christian Recorder*, an African American newspaper published in Philadelphia, warned that the estimated 50,000 Chinese then in California were "but the advance guard of what may turn out a mighty eastward movement from the most populous hive of humanity in the world." It was a migration akin to "the march of diminutive animals, rats, locusts, army worms, squirrels, [and] ants, in vast numbers." It was similar to "the migrations of Goths, Vandals, and Saracens, and like the movements of rebellious hordes in China itself." It was a movement so strong that it "may be utterly beyond the control of the more civilized, but numerically weaker races," the *Recorder* worried. "Shall we beckon this heathen mass to our shores?" If so, would it force a tolerance of polygamy upon the nation in the guise of religion, similar to that already countenanced in Utah due to the "persistent apathy of our politicians." "Is a combination of Chinese and of Mormon interests such an impossible thing in the future?" it mused.[62]

In 1876 the *Chicago Journal of Commerce* actually suggested that the Mormons in Utah should welcome an influx of Chinese migrants and use them as agents of colonization. The resulting "mixture of races," it predicted, would be beneficial to the Mormons. The *Deseret News* quickly dismissed the idea, stating that an "amalgamative mixture of population" was "not likely to prevail to any extent in Utah." There were already Chinese in the territory, the paper noted, "but their presence has not had any appreciable influence here in the direction mentioned." It rejected "anything of the kind among the probabilities."[63]

Others were not so sure. In 1882 as Congress debated both the Chinese Exclusion Act and the Edmunds Act aimed at Mormon polygamy, the *Boston Daily Advertiser* published an editorial that predicted dire consequences within twenty years if Congress did not address both "problems" then before it. The *Advertiser* suggested that if left unchecked, the Mormons and Chinese would continue to spread geographically and increase numerically until they occupied sites as far east as Omaha, Nebraska. The paper predicted that by 1896 the two groups combined would have sufficient population to control politics, even in the Great Plains. In an imagined future election in Omaha between a "Caucasian," a "Chinese," and a "latter-day saint," the *Advertiser* posited a scenario whereby the Chinese candidate might win. The Chinese office seeker need only promise political appointments to polygamists once elected and thereby secure Mormon votes. In the future this "Chinese-Mormon combination" might resort to underhanded methods, such as the distribution of "opium and crackers" to curry favor and beguile electors. It was an imagined scenario designed to heighten fear of both Mormons and Chinese and to prod Congress to act forcefully against both.[64]

Legislators across the American West did not wait for Congress to act when it came to the fear of a disappearing white race. In 1861 Nevada territory was first to name "Chinese" in an antimiscegenation law that made it a crime for whites and Chinese to marry. Other western states and territories soon followed, with Idaho, Arizona, Wyoming, and Oregon all passing marriage bills before 1869. California adopted the term "Mongolian" in its 1880 law, a word that in the minds of some California legislators encompassed all Asians, not merely Chinese. Utah lawmakers did not join the trend until 1888 when its first antimiscegenation law prohibited whites from marrying both "Mongolians" and blacks. Mormon legislators united with their counterparts of other faiths to vote the provision into law. It was a sign of their willingness to follow the lead of other western states in preserving whiteness in the face of a perceived yellow threat, as well as a way for Mormons to assert their whiteness against persistent efforts to color them yellow.[65]

The most significant way in which Mormons and Chinese were conflated in the nineteenth century was in the political arena, where they were both viewed as pressing national "problems" or "questions" in American politics, especially in the late 1870s and early 1880s. In February 1879, the San Francisco *Wasp* made the link explicit in one of at least four political cartoons that featured Mormons and Chinese over the ensuing seven years. The 1879 picture, titled "Uncle Sam's Troublesome Bed Fellows," featured a cast of multiracial Americans crowding Uncle Sam in his bed. It was a representation of a teeming nation filled with increasingly undesirable inhabitants (see figure 8.5). A drunk Irishman slept off his alcohol on the farthest edge of the bed, oblivious to the "trouble" he created for a nation worried about its whiteness. A contented black "Sambo" character sat next to him, apparently pleased that there was room at all for him in Uncle Sam's bed. A wily Indian harassed Uncle Sam with a finger in his ear, an annoyance but not necessarily a threat. The most "troublesome" of the bedfellows,

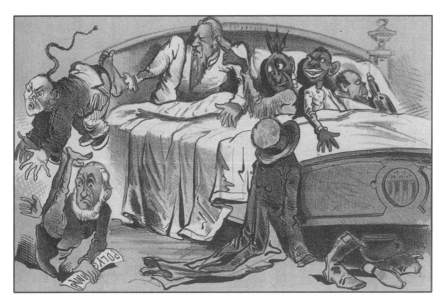

Figure 8.5 "Uncle Sam's Troublesome Bed Fellows." Reprinted from *Wasp*, 8 February 1879. Library of Congress.

however, were no longer welcome at all. Uncle Sam already kicked the Mormon polygamist from the country and was in the process of booting the Chinese.[66]

It was a cartoon filled with deep imagery and rich irony. It captured the marginalized and suspect status of each of the groups it portrayed. In the case of the booted Mormon it also signaled a loss of status, not merely in the act of being excluded from Uncle Sam's bed but also in being put to bed with the other nonwhites in the first place. Association with suspect groups made one suspect as well. Of all of the groups depicted, only the Mormon needed a label to distinguish himself. A bottle of alcohol was a recognizable symbol for the Irish, but an otherwise nondescript white Mormon had to be denoted with a "polygamy" placard in his hand.

Mormons' unfitness for citizenship also infused the landmark US Supreme Court decision, *Reynolds v. United States*, which was handed down less than three months following the *Wasp* cartoon. George Reynolds, a secretary to Brigham Young and a polygamist, agreed to offer himself up for a legal test case. Mormons long insisted that the Morrill Anti-Bigamy Bill of 1862 that made polygamy a crime was an unconstitutional violation of the free exercise of their religion. Plural marriage, they argued, was a religious requirement to reach the highest degree of the LDS heaven. Any law against plural marriage was therefore a violation of their religious freedom.[67]

In 1879 the Supreme Court unanimously disagreed. In doing so, it relied in part upon racial arguments commonly in circulation in America. Political philosopher and professor Francis Lieber put forth some of those ideas as early as 1855, when he argued that polygamy was racial and a mark of a group's incapacity for self-rule. Charles Sinclair, a federally appointed district judge for Utah Territory, made a similar argument in 1858. He noted that in ancient Greece polygamy was regarded "as the practice of barbarians" and asserted that it was "exclusively the feature of Asiatic manners, and of half civilized life." Chief Justice Morrison Waite wrote the Supreme Court's opinion in *Reynolds* and referenced these earlier ideas, even citing Lieber by name. "Polygamy has always been odious among the northern and western nations of Europe," Waite contended, "and, until the establishment of the Mormon Church, was almost exclusively a feature of the life of Asiatic and of African people." Drawing upon Lieber, Waite further argued that polygamy was grounded in "the patriarchal principle," a system that fettered "people in stationary despotism."[68]

Religious liberty had its limits, Waite concluded, and polygamy was one of them. To make his point more explicit, Waite drew upon other examples from Eastern traditions. What if a person believed that "human sacrifices were a necessary part of religious worship," or "if a wife religiously believed it was her duty to burn herself upon the funeral pile of her dead husband?" Lieber drew upon the same example of suttee in 1855, as did other commentators over the ensuing decades. One Protestant minister argued in 1871 that "the law of limitation is just as applicable to marriage as it is to any form of worship." As an example, he said, "the Hindoo may come here and read his Shasta, but he shall not burn the widow on the funeral pile." In similar fashion Congress had a right to "interfere" in Mormon polygamy. Chief Justice Waite made a comparable point that if the free exercise clause of the Constitution did not protect such Asiatic "religious" practices as suttee, then it should not protect polygamy.[69]

The conflation between the Mormon and Chinese questions only intensified following the *Reynolds* decision, especially as Congress debated various solutions to both problems in the spring of 1882. The result of their deliberations were two bills, signed into law less than two months apart, and heralded by some commentators as long-sought-for answers to both oriental diseases then plaguing the American body politic. The day after President Chester A. Arthur signed the Edmunds Act into law, a bill that created the new crime of "unlawful cohabitation," as well as barred polygamists from voting, holding office, or serving on juries, the *Wasp* again captured national sentiment in pictorial form (see figure 8.6). This time the "Chinese question" and "polygamy" weighed heavily upon the nation and gave Uncle Sam nightmares. Chinese hordes with long queues haunted the head of the national bed while a polygamist mountain goat with its plural ewes pushed in from the side. With such substantial questions troubling the nation, it seemed unlikely Uncle Sam could muster the strength to rise from his bed and throw off the pressing problems.[70]

Figure 8.6　Keller, "Uncle Sam's Nightmare." Reprinted from *Wasp*, 24 March 1882.
Library of Congress.

In the years leading up to the congressional debates over both bills (and during the debates themselves) politicians, clergy, and social commentators across the nation linked the two issues. Newspapers referred to them as "the vexed Chinese and Mormon questions," "the Mormon and Chinese curses," and "the Chinese and Mormon problems."[71] Sometimes they debated which was worse, the Mormons or the Chinese, and how to best handle both. One newspaper called for broad immigration reform to exclude Mormons and Chinese, while another argued that "it is vastly more important to suppress Mormon than Chinese immigration, so far as the moral welfare of the nation is concerned." Yet another acknowledged that the two problems were alike, although it deemed the Mormon problem "more difficult." One California headline declared "CHINESE AND MORMONS. TWO CLASSES OF PEOPLE WHO MUST BE MADE TO GO." A newspaper in a Utah mining town concurred: "Polygamy and the Chinese must go," it affirmed. A report from Arizona announced, "We can stand the Chinese, but no Mormon polygamists," while a letter in the *Salt Lake Tribune* made a similar point: "If there is any sound reason for the exclusion of the Chinese from this country, there is for the exclusion of the Mormons." A Kansas newspaper meanwhile urged Congress to take "prompt action on the Chinese immigration question" and "the subjection of Mormonism to the laws of the nation." More lighthearted, the *National Republican* joked, "There is one good thing that can be said about the Chinese—None of them are Mormons."[72]

At least one California newspaper, the *Argonaut*, resisted the seemingly end-less comparisons: "The analogies between Mormons and Chinese do not hold good in any single particular," it reasoned. "Mormons are not of distinctive race; they can and do assimilate with us; they come from branches of the human family to which we belong." With the Mormons it was only polygamy that set them apart, something serious enough to demand action against the root of the problem. "The civilization of this age is a Christian civilization," the *Argonaut* de-clared, and "Monogamy is the law of this civilization." If Mormons did not con-form, the consequences should be severe: "If it breaks up families, wounds the sensibilities of women, brings confusion to domestic circles, and works hard-ships, cruelty, and distress to communities," the law should be enforced. "We would destroy polygamy and drag it out of the soil by the roots, though blood flowed from every broken fibre [*sic*]," the *Argonaut* urged.[73]

In the end, the process was not bloody like some predicted, but it was wrench-ing for the Mormons. In 1890, after the Supreme Court opened the way for the confiscation of Mormon temples, the Mormons began a complicated process of abandoning polygamy. As they "Americanized" and gave up the things that out-siders insisted made them oriental, Mormons adopted orientalization rhetoric of their own in order to distinguish themselves from Asians on the outside and mark themselves as Western and white from within.

*   *   *

Unlike their understanding of Indians and blacks, Mormons did not have a special theological vision of the Chinese, other than viewing them as poten-tial converts. In the 1850s Mormons evangelized among Chinese in California, Hawaii, and mainland China for a brief time. By the 1880s, as nationwide anti-Chinese rhetoric grew in intensity, Mormons largely ignored the Chinese who were by then living in Utah Territory. It was a transition over time best under-stood within the larger context of whiteness, a move from East to West and from yellow to white.[74]

Brigham Young first called missionaries to Asia in 1852. They struggled in their various fields of labor—India, Thailand, and China—with little success to show for their efforts. Language presented a significant barrier, as did weather, climate, culture, transportation, poverty, sickness, and religion. They did win about seventy converts but most of them were European expatriates. By 1856 Mormon leaders ended evangelizing efforts in Asia for lack of success.[75]

Those who went to China also had to confront violence on the mainland caused by the Taiping Rebellion, a civil war in southern China that left twenty million people dead. One of the missionaries, Hosea Stout, described the situation to Brigham Young: "The only safe place was Hong Kong owing to the Revolution spreading through that Country," he wrote. Even in Hong Kong the missionaries found it difficult to find people willing to listen. "A few of our lectures were very well attended [and] many stopped to hear us," Stout wrote, "but soon our congregations dwindled down till not . . . a soul would stop or attend." Undaunted they continued to preach, but described it as merely "batting the air." They visited individuals and distributed books and pamphlets "as long as one person would hear." Yet, they were unable to find a single proselyte who was "interested in our message." They "visited the Chinese who could speak English" but were told that "they had no time to talk a Religion." Stout acknowledged that "The people are all remarkably friendly & courteous" but said that they "care nothing about religious affairs." He described them as "the least likely" people, "above all others . . . to receive the gospel." Discouraged, the missionaries returned to America.[76]

The first Chinese converts to Mormonism came in Hawaii in 1854. Mormons also encountered Chinese immigrants in California and saw the influx of Chinese there as opportunity for evangelizing. In 1854 apostle Parley P. Pratt predicted that "there will soon be a hundred thousand of these people on these shores," and then described a Chinese man "of the intelligent sort" who knew English and was reading the Book of Mormon. Alexander Badlam, another Mormon then in California, predicted that if the man indeed converted, he could return to China and "be the first Missionary to his race."[77]

Badlam viewed the Chinese in California with openness and missionary zeal. "The Chinese are approachable and the Language is attainable," he wrote to Brigham Young in 1854. He expected to devote "at least one half" of his time to work with Chinese immigrants, people he described as "great and truly wonderful." He acknowledged that "the work will require years of faithful Application by those who will not feel it a burden but a delight to Spread the gospel Even to the darkest corners of the Earth." A year later, after working among the Chinese, Badlam's enthusiasm had not dissipated: "The more I learn about them, the more highly I esteem them" he wrote. They are a people full of energy, Industry, and determination." He felt "a strong desire that the time may soon come when the gospel of Salvation shall salute their ears."[78]

Despite such enthusiasm, there were few converts. The LDS nonetheless remained relatively positive amidst broader anti-Chinese sentiment. In May 1869 the *Deseret News* extolled the "good temper, patience, docility and intelligence" of the Chinese and railed against those who "chased, abused, robbed and abominably maltreated" them. The following month it responded to "rumors from the Pacific slope" regarding the formation of "societies who design to prevent the migration of Asiatics to America." The *News* argued that such sentiments were "in direct antagonism to the genius of American institutions" and were "dictated by a narrow, selfish policy engendered by ignorance." It contended that "the country is large enough for all." It hoped for the day "when all citizens, whether black, yellow or white, will be able to live without fear or molestation if they live by the fruits of honest toil." In July it again spoke out against national voices then decrying an Asiatic invasion. "There is no class, American, European or Asiatic, the influx of which can harm" the people of Utah, it announced.[79]

By the 1880s, however, the level of enthusiasm toward the Chinese had dissipated among some Mormons in Utah. By that point Chinese laborers had moved to Utah to help build the transcontinental railroad and work in the mining industry and thus competed for jobs. The 1890 federal census counted 806 Chinese in the state that year. According to historian Reid Neilson, the generally missionary minded Mormons did "next to nothing to fellowship and evangelize" them, even as Protestant churches in Utah did.[80]

By the 1890s some LDS publications began to racialize Asians, an indication that Mormons were in many ways part of the cultural mainstream. This orientalization process, even subconsciously, positioned Mormons as white and Western and simultaneously marked their transition out of polygamy. In 1892 the Young Woman's Journal, a publication aimed at the female youth of the church, indicated a continued missionary focus toward the Chinese but in a much more paternalistic spirit of superiority than expressed by Badlam in the 1850s. One article reported a visit to a "Chinese Joss house when the devout were prostrated before their Joss." The author recalled bowing her head in prayer to petition God "to send them the light and truth and to give them faith in Him instead of in graven images." Another article the following year, somewhat derisively described Chinese medical practices, including the use of "frog's eyes, snake's fat, and the dried wings of dragon flies." It expressed shock at the "superstition" of Chinese medicine with no real consideration for the ways in which outsiders also described Mormon faith healing and herbal remedies as equally superstitious.[81]

In 1893 and 1894 the Contributor, a publication aimed at the young men of the church, ran a sixteen-part series, "Ramblings Around the World," with the first twelve reports from Asian countries. G. H. Snell, a Mormon from Salt Lake City, took a journey to the Near and Far East and filed monthly reports about the peoples and cultures he encountered.[82] Snell's first impression of the Chinese came on board ship before he ever reached Asia. He described the Chinese passengers he met as a "mongrel," "motley," and "villainous . . . horde." His travels to mainland China did little to convince him otherwise. Even though he was favorably impressed with the Chinese reverence for their parentage, his views of their religious practices in general were dismissive. He called the Chinese people superstitious idol worshipers and heathens. He also found China to be a "very filthy empire," filled with citizens who were "bloody, cruel and cold to each other." The smells were also exotic, foreign, and foul. The incense from the "thousands of temples and pagodas" combined in his nostrils with smells wafting from "the sewers, reeking streets, itinerary restaurants, opium smoking and . . . the oder [*sic*] of nationality." It produced in Snell's mind a combination of smells "that the traveler may refuse to appreciate but cannot ignore." When he finally left China, he described himself as "tired out and disenchanted with the whole Chinese Empire and its almond-eyed race."[83]

His view of Turkey was hardly any more positive. In fact his description of a seraglio was nearly identical to the disparaging reports about Mormon harems that permeated the nineteenth century: "If walls had tongues as well as ears, what tales of romance, love and lust, treachery and murder those walls could tell of its inmates," Snell opined. "When a maiden enters an Eastern harem," he reported, "her face is never seen again, she is dead to the world as if the grave had already closed above her; fair limbed women with fettered feet." The "sanctity of the harem" was guarded with "rude force and savage pain," and its patriarchs showed "no mercy" to intruders, he declared.[84] In sum, Snell's series constructed Eastern locations and peoples as exotic. It was a way for Mormons to draw distinct boundaries between themselves and the peoples of Asia with whom they had been so thoroughly conflated throughout the nineteenth century.[85]

At least a portion of the Mormon effort to gain acceptance and legitimacy thus came at the expense of other marginalized groups. As the Mormons underwent the difficult challenge of leaving polygamy behind, they marked themselves white and worthy of assimilation by contrasting themselves with those who were eastern and "other." Even if only among themselves, the message was designed to shore up a Western identity measured in distance from oriental peoples.[86]

*   *   *

When Reverend Thomas DeWitt Talmage spoke about the Chinese and Mormon problems, he was only one of many nineteenth-century commentators to juxtapose the two groups. He was unusual, though, in not lumping Mormons and Asians together as indistinguishable oriental perils whose very presence in the American West threatened to sap the strength of the nation's burgeoning democracy.

The conflations began early with religious comparisons between Mormonism and Islam. Conflations with Islam were designed to mark Mormons out, to make them so oriental that they did not fit prevailing ideas about what it meant to be a Christian, let alone what it meant to be white and American.[87] Outsiders also orientalized Mormon geography and thereby imagined tyrannical sultanates run amok in the Great Basin. Some intellectuals, politicians, and the US Supreme Court argued that monogamy was racial, white, and Western, while polygamy marked those who practiced it as racially inferior and susceptible to despotic rule.

Some Mormon leaders initially defended Asian civilizations as superior to those in Europe; yet when Mormons abandoned polygamy, a repositioning occurred. The old defenses of "polygamic races" crumbled in the wake of "the one-wife system," a system that Mormon leader George Q. Cannon had derided as detrimental to the success of nations only a few decades earlier. It was a dramatic transition for Mormons, a move from monogamy to polygamy and back to monogamy in roughly sixty years. This process played out against an American racial backdrop that sometimes made sense of the Mormons in oriental terms. Thus monogamy became a key facet of the Mormon racial passage, a signal to a suspicious Protestant majority that Mormons were willing to perform whiteness if that is what it meant to be white.

From Not White to Too White: The Continuing Contest over the Mormon Body

When *Life* magazine published a cartoon of Mormon Elder Berry in April 1904, it was less than two months following Joseph F. Smith's testimony before the US Senate in the Reed Smoot investigation. It was hardly a stretch of the imagination to suggest that Elder Berry was intended to be a Joseph F. Smith lookalike (see figure 9.1). In that vein, Elder Berry's mythical multiracial family stood in for all Mormon families. An attack on him was meant to be an attack on Mormon whiteness, Mormon polygamy, and Mormonism as a system of racial decline.

At the same time that outsiders criticized Mormon impurity, Latter-day Saints clamored for acceptance and respectability. They were rewarded when President Theodore Roosevelt entered the debate on the side of Reed Smoot. Roosevelt, in part at least, viewed Smoot as an opportunity to secure votes for the Republican Party in the intermountain West. It marked a political transition for Mormons, from Democrats to Republicans and from politically suspect to politically desirable, but it also marked a racial transition. As *Life* magazine summarized the previous century's themes of racialization, some Mormons voiced ongoing efforts to secure a racially beneficial identity for the Saints.[1]

Roosevelt had long been an open critic of what he termed "race suicide," which was a percolating fear that the new wave of immigrants flooding to America from southern and eastern Europe with their dark skins and suspect religions were out reproducing old stock Americans from northern and western Europe. As Roosevelt saw it, Americans of northern and western European descent were committing race suicide when they chose to have fewer children than their undesirable counterparts. "If the average married couple . . . has only two children," Roosevelt warned Americans, "the whole race will disappear in a very few generations."[2]

Figure 9.1 Joseph F. Smith. Photograph courtesy of Church History Library, the Church of Jesus Christ of Latter-day Saints, Salt Lake City, Utah.

For once, the Mormons represented a potential solution rather than a problem. In May 1903 the *Salt Lake Herald*, an unofficial Mormon newspaper, tapped into Roosevelt's "race suicide" rhetoric for its own purposes. It trumpeted Mormon fertility and Mormon whiteness in an effort to garner Roosevelt's approval. In its Sunday edition, the *Herald* ran a cartoon that imagined what the scene would look like "when Roosevelt Reaches Utah," a picture that anticipated the president's scheduled visit later that month (see figure 9.2). The scene depicted Mormon men greeting Roosevelt with outstretched arms and surrounded by women and children. The Mormons declared their intent to vote for Roosevelt, which was a decision tied to their appreciation for his stance on race suicide. A large placard proudly welcoming Roosevelt proclaimed, "No Race Suicide Here."[3] It was a signal that Mormon polygamy produced what Roosevelt desired, white children, something that should have earned the nation's respect, not its racial scorn.

In advance of Roosevelt's visit another news account emphasized a similar theme. It pointed to Utah pioneer Lorin Farr, the former mayor of Odgen, as

Figure 9.2 "When Roosevelt Reaches Utah: 'Glad to Meet Ye, Brother Roosevelt. We're All Goin' to Vote for Ye 'Round Here. We Like What You Said 'Bout Race Suicide.'" Reprinted from *Salt Lake Herald*, 3 May 1903. L. Tom Perry Special Collections, Harold B. Lee Library, Brigham Young University, Provo, Utah.

an example of Mormon fruitfulness. Farr had six wives with whom he fathered twenty sons and nineteen daughters. His total descendants numbered 326, including his grandchildren and great-grandchildren. If one factored in the progeny of his two brothers, the combined descendants of the three Farrs rose to 553. One Arizona newspaper published the story as evidence designed to combat "President Roosevelt's race suicide theory." The article suggested that Mormons were certainly doing their part for the survival of the "race."[4]

The following year when the Smoot hearing once more called Mormon whiteness into question, the *Salt Lake Herald* responded. It ran on its front page a cartoon of the delighted president reading a news account of the testimony in the Smoot case (see figure 9.3). The "Daily Paper" that Roosevelt clutched announced that President Joseph F. Smith admitted to fathering forty-two children in his Senate testimony. It also noted that Apostle Marriner W. Merrill had thirty-eight children in his family as well as over a hundred nieces and nephews. Roosevelt was noticeably pleased at learning such news, so much so that he exclaimed, "That's Bully! No Race Suicide There!"[5]

Even some Protestants acknowledged somewhat begrudgingly that Mormon fertility was a constructive aspect of the religion, a rather dramatic change from the previous century. One 1913 tract referred to the rate of growth among Mormons as unprecedented "in the history of any sect or cult." It noted that babies had always been "Utah's best crop" and that Mormons claimed the highest birth rate and lowest death rate in the nation. Gone were the accusations of sickly and degenerate children and high infant mortality. Instead the report observed that the "charge of race suicide has never been preferred against the Mormon people."[6]

Figure 9.3 "Roosevelt—That's Bully! No Race Suicide There!" Reprinted from *Salt Lake Herald*, 10 March 1904. Special Collections, J. Willard Marriott Library, University of Utah, Salt Lake City.

Mormons thus used Roosevelt's fears of race suicide to aid their acceptance and integration. Utah statehood in 1896 ushered Mormons into the sisterhood of states and signaled a political and legal acknowledgement of their rights as citizens. They could vote in presidential elections, elect their governor and state leaders, and elect people of their choosing to represent them in Congress. In short, they were full-fledged citizens.

* * *

Beyond political rights, citizenship and inclusion was a racial process heavily invested in whiteness. In the fluid and illogical racial context of nineteenth-century America, Mormons were forced to fight for their status as American citizens. This was a battle that required them to assert their whiteness in an effort to distinguish themselves from other marginalized racial groups. National racial segregation marred the era of Mormon integration into the American mainstream and left its mark upon Mormonism as well. This period of racial transition for Mormons spanned the first half of the new century. When the Senate voted in 1907 to allow Smoot to retain his seat, it signaled a clear move toward integration and acceptance, as did Smoot's subsequent thirty-year tenure in the Senate.

Even still, the transition was rocky and was hampered by lingering suspicions about Mormon whiteness. Novelist Jack London, best known for his tales of adventure set in the American West, published a short story in 1915 involving an overland immigrant train attacked by Indians and Mormons, a clear parallel to the Mountain Meadows massacre. When one of the characters referred to the Mormons as "'white like us,'" another character immediately replied, "'They ain't whites,' . . . 'They're Mormons.'"[7] It was an echo from the past that reverberated at various times and places across the first half of the new century. Outsiders continued to emphasize many of the same themes as before, but after Mormon leaders officially ended polygamy, the virility of the attacks diminished and transformed into an underlying wariness. Mormons may have abandoned polygamy and gained statehood, but their true nature sometimes lurked just beneath their white skins.[8]

The Mountain Meadows massacre continued to evoke such perceptions. One 1908 publication informed its readers that the attack was carried out by "a band of Indians, who subsequently proved to be a band of painted Mormons." Likewise, in 1922 eighty-one-year-old Elisha Brooks sat down to write a remembrance of his family's overland journey seventy years earlier. By that point his recollection was tainted by his understanding of the Mountain Meadows massacre, which took place five years after his own migration. As he recalled it, "North of Salt Lake we were harassed by the hostile Shoshones spurred on by the Mormons." He then inserted the massacre into his memory of the Mormons: "You have heard of the Mountain Meadows massacre led by Brigham Young's Danites?" he prodded his reader. There were "many" other such deeds left "unrecorded," he went on to say, deeds for which the Mormons would have to answer once "the Judgment Books are opened." Then his memory returned seamlessly to 1852 and noted that as his wagon train traveled westward, it deliberately avoided Utah. As a result of Mormon "reputed hostility," Brooks wrote, "We dared not go through Salt Lake" but rather "passed around to the North." More than a precise account of the overland trail, the remembrance demonstrated how completely the massacre had impacted public memory of the Mormons by 1922. The massacre created enduring misgivings over Mormon whiteness that continued to surface at moments when the national spotlight shone on the Saints.[9]

The Mormon-oriental discourse also transitioned over the same period, with lingering critiques. In one case the allegation of a Mormon-Chinese combination came together in Hawaii in the person of Goo Akuna. Similar to the "Mormon Coon," Hawaiian newspapers brought the two undesirable groups together in the actions of a polygamist Chinese man. The 1906 headlines announced, "CHINESE MORMON IS BEING TRIED," "CHINESE MORMON GIVEN SENTENCE," and "THE FEDERAL GRAND JURY INDICTS THE CHINESE MORMON OF MAUI." There was no evidence that Akuna was actually Mormon, but in the eyes of the press he acted Mormon when he married two women, lived with a third, and fathered a combined total of twenty-two children. He pled guilty to the charge of "illicit cohabitation" and was sentenced to three months in jail and fined $300.[10]

Nonetheless, calling Akuna a "Chinese Mormon" was a much milder form of denigration than when Reverend DeWitt Talmage thundered from the Brooklyn Tabernacle that the Chinese could stay but the Mormons must go. By the early twentieth century the term "Mormon" was still used as shorthand for sexual excess, large families, and multiple wives, but the fictional threat of a full blown interracial merger between the Mormons and the Chinese had disappeared.

The imagined link to Islam continued unabated for the time being. In 1912 Bruce Kinney, the former superintendent of Baptist Missions in Utah, published *Mormonism, the Islam of America*. Designed as an "Interdenominational Home Mission Study Course," it was quickly adopted by church groups in various locations across the country and was advertised as a subject "vital to the nation." In Washington, DC, "women of all denominations" were encouraged to attend four sessions of training so they could then conduct classes of their own in their individual congregations.[11] The textbook largely focused upon Mormonism, with few direct comparisons to Islam, and was geared toward religious topics. It nonetheless echoed familiar racial themes such as an inherent "sensualism" in Mormonism, a faith filled with "unlimited carnality," which was also "obscene and immoral." It was more Eastern than Western, a revival of "the ancient Phallic religion or equivalent to the introduction into America of the worship of the Hindu Siva." Its adherents were incapable of self-rule; they were at base "superstitious and priest-ridden," people whom an "all powerful hierarchy" controlled "absolutely."[12] These were all old ideas repackaged for the new century. By the time of the book's publication Mormon leaders had actively excommunicated Latter-day Saints who took additional plural wives and at least made efforts toward political neutrality. However, internal policies continued to do little to combat views from the outside.

The most complicated—and complete—transition took place at the nexus between black and white, both in terms of public perception from the outside and racial understanding on the inside. During the Reed Smoot hearings comparisons between Mormonism and Southern slavery persisted, but the rhetoric was already moving in a different direction. At the hearings, Senator Frederick T. Dubois from Idaho, an avid anti-Mormon, used segregationist rhetoric and sentiments of white supremacy to his advantage against the Mormons. He believed that it was his duty to speak out against Mormonism, just like a Southern senator would support "American white citizenship" against the threat of black ascendancy. "Negro domination in the South would not be tolerated by the white man," he asserted, just like non-Mormons could not bear to live under "the political control of the Mormon hierarchy." Dubois' wife, Edna M. Whited, used a similar comparison in pursuing her own campaign against Mormonism. In her mind Mormonism was a "greater blot than was slavery" and would require the same courage to fight against it as the abolitionists "displayed in the cause of freedom."[13]

Even as comparisons to slavery persisted, as early as the 1880s public opinion began to envision a white Mormonism shorn of its black members altogether. Some outsiders wondered if black Mormons existed at all. A report from Salt Lake City published in a Nebraska paper refuted the claim that "nobody ever saw a negro Mormon" and suggested that "any one interested can find a number of colored 'Saints' in Salt Lake City." The story nonetheless clarified that the presence of black Mormons did not automatically signal that Mormons tolerated racial mixing: "Some few cases of miscezination [*sic*] have occurred in this territory, but public feeling amongst the majority is strongly opposed to such unions." One 1882 story in the *Los Angeles Herald* announced that "there are negro Mormons in Utah, and that there have been colored followers of Brigham Young almost from the very foundation of the church." It correctly reported that Young "made no distinction as to race, color or previous condition of servitude among his proselytes, but he had a prejudice against colored saints taking unto themselves white wives." The following year a report from Nebraska said that "a dozen colored Mormons arrived last week at Salt Lake," while a year later a Minnesota paper wrote that three blacks had converted to Mormonism in Tennessee and left for Utah; the paper described them as "the first colored Mormons" the faith had known.[14] With such confusion dominating news accounts, it is little wonder that the general public lacked understanding regarding the racial stance Brigham Young adopted in 1852 and the evolving priesthood and temple bans. Where lack of information prevailed, outsiders did not hesitate to offer possibilities.

In the meantime, Mormon leaders deliberately curtailed or stopped missionary activity among blacks. It was another cost associated with whiteness, which only served to reinforce the growing impression that there were no black Mormons. Especially in the era of racial segregation during the first half of the twentieth century, missionary efforts among blacks suffered, even in the northern United States. One 1909 mission report from the Northern States Mission, for example, recounted three black Mormon families, in Minneapolis, Minnesota; Oshkosh, Wisconsin; and South Bend, Indiana. Family members were deemed "good faithful people," but their blackness was "so much in evidence" at Sunday services that white investigators stayed away. As a result, missionaries quit proselyting "among the colored people" and had done so for the past seven years.[15]

Although church leaders never did adopt a segregationist policy for weekly Sunday worship, in some locations de facto segregation existed. Leaders in Salt Lake City did not instigate it, but they did not eradicate it either. In the early decades of the new century, Len and Mary Hope converted to Mormonism in Alabama. Outsiders resented the fact that they had joined a "white church" and threatened Len's life if he did not withdraw. Len had his name removed from local records but ensured that he would be retained on official rolls in Utah. Following World War I, the Hopes moved to Cincinnati, Ohio, where they again experienced prejudice, this time from fellow Mormons. White members of the congregation refused to worship with black people, and so the Hopes were advised to stay away. Once a month local leaders and missionaries brought the Lord's Supper to their home and held an intimate service with the family. After World War II, the Hopes moved to Salt Lake City and attended services in their local congregation. Similar experiences were repeated in various locations during the first half of the new century, with some congregations welcoming black members at Sunday services and others enforcing a local version of segregation.[16]

Such issues were only exacerbated later in the century as the church moved into international locations with large mixed-race populations such as Brazil. Initially missionaries concentrated on those with European ancestry, but over time they adopted various methods to ferret out a person's racial heritage, including asking to see pictures of potential proselytes' progenitors. Enforcing a "one drop" policy was impossible, however, and "mistakes" were inevitable. As the LDS First Presidency admitted in 1947, "the races are badly mixed in Brazil, and no color line is drawn among the mass of the people. The result is . . . that a great part of the population of Brazil is colored." In some circumstances it led to stripping men of their priesthood when their ancestry was discovered.[17]

Such internal transitions reinforced outside perceptions that Mormons were white and had always been so. Ironically, a similar confusion and historical forgetfulness dominated the way Mormons told their racial story on the inside as well. By the early twentieth century they too forgot their own black pioneers and became especially adept at erasing black priesthood holders from Mormon collective memory.

The new story for the new century was one of uncomplicated whiteness. Joseph Smith implemented the priesthood restriction from the beginning, and it was irreversible until God commanded it. Ben E. Rich, president of the Southern States Mission, articulated his understanding of "just where the negros come from" in a letter to a fellow Saint in 1898. As he expressed it, the exact origins of black people were "a hard matter to prove from holy writ" except that they were "descendants of Caine." He then linked their coming to earth as Cain's progeny to the neutrality of blacks in a premortal war in heaven, a cosmic struggle between the followers of Jesus and Satan ending with Satan's expulsion (Revelation 12:7–9). As a result of remaining neutral in that war, Rich said that blacks "were given an inferior body, in fact the most obnoxious of all human bodies, and the right was taken from them to hold the Priesthood." Rich admitted that a person could not "prove this from the bible" but nonetheless stated that it was "doctrine received from the Prophet Joseph, and which we believe came from God."[18] Attributing the ban and its supporting "doctrine" to Smith—and then from Smith to God—became standard practice, an invented memory that came to dominate Mormon collective thinking on blacks moving forward.

Even still, there was no unified justification for the restriction. The idea of black neutrality was not universally accepted. In 1907 Joseph Fielding Smith, then assistant church historian (and son of Joseph F. Smith and grandnephew of Mormon founder Joseph Smith), admitted that "there is nothing in our standard works, nor any authoritative statement to the effect that one third of the hosts of heaven remained neutral in the great conflict and that the colored races are of that neutral class." The belief was "quite general" among Latter-day Saints, however, "that the Negro race has been cursed for taking a neutral position in that great contest." Yet the view was admittedly speculative. "This is not the official position of the Church, merely the opinion of men," Smith said.[19]

Nevertheless, explanations tied to the premortal life slowly supplanted the curse of Cain justification even as the premortal reasoning experienced a modification of its own, from "neutral" to "less valiant." Apostle Joseph Fielding Smith is perhaps indicative of this transition. In his influential publication *The Way to Perfection* (1931), Smith tied the priesthood restriction to the curse of Cain and drew upon the books of Moses and Abraham to sustain his position. Decades later, in his *Answers to Gospel Questions,* he turned primarily to the premortal realm for explanation, elaborating upon the war in heaven, a conflict in which he claimed some premortal spirits "were not valiant." As a result of "their lack of obedience," blacks came to earth "under restrictions," including a denial of the priesthood. Bruce R. McConkie, as a member of the church's third-tier leadership, published similar views in *Mormon Doctrine* (1958); the popularity of his book and its authoritative title gave such ideas greater legitimacy. It continued to be published, racist ideas intact, up through 2010 before its church-owned distributor allowed it to quietly go out of print.[20]

The crucial element used to give authority and weight to justifications for the priesthood restriction was an effort to tie it to Joseph Smith and his revelatory access to heaven. If the ban could be connected to Smith, the reasoning likely went, then it must be of divine origins and thus a restriction mortals could not interfere with. Joseph Fielding Smith's *The Way to Perfection* was particularly emphatic on this point. After developing an extensive explanation regarding the curse of Cain, Fielding Smith attributed the teachings to his great-uncle Joseph Smith. "Millions of souls have come into this world cursed with a black skin and have been denied the privilege of Priesthood and the fullness of the blessings of the Gospel," he wrote. "These are the descendants of Cain." After tracing Cain's supposed descendants through Ham and the great flood, Smith asserted that the priesthood "doctrine did not originate with President Brigham Young but was taught by the Prophet Joseph Smith." He then cited secondhand reports from decades later of what people reputedly recalled Joseph Smith saying. His sole contemporary source was a brief entry from 1842 recorded in Joseph Smith's journal, which summarized a debate with John C. Bennett. Joseph Smith's clerk, Willard Richards, captured the entire debate in one sentence: Joseph, he said, sought to "shew that the Indians have grater cause to complain of the treatment of the whites than the Negroes or Sons of Cain." In such a truncated entry, not written by Joseph Smith himself, it is unclear whether the term "Sons of Cain" was coined by Smith, Richards, or Bennett. More to the point, the entry said nothing about priesthood, let alone a divine curse or black skin. For Fielding Smith, however, it was enough evidence to conclude that "it is due to [Joseph Smith's] teachings that the Negro today is barred from the Priesthood."[21]

When Milton R. Hunter, another LDS leader, published his *Pearl of Great Price Commentary* in 1949, he used the same argument and evidence. "Joseph Smith identified the negroes as the descendants of Cain," Hunter wrote. He further asserted that Joseph Smith taught the "doctrine" to Brigham Young, even though Young himself did not evoke Smith as the source for his ideas on priesthood and race. In fact, to date there is no known statement from Joseph Smith wherein he articulated a race-based priesthood or temple restriction.[22]

When the LDS First Presidency issued a statement on the priesthood ban in 1949, it moved beyond Smith to God for its rationale. It declared that the restriction was "always" in place: "The attitude of the Church with reference to Negroes remains as it has always stood. It is not a matter of the declaration of a policy but of direct commandment from the Lord." The "doctrine of the Church" on priesthood and race was in place "from the days of its organization," the First Presidency declared. The ban, it said, began when Mormonism began and would remain in place until some future time when "that race will be redeemed and possess all the blessings," which the rest of the Latter-day Saints then enjoyed. The statement said nothing of the original black priesthood holders, an indication of how thoroughly reconstructed memory had come to replace verifiable facts.[23]

The first presidency reiterated this view in another statement in 1969 when it linked the ban to "Joseph Smith and all succeeding presidents of the Church." The reasons this time were "known to God" but were "not made fully known to man." The then president of the church, David O. McKay, said that the "seeming discrimination by the Church toward the Negro is not something which originated with man; but goes back into the beginning with God." Gone as explanations were the curse of Cain and subpar valiancy in the preexistence. In their place was a new "we don't know" explanation, which in the twenty-first century came to replace the earlier rationales.[24]

*   *   *

Even as LDS leaders evolved in their official declarations regarding the priesthood restriction, so too did public perception evolve concerning Mormons. Although the shift was erratic, a growing admiration for Mormons emerged. Mormon efforts to care for their own during the Great Depression, including a highly touted welfare system anchored in ideals of self-sufficiency, gained national attention and respect. The Mormon Tabernacle Choir became goodwill ambassadors for the church. The choir's popularity increased after its radio broadcast, *Music and the Spoken Word*, began a weekly program in 1929, to date the longest continuous broadcast in radio history.[25]

Between the 1950s and 1970s the Mormons successfully made themselves over into white monogamist über Americans. In the words of religious historian Jan Shipps, they were "more American than the Americans." So effective were they at merging their version of the ideal family with the post–World War II *Leave it to Beaver* version of the American family that *Coronet* magazine ran an article in 1952 simply titled "Those Amazing Mormons." Within a year, sitting LDS Apostle Ezra Taft Benson was tapped by President Dwight D. Eisenhower to serve as US Secretary of Agriculture. Benson did not face the same type of political and public consternation that Smoot had faced fifty years earlier. In fact, Benson, while sometimes controversial, served in Eisenhower's cabinet for eight years. The *Saturday Evening Post* featured Benson in an article that highlighted his faith and strong family values. The Mormon family in many ways had become a model for the American family—white, middle class, and successful.[26]

The irony of this convergence was its timing. Almost as soon as Mormons became securely white, the nation began moving in a different direction. The postwar shift toward integration and civil rights gained significant momentum following the landmark 1954 US Supreme Court decision *Brown v. Board of Education,* which struck down the segregationist doctrine of "separate but equal." The nation lurched toward civil rights for blacks even as the South clung tenaciously to white supremacy. Mormon leaders also dug in their heels, arguing in 1949 that "there is no injustice whatsoever" involved in withholding the priesthood from blacks.[27]

In 1954 Mormon Apostle Mark E. Petersen demonstrated a willingness to shore up segregation in the face of national efforts otherwise. In a speech at Brigham Young University to college-level Mormon religion teachers, he quoted from a recent interview with Adam Clayton Powell Jr., a prominent black leader and US Congressman from New York City. Powell spoke out strongly in favor of "social equality," including "intermarriage" between whites and blacks. For Petersen it was a clear indication of "what the negro is after." It was not merely integrated lunch counters, streetcars, and theaters, but as Petersen viewed it, "The negro seeks absorption with the white race. He will not be satisfied," Petersen worried, "until he achieves it by intermarriage."[28]

Petersen insisted that God favored segregation of peoples and races: "He certainly segregated the descendants of Cain when he cursed the Negro as to the Priesthood, and drew an absolute line." As for intermarriage, Petersen was most emphatic. "We must not intermarry with the Negro," he admonished. "If I were to marry a Negro woman and have children by her, my children would all be cursed as to the priesthood.... If there is one drop of Negro blood in my children ... they receive the curse." He worried that if the estimated fifty million blacks in the United States achieved "complete absorption with the white race ... where would the priesthood be? Who could hold it, in all America?"[29]

It was clearly an exaggerated fear. Petersen based his concern upon the premise that all blacks wanted to marry all whites and that all whites wanted to marry all blacks rather than letting love and mutual attraction prevail. Petersen also falsely assumed that black-white marriages in the general population would somehow facilitate the spreading of the Mormon priesthood curse across "all America." It was a remote possibility given that the majority of African Americans were not Mormon and that the majority of Mormons were not black. Even still, it was an indication of how deeply entrenched the ban was in the mind of at least one member of the LDS hierarchy. It also signaled a defensive posture from Salt Lake City as the nation begrudgingly, slowly, sometimes violently lurched toward civil rights.

By the 1960s outsiders increasingly perceived that the LDS Church was out of step with changes taking place nationally. The civil rights movement sought racial equality in all walks of life, and the church quickly became an object of scorn for a priesthood and temple policy that denied such equality within Mormonism. The sweep of change was already evident in 1963, when the Utah state legislature repealed the state's antimiscegenation law, allowing residents to marry without racial concerns. Eager for further change, the Utah chapter of the National Association for the Advancement of Colored People (NAACP) lobbied the church to rescind its priesthood ban. Adding pressure, some college sports teams boycotted or protested when their schools played Brigham Young University. In response, the church released a statement in which it decried the "moral evil" of denying "any human being the right to gainful employment, to full educational opportunity, and to every privilege of citizenship."[30]

The church, in essence, adopted a difficult position to defend, one that argued for full civil rights for blacks in American society at the same time that it denied priesthood and temple access to blacks within Mormonism. In 1969 the First Presidency again affirmed civil rights for blacks: "We believe the Negro, as well as those of other races, should have full Constitutional privileges as members of society." Yet priesthood restriction, as a religious matter, "has no bearing on matters of civil rights" and could not change without a revelation from God: "Were we the leaders of an enterprise created by ourselves and operated only according to our own earthly wisdom, it would be a simple thing to act according to popular will. But we believe that this work is directed by God and that the conferring of the priesthood must await His revelation."[31]

At the same time, Hugh B. Brown, a counselor in the First Presidency, pressed to have the priesthood ban rescinded. Brown viewed the restriction as an administrative policy that did not begin with revelation and was therefore subject to modification with no revelation necessary. In contrast, McKay, as president, believed divine intervention necessary regardless of the restriction's origin, something he reportedly sought but did not receive. In the meantime the ban came under historical scrutiny when two influential publications undermined entrenched assumptions regarding its origins. Lester Bush's seminal 1973 article, "Mormonism's Negro Doctrine," was especially persuasive in modifying opinions.[32] When the quiet, unassuming Spencer W. Kimball became prophet/president of the church that same year, the climate was thus conducive for change. As early as 1963 Kimball signaled his open attitude: "The doctrine or policy has not varied in my memory," Kimball acknowledged, "I know it could. I know the Lord could change his policy and release the ban and forgive the possible error which brought about the deprivation."[33]

That forgiveness came in June 1978 with Kimball at the helm. He stunned Mormons and outsiders alike when he announced a revelation reversing the priesthood ban and by implication the temple ban. It was a revelation, he said, premised upon "the promises made by the prophets and presidents of the Church" who preceded him, that at some time "all of our brethren who are worthy may receive the priesthood." For Kimball, the promises he focused on were those that suggested a day of redemption for blacks and not those that reified divine curses. The true redemption Kimball ushered in was for the church he led and its mission to share a universal gospel message. It was a mission he guided back from a 130-year detour toward whiteness. Kimball's revelation returned Mormonism to its universalistic roots and ushered in dramatic transformations.[34]

The change was almost unanimously welcomed, both from within the church and also from outside it. Mormon leaders moved swiftly to reintegrate the priesthood and to throw open the doors of their temples to black men and women. Temple rituals and priesthood ordinations for blacks quickly ensued. Mixed-race temple marriages followed with no proscription against their practice, although lingering cultural attitudes persisted. When Mary Sturlaugson, the first black woman to serve as a missionary for the church, returned from her mission and started to date a white man, some of her acquaintances counseled her against it. She sought a personal interview with Kimball to learn from him directly. "I expressed to him my sincere desire to know the Lord's will on interracial marriage," she recalled. He reached out and gently embraced her, as "tears slowly rolled down his face." He "quietly but emphatically whispered, 'My child, it is not wrong. It is not wrong.'" Interracial marriage was not incompatible with the gospel, he told her.[35]

In this regard, Mormon Elder Berry's family was a century ahead of its time.This was a point made even more evident in 2010 when the LDS Church launched its "I'm a Mormon" media campaign. It was a multiyear public relations blitz in key market areas, including New York City and London; and it looked a lot like Elder Berry's imagined family from a century ago. It included Mormons from around the globe: Taiwan, Austria, Russia, Brazil, England, Japan, Ukraine, New Zealand, Guatemala, Australia, Switzerland, Hong Kong, Ireland, Costa Rica, Puerto Rico, Germany, the Dominican Republic, France, and other places, as well as a racially diverse group of Americans. The participants all shared short biographies of themselves, their vocations and avocations, and their strong family values. Then they ended with a string of identifiers such as "My name is Joe Saint, I'm a scientist, marathon runner, husband, father, and I'm a Mormon." The spots were designed to normalize Mormons and turn them into everyday people one might encounter at work, at the gym, in the theater, or in the classroom.

Of particular note, the campaign included a variety of mixed-race couples who were selected to represent the twenty-first-century faces of Mormonism. It was a dramatic divergence from Brigham Young's response in 1847 to news of Enoch Lewis and Mary Webster's mixed-race marriage at Lowell, Massachusetts. This time the "I'm a Mormon" campaign marked Mormons as progressive in terms of their lack of concern over mixed marriages, especially compared to more conservative segments of American society. In 1998, for example, a Christian liberal arts school in South Carolina, Bob Jones University, refused to admit white student James Landrith when the school learned of his marriage to a black woman. As late as 2013, the American cereal maker General Mills received a backlash of negative reaction when it ran a Cheerios commercial featuring a mixed-race family promoting its breakfast cereal.[36]

In contrast, the "I'm a Mormon" campaign included Saratoga Springs mayor Mia Love before she declared her candidacy in 2012 for US Congress. Love was a convert to Mormonism of Haitian descent and the first female black mayor in Utah history. Some called her a rising political star in the Republican Party, especially after she spoke at the national convention. Prior to her political campaign, she was featured in the Mormon ads alongside her white husband and their children, as were other couples of a variety of blended backgrounds. The departure from the nineteenth century was dramatic.[37]

Earlier trepidation regarding proselytizing in traditionally black areas in the United States and internationally also vanished. Missionaries were called to serve in Africa, and temples were later built in Nigeria and Ghana, all signs of church growth among black Africans. Domestically the church moved into black inner-city locations to establish congregations in places such as Harlem, Atlanta, and Oakland. In 1990 church leaders ordained Helvécio Martins from Brazil as the church's first black general authority. In 2009, Joseph Wafula Sitati, a black African, was ordained as a member of the First Quorum of the Seventy, and in 2013, Edward Dube from Zimbabwe was ordained to the same quorum. On a local level, black women and men served in every leadership capacity possible— bishops, Relief Society presidents, stake presidents, Young Women presidents, area authorities, Primary presidents—in integrated congregations across the globe.[38]

*   *   *

In the 1830s, Missourians excused the murder and expulsion of people who looked like themselves in part by suggesting that Mormons were less white. Residents of Illinois did the same less than a decade later. To explain these events, historians have traditionally pointed to Mormon communitarianism, clannishness, bloc voting, a general stance against slavery, and distinct religious principles that members of the Missouri and Illinois majority deemed an affront to what it meant to be an American. Beyond those answers, a blatant land grab on the part of some Missourians and the concentration and growth of Mormon political and economic power in both Missouri and Illinois offer the most compelling explanations. Although those reasons account for the tension and violence between Mormons and outsiders, they do not fully explain the rationalizations behind the actions and fail to account for the ways in which some Missouri and Illinois residents constructed distinct Mormon bodies on which to inscribe their hatred.[39]

The Mormon story highlights the racialization process at play from its beginnings and the ramifications of whiteness in the history of an American-born faith. Certainly if people of such white ancestry as the Mormons could be so thoroughly racialized as red, black, yellow, and less white, then race truly is a "hideous monster of the mind."[40] Outsiders imagined disparate identities for the "Mormonites," identities that little resembled the people being racialized but that were deployed nonetheless to justify religious discrimination, violence, murder, and expulsion. Religious freedom in America met its limits in the Mormons, but not without racial validations.

The Mormon story lays bare, in all of its ugly and naked defenselessness, the self-interested and manipulative nature of racial identity construction. Outsiders invented the derogatory label "Mormonites," which quickly accumulated a shared set of group characteristics—deluded, fanatical, dumb, susceptible to despotic rule, poor, lazy, and brutish—in the minds of those who used it. It was a racialization process that began before Mormons practiced polygamy. Polygamy only confirmed and gave new life to a racial progression already underway. As the "Mormonite" label morphed to "Mormon" and then "Mormon race," so too did the associated racial characteristics.

Beginning in the 1850s, in fact, some American thinkers argued that marriage was racial. The development theory of civilizations, so prevalent in nineteenth-century thought, dictated that all societies progressed from primitive savagery, to barbarism, and then to civilization. As societies moved along that upward trajectory they left polygamy behind. Monogamy was thus white and civilized, while polygamy was a sign of barbarism or savagery.

In 1852 when Mormons openly acknowledged plural marriage and defended it as a religious principle protected under the free exercise clause of the US Constitution, the floodgates were opened. Outsiders imagined Mormonism giving birth to civilization's decay. To make matters worse, the threat was from within: these were white people who looked no different than their neighbors. Racial thinkers contended that plural marriage was the special preserve of Asiatic and African societies and therefore a step backward toward barbarism. From there the racialization process spiraled dramatically out of control. The medical community and the pseudosciences of phrenology and physiognomy added "scientific" certainty to the evolving argument. Mormonism was a racial threat from the inside and a deterioration of whiteness that might ultimately lead to democracy's demise.

Here the Mormon experience exposes a crucial lesson in racial imagination and the powerful role that performance played in giving rise to a "new race." In many regards it is the proverbial chicken-and-egg argument: which came first, race or its assumed set of characteristics? Nineteenth-century observers believed that being black, red, or yellow each carried with them a collection of (ever-shifting) racial attributes. Race, in other words, produced undesirable behavior—laziness, sexual promiscuity, brutality, filthiness, and so forth. Nineteenth-century Americans believed that the people who belonged to the various "races" were biologically incapable of rising above such behavior.

In the case of the Mormons, the argument was reversed. Mormon behavior—fanaticism, adherence to theocratic rule, ignorance, sexual promiscuity, plural marriage, fawning subservience, and violence—produced race. Polygamy, when combined with Mormon isolation spawned a "new race." As outsiders viewed it, Mormon race was a performance; that is, Mormons *acted* racially degenerate, therefore they *were* racially degenerate. It was a self-fulfilling observation that brings the socially constructed nature of race in American history into sharp focus.

Mormons then were born into a complex and fluid racial culture and did not escape its consequences. Scholars of Mormon race have largely focused on the way in which Mormons racialized others, especially blacks and Indians. However, it is impossible to fully understand that story without first understanding that race is something ascribed from the outside as well as aspired to from within. Mormons were persistently defined as "in-between" people, neither securely white, nor nonwhite. In response, they moved unevenly across the course of the nineteenth century toward whiteness. It was a transition for which they paid a high price.

Mormons were mostly white like their American and European neighbors, yet they struggled to claim the blessings of whiteness in their lives. From a twenty-first- century perspective, the racialization of the Mormons at the hands of outsiders was illogical and even absurd. It is impossible, after all, for a marriage practice to produce a new race. Such a frank acknowledgement requires an equally frank confrontation with the ways in which Mormons themselves imagined racial identities for "others." They participated in the same racial culture that denigrated them but turned their focus on other marginalized groups, especially blacks and Indians, in their own quest for whiteness. Mormons reinforced their ideas with scripture and prophetic proclamations, which led them to believe that black and red skin were divine curses. Those curses, however, carried starkly different paths toward redemption. Indians, as fallen descendants of ancient Israel, were subject to racial uplift and could become "white and delightsome" after conversion. In contrast, Mormons eventually imagined blacks as beyond the redemptive power of their gospel plan: they were people who bore the mark of Cain and therefore fell outside the great chain of being, a cosmological web that bound the human family together leading back to Father Adam. Blacks were welcomed into membership in the Mormon kingdom but were eventually barred from its priesthood and the full saving rites of temple worship. Mormons thus sought to bring Indians with them on their journey toward whiteness while they left blacks behind. Whiteness, after all, was measured in distance from blackness, and Mormons moved increasingly across the course of the nineteenth century toward segregated priesthood and temples and away from their own black members.

* * *

Whiteness historians sometimes speak of moments or periods when minority groups achieved whiteness and assimilated into the American family. With Mormons it is more accurate to speak of the ebb and flow of whiteness, periods when they blended and times and places when they did not. Especially at moments in the spotlight, old suspicions sometimes resurfaced in new ways to once again call the Mormon body into question. Yet by the twenty-first century the terms of the struggle had shifted. There was a transition from a racial *and* religious contest over Mormon whiteness to primarily a religious skirmish over the

Mormon body. The racial struggle that remained underwent a transition of its own, from not white to too white.[41]

In 2008 Arvella George, a Mormon docent at the Church of Jesus Christ of Latter-day Saints' office tower in Salt Lake City, led a tour of visitors through that building. As was typical, George took her group to the twenty-sixth floor of the high rise and from that vantage point noted historical structures and landmarks in the vicinity of downtown Salt Lake City. As the tour ended and the group waited to board the elevator, one particular woman hung back and rather hesitantly approached George with a request: "I would like to see a Mormon," she stated. Somewhat taken aback, George contemplated a "variety of sassy answers," but not wanting to embarrass the tourist she instead explained that the majority of men and women in business attire she had observed on the tour were Mormons. The tourist got on the elevator before George could query her as to what she expected a Mormon to look like. Perhaps she had confused Mormons with Amish, or maybe she envisioned women in plain-style prairie dresses and men in long-sleeved western shirts and jeans. Whatever the tourist's expectation, her question highlighted the way in which the Mormon body, even in the twenty-first century, was sometimes perceived as something different. It reminded George of an experience in 1956 when she moved to the Boston suburb of Burlington while her husband attended Boston University. She quickly made friends with her neighbors, the majority of whom were Catholic. When one friend learned that George was Mormon the friend later admitted, "She was so surprised, as she had been told the Mormons had horns!"[42]

The belief that Mormons still practiced polygamy animated public perceptions in the twenty-first century, spurred on by news events as well as by popular culture. The success of HBO's series *Big Love* as well as TLC's *Sister Wives* only added to the confusion. In 2008 when the state of Texas raided the Yearning for Zion (YFZ) ranch outside of Eldorado, Texas, it highlighted lingering misunderstandings. The Fundamentalist Church of Jesus Christ of Latter-day Saints (FLDS) owned the YFZ Ranch under the leadership of Warren Jeffs, and the raid was undertaken due to allegations of child sexual abuse. Contemporary members of the FLDS communities in Texas, Utah, Arizona, and Canada were never members of the Church of Jesus Christ of Latter-day Saints headquartered at Salt Lake City. The split between the groups took place after 1904, when the mainstream LDS Church began to actively excommunicate members who took additional plural wives. Those who refused to abandon future plural marriages were cut off and eventually formed their own churches.[43]

The splinter group that adopted the moniker "FLDS" settled along the Utah-Arizona border in the sister cities eventually named Hildale and Colorado City. Over time the FLDS community turned dramatically inward, while the LDS community increasingly expanded its vision outward. In the 1940s, as one facet of a broader retrenchment from the outside world, members of the FLDS community adopted a distinct manner of dress and grooming. Women typically wore plain prairie-style dresses, no makeup or pants, with their hair pulled away from their faces. Men tended to wear long-sleeve western-style shirts and jeans. The LDS community meanwhile followed American fashion trends, always tempered by "modesty." As evidence of its global outreach, by the twenty-first century, the Church of Jesus Christ of Latter-day Saints boasted more members who lived outside of the United States than within; by 2013 it counted over 29,000 congregations worldwide. The FLDS community in contrast did not send missionaries to outside locales but established increasingly insular compounds in remote locations and relied primarily upon internal increase. The LDS Church counted its membership in millions, while the FLDS did so in thousands. The distinctions between the two groups, however, were easily lost on outsiders, and once again the Mormon body became one focus of the struggle among Salt Lake City–based Mormons to define themselves—religiously, not necessarily racially.[44]

Following the raid in Texas and the subsequent arrest of FLDS leader Warren Jeffs, news sources were not always precise in distinguishing between the FLDS and LDS churches. The term "Mormon" was sometimes used interchangeably for both. For example, cable news channel CNN superimposed Jeffs's arrest picture over a large image of the Salt Lake Temple, a blunder that angered LDS authorities at Salt Lake City and sent them scrambling to distinguish their church from the group led by Jeffs. Jeffs was never a member of the Church of Jesus Christ of Latter-day Saints and had never been in the Salt Lake Temple. His ancestors were excommunicated from the LDS Church for continuing to take additional plural wives and refusing to abandon the practice.[45]

In an effort to clarify a distinction, the Houston director of public affairs for the Church of Jesus Christ of Latter-day Saints issued a press release regarding the "improper use of the term 'Mormon' by media." It complained that "associating the term *Mormons* with polygamists blurs what should be a crystal-clear distinction between organizations that are entirely separate." A local LDS leader insisted that "Mormons do not look like members of the polygamous group in Texas. They do not dress like them, worship like them, or believe the same things." It was a point that LDS apostle Quentin L. Cook also sought to clarify. As reported by the *Salt Lake Tribune,* Cook stipulated that "Mormons do not live in isolated compounds, arrange marriages, dress in old-fashioned clothing or wear unusual hairstyles."[46]

Meanwhile, individual Mormons created responses of their own to defend a particular vision of who Mormons were and what they looked like. One e-mail titled "Just for the record . . ." made the rounds electronically in Mormon circles. "For those of you who have been watching the news," it began, "this will set the

record straight." What followed was a string of pictures of nationally prominent Mormons interspersed with short introductions. "Some Mormon women
sing," it said, followed by a picture of Gladys Knight, the Grammy Award–winning Motown rhythm-and-blues artist who converted to Mormonism in 1997.
"Some Mormon women write scary stories," it continued, followed by a picture
of Stephenie Meyer, author of the wildly popular *Twilight* vampire series. "Some
Mormon women have lots of money and really great hair," with Marie Osmond
as the case in point. Other such illustrations were used to the same ends. The
string of examples then ended with the line, "None of the Mormon women I
know look like this . . ." followed by a picture of FLDS women in prairie dresses
being escorted onto a bus by Texas law enforcement officers.[47]

The e-mail deployed a similar pattern for Mormon men. To illustrate the
point, it used Steve Young, former Super Bowl quarterback for the San Francisco 49ers; Andy Reid, then head coach of the Philadelphia Eagles football
team; John Heder, actor of *Napoleon Dynamite* fame; and Mitt Romney, former
governor of Massachusetts then seeking the Republican nomination for president of the United States. It ended, "None of the Mormon men I know look like
this . . ." with a picture of FLDS leader Warren Jeffs, chained, handcuffed, and in
prison garb.[48] Clearly, what Mormons looked like was still a relevant concern.

Mitt Romney's run for the US presidency in the twenty-first century suggested that although the racial discourse had changed, the Mormon body was
still suspect. A Gallop poll prior to the 2008 primary season queried potential
voters as to who they might support for president: a woman (with Hillary Clinton seeking the Democratic nomination), a black (with Barack Obama also
running as a Democrat), or a Mormon. The Mormon finished behind the hypothetical woman and black, with similar results in 2012. Some of the consternation revolved around continuing confusion over polygamy, suspicions about
Mormon loyalty, and old fears regarding a lurking religious "cult" with secret
rituals and bizarre beliefs.[49]

Even still, Mitt Romney's body and, by extension, the collective Mormon
body did not escape critique. One political blogger wrote: "I don't get why some
Republicans like Mitt Romney. . . . For me and others, interest in Romney ended
when we discovered he's one of those weird underwear-wearing Mormons," a
reference to undergarments worn by temple-attending Latter-day Saints. "Look
at the dude. Lantern-jawed, excellent physical shape, jet black hair with graying
temples, crisp suit, and too long in the tanning booth," the blogger wrote. "He's
a caricature of your slick and soulless politician. Plus, a girl on MTV couldn't
possibly ask him whether he prefers boxers or briefs because he's got that freaky
religious underwear on all the time."[50]

New York Times columnist Charles M. Blow, pop singer Cher, and political
pundit Bill Maher also took pot shots at Romney's underwear. Blow, a single

parent, simply wanted Romney to stick his comment about single parents during one of the presidential debates in his "magic underwear." Meanwhile, Maher told David Letterman that he planned to vote for Romney: "If our enemies get past all our other defenses, at least our leader has the magic underwear on," he mocked. More caustically, Cher called Romney an "Uncaring Richy Rich! The whitest man in MAGIC UNDERWEAR in the W[hite] H[ouse]."[51]

Mormons responded with efforts to normalize their bodies and explain the religious significance of their undergarments. One Mormon founded a website, Mormon-underwear.com, designed to counter the mocking "magic underwear" moniker. An official church website for press releases and media interaction, Mormonnewsroom.org, also included an explanation designed to historicize and spiritualize what outsiders ridiculed as "magic."[52]

As such sources explained, temple-going Mormons wear sacred "garments" designed to remind them of the covenants they make in LDS temples. Similar to Jewish prayer shawls, a Jewish yarmulke, a priest's collar, or other religious vestments, Mormon "garments" served as physical symbols of spiritual commitments, in this case promises to walk a Christian path and follow the example of Jesus Christ. One LDS Church statement simply called the garments "an outward expression of an inward commitment to follow the Savior." Mormons view their garments as physical reminders of spiritual covenants and hold them sacred, as a way to privately mark their bodies as different and committed to a Christian path. A church statement indicated that public ridicule of such private matters was offensive to Mormons and requested media representatives to "report on the subject with respect, treating Latter-day Saint temple garments as they would religious vestments of other faiths."[53]

Public ridicule of so-called magic underwear and confusion between FLDS and LDS once again caught the Mormon body in its crosshairs. The terms of the denigrations and the terms of the Mormon responses, however, had changed. The effort to differentiate between an LDS body and an FLDS body centered on religious beliefs and practices more than racial notions about Asiatic or African societies and a backward slide into barbarism. The distinction was between churches, not Western and Eastern civilizations. Mormon responses to ridicule of their temple garments also sought to claim religious legitimacy and inclusion. Mormons attempted to situate LDS vestments alongside "religious vestments of other faiths," to demystify them and claim for Mormons the same respect offered other believers. Clearly Mormons still struggled for a place at the religious table, and their bodies remained a battleground; however, the racial struggle had transformed.

The juxtapositions between the nineteenth and the twenty-first centuries were striking. The terms "Mormonite" and "Mormon" were deployed derisively in the nineteenth century to distinguish between adherents to the new faith and "citizens" of Ohio and Missouri. Labeling "Mormons" as collectively distinct was the first step in the racialization process. By the twenty-first century, the institutional church embraced the term "Mormon" and even claimed it as an exclusive identifier for the Church of Jesus Christ of Latter-day Saints. The church established a web presence at Mormon.org and launched an international public relations campaign.[54] Likewise, in the nineteenth century Mormons defended the polygamist body as elevated, celestial, and divine; in the twenty-first century, they defined the monogamist body as their new ideal. In the wake of Warren Jeffs's arrest, Mormons wanted the world to know that they no longer practiced polygamy and offered outward proof that they did not look like those who did. Their bodies were beautiful, successful, integrated, indistinguishable, even famous, but they were certainly not clothed in prairie dresses and holed up in compounds. It was a historical evolution that was nothing short of astonishing.

In some cases, perhaps, Mormons have won the long struggle over their bodies. LDS proscriptions against alcohol, tobacco, harmful drugs, coffee, and tea, along with admonitions toward healthy eating and exercise, have gained national attention and earned Mormon bodies a reputation for being strong and wholesome. In 2005, *Men's Fitness* magazine, in conjunction with *Princeton Review*, conducted a nationwide survey of college campuses to determine the "fittest" student body in America. Brigham Young University (BYU), at Provo, Utah, the flagship school in the LDS Church's higher-education system, ranked number one. On average 13,000 students a year enrolled in campus intermural sports teams, and university programs promoted healthy eating and lifestyles. "We're encouraged to take care of our bodies," one student told the Associated Press when news of the ranking broke.[55]

In 2013, in a different survey, BYU was ranked as the most "stone-cold sober" campus in the nation for the sixteenth year in a row. The rank was established in a survey conducted by the *Princeton Review* based upon student reported daily study hours, levels of alcohol and drug use on campus, and popularity of fraternities and sororities. It was a national standing for which BYU remained proud. In 2013 *Business Insider* magazine placed BYU first in the nation "where students are both hot and smart." It was a dramatic reversal from nineteenth-century descriptions of Mormon bodies as repulsive, debased, and stupid. As Jennifer Polland at *Business Insider* put it, "Everyone at BYU is very attractive; I've yet to see an ugly person here." She found the men to be "clean shaven and well groomed" and the women "dressed modestly." This, combined with BYU's "strong academic program," earned the school its top spot.[56]

*   *   *

BYU's notoriety for "hot," healthy, and temperate student bodies, however, reinforced a different reputation that Mormon leaders preferred to leave behind—that Mormons were universally white and lived in Utah. Despite a return to Mormonism's universalistic roots ushered in by the 1978 revelation, public perception regarding Mormons tended to be stuck in a pre-1978 time warp. By the time the revelation was announced, the evolution in public perception was already complete. Mormons, in the eyes of some outsiders faced a new struggle with whiteness in the twenty-first century, one marked by an effort to claim an international and racially diverse identity for themselves.[57]

In May 2012 *New York Times* reporter Susan Saulny published the story "Black Mormons and the Politics of Identity," which was an investigation into how black Latter-day Saints grappled with their choice between Mitt Romney, a Mormon Republican, and Barack Obama, a black Democrat, in the 2012 presidential election. The online version of the story featured a four-minute video in which a fellow reporter from the *Times* interviewed Saulny about her story. The conversation began with an expression of "surprise" that there were in fact black Mormons for Saulny to interview. The exchange then entertained a bit of speculation over how many black Mormons there were in the United States, with a "very small number," a "couple of thousand max," and "500 to 2,000" offered as possibilities.[58]

Likewise, in 2012 Jon Stewart's *The Daily Show* sent reporter Jessica Williams to Utah to interview black Mormons on the pending election. When Williams met with five black Latter-day Saints she called black Mormons "mythical creatures, the unicorns of politics" and asked if the five she had assembled comprised the entire population of black people in the Church of Jesus Christ of Latter-day Saints. Even after her guests explained that there were many black Saints in Utah and elsewhere, Williams still joked that there were only seventeen more. It was a satirical interview to be sure, but one based on a popular perception that Mormons were universally white. Not to be outdone, Jimmy Kimmel simply asked on *Jimmy Kimmel Live*, "Are there black Mormons? I find that hard to believe."[59]

The LDS Church does not track members of record by race, making estimates of black membership impossible to verify, yet some empirical data does exist. According to a 2009 study conducted by the Pew Research Center, African Americans comprised 3% of US church membership that year (around 180,000 members) and one in ten converts to the faith was black. Meanwhile, in 2011 the church reported members residing in thirty-four African countries with a total membership across the continent of 320,000. Factoring in black membership in the Caribbean and South America, in particular Brazil, the number is likely bigger still.[60] In the United States, the Pew survey noted that 86% of Mormons were white, an indication that US Mormonism is more racially diverse than mainline Protestant churches (91% white), Jews (95% white), and Orthodox Christians (87% white). Catholics, Jehovah's Witnesses, and Muslims were all much more racially diverse.[61]

Such evidence notwithstanding, as late as 2012 the perception persisted in some corners that Mormons were racist and that there were few or no black Mormons. It was a new racial problem for Mormonism, which was the opposite dilemma it faced almost two centuries previously. In the 1830s reports of the integrated and charismatic nature of Mormon worship services in Kirtland, Ohio, made news in New York and Pennsylvania within months of Black Pete's conversion to the new faith. In Missouri, the perception that Mormons invited freed blacks to move to that state in order to incite a slave rebellion and violate white women only fueled interracial rumors.

As outsiders perceived it, in the 1830s and 1840s, Mormons were too inclusive. The allegations leveled against them complained that they accepted a variety of unacceptable people. Outsiders variously suggested that the Mormons had "opened an asylum for rogues and vagabonds and free blacks," embraced "all nations and colours," that they maintained "communion with the Indians," walked out with "colored women," welcomed "all classes and characters," and received "aliens by birth," as well as people from "different parts of the world" into their communities and congregations. Edward Strutt Abdy, the British official who toured the United States in the early 1830s, specifically highlighted the Book of Mormon ideal that "all are alike unto God" (2 Nephi 26:33) as a potential source of agitation with the surrounding society. As Abdy saw it, such a universalistic principle placed Mormons out of sync with national culture. America was in the midst of its own racial struggle centered on the exclusion of those who were not white. It was a struggle that created a distorted racial lens through which to view the Mormons and find them wanting.[62]

The spotlight that Romney brought to Mormonism in 2008 and 2012 exposed the near polar opposite racial problem for the faith. In 2008 when Romney unsuccessfully sought the Republican nomination for president, one political blog made fun of the Romney Christmas card, which was a picture of Ann and Mitt Romney surrounded by their very white and polished children and grandchildren. The blogger suggested that the Romney family represented "the melting pot that is Utah." He electronically pasted an African American man into the otherwise white Romney family photo and then asked, "Who do you think is the non-Romney . . . in this photo?"[63]

By the 2012 election, the issue was more salient. In February of that year, *Washington Post* journalist Jason Horowitz ran a lengthy article on the historical priesthood ban and the ways it might shape public perceptions of Mitt Romney and his faith. When Horowitz interviewed BYU religion professor Randy Bott, he found a relic of racial justifications from the past. Bott told Horowitz that "God has always been discriminatory" in distributing priesthood authority. Bott then trotted out a variety of racist justifications for the historical ban as if he were really Brigham Young and it was still the nineteenth century. It was a stinging

black eye for LDS leaders. They had moved swiftly to change policy and practices following the 1978 revelation but had also never bothered to repudiate old
teachings used to justify the priesthood and temple bans.[64]

Bruce R. McConkie, an LDS apostle who was personally responsible for
some of the church's most egregious racial justifications, did attempt to dismiss
his own and other leaders' teachings to an LDS audience at BYU within months
of the 1978 revelation. "It doesn't make a particle of difference what anybody
ever said about the Negro matter before the first day of June of this year," Mc-
Conkie said. He asked his audience to "[f]orget everything that I have said, or
what President Brigham Young or George Q. Cannon, or whomsoever has said
in days past that is contrary to the present revelation. We spoke with a limited
understanding and without the light and knowledge that now has come into
the world."[65] It was a statement that suggested that prior teachings on race were
devoid of the "light and knowledge" that revelation represented to Latter-day
Saints. Even still, the speech was delivered to a limited audience and was unknown to most Latter-day Saints. Its sentiment was never repeated in a worldwide "general conference" setting.

In the wake of Horowitz's *Washington Post* article, an episode quickly dubbed
"Bottgate" by Mormon watchers, the church did issue two statements. It distanced itself as much as possible from Bott, who was no longer employed at BYU
after that semester. "The positions attributed to BYU professor Randy Bott in
a recent *Washington Post* article absolutely do not represent the teachings and
doctrines of The Church of Jesus Christ of Latter-day Saints," one statement
read. "We condemn racism, including any and all past racism by individuals both
inside and outside the Church."[66] In a separate statement, the church referred
to the Book of Mormon verse, "all are alike unto God," including "black and
white," the very verse that British officer Edward Strutt Abdy cited in the 1830s
to suggest that Mormonism represented an open racial vision too progressive for
nineteenth-century Americans to stomach. Mormon leaders in the twenty-first
century gave that verse new life in an effort to reclaim the universalism they lost
in their search for whiteness. In 2013 they again cited the same verse in an introduction to Kimball's 1978 revelation, this time to be included in new editions
of LDS scriptures. They also officially acknowledged that a few black men were
ordained to the priesthood during Joseph Smith's lifetime.[67] In December 2013,
they went even farther, posting an essay to their website that for the first time
disavowed "that black skin is a sign of divine disfavor or curse, or that it reflects
actions in a premortal life; that mixed-race marriages are a sin; or that blacks or
people of any other race or ethnicity are inferior in any way to anyone else."[68]

Public perception nonetheless lagged behind. Mitt Romney's run for the
presidency again highlighted the gap. In an opinion piece for the *New York Times*,
culture critic Lee Siegel went so far as to call Romney "the whitest white man to

run for president in recent memory." For Siegel it was "a whiteness grounded in a retro vision of the country, one of white picket fences and stay-at-home moms and fathers unashamed of working hard for corporate America." As Siegel viewed it, there was "no stronger bastion of pre-civil-rights-American whiteness than the Church of Jesus Christ of Latter-day Saints." It was a designation that Mormons craved a century ago but one that came as a liability for Romney in 2012, especially as the Republican Party grappled with a white identity crises of its own.[69]

Mormons again found themselves on the wrong side of white. In the nineteenth century they were denigrated as not white enough. By the twenty-first century, they had become too white. In the nineteenth century Mormons moved away from diversity toward whiteness. In 1978 they reversed course with a revelation that signaled an effort to reclaim a lost diversity. Through it all, the Book of Mormon maintained that "all are alike unto God," a scriptural imperative that met its match in an American religious and racial culture which insisted otherwise.

NOTES

Introduction

1. The Church of Jesus Christ of Latter-day Saints is the official name of the church under study here. The term "Mormon" was a nickname first used derisively in the nineteenth century to refer to members of the new faith and derived from their belief in a new book of scripture, the Book of Mormon. Over time, the term "Mormon" was embraced by members of the faith and is the most readily recognized label associated with the church and its members. The church in the twenty-first century owns and operates a website at Mormon.org geared toward curious outsiders and those with questions about the faith. Its official site aimed at its members is LDS.org. Members are sometimes referred to as Mormons, Latter-day Saints, Saints, or LDS, and their belief system as Mormonism. This study will use those terms interchangeably to refer to members of the church.

2. "Mormon Elder-Berry—Out With His Six-Year-Olds, Who Take After Their Mothers," *Life,* vol. 43, 28 April 1904, 404; Michael Harold Paulos, "Under the Gun at the Smoot Hearings: Joseph F. Smith's Testimony," *Journal of Mormon History* 34 (Fall 2008): 181–225; Michael Harold Paulos, ed., *The Mormon Church on Trial: Transcripts of the Reed Smoot Hearings* (Salt Lake City, UT: Signature Books, 2008), 19–142, 177–184.

3. For the "I'm a Mormon" campaign see Mormon.org; and Eric Marrapodi, "With 'I'm a Mormon' Campaign, Church Counters Lily-white Image," CNN Belief Blog, <http://religion.blogs.cnn.com/2011/11/02/with-im-a-mormon-campaign-church-counters-lily-white-image> (accessed 14 May 2013).

4. Thomas G. Alexander, "The Odyssey of a Latter-day Prophet: Wilford Woodruff and the Manifesto of 1890," *Journal of Mormon History* 17(1991): 169–206; *LDS Conference Reports, Seventy-Fourth Annual Conference of the Church of Jesus Christ of Latter-day Saints, Held in the Tabernacle, Salt Lake City, April 3rd, 4th and 6th, 1904, with a full Report of the Discourses* (Salt Lake City, UT: Deseret News, 1904), 75.

5. Kathleen Flake, *The Politics of American Religious Identity: The Seating of Senator Reed Smoot, Mormon Apostle* (Chapel Hill: University of North Carolina Press, 2004); J. Spencer Fluhman, *"A Peculiar People": Anti-Mormonism and the Making of Religion in Nineteenth-Century America* (Chapel Hill: University of North Carolina Press, 2012); Walter Kirn, "Mormons Rock!" *Newsweek,* 5 June 2011, as posted at <http://www.thedailybeast.com/newsweek/2011/06/05/mormons-rock.html> (accessed 18 May 2013); Michael H. Paulos, "Political Cartooning and the Reed Smoot Hearings," *Sunstone* 144 (December 2006): 36–40.

6. Flake, *The Politics of American Religious Identity,* 1–33; Jonathan H. Moyer, "Dancing with the Devil: The Making of the Mormon-Republican Pact" (PhD diss., University of Utah, 2009); Harvard S. Heath, "Reed Smoot: First Modern Mormon," (PhD diss., Brigham Young University, 1990), 84–197; Milton R. Merrill, *Reed Smoot: Apostle in Politics* (Logan: Utah State University Press, 1990); Gustive O. Larson, *The "Americanization" of Utah for Statehood* (San Marino, CA: Huntington Library, 1971).

7. Thomas Alexander, *Mormonism in Transition: A History of the Latter-day Saints, 1890–1930* (Urbana: University of Illinois Press, 1986); Ethan R. Yorgason, *Transformation of the Mormon Culture Region* (Urbana and Chicago: University of Illinois Press, 2003).

8. Parley P. Pratt, *Late Persecution of the Church of Jesus Christ of Latter-day Saints* (New York: J. W. Harrison, 1840), 59; "Speech Delivered by Heber C. Kimball," *Times and Seasons*, 15 July 1845.

9. Kenneth H. Winn, *Exiles in a Land of Liberty: Mormons in America, 1830–1846* (Chapel Hill: University of North Carolina Press, 1989); Terryl L. Givens, *The Viper on the Hearth: Mormons, Myths, and the Construction of Heresy* (New York: Oxford University Press, 1997); Sarah Barringer Gordon, *The Mormon Question: Polygamy and Constitutional Conflict in Nineteenth-Century America* (Chapel Hill: University of North Carolina Press, 2002); Megan Sanborn Jones, *Performing American Identity in Anti-Mormon Melodrama* (New York: Routledge, 2009); Patrick Q. Mason, *The Mormon Menace: Violence and Anti-Mormonism in the Postbellum South* (New York: Oxford University Press, 2011); Christine Talbot, *A Foreign Kingdom: Mormons and Polygamy in American Political Culture, 1852–1890* (Urbana: University of Illinois Press, 2013); Fluhman, "A Peculiar People."

10. Givens's *The Viper on the Hearth*, comes the closest to this study, yet his focus is on anti-Mormon novels and the construction of heresy. This study explores vast swaths of cultural sources and argues that race is what outsiders ultimately constructed. Historians of Mormonism have explored physical characterizations of Mormons in the past but not in the context of race and whiteness. See Davis Bitton and Gary L. Bunker, "Double Jeopardy: Visual Images of Mormon Women to 1914," *Utah Historical Quarterly* 46 (Spring 1978): 184–202; Gary L. Bunker and Davis Bitton, "Illustrated Periodical Images of Mormons, 1850–1860," *Dialogue: A Journal of Mormon Thought* 10 (Spring 1977): 82–94; Davis Bitton and Gary L. Bunker, "Mischievous Puck and the Mormons," *BYU Studies* 18 (Summer 1978): 504–519; Gary Bunker and Davis Bitton, *The Mormon Graphic Image, 1834–1914: Cartoons, Caricatures, and Illustrations*, University of Utah Publications in the American West, vol. 16 (Salt Lake City: University of Utah Press, 1983); Davis Bitton and Gary L. Bunker, "Phrenology Among the Mormons," *Dialogue: A Journal of Mormon Thought* 9 (Spring 1974): 42–61; Gary L. Bunker and Davis Bitton, "Polygamous Eyes: A Note on Mormon Physiognomy," *Dialogue: A Journal of Mormon Thought* 12 (Autumn 1979): 114–119; Terryl Givens, "Caricature as Containment: Orientalism, Bondage, and the Construction of Mormon Ethnicity in Nineteenth-century American Popular Fiction," *Nineteenth-Century Contexts* 18.4 (1995): 385–403. Whiteness historians have neglected Mormon examples altogether.

11. Roediger, *Working Toward Whiteness*, 4–5.

12. Matthew Guterl, *The Color of Race in America, 1900–1940* (Cambridge, MA: Harvard University Press, 2001), 15–19; Matthew L. Basso, *Meet Joe Copper: Masculinity and Race on Montana's World War II Home Front* (Chicago and London: University of Chicago Press, 2013), 29–30; Bruce Dain, *A Hideous Monster of the Mind: American Race Theory in the Early Republic* (Cambridge, MA: Harvard University Press, 2002), vii–viii; Mark M. Smith, *How Race is Made: Slavery, Segregation, and the Senses* (Chapel Hill: University of North Carolina Press, 2006), 46–47, 68. On the negative connotations of "Celt" as applied to Irish-Catholics see Nell Irvin Painter, *The History of White People* (New York: W. W. Norton, 2010), chapter 9.

13. David R. Roediger, *Working Toward Whiteness: How America's Immigrants Became White* (New York: Basic Books, 2005).

14. Roediger, *Working Toward Whiteness*, 12.

15. Patricia J. Williams, *The Alchemy of Race and Rights* (Cambridge, MA, and London: Harvard University Press, 1991); Patricia J. Williams, *Seeing a Color-Blind Future: The Paradox of Race* (New York: Noonday Press, 1997).

16. *Congressional Globe*, 30th Cong., 1st Sess. (Washington, DC: Blair and Rives, 1848), 53–56; 96–100.

17. *Congressional Globe*, 30th Cong., 1st Sess., 98.

18. *Congressional Globe*, 30th Cong., 1st Sess., 98–99.

19. For population and demography of the Mormons see Dean L. May, "A Demographic Portrait of the Mormons, 1830–1980," in *The New Mormon History: Revisionist Essays on the Past*, ed. D. Michael Quinn (Salt Lake City, UT: Signature Books, 1992). May finds (p. 124) that by 1850 53% of "western Mormons were British."

20. Todd M. Kerstetter, *God's Country, Uncle Sam's Land: Faith and Conflict in the American West* (Urbana: University of Illinois Press, 2006), 80.

21. "An Act to Establish an Uniform Rule of Naturalization," 1st Cong., 26 March 1790, Sess. II, chap. 3, 1 stat 103; *Congressional Globe*, 30th Cong., 1st Sess., 98; *Scott v. Sandford*, 60 US 393, p. 407; *Political Debates Between Hon. Abraham Lincoln and Hon. Stephen A. Douglas, in the Celebrated Campaign of 1858, in Illinois* (Columbus, OH: Follett, Foster and Company, 1860), 136.

22. Painter, *The History of White People*, 132; Matthew Frye Jacobsen, *Whiteness of a Different Color: European Immigrants and the Alchemy of Race* (Cambridge, MA: Harvard University Press, 1998), 41.

23. Jacobsen, *Whiteness of a Different Color*, 37–38; Painter, *The History of White People*, 132–150.

24. Painter, *The History of White People*, 132–150, 190–191; Jacobson, *Whiteness of a Different Color*, 7, 31–68.

25. Matthew Frye Jacobson, *Barbarian Virtues: The United States Encounters Foreign Peoples at Home and Abroad, 1876–1917* (New York: Hill and Wang, 2000), 140–149.

26. Metta Victoria Fuller, *Mormon Wives: A Narrative of Facts Stranger than Fiction* (New York: Derby and Jackson, 1856), viii.

27. George A. Smith Papers, 1834–1875, "History of George A. Smith," MS 1322, box 1, folder 1, 79, CHL.

28. Alexander Majors, *Seventy Years on the Frontier: Alexander Majors' Memoirs of a Lifetime on the Border*, ed. Prentiss Ingraham (Chicago: Rand, McNally, 1893; repr, Lincoln: University of Nebraska Press, 1989), 45.

29. George Q. Cannon, "Word of Wisdom—Fish Culture—Dietetics," 7 April 1868, *Journal of Discourses*, vol. 12 (London and Liverpool: Latter-day Saints' Book Depot, 1869), 224; B. Carmon Hardy, *Solemn Covenant: The Mormon Polygamous Passage* (Urbana and Chicago: University of Illinois Press, 1992), 84–126.

30. Reginal Horsman, *Race and Manifest Destiny: The Origins of American Racial Anglo-Saxonism* (Cambridge, MA: Harvard University Press, 1981); Armand L. Mauss, *All Abraham's Children: Changing Mormon Conceptions of Race and Lineage* (Urbana and Chicago: University of Illinois Press, 2003), 23.

31. Bryan J. Grant, "The Church in British Isles," in *Encyclopedia of Mormonism*, ed. Daniel H. Ludlow, 5 vols. (New York: Macmillan, 1992), 1, 227–232; *Doctrine and Covenants of the Church of Jesus Christ of Latter-day Saints* (Salt Lake City, Utah: Church of Jesus Christ of Latter-day Saints, 1981), 4:4.

32. Here, I am influenced by Eric L. Goldstein's insights in *The Price of Whiteness: Jews, Race, and American Identity* (Princeton, NJ: Princeton University Press, 2006).

33. Abraham Owen Smoot, diary, 28 May 1836, MSS 896, vol. 1, LTPSC. I am indebted to Jonathan Stapley for this reference.

34. See Fluhman, *"A Peculiar People,"* Givens, *The Viper on the Hearth,* and Talbot, *A Foreign Kingdom* for explorations of religious anti-Mormonism.

Chapter 1

1. On the Utah War see Richard D. Poll and William P. MacKinnon, "Causes of the Utah War Reconsidered," *Journal of Mormon History* 20 (Fall 1994): 16–44; Todd M. Kerstetter, *God's Country, Uncle Sam's Land: Faith and Conflict in the American West* (Urbana: University of Illinois Press, 2006); William P. MacKinnon, *At Sword's Point, Part 1: A Documentary*

History of the Utah War to 1858 (Norman, OK: The Arthur H. Clark Company, 2008); Norman F. Furniss, *The Mormon Conflict, 1850–1859* (New Haven, CT: Yale University Press, 1960); Matthew J. Grow, *"Liberty to the Downtrodden": Thomas L. Kane, Romantic Reformer* (New Haven, CT: Yale University Press, 2009); David L. Bigler and Will Bagley, *The Mormon Rebellion: America's First Civil War, 1857–1858* (Norman: University of Oklahoma Press, 2011).

2. Lester E. Bush Jr., "A Peculiar People: The Physiological Aspects of Mormonism, 1850–1875," *Dialogue: A Journal of Mormon Thought* 12 (Fall 1979): 61–83; Lester E. Bush Jr., "Mormon 'Physiology,' 1850–1875," *Bulletin of the History of Medicine* 56:2 (Summer 1982), 218–237.

3. US Senate, *Statistical Report on the Sickness and Morality in the Army of the United States, compiled from the Records of the Surgeon General's Office; Embracing a Period of Five Years from January 1, 1855, to January, 1860*, Senate Executive Document 52, 36th Cong., 1st Sess., 301—302.

4. US Senate, *Statistical Report*, 301–302.

5. US Senate, *Statistical Report*, 301–302.

6. US Senate, *Statistical Report*, 301–302.

7. Bush, "Mormon 'Physiology,'" 224.

8. "Hereditary Descent; or, Depravity of the Offspring of Polygamy Among the Mormons," *DeBow's Review* 10, no. 2 (January 1846), 206–216.

9. "Hereditary Descent," 207–208.

10. "Hereditary Descent," 210–212.

11. "Hereditary Descent," 212–216.

12. John F. Kvach, *DeBow's Review: The Antebellum Vision of a New South* (Lexington: University Press of Kentucky, 2013), 5.

13. "Hereditary Descent," 206, 208; Bush, "Mormon 'Physiology,'" 224.

14. Charles C. Furley, "Physiology of Mormonism," *British Medical Journal* 2 (18 July 1863), 66; Bush, "Mormon 'Physiology,'" 224, 227–228. For a brief biography of Furley see David Dary, *Frontier Medicine: From the Atlantic to the Pacific, 1492–1941* (New York: Alfred A. Knopf, 2008), 200–201.

15. Roberts Bartholow, "The Physiological Aspects of Mormonism, and the Climatology, and Diseases of Utah and New Mexico," *Cincinnati Lancet and Observer*, 1 April 1867; Bush, "Mormon 'Physiology,'" 230–231.

16. "Report of Surgeon E. P. Vollum, USA," in John Shaw Billings, *War Department Surgeon Generals' Office Circular No. 8, Report on the Hygiene of the United States Army*, 1 May 1875 (Washington, DC, 1875), 342–343; Bush, "Mormon 'Physiology,'" 234–236.

17. See J. Spencer Fluhman, *"A Peculiar People,": Anti-Mormonism and the Making of Religion in Nineteenth-Century America* (Chapel Hill: University of North Carolina Press, 2012). Specifically see chapters two and three for insightful discussions of "delusion" and "fanaticism" as markers designed to exclude Mormonism as a religion.

18. For another assessment of "Mormonite" rhetoric see Michael W. Homer, *On the Way to Somewhere Else: European Sojourners in the Mormon West* (Spokane, WA: The Arthur H. Clark Company, 2006), chap. 1.

19. "Latest from the Mormonites," *New York American*, 10 June 1831; A. W. B. "Mormonites," *Evangelical Magazine and Gospel Advocate* (Utica, NY), 9 April 1831; "The Mormonites," *Village Chronicle* (17 May 1831); "The Mormonites," *Geauga Gazette* (Painesville, OH) 21 June 1831, repr. in *Western Reserve Chronicle* (Warren, OH), 30 June 1831; P.H.B, "The Mormonites," *Ohio Eagle* (Lancaster, OH) 20 April 1833; "Mormonites," *Republican Advocate* (Wooster, OH), 16 July 1831; J. Newton Brown, "Mormonites," *Encyclopedia of Religious Knowledge* (Boston: Shattuck and Company, 1835), 844; *Niles' Weekly Register* (Baltimore, MD), 7 June 1834). For other examples deploying "Mormonites" see "The Mormonites," *New York Spectator*, 27 September 1831; "Mormonites," *Working Man's Advocate* (New York, NY), 14 May 1831; "Mormon Religion—Clerical Ambition—Western

New York—The Mormonites Gone to Ohio," *Morning Courier and New-York Enquirer* (New York, NY), 1 September 1831; "Mormonites," *Trumpet and Universalist Magazine* (Boston, MA), 22 October 1831; "The Mormonites" *Christian Intelligencer and Eastern Chronicle* (Gardiner, ME) 18 November 1831; "The Mormonites," *Baptist Chronicle and Literary Register* (Georgetown, KY), December 1831; "Mormonites," *Gospel Luminary* 6, no. 8 (May 1833), 263–265; "'Regulating' the Mormonites," *Niles' Weekly Register*, 14 September 1833; "Mormonites," *Christian Review* 2 (June 1837), 203; "The Book of Mormon and the Mormonites," *Athenaeum, Museum of Foreign Literature, Science and Art* 42 (July 1841), 370–374; *Doctrine of the Mormonites* (London: J. Wertheimer and Company, 1842), 1–4. For a Mormon defense against such descriptions see Parley P. Pratt, "The Mormonites. To the Editor of the New Era," *Times and Seasons* (Commerce, IL), January 1840.

20. "To His Excellency, Daniel Dunklin, Governor of the State of Missouri," *The Evening and the Morning Star* (Kirtland, OH), December 1833.

21. "The Mormons," *Sangamo Journal* (Springfield, IL), 7 December 1833.

22. "Kirtland, O. July 5th, 1836," *The Far West* (Liberty, MO), 11 August 1836.

23. "Public Meeting," *Latter Day Saints' Messenger and Advocate* (Kirtland, OH), August 1836, 353–354.

24. John W. Price and Wm. K. Logan, Report of the committee of Chariton County, in *Document Containing the Correspondence, Orders, &C. In Relation To The Disturbances With The Mormons; And The Evidence Given Before The Hon. Austin A. King* (Fayette, MO: Office of the Boon's Lick Democrat, 1841), 36.

25. To the Citizens of Howard County, 7 October 1838, in *Document Containing the Correspondence*, 40.

26. W. A. Cowdery, "Freedom," *Evening and Morning Star* (Kirtland, OH), September 1834.

27. "An Appeal," *Evening and Morning Star*, August 1834.

28. Parley P. Pratt, *Late Persecution of the Church of Jesus Christ of Latter-day Saints* (New York: J. W. Harrison, 1840), 59.

29. "Important from the Mormon County," *New York Weekly Herald*, 7 August 1841, emphasis in original. The Mormon newspaper at Nauvoo picked up the same column that it claimed first appeared in the *New York Journal of Commerce* and was then "copied in many of the eastern papers." Mormons denied the charges and appealed to their rights, which "the constitution guarantees to all its citizens." See "The Mormons—Arrest of Jo. Smith," *Times and Seasons*, 15 July 1841.

30. Simon G. Whitten, La Harpe, Illinois, to Mary B. Whitten, Parsonsfield, Maine, June 22 1844, Mormon File, HL.

31. Captain Frederick Marryatt, *Monsieur Violet. His Travels and Adventures among the Snake Indians and Wild Tribes of the Great Western Prairies* (London: Thomas Hodgson, 1849), 275.

32. E. S. Abdy, *Journal of a Residence and Tour in the United States of North America, From April, 1833, to October, 1834*, 3 vols. (London: John Murray, 1835), 1:324–325; 3:40–42, 54–59.

33. John C. Bennett, *The History of the Saints; or, an Exposé of Joe Smith and Mormonism*, (Boston: Leland and Whiting, 1842), 193, emphasis in original.

34. "The Mormons," *New York Herald*, 23 September 1843, quoting "The Mormons and Anti-Mormons" from the St. Louis *New Era*, 12 September 1843.

35. "The Mormon War," *Cleveland Herald* (Cleveland, OH), 27 June 1844.

36. "Report of Gov. Ford in relation to the Mormon Disturbances," *Ottawa Free Trader* (Ottawa, IL), 10 January 1845.

37. "Conference Minutes," *Times and Seasons*, 1 November 1845. I am indebted to David Grua for this reference.

38. "Speech Delivered by Heber C. Kimball," *Times and Seasons*, 15 July 1845.

39. "Conference Minutes," *Times and Seasons*, 1 November 1845.

40. Warren Foote, "Autobiography of Warren Foote, son of David Foote a decendant [sic] of Nathaniel Foote the Settler who came from England about 1633 and was one of the

First settler of Weathersfield Conectticut," [*sic*] vol 1., 96, microfilm holograph. Archives, CHL.

41. "Uncle Tom in Germany," *Frederick Douglass Paper* (Rochester, NY), 18 February 1853.
42. For a collection of such travel narratives from Prussia, Germany, Italy, Belgium, and France, see Michael W. Homer, *On the Way to Somewhere Else: European Sojourners in the Mormon West* (Spokane, WA: The Arthur H. Clark Company, 2006).
43. Olympe de Joaral Audouard, *Crossing America: The Far West*, trans. by Hugh MacNaughton, as in Homer, *On the Way to Somewhere Else*, 123–145.
44. "Highway Gleanings to California," *The Christian Recorder* (Philadelphia, PA), 29 November 1883.
45. Sherrie Lynne Lyons, *Species, Serpents, Spirits, and Skulls: Science at the Margins in the Victorian Age* (Albany: State University of New York Press, 2009), 51–52, 71–77.
46. Joseph Simms, *Nature's Revelations of Character; or, Physiognomy Illustrated. A Description of the Mental, Moral and Volitive Dispositions of Mankind, as Manifested in the Human Form and Countenance*, 3d ed. (New York: D. M. Bennett, Liberal and Scientific Publishing House, 1879), x–xi.
47. "Outline of the Science of Man, according to Phrenology, Physiology, Physiognomy, and Psychology," *The Phrenological Journal and Life Illustrated* 52, no. 1 (January 1871): 77–80. The number of faculties was either twenty-seven or thirty-five depending upon the phrenologist; see Lyons, *Species, Serpents, Spirits, and Skulls*, 72.
48. Lyons, *Species, Serpents, Spirits, and Skulls*, chap. 3.
49. Davis Bitton and Gary L. Bunker, "Phrenology Among the Mormons," *Dialogue: A Journal of Mormon Thought* 9 (Spring 1974): 42–61; Gary L. Bunker and Davis Bitton, "Polygamous Eyes: A Note on Mormon Physiognomy," *Dialogue: A Journal of Mormon Thought* 12 (Autumn 1979): 114–119; Joseph Smith, History, 1838–1856, vol. C-1, 2 July 1842; handwriting of Thomas Bullock, Franklin D. Richards, Jonathan Grimshaw, and Leo Hawkins, pp. 1352–1354, as archived at JosephSmithPapers.org; Bitton and Bunker, "Phrenology Among the Mormons," 43–44; Nauvoo *Wasp*, 2 July 1842.
50. Joseph Smith, History, 1838–1856, vol. C-1, 2 July 1842; Bitton and Bunker, "Phrenology among the Mormons," 45–50, 52.
51. Bitton and Bunker, "Phrenology Among the Mormons," 52; "The Mormons: Who and What They Are," *The Phrenological Journal and Life Illustrated* 52 (January 1871), 42–43.
52. Although the *Journal* used the percent of men in polygamy as its gauge, historians now use percent of households to measure rates of participation in polygamy. Historian B. Carmon Hardy suggested that somewhere between 15 and 30% of households were polygamous in the nineteenth century while Kathryn Daynes found 36% of Manti, Utah, households to be polygamous in 1870, a rate in dramatic decline over the next three decades. In any case, the *Journal* was correct to suggest that the majority of Mormons chose monogamy over polygamy, an unusual assertion among those who looked in on the Mormons and imagined polygamy and sexual excess run amok. See Kathryn M. Daynes, *More Wives than One: Transformation of the Mormon Marriage System, 1840–1910* (Urbana and Chicago: University of Illinois Press, 2008), 101; B. Carmon Hardy, "That 'Same old Question of Polygamy and Polygamous Living:' Some Recent Findings Regarding Nineteenth and Early Twentieth-Century Mormon Polygamy," *Utah Historical Quarterly* 73 (Summer 2005), 215.
53. "The Mormons: Who and What They Are," 42, 44.
54. "The Mormons: Who and What They Are," 44–45.
55. This is an observation based upon the monthly publications between 1866 and 1876 (absent 1867) of the *Phrenological Journal*. It included an article by Rev. S. H. Platt on the Presbyterian minister "Thomas De Witt Talmadge," *The Phrenological Journal and Life Illustrated*, 52, no. 3 (March 1871), 168–170; it also included the article "The 'Christian' Church and its Eminent Preachers," 52 (February 1871): 92–103; and "Women in the Presbyterian Pulpit," 55 (September 1872): 165–166. Shakers (featured seven times: 54,

no. 6 [June 1872], 400–401; 55, no. 6 [December 1872]: 426; 56, no. 5 [May 1873]: 358; 56, no. 6 [June 1873]: 410–411; 57, no. 1 [July 1873]: 42–44; 57, no. 2 [August 1873]: 111–115; 61, no. 2 [August 1875]: 138), Jews and "the Hebrew Race" (featured five times: 43, no. 3 [March 1866], 75; 47, no. 4 [April 1868]: 147–148; 47, no. 4 [April 1868]: 144–147; 61, no. 2 [August 1875]: 138; 62, no. 5 [May 1876]: 377–379) and Swedenborgians (three times: 49, no. 6 [June 1869]: 223; 55, no. 5 [November 1872]: 300–302; 60, no. 4 [April 1875]: 218–223), were each featured three times or more during this same time frame. "A Quaker Wedding" (47, no. 1 [January 1868]: 34–35), "Eminent Roman Catholic Clergymen" (48, no. 1 [July 1868]: 12–15), "Two Colored [Episcopal] Bishops" (60, no. 1 [January 1875]: 13–16), "Church of United Brethren" (57, no. 5 [November 1873]: 355–365), and "John H. Noyes and the Oneida Community" (44, no. 4 [October 1866]: 97–101) garnered one article each. The Mormons were either featured in articles or were noted at least nine times in addition to the five articles appearing in 1871 (an atypical year for its number of articles on Mormons). Baptists and Methodists were never featured as distinct religious communities. The single article on Presbyterian women did not discuss phrenological features. If this nine-year sampling is representative, mainstream Protestant communities were not treated as separate groups worthy of phrenological study the same as Mormons, Shakers, and Jews. For the articles on Mormons see 43, no. 6 (June 1866): 196; 44, no. 4 (October 1866): 111; 44, no. 5 (November 1866): 144–151; 49, no. 2 (February 1869): 82–83; 55, no. 3 (September 1872): 165–166; 59, no. 5 (November 1874): 325; 61, no. 3 (March 1873): 203–204; 61, no. 6 (June 1873): 423–424; and 62, no. 6 (December 1873): 391–393.

56. "Japan—A Sketch of Its Present Condition," 52 (March 1871): 197–199; "Italians in New York—Who and What they Are," 52 (April 1871): 242–250; "The Jews—Their Peculiarities," 52 (April 1871): 262–264; John P. Jackson, "The Last of the Tasmanians," 53 (July 1871): 16–19; "Street Sights in China," 53 (August 1871): 102–104; "N. A. Indians—Can they be Civilized?" 53 (August 1871): 104–105; Francis Gerry Fairfield, "A New Guessing of an Old Puzzle, or the Chinese Labor Question," 53 (August 1871): 107–110; F. Lawrence Miles, "Causes of Grecian Greatness," 53 (September 1871): 199–201; "Street Signs in China—No. 2," 53 (October 1871): 254–256; "Physical Structure of the Italians," 53 (October 1871): 256. On the Mormons see "The Mormons: Who and What they Are," 38–45; "The Mormons," 52 (January 1871): 53–54; "The Utah Gentiles—Who and What they Are," 52 (May 1871): 337–343; "Leaders in the Mormon Reform Movement—With Portraits," 53 (July 1871): 30–40; and "The Mormon Question," 53 (December 1871): 394–395.

57. Simms, *Nature's Revelations of Character*, 158–159, 163–164.

58. Simms, *Nature's Revelations of Character*, 158–159, 163–164; John Matteson, *The Lives of Margaret Fuller: A Biography* (New York: W.W. Norton, 2012).

59. *Harper's Weekly* 2 (4 December 1858), 782.

60. *Harper's Weekly* 1 (11 July 1857), 442.

61. Samuel Bowles, *Across the Continent: A Summer's Journey to the Rocky Mountains, the Mormons, and the Pacific States, with Speaker Colfax* (Springfield, MA: Samuel Bowles and Company; New York: Hurd and Houghton, 1865), 87.

62. Robert Richards, *The California Crusoe* (London: J. H. Parker, 1854), 60.

63. *Mormonism Dissected, or, Knavery "On Two Sticks," Exposed* (Bethania, PA: Printed by Reuben Chambers, 1841), 7; Henry Caswall, *The Prophet of the Nineteenth Century; or, the Rise, Progress, and Present State or The Mormons, or Latter-Day Saints: To which is appended, An Analysis of the Book of Mormon* (London: J. G. F. and J. Rivington, 1843), 223.

64. T. W. P. Taylder, *The Mormon's Own Book; or, Mormonism Tried by its own Standards—Reason and Scripture, with an Account of its Present Condition.* (London: Partridge and Co., 1857), xiv–xv.

65. Bowles, *Across the Continent*, 86.

66. "The Mormon Apostle," *Portland Transcript* (Portland, MA), 5 February 1870, 356.

67. *The Mysteries of Mormonism. A Full Exposure of Its Secret Practices and Hidden Crimes By An Apostle's Wife. Fully Illustrated.* (New York: Richard K. Fox, Proprietor Police Gazette, 1882), 16.

68. "The Cephalopod of the Great Basin.—Genus Polypi Mormoni Priesthoodi," *Enoch's Advocate*, 11 May 1874, 1.

69. Bowles, *Across the Continent*, vi.

70. Mrs. Benjamin G. Ferris, *The Mormons at Home; With some Incidents of Travel from Missouri to California, 1852–3. In a Series of Letters.* (New York: Dix and Edwards, 1856), 147.

71. On Mormon gender imbalance see Bush, "Mormon 'Physiology,'" 232; "The Crazy Quilt," *St. Johns Herald* (St. Johns, AZ), 27 August 1885.

72. John Hyde Jr., *Mormonism: Its Leaders and Designs* (New York: W. P. Fetridge and Company, 1857), 54–58. On Hyde's exodus from Mormonism see Edward L. Hart, "John Hyde, Junior—An Earlier View," *BYU Studies* 16, no. 2 (1976): 305–312.

73. Memorial of Mrs. Angie F. Newman, Remonstrating Against the Admission of Utah Territory into the Union as a State so Long as the Administration of the Affairs of that Territory Continues in the Hands of the Mormon Priesthood, 50th Cong., 1st Sess., Senate. Mis. Doc. No. 201, 21 September 1888, 2.

74. "The Beauties of Polygamy," *Anti-Polygamy Standard* (Salt Lake City), May 1880.

75. Hyde, *Mormonism*, 58, 63, 69.

76. Ferris, *The Mormons at Home*, 153.

77. "Incidents of Life in Utah," *Anti-Polygamy Standard* 2, no. 2 (May 1881): 12.

78. J. W. R., "Polygamy: The Thrilling Story of Mrs. Brig Hampton as told in Her Prayer for Divorce," *Inter Ocean*, 30 May 1881.

79. "The Woman's National Anti-Polygamy Society," *Anti-Polygamy Standard* 1, no. 5, (August 1880): 33.

80. Mark Twain, *Roughing It* (Hartford, CT: American Publishing Company, 1872), 117–118.

81. *Liberty Weekly Tribune*, 17 April 1863.

82. Ferris, *The Mormons at Home*, 199–200; see also "Mormonism," *New York Independent*, 14 July 1870.

83. John G. Fackler, "Brief Notes of Travils a cross the Plains from St. Joseph Mo. To California in 1864," Archives, Missouri Historical Society, 85–90, as in *Doing the Works of Abraham: Mormon Polygamy, its Origin, Practice, and Demise*, ed. B. Carmon Hardy (Norman, OK: The Arthur H. Clark Company, 2007), 208.

84. Harold D. Langley, *To Utah with the Dragoons and Glimpses of Life in Arizona and California, 1858–1859* (Salt Lake City: University of Utah Press, 1974), 66.

85. "For the Christian Recorder," *The Christian Recorder* (Philadelphia, PA) 3 October 1863.

86. Bartholow, "The Physiological Aspects of Mormonism," 195.

87. Hyde, *Mormonism*, 74–76.

88. Margaret M. Hecox, *California Caravan: The 1846 Overland Travel Memoir of Margaret M. Hecox* (San Jose, CA: Harlan-Young Press, 1966), 24; Metta Victoria Fuller, *Mormon Wives: A Narrative of Facts Stranger than Fiction* (New York: Derby and Jackson, 1856), xi–xii.

89. T. W. P. Taylder, *The Mormons Own Book*, 202; Hyde, *Mormonism*, 77; Ferris, *The Mormons at Home*, 145; Fackler, "Brief Notes of Travils," in *Doing the Works of Abraham*, 208; "What a Mormon Baby is Like," *Harper's Weekly*, 21 February 1857, 118; "The Woman's National Anti-Polygamy Society," 33.

90. E. Jump, "B. Y. the Great American Family Man," *Wild Oats* (New York, NY), 28 March 1872. For another example of the deformed offspring of polygamy see Matt Morgan, "The Mormon Problem Solved," *Leslie's Weekly*, 11 November 1871; and for another attack on Young's family see *Wild Oats*, 29 February 1872.

91. E. D. Howe, *Mormonism Unvailed* (Painesville, OH: Printed and Published by the Author, 1834), 65.

92. Gary F. Jensen, *The Path of the Devil: Early Modern Witch Hunts* (Lanham, MA: Rowman and Littlefield, 2006), 155–156; Joshua Trachtenberg, *The Devil and the Jews* (New Haven,

CT: Yale University Press, 1943), 44–47; Robert Bonfil, "The Devil and the Jews in the Christian Consciousness of the Middle Ages," in *Antisemitism Through the Ages*, ed. Shmuel Almog, trans. Nathan H. Reisner (New York: Pergamon Press, 1988), 93–95.

93. William Harris, *Mormonism Portrayed; its Errors and Absurdities Exposed, and the Spirit and Designs of its Authors Made Manifest* (Warsaw, IL: Sharp and Gamble, Publishers, 1841), p. 3 of unnumbered introduction.

94. "Conference Minutes," *Times and Seasons* (Nauvoo, IL), 1 August 1844.

95. William Smith, Bordentown, New Jersey, to William W. Phelps, Nauvoo, Illinois, 10 November 1844, in *The Prophet* (New York), 23 November 1844; repr. as "Correspondence," *Times and Seasons*, 1 January 1845.

96. Foote, "Autobiography," 1:97.

97. "Ye Popular Idea of Brigham Young and his Followers," *Yankee Notions*, April 1858; "Latest from Polygamutah," *Vanity Fair*, 11 February 1860, 100.

98. "Mormon Immigrants," *Austin Weekly Statesman* (Austin, TX), 22 November 1883.

99. "One Way to Solve the Mormon Problem," *Sam the Scaramouch* (Cincinnati, OH), 23 May 1885.

100. "At the Tabernacle," *Salt Lake Herald*, 3 August 1886.

101. "'Mayor' Anderson," *Salt Lake Herald*, 23 July 1892.

102. Armand L. Mauss, *All Abraham's Children: Changing Mormon Conceptions of Race and Lineage* (Urbana and Chicago: University of Illinois Press, 2003), 17–19.

103. Reginal Horsman, *Race and Manifest Destiny: The Origins of American Racial Anglo-Saxonism* (Cambridge, MA: Harvard University Press, 1981); Mauss, *All Abraham's Children*, 19–22.

104. Nell Irvin Painter, *The History of White People* (New York: W. W. Norton, 2010), 132; Matthew Frye Jacobsen, *Whiteness of a Different Color: European Immigrants and the Alchemy of Race* (Cambridge, MA: Harvard University Press, 1998), 132–150.

105. Mauss, *All Abraham's Children*, 21–24.

106. Richard S. Van Wagoner, *The Complete Discourses of Brigham Young.* 5 vols. (Salt Lake City: The Smith-Pettit Foundation, 2009), 3:1677, 1718; 4:2122.

107. Van Wagoner, *The Complete Discourses*, 4:2122.

108. Hyde, *Mormonism*, 79.

109. Mary Jane Mount Tanner, *A Fragment: The Autobiography of Mary Jane Mount Tanner*, ed. Margery W. Ward (Salt Lake City: University of Utah Tanner Trust, 1980), 188; Mary Jane Mount Tanner to Hubert Howe Bancroft, 29 October 1880, as in Hardy, *Doing the Works of Abraham*, 91.

110. George Q. Cannon to journalists, 20 March 1882; Eliza R. Snow, "Sketch of My Life," 17; and Catherine Bates, *Year in the Great Republic*, 2:225, 228, all in Hardy, *Doing the Works of Abraham*, 91 and 91 note 39.

111. B. Carmon Hardy and Dan Erickson, "'Regeneration—Now and Evermore!': Mormon Polygamy and the Physical Rehabilitation of Humankind," *Journal of the History of Sexuality* 10 (January 2001): 40–61.

112. Van Wagoner, *Complete Discourses*, 28 July 1847, 1:236.

113. Charles W. Penrose, "Physical Regeneration," *Millennial Star*, 10 August 1867, in Hardy, *Doing the Works of Abraham*, 92–93.

114. Albert Carrington, "Plurality of Wives—Physiologically and Socially," *Deseret News* [*Weekly*], 29 March 1866; Hardy, *Doing the Works of Abraham*, 94–95.

115. Orson Hyde, "Common Salvation," 24 September 1853, *Journal of Discourses* 2 (London and Liverpool: Latter-day Saints' Book Depot, 1855), 112–120.

116. George Q. Cannon, "The Improvement of Our Species," *Western Standard* (San Francisco, CA), 7 August 1857.

117. Benjamin Morgan Palmer, *Mormonism: A Lecture Delivered Before the Mercantile Library Association of Charleston, S.C. By B. M. Palmer, D. D. January 26, 1853* (Columbia, SC: Printed by I. C. Morgan, 1853), 32.

118. "Our Reporter Visits the Mormons," *New York Times*, 29 March 1856.
119. "A Mormon Conventicle in Wales," *Glasgow Herald*, 22 June 1863.
120. "Mormonism," *New York Independent*, 14 July 1870.
121. Bartholow, "The Physiological Aspects of Mormonism," 194, 197.
122. "Hereditary Descent," 208, 210.
123. William M. Evarts, Department of State, Washington, DC, 9 August 1879, Circular No. 10, Sent to Diplomatic and Consular Officers of the United States, *Papers Relating to the Foreign Relations of the United States, Transmitted to Congress, with the Annual Message of the President, 1879* (Washington, DC: Government Printing Office, 1880), 11–12; William Mulder, "Immigration and the 'Mormon Question': An International Episode," *The Western Political Quarterly* 9 (Jun 1956): 416–433; Ardis E. Parshall, "A 'Gathering Storm': The US State Department's Worldwide War on Mormonism," Parts 1–3, as archived at <http:// www.keepapitchinin.org>. I am indebted to Ardis E. Parshall for the source material concerning Evarts and the foreign response.
124. Evarts, 9 August 1879.
125. R. R. Hitt, Legation of the United States, Paris, France, to Evarts, 1 November 1879, in *Papers Relating to the Foreign Relations*, 349–350; Mulder, "Immigration and the 'Mormon Question,'" 423–425; Ardis E. Parshall, "A 'Gathering Storm," parts 2–3.
126. "Notes from Washington," *New York Times*, 25 May 1883; "Pauper Mormons from Switzerland," *New York Times*, 26 May 1883; "The Coming Swiss Mormons," *New York Times*, 27 May 1883.
127. "The Mormon Immigrants," *New York Times*, 28 May 1883.
128. "Mormon Immigrants, *Salt Lake Tribune*, 7 July 1883, 4. For additional coverage of the steamship *Nevada*'s passengers in the local and national press see "Safe Voyage of Emigrating Saints—Birth on the Way," *Millennial Star*, 1 June 1883; "Pauper Immigrants," *New York Times*, 4 June 1883; "Mormon Proselytes," *Salt Lake Tribune*, 5 June 1883; "Attempt to Stop the Emigrants," *Millennial Star*, 18 June 1883; "A Batch of Mormon Converts," *New York Times*, 2 July 1883; "Don't Be Hasty," *Salt Lake Herald*, 4 July 1883;
129. William Jarman, *U. S. A. Uncle Sam's Abscess, or Hell Upon Earth for U. S. Uncle Sam* (Exeter, UK: H. Leduc's Steam Printing Works, 1884), 39.
130. Thomas Nast, "Pure White 'Mormon Immigration' on the Atlantic Coast," *Harper's Weekly*, 25 March 1882, 191; "The Twin Relic of Barbarism," *Frank Leslie's Illustrated Newspaper*, 15 December 1883.
131. "Woman's Bondage in Utah," *Frank Leslie's Illustrated Newspaper*, 11 March 1882.
132. David R. Roediger, *The Wages of Whiteness: Race and the Making of the American Working Class* (New York: Verso, 1991; repr. 2007), 82–87.
133. "The True Dignity of Labor," *The National Era* (Washington, DC), 21 May 1857.
134. Parshall, "A 'Gathering Storm,'" part 3; see also Mr. Doty, consulate of the United States, Tahiti, to Mr. Uhl, Washington, DC, 11 May 1895; Frank Cutler, Papute, Tahiti, to J. L. Doty, Papeete, Tahiti, 29 April 1895; Mr. Uhl, Department of State, Washington, DC, to Mr. Doty, Papeete, Tahiti, 25 June 1895, in *Papers Relating to Foreign Relations, 1898*, 347–353.
135. Julian Ralph, "A Week with the Mormons," *Harper's Weekly*, 8 April 1893, 327.
136. "Only Human," *Denver Evening Post*, 18 October 1897.

Chapter 2

1. For an overview of Sevier's Indian campaigns see Carl S. Driver, *John Sevier: Pioneer of the Old Southwest* (Chapel Hill: University of North Carolina Press, 1932), chapters 2 and 3, especially p. 28 for the campaign into North Carolina. For the "nits make lice" comment, see E. Raymond Evans, "Notable Persons in Cherokee History: Bob Benge," *Journal of Cherokee Studies* 1 (Fall 1976): 98–106; Michelle Daniel, "From Blood Feud to Jury System: The Metamorphosis of Cherokee Law from 1750 to 1840," *American Indian Quarterly* 11

(Spring 1987), 103; Grace Steele Woodward, *The Cherokees* (1963; repr. Norman: University of Oklahoma Press, 1982), 125.

2. Quoted in Katie Kane, "Nits Make Lice: Drogheda, Sand Creek, and the Poetics of Colonial Extermination," *Cultural Critique* 42 (Spring 1999), 84.

3. Kane, "Nits Make Lice," 85.

4. Ronald Takaki, "The Tempest in the Wilderness: The Racialization of Savagery," *Journal of American History* 79 (December 1992): 893; James Muldoon, "The Indian as Irishman," *Essex Institute Historical Collections* 111 (October 1975): 267–289; Wayne E. Lee, *Barbarians and Brothers: Anglo-American Warfare, 1500–1865* (New York: Oxford University Press, 2011).

5. Nicholas P. Canny, "The Ideology of English Colonization: From Ireland to America," *William and Mary Quarterly* 30 (October 1973): 596.

6. Kane, "Nits Make Lice," 85, 86; Takaki, "The Tempest in the Wilderness," 892–912.

7. *History of Caldwell and Livingston Counties, Missouri* (St. Louis. MO: National Historical Company, 1886), 149.

8. James Eldridge Quinlan, *Tom Quick, the Indian Slayer: and the Pioneers of Minisink and Warwarsink* (Monticello, New York: Devoe and Quinlan, 1851); republished in 1894 as *The Original Life and Adventures of Tom Quick, the Indian Slayer* (Deposit, NY: Deposit Journal, 1894); republished under the original title by Howard E. Case, Sussex, New Jersey, in 1975.

9. Vernon Leslie, *The Tom Quick Legends* (Middletown, NY: T. Emmett Henderson, 1977), chap. 7.

10. On the Sand Creek Massacre see Ari Kelman, *A Misplaced Massacre: Struggling Over the Memory of Sand Creek* (Cambridge, MA: Harvard University Press, 2013); David Svaldi, *Sand Creek and the Rhetoric of Extermination: A Case-Study in Indian-White Relations* (Lanham, MD: University Press of America, 1989); Stan Hoig, *The Sand Creek Massacre* (Norman: University of Oklahoma Press, 1961); Duane Schultz, *Month of the Freezing Moon: The Sand Creek Massacre, November 1864* (New York: St. Martin's Press, 1990).

11. Kane, "Nits Make Lice," 95, 99.

12. See, for example, Robert F. Berkhofer Jr., *The White Man's Indian: Images of the American Indian from Columbus to the Present* (New York: Alfred A. Knopf, 1978); Philip J. Deloria, *Playing Indian* (New Haven, CT: Yale University Press, 1998); and Ward Churchill, *A Little Matter of Genocide: Holocaust and Denial in the Americas 1492 to the Present* (San Francisco, CA: City Lights Books, 1997) especially pp. 129–288, the essay titled "'Nits Make Lice': The Extermination of North American Indians, 1607–1996."

13. David Lewis, petition to Congress, in *Mormon Redress Petitions: Documents of the 1833–1838 Missouri Conflict*, ed. Clark V. Johnson (Provo, Utah: Religious Studies Center, Brigham Young University, 1992), 276; on the Hawn's Mill massacre (recent scholarship suggests that the spelling should be "Hawn") see Thomas M. Spencer, "'Was This Really Missouri Civilization?': The Haun's Mill Massacre in Missouri and Mormon History," in *The Missouri Mormon Experience*, ed. Thomas M. Spencer (Columbia: University of Missouri Press, 2010), 100–118; Beth Shumway Moore, *Bones in the Well: The Haun's Mill Massacre, 1838, A Documentary History* (Norman, OK: Arthur H. Clark Company, 2006); Alexander L. Baugh, *A Call to Arms: The 1838 Mormon Defense of Northern Missouri*, Dissertations in Latter-day Saint History (Provo, Utah: Joseph Fielding Smith Institute for Latter-day Saint History and BYU Studies, 2000), 116–127; Stephen C. LeSueur, *The 1838 Mormon War in Missouri* (Columbia: University of Missouri Press, 1987), 162–168.

14. *History of Caldwell and Livingston Counties,* 149; Alexander L. Baugh, "Joseph Young's Affidavit of the Massacre at Haun's Mill," *BYU Studies* 38, no. 1 (1999): 188–202; Nathan Kinsman Knight, "Autobiographical Sketch, 1870," MS 2852, CHL; Spencer, "'Was This Really Missouri Civilization?,'" 105–106.

15. Canny, "The Ideology of English Colonization," 596; Kane, "Nits Make Lice," 98. In the Irish and Native American contexts, Kane argues that bound up in the "nits make lice"

metaphor, "the colonized territory, and by extension the empire as a whole is transformed into a host body, infested by parasitic vermin. The indigenous peoples, the Irish or the Native Americans, in the turning of the metaphor become parasites who take their sustenance from a national body to which they offer nothing in exchange." As explained here the Mormon experience at Hawn's Mill does not fit Kane's colonial model perfectly.

16. See Deloria, *Playing Indian*, 8, 40, for insightful questions that inspired those asked here.

17. Richard Lyman Bushman, *Joseph Smith, Rough Stone Rolling: A Cultural Biography of Mormonism's Founder* (New York: Alfred A. Knopf, 2005), 94–99; Terryl L. Givens, *By the Hand of Mormon: The American Scripture that Launched a New World Religion* (New York: Oxford University Press, 2002); Royal Skousen, ed., *The Book of Mormon: The Earliest Text* (New Haven, CT: Yale University Press, 2009); Armand L. Mauss, *All Abraham's Children: Changing Mormon Conceptions of Race and Lineage* (Urbana: University of Illinois Press, 2003), 48–52.

18. Bushman, *Joseph Smith*, 98.

19. Skousen, *The Book of Mormon*, 90.

20. Brigham Young to George A. Smith, 29 May 1856, BYC, CR1234/1, box 17, folder 24 (reel 26); Amasa M. Lyman, Deseret Valley, Nevada, to Brigham Young, Salt Lake City, 20 January 1858, BYC, CR1234/1, box 40, folder 22 (reel 53); Brigham Young to Amasa M. Lyman, 4 February 1858, BYC, CR1234/1, box 18, folder 10 (reel 26).

21. Bushman, *Joseph Smith*, 94–99; Skousen, *The Book of Mormon*, 148.

22. Theda Perdue and Michael D. Green, eds., *The Cherokee Removal: A Brief History with Documents*. 2nd ed. (Boston: Bedford/St. Martin's, 2005), 15–19, 123–128.

23. Lewis Cass, "Removal of the Indians," January 1830, in Perdue and Green, *The Cherokee Removal*, 114–121.

24. Robin Scott Jensen, Robert J. Woodford, Steven C. Harper, *The Joseph Smith Papers: Revelations and Translations, Manuscript Revelation Books*, Facsimile Edition (Salt Lake City: The Church Historian's Press, 2009), 10–11, 53, 55, 583–585; Joseph Smith Jr., comp., *Doctrine and Covenants of the Church of Jesus Christ of Latter-day Saints: Containing Revelations Given to Joseph Smith, the Prophet, with Some Additions by His Successors in the Presidency of the Church* (Salt Lake City, UT: Church of Jesus Christ of Latter-day Saints, 1981), 3: 20; 28:8; 30:5; 32:2–3; see also, Leland H. Gentry, "Light on the 'Mission to the Lamanites,'" *BYU Studies* 36, no. 2 (1996–1997): 226–234; Ronald E. Romig, "The Lamanite Mission," *John Whitmer Historical Association Journal* 14 (1994), 25–33; Terryl L. Givens and Matthew J. Grow, *Parley P. Pratt: The Apostle Paul of Mormonism* (New York: Oxford University Press, 2011), 42; Mark Roscoe Ashurst-McGee, "Zion Rising: Joseph Smith's Early Social and Political Thought, (PhD diss., Arizona State University, 2008), chap. 6.

25. Bushman, *Joseph Smith*, 123; Ronald Walker, "Seeking the 'Remnant': The Native American During the Joseph Smith Period," *Journal of Mormon History* 19 (Spring 1993): 6–10.

26. Gentry, "Light on the 'Mission to the Lamanites,'" 226–234; "Fanatics," *Vermont Watchman and State Gazette* (Montpelier, VT), 14 December 1830.

27. Parley P. Pratt, *The Autobiography of Parley Parker Pratt*, ed. by Parley P. Pratt Jr. (New York: Russell Brothers, 1874; reprint, Salt Lake City: Deseret Book Company, 1985), 41–44; Givens and Grow, *Parley P. Pratt*, 37–47.

28. Romig, "The Lamanite Mission," 25–33; Pratt, *Autobiography*, 44; Givens and Grow, *Parley P. Pratt*, 46–47; Walker, "Seeking the 'Remnant,'" 10–15.

29. Eber D. Howe, *Mormonism Unvailed* (Painesville, OH: Telegraph Press, 1834), 175–221.

30. Booth's letters are published in *The Ohio Star* (Ravenna, OH) as follows: "For the Ohio Star," 13 October 1831; "Mormonism—No II," 20 October 1831; "Mormonism—No. III," 27 October 1831; "Mormonism—No. IV.," vol. 2, no. 44, 3 November 1831; "Mormonism—No. V.," vol. 2, no. 45, 10 November 1831; "Mormonism—No. VI.," vol. 2, no. 46, 17 November 1831; "Mormonism—No. VII.," vol. 2, no. 47, 24 November 1831; "Mormonism—Nos. VIII–IX," 8 December 1831. The third, sixth, eighth, and ninth letters have Indian relations as key themes.

31. "Reuben P. Harmon," *Naked Truths about Mormonism: Also a Journal for Important, Newly Apprehended Truths, and Miscellany* (Oakland, CA) 1, no. 2 (April 1888): 1.

32. Josiah Jones, "History of the Mormonites," *The Evangelist,* June 1841, as reproduced in Milton V. Backman Jr., "A Non-Mormon View of the Birth of Mormonism in Ohio," *BYU Studies* 12, no. 3 (1972): 1–4.

33. John Corrill, *A Brief History of the Church of Christ of Latter Day Saints, (Commonly Called Mormons) Including an Account of Their Doctrine and Discipline; with the Reasons of the Author for Leaving the Church by John Corrill, A Member of the Legislature of Missouri* (St. Louis: Printed for the Author, 1839), 9.

34. "Mormonism—No. III," *Ohio Star,* 27 October 1831.

35. "Mormonism—No. VI," *Ohio Star,* 17 November 1831; Howe, *Mormonism Unvailed,* 196–200.

36. "Mormonism—No. VI," *Ohio Star,* 17 November 1831; Howe, *Mormonism Unvailed,* 196–200.

37. Bushman, *Joseph Smith,* 94–99.

38. Increase and Maria van Deusen, *Spiritual Delusions: Being a Key to the Mysteries of Mormonism, Exposing the Particulars of that Astounding Heresy, the Spiritual-Wife System, as Practiced by Brigham Young, of Utah* (New York: Self-published, 1854), 10.

39. Captain Frederick Marryatt, *Monsieur Violet. His Travels and Adventures among the Snake Indians and Wild Tribes of the Great Western Prairies* (London: Thomas Hodgson, 1849), 285.

40. Catherine Lewis, *Narrative of some of the Proceedings of the Mormons: Giving an Account of their Iniquities, with particulars concerning the training of the Indians by them, Description of the Mode of Endowment, Plurality of Wives, &c., &c.* (Lynn, UT: Self-published, 1848), 13.

41. Jensen, et al., *The Joseph Smith Papers: Revelations and Translations,* 291; Smith, comp., *Doctrine and Covenants* 87: 5, 8.

42. Jensen, et al., *The Joseph Smith Papers: Revelations and Translations,* 10–11, 135; Smith, comp., *Doctrine and Covenants,* 3:20, 49:24.

43. "Mormonism—Nos. VIII – IX," *Ohio Star,* 8 December 1831; H. Michael Marquardt, *The Joseph Smith Revelations: Text and Commentary* (Midvale, UT: Signature Books, 1999), 374–376. On historical debates surrounding the purported revelation see David J. Whittaker, "Mormons and Native Americans: A Historical and Biographical Introduction," *Dialogue: A Journal of Mormon Thought* 18 (Winter 1985): 35; Richard S. Van Wagoner, *Mormon Polygamy: A History* (Salt Lake City, UT: Signature Books, 1989), 3:12–13 n. 2; Lawrence Foster, *Religion and Sexuality: The Shakers, the Mormons, and the Oneida Community* (New York: Oxford University Press, 1981), 134–135, 299. I am indebted to Todd Compton for his assistance with this context.

44. "Mormonism—Nos. VIII–IX," *Ohio Star,* 8 December 1831.

45. For an analysis of this during the Mormon expulsion from Missouri, see T. Ward Frampton, "'Some Savage Tribe': Race, Legal Violence, and the Mormon War of 1838," *Journal of Mormon History* 40 (Winter 2014): 175–207.

46. "To His Excellency, Daniel Dunklin," *Evening and the Morning Star,* December 1833, 114–115; "Mormonism!," *Missouri Intelligencer* (Columbia, MO), 10 August 1833.

47. Canny, "The Ideology of English Colonization," 596.

48. Joseph Smith to W. W. Phelps, 31 July 1832, in *The Personal Writings of Joseph Smith,* comp. and ed. Dean C. Jessee (Salt Lake City, UT: Deseret Book, 1984), 247.

49. Frederick G. Williams, Kirtland, Ohio, to the Missouri Saints, 10 October 1833, Joseph Smith Collection, Letterbook 1, 59, as archived at <http://josephsmithpapers.org/paper-Summary/letterbook-1?dm=image-and-text&zm=zoom-inner&tm=expanded&p=71&s=undefined&sm=none> (accessed 11 September 2013).

50. Isaac McCoy, "The Disturbances in Jackson County," *Daily Missouri Republican* (St. Louis, MO), 20 December 1833.

51. "Public Meeting," *The Latter Day Saints' Messenger and Advocate,* August 1836, 353–355; Sidney Rigdon, Joseph Smith Jr., et al., in Kirtland, Ohio, to John Thornton et al., in Liberty, Missouri, 25 July 1836, in *Latter Day Saints' Messenger and Advocate,* August 1836, 356.

52. Rigdon, et al. to Thornton et al., 25 July 1836, 357; "Public Meeting," 360.

53. Daniel Dunklin to William Wines Phelps, 18 July 1836, Collection of Missouri Documents, 1833–1837, MS 657, folder 8, item 5, CHL, emphasis in original.

54. "Public Meeting," 354.

55. Andrew Jackson, "State of the Union Address," 6 December 1830, in Perdue and Green, *The Cherokee Removal*, 127–128.

56. Stephen C. LeSueur, "Missouri's Failed Compromise: The Creation of Caldwell County for the Mormons," *Journal of Mormon History* 32 (Fall 2005): 113–144; Leland H. Gentry and Todd M. Compton, *Fire and Sword: A History of the Latter-day Saints in Northern Missouri, 1836–39* (Salt Lake City: Greg Kofford Books, 2011), chap. 2; LeSueur, *The 1838 Mormon War*, 25–27; Baugh, *A Call to Arms*, 13; H. E. Robinson, "Mormons in Missouri," *The State Republican* (Jefferson City, MO), 7 February 1895, 1, reprinted from the *Maryville Republican*.

57. LeSueur, *The 1838 Mormon War*, 28–53; Walker, "Seeking the 'Remnant,'" 16–20.

58. Daniel Ashby, James Keyte, and Sterling Price to Governor Boggs, 1 September 1838, in *Document Containing the Correspondence, Orders, &C. In Relation To The Disturbances With The Mormons; And The Evidence Given Before the Hon. Austin A. King* (Fayette, MO: Office of the Boon's Lick Democrat, 1841), 16.

59. John Sapp, affidavit, 4 September 1838, in *Document Containing the Correspondence*, 17.

60. "The Mormon Difficulties," *Niles' National Register*, 13 October 1838, 103.

61. Parley P. Pratt, *Late Persecution of the Church of Jesus Christ of Latter-day Saints. Ten Thousand American Citizens Robbed, Plundered, and Banished; Others Imprisoned, and Others Martyred for their Religion. With a Sketch of their Rise, Progress and Doctrine. By P. P. Pratt, Minister of the Gospel: Written in Prison* (New York: J. W. Harrison, 1840), xii.

62. General Parks to General Atchison, Carroll County, 7 October 1838, in *Documents Containing the Correspondence*, 37–38.

63. Governor Lilburn W. Boggs, to General John B. Clark, 27 October 1838, in *Documents Containing the Correspondence*, 61. There is no evidence to suggest that the Missouri militiamen who conducted the massacre at Hawn's Mill knew of the extermination order.

64. Peter Crawley, "Two Rare Missouri Documents," *BYU Studies* 14 (Summer 1974): 502–527; Sidney Rigdon, *Oration Delivered by Mr. S. Rigdon, on the 4th of July, 1838 at Far West, Caldwell County, Missouri* (Far West: Journal Office, 1838), 12; Jared Farmer, *On Zion's Mount: Mormons, Indians, and the American Landscape* (Cambridge, MA: Harvard University Press, 2008), 71.

65. Richard Slotkin, *The Fatal Environment: The Myth of the Frontier in the Age of Industrialization, 1800–1890* (Norman: University of Oklahoma Press, 1985), 275–276, 320–321, 449–450.

66. Jedediah M. Grant, *A Collection of Facts Relative to the Course Taken by Elder Sidney Rigdon in the States of Ohio, Missouri, Illinois and Pennsylvania* (Philadelphia: Brown, Bricking and Guilbert, Printers, 1844), 11.

67. "Continuation of Elder Rigdon's Trial," *Times and Seasons*, 1 October 1844, 667. Young's and Grant's remarks should be understood within the context of Rigdon's efforts to assume control over the LDS Church following the murder of Joseph Smith Jr. Young and Rigdon engaged in a power struggle over succession, and his and Grant's comments regarding Rigdon's speech grow out of efforts to discredit Rigdon's claims to leadership, yet they still indicate an awareness of the Mormons' precarious position as a minority in Missouri in 1838 and the impact Rigdon's speech had on the unraveling there.

68. Anderson, "Atchison's Letters," 3–47; Rigdon, "Oration," 12; Pratt, *Late Persecution*, 59.

69. *Warsaw Signal* (Warsaw, IL), 12 June 1844, 1, emphasis in original.

70. "Extra," *Warsaw Signal*, 14 June 1844, 1.

71. "The Mormon Question: Shall We Admit Into the Union An Anti-Christian and Barbarous State?" *Christian Advocate and Journal*, 19 July 1855.

72. Joseph Smith to the Pottawattamie Indians, 28 August 1843, Joseph Smith Papers, Letters Sent, Box 2, folder 6, CHL.

73. Henry King, Keokuk, Iowa Territory, to Gov. John Chambers, Burlington, Iowa, 14 July 1843, Iowa Superintendency, 1838–49, Letters Received by the Office of Indian Affairs, 1824–81, BIA Microfilm #363, 357–360; see also, Chambers to T. Hartley Crawford, Washington, DC, 7 August 1843, 361–362.

74. "Mormon Affairs," *New York Daily Tribune*, 13 November 1844, 2.

75. Lewis, *Narrative of some of the Proceedings of the Mormons*, 15–16.

76. William P. Richards, "Great Western Move," and "An Act for the Relief of the People Called Mormons, or Latter Day Saints," *Nauvoo Neighbor* (Nauvoo, IL), 26 February 1845.

77. "Answer to a Letter," *Nauvoo Neighbor*, 26 February 1845; Annette P. Hampshire, "Thomas Sharp and Anti-Mormon Sentiment in Illinois, 1842–1845," *Journal of Illinois State Historical Society* 72 (May 1979), 98–100. I am indebted to Alan Morrill for bringing the latter reference to my attention.

78. Hampshire, "Thomas Sharp," 98–100.

79. Brigham Young, "The Constitution and Government of the United States—Rights and Policy of the Latter-Day Saints," 18 February 1855, *Journal of Discourses* 2 (London and Liverpool: Latter-day Saints' Book Depot, 1855), 172–173.

80. Warren Foote, "Autobiography of Warren Foote, son of David Foote a decendant [*sic*] of Nathaniel Foote the Settler who came from England about 1633 and was one of the First settlers in Weathersfield Conectticut [*sic*]," vol. 1: 96, microfilm holograph, CHL.

Chapter 3

1. Richard F. Burton, *The City of the Saints and Across the Rocky Mountains to California* (New York: Harper and Brothers Publishers, 1862), 2, 208, 339; *Reports of Explorations and Surveys, to Ascertain the Most Practicable and Economical Route for a Railroad from the Mississippi River to the Pacific Ocean. Made under the Direction of the Secretary of War, in 1853–4, According to acts of Congress of March 3, 1853, May 31, 1854, and August 5, 1854*. Vol. 2 (Washington, DC: Beverley Tucker, Printer, 1855), 74, Senate Ex. Doc. No. 78, 33rd Cong., 2d Sess. See also: Andrew Joseph Gunnison, San Francisco, to Martha A. Delony Gunnison, 16 March 1854, Gunnison Collection, box 1, HM 17093, HL; Brigham Young, Salt Lake City, to Mrs. J. W. Gunnison, Grand Rapids, Michigan, 30 November 1853, BYC, CR1234/1, box 17, folder 10 (reel 25), CHL; and Ronald W. Walker, "President Young Writes Jefferson Davis about the Gunnison Massacre Affair," *BYU Studies* 35, no. 1 (1995): 147–170.

2. Colin G. Colloway, "Neither White Nor Red: White Renegades on the American Indian Frontier," *Western Historical Quarterly* 17 (January 1986): 43–66.

3. W. Paul Reeve, *Making Space on the Western Frontier: Mormons, Miners, and Southern Paiutes* (Urbana: University of Illinois Press, 2006), 66–67.

4. JH, 7 May 1849, 1–2; Robert Glass Cleland and Juanita Brooks, eds., *A Mormon Chronicle: The Diaries of John D. Lee, 1848–1876* (San Marino, CA: Huntington Library, 1955; Salt Lake City: University of Utah Press, 1983), 108.

5. Brigham Young, to the Saints in Parowan and Cedar City and the regions around Iron County, October–November 1851, BYC, CR1234/1, box 16, folder 22 (reel 25), CHL; Jared Farmer, *On Zion's Mount: Mormons, Indians, and the American Landscape* (Cambridge, MA: Harvard University Press, 2008), 54–82; Howard A. Christy, "Open Hand and Mailed Fist: Mormon-Indian Relations in Utah, 1847–52," *Utah Historical Quarterly* 46 (Summer 1978): 216–235; Howard A. Christy, "The Walker War: Defense and Conciliation as Strategy," *Utah Historical Quarterly* 47 (Fall 1979): 395–420.

6. Young to the Saints in Parowan and Cedar City, October–November 1851.

7. JH, 16 May 1851, 1; Wilford Woodruff, *Wilford Woodruff's Journal, 1833–1898*, vol. 4, ed. Scott G. Kenney (Midvale, UT: Signature Books, 1983), 26; Elder Marion J. Shelton, Harmony, Washington Co., Utah, to George A. Smith, Salt Lake City, JH, 18 December 1858, 2–3. For a detailed examination of the robbers as cultural discourse, see W. Paul Reeve, "'As

Ugly as Evil' and 'As Wicked as Hell': Gadianton Robbers and the Legend Process among the Mormons," *Journal of Mormon History* 27 (Fall 2001): 125–149.

8. For broader context on Indian conversions reconceived as "affiliations" and "hybrid" religious cultures see Linford D. Fisher, *The Indian Great Awakening: Religion and the Shaping of Native Cultures in Early America* (New York: Oxford University Press, 2012) and Tracy Neal Leavelle, *The Catholic Calumet: Colonial Conversions in French and Indian North America* (Philadelphia: University of Pennsylvania Press, 2012).

9. Brigham Young, Salt Lake City, to Chief Walker, 14 May 1849, BYC, CR1234/1, box 16, folder 17 (reel 24), CHL; Lawerence Coates, review of *Blood of the Prophets*, by Will Bagley, *BYU Studies* 42.1 (2003): 156; Scott Christensen, *Sagwitch: Shoshone Chieftan, Mormon Elder, 1822–1887* (Logan: Utah State University Press, 1999); James G. Bleak, "Annals of the Southern Utah Mission," vol. B, typescript, 401, 403–404, 407–416, Special Collections, JWML; JH, 24 March 1850, 9 June 1850, 1; Young to Walker, 9 April 1852, BYC, 1234/1, box 17, folder 1 (reel 25), CHL; Reeve, *Making Space*, 75–77.

10. Christy, "The Walker War."

11. David L. Bigler, *Fort Limhi: The Mormon Adventure in Oregon Territory, 1855–1858* (Spokane, WA: Arthur H. Clark Company, 2003); Gregory E. Smoak, *Ghost Dances and Identity: Prophetic Religion and American Indian Ethnogenesis in the Nineteenth Century* (Berkeley: University of California Press, 2006), 71–80.

12. John Alton Peterson, *Utah's Black Hawk War* (Salt Lake City: University of Utah Press, 1998).

13. Council, North Bank, Platt River, to John Smith, Winter Quarters, 4 May 1847, BYC, CR 1234/1, box 16, folder 12 (Reel 24), CHL; Orson Hyde, Council Bluffs, to H. Felt, 21 June 1847, BYC, CR1234/1, box 39, folder 17 (reel 53), CHL; George A. Smith and Ezra T. Benson, Winter Quarters, to Brigham Young, 28 June 1848, BYC, CR1234/1, box 42, folder 3 (reel 55), CHL; James Bridger, Blacks Fork, to Brigham Young, 16 July 1848, BYC, CR1234/1, box 21, folder 10 (reel 30), CHL; Stanley B. Kimball, "The Captivity Narrative on Mormon Trails, 1846-65," *Dialogue: A Journal of Mormon Thought* 18 (Winter 1985), 82, found "very little fear of Indians" manifest in the trail journals he studied.

14. Brigham Young, et al., to President of the United States, 15 April 1850, BYC, CR1234/1, miscellaneous letterbook, 1844-1853 (Romney typescript), CHL; Brigham Young to Abner Morton, 29 May 1852, BYC, CR1234/1, box 17, folder 1 (reel 25), CHL; Brigham Young, Salt Lake City, to John M. Bernhisel, Washington, DC, 27 May 1852, BYC, CR1234/1, box 60, folder 2 (reel 70), CHL; Brigham Young to Millard Fillmore, 11 June 1852, BYC, CR1234/1, box 51, folder 3 (reel 64), CHL.

15. Brigham Young, Salt Lake City, to John M. Bernhisel, Washington, DC, 28 February 1852, BYC, 1234/1, box 60, folder 2 (reel 70), CHL (this letter is to Bernhisel, a Mormon, but was designed to influence the narrative that Bernhisel constructed to influence politicians in Congress).

16. Brigham Young to Stephen B. Rose, 10 February 1854, BYC, CR1234/1, box 50, Gubernatorial Letterbook, pp. 53–54 (reel 63), CHL.

17. Brigham Young to Jefferson Davis, 29 April 1854, BYC, CR1234/1, box 50, Gubernatorial Letterbook, pp. 82–83 (reel 63), CHL. This was a message the Saints continued to repeat, especially for an outside audience. See, for example, George Q. Cannon's speech when US Congressman James M. Ashley from Toledo, Ohio, was present and Utah Territorial Delegate, William H. Hooper's speech to Congress: "Celebration of the Fourth," *Deseret News* (Salt Lake City, UT), 5 July 1865, 4; "Extension of Boundaries, Speech of Hon. William H. Hooper, of Utah, Delivered in the House of Representatives, February 25, 1869," *Congressional Globe and Appendix*, 40th Cong., 3d Sess., pt. 3, Appendix (Washington, DC: F. and J. Rives and George A. Bailey, 1869).

18. Margaret D. Jacobs, "The Eastmans and the Luhans: Interracial Marriage between White Women and Native American Men, 1875–1935," *Frontiers: A Journal of Women Studies* 23:3 (2002): 32, 50 n.13.

19. Kimball, "Captivity Narrative," 82; Heber C. Kimball, Journal, 14 October 1845, Heber Chase Kimball Collection, MS 652, box 1, folder 19, Special Collections, JWML.

20. Richard E. Bennett, "Cousin Laman in the Wilderness: The Beginnings of Brigham Young's Indian Policy," *Nebraska History* 67 (Spring 1986): 68–82; Richard E. Bennett, *Mormons at the Missouri: Winter Quarters, 1846–1852* (1987; repr., Norman: University of Oklahoma Press 2004), 95.

21. Scott G. Kenney, ed., *Wilford Woodruff's Journal*, 28 July 1847 (Midvale, UT: Signature Books, 1985), 3: 240–241 (I am indebted to Barbara Jones Brown for bringing this reference to my attention); Will Bagley, "The Pioneer Camp of the Saints: The 1846 and 1847 Mormon Trail Journals of Thomas Bullock" (Logan: Utah State University Press, 1997), 243; for other iterations of the same speech see Richard S. Van Wagoner, *The Complete Discourses of Brigham Young*, vol. 1 (Salt Lake City, UT: The Smith-Pettit Foundation, 2009), 234–238.

22. James S. Brown, *Giant of the Lord: Life of a Pioneer* (Salt Lake City, UT: Bookcraft, 1960), 320–321; Richard Darrell Kitchen, "Mormon-Indian Relations in Deseret: Intermarriage and Indenture, 1847 to 1877," (PhD diss., Arizona State University, 2002), 22–24.

23. Brigham Young to James Brown, 14 June 1855, BYC, CR1234/1, Letterbook 2, (Romney typescript), pp. 202–204, CHL; Kitchen, "Mormon-Indian Relations in Deseret," 139–150.

24. Juanita Brooks, ed., *On the Mormon Frontier: The Diary of Hosea Stout, 1844–1861* (Salt Lake City: University of Utah Press and Utah State Historical Society, 1964), 2:516–517.

25. Henry Weeks Sanderson, Diary of Henry Weeks Sanderson, MS photocopy, 97, LTPSC.

26. Elder Marion J. Shelton, Harmony, Washington Co., Utah, to George A. Smith, Salt Lake City, JH, 18 December 1858, 2–3.

27. Todd M. Compton, *A Frontier Life: Jacob Hamblin, Explorer and Indian Missionary* (Salt Lake City: University of Utah Press, 2013), 170–173, 487; Kitchen, "Mormon-Indian Relations in Deseret," 233–237.

28. Mrs. B. G. Ferris [Elizabeth Cornelia Woodcock Ferris] *The Mormons at Home; With some Incidents of Travel from Missouri to California, 1852–3. In a Series of Letters.* (New York: Harper and Brothers, 1854; Dix and Edwards, 1856), 165–167.

29. JH, 23 June 1854, 2; Peter Gottfredson, *History of Indian Depredations in Utah* (Salt Lake City, UT: Skelton Publishing, 1919), 77–78; Paul Bailey, *Walkara: Hawk of the Mountains* (Los Angeles: Westernlore Press), 164; Gustive O. Larson, "Wákara's Half Century," *Western Humanities Review* 6 (Summer 1952): 255–257; Terryl L. Givens and Matthew J. Grow, *Parley P. Pratt: The Apostle Paul of Mormonism* (New York: Oxford University Press, 2011), 262, 277–278; for a different version of the story see Austin N. Ward, *The Husband in Utah; or, Sights and Scenes among the Mormons: with remarks on their moral and social economy by Austin N Ward. Edited by Maria Ward, Author of "Female Life Among the Mormons."* (New York: Derby and Jackson, 1857), 281.

30. Ward, *The Husband in Utah*, 33–34, 66–67.

31. John Demos, *The Unredeemed Captive: A Family Story from Early America* (New York: Vintage Books, 1995); Fairfax Downey, *Indian-Fighting Army* (New York: Charles Scribner's Sons, 1944), 99; "Affairs at Salt Lake City," *Harper's Weekly*, 1 May 1858.

32. Mark Twain, *Roughing It* (Berkeley and Los Angeles: Mark Twain Project of the Bancroft Library and University of California Press, 1995), 103–104.

33. J. H. Beadle, "The Mormon Theocracy," *Scribners Monthly: An Illustrated Magazine for the People* 14.3 (July 1877): 394.

34. Joan Smyth Iversen, *The Antipolygamy Controversy in U.S. Women's Movements, 1880–1925: A Debate on the American Home* (New York: Routledge, 1997), 108–111; "The Beauties of Polygamy," *Anti-Polygamy Standard* (Salt Lake City, UT), April 1880, 1.

35. San Pete, "Eds. Standard," *Anti-Polygamy Standard*, October 1880, 45.

36. See Patricia Nelson Limerick, *The Legacy of Conquest: The Unbroken Past of the American West* (New York: W. W. Norton, 1987), chap. 3 and Earl S. Pomery, *The Territories and the United States, 1861–1890: Studies in Colonial Administration* (Philadelphia: University of

Pennsylvania Press, 1947) for further evidence of frustration with the territorial system and its weaknesses.

37. Richard D. Poll and William P. MacKinnon, "Causes of the Utah War Reconsidered," *Journal of Mormon History* 20 (Fall 1994): 16–44.

38. On the negotiated peace, see Matthew J. Grow, *"Liberty to the Downtrodden": Thomas L. Kane, Romantic Reformer* (New Haven, CT: Yale University Press, 2009), chapters 9 and 10.

39. Ronald W. Walker, Richard E. Turley Jr., and Glen M. Leonard, *Massacre at Mountain Meadows: An American Tragedy* (New York: Oxford University Press, 2008); Juanita Brooks, *Mountain Meadows Massacre* (Norman: University of Oklahoma Press, 1950); Will Bagley, *Blood of the Prophets: Brigham Young and the Massacre at Mountain Meadows* (Norman: University of Oklahoma Press, 2002).

40. Robert H. Briggs, "The Mountain Meadows Massacre: An Analytical Narrative Based on Participant Confessions," *Utah Historical Quarterly* 74 (Fall 2006): 313–333; Will Bagley, et al., and Robert Briggs, "Letters," *Utah Historical Quarterly* 75 (Summer 2007): 292–295; Shannon A. Novak, *A House of Mourning: A Biocultural History of the Mountain Meadows Massacre* (Salt Lake City: University of Utah Press, 2008), 174–177; Gary Tom and Ronald Holt, "The Paiute Tribe of Utah," in *A History of Utah's American Indians*, ed. Forrest S. Cuch (Salt Lake City: Utah State Division of Indian Affairs and Utah State Division of History, 2000), 131–139; David L. Bigler and Will Bagley, *Innocent Blood: Essential Narratives of the Mountain Meadows Massacre* (Norman, OK: Arthur H. Clark Company, 2008), 453–460.

41. Homer Brown diary, 20 September 1857, MS 2181 1, CHL; John D. Lee speech, Utah Stake minutes, LR 9629 11, 27 September 1857, CHL; Samuel Pitchforth, diary, 30 September 1857, typescript, CHL; Andrew Hunter Scott, diary, entry for 12 September–1 October 1857, in *Susan Tate Laing*, ed. *Andrew Hunter Scott: Builder in the Kingdom* (Provo, Utah: The Andrew Hunter Scott Genealogical Association, 2001), 530; Historian's Office journal, 28 and 29 September 1857, CHL; John D. Lee, Harmony, Utah, to Brigham Young, Salt Lake City, 20 November 1857, BYC, CR1234/1, box 25, folder 14 (reel 35), CHL; Brigham Young, Salt Lake City, to William J. Cox, San Bernardino, California, 4 December 1857, BYC, CR1234/1, Letterpress copybook 3, p. 929–932 (Romney typescript); George A. Smith, Parowan, Utah, to Brigham Young, Salt Lake City, 17 August 1858, BYC, CR1234/1, box 42, folder 6 (reel 55).

42. J. Cecil Alter and Robert J. Dwyer, eds. "Journal of Captain Albert Tracy," 19 March 1859, *Utah Historical Quarterly* 13 (1945): 58.

43. James Henry Carleton, *Report on the Subject of the Massacre at Mountain Meadows in Utah Territory in September 1857* (Little Rock, AR: True Democrat Steam Press Print, 1860), 19–20.

44. Report of the Secretary of the Interior, 36th Cong., 1st Sess., 1859, *The Congressional Globe: Containing the Debates and Proceedings of the First Session of the Thirty-Sixth Congress* (Washington, DC: John C. Rives, 1860), Appendix, 29.

45. Peter Shirts statement, [*ca.* 1876], Bureau of American Ethnology, MS 3141, National Archives; Annie Elizabeth Hoag, testimony, *United States v. John D. Lee*, First Trial, Boreman Collection, 4:28–29, HL; Nephi Johnson, testimony, *United States v. John D. Lee*, Second Trial, Jacob S. Boreman Transcript, Jacob S. Boreman Collection, 1:45, HL. I am indebted to Michael Shamo for his generous assistance on this and the next two paragraphs.

46. Walker, et al., *Massacre at Mountain Meadows*, 206.

47. James Henry Carleton, Report on the Subject of the Massacre at the Mountain Meadows in Utah Territory in September 1857 (Little Rock, AR: True Democrat Steam Press Print, 1860), 19–20; John Cradlebaugh, "Utah and the Mormons," Delivered in the House of Representatives, 7 February 1863, 17–19; W. H. Rogers, "The Mountain Meadows Massacre: Statement of Mr. Wm. H. Rogers," *The Valley Tan*, 29 February 1860 also quoted in Juanita Brooks, *The Mountain Meadows Massacre* (1950; repr. Norman: University of Oklahoma Press, 1991), 274; James Lynch, affidavit, US Senate, Message of the President of

the United States Communicating, In Compliance with a Resolution of the Senate, Information in Relation to the Massacre at Mountain Meadows, and Other Massacres in Utah Territory, 36th Cong., 1st Sess., 1860. Sen. Ex. Doc. 42. Serial 1033, 81–85.

48. Walker, et al., *Massacre at Mountain Meadows*, 268, 349–350, note 77; C. F. McGlashan, "The Mountain Meadows Massacre," *Sacramento Daily Record*, 1 January 1875; "Our Los Angeles Correspondence," *Daily Alta California*, 27 October 1857.

49. Richard E. Turley Jr. and Ronald W. Walker, *Mountain Meadows Massacre: The Andrew Jenson and David H. Morris Collections* (Provo, UT: Brigham Young University Press, 2009), 185–187. See also p. 175 for the Joseph Clewes account. Bull Valley Snort [John M. Higbee], statement, Feb. 1894, 2–3, Mountain Meadows Massacre collected material, CHL; also quoted in Brooks, *The Mountain Meadows Massacre*, 227.

50. None of the historians who have studied the massacre to date have taken into account the stories of Mormons dressing as Indians as a cultural discourse that predated the massacre. John Unruh Jr. does discuss allegations of white Indians that predate the massacre but does not make the same connections made here. See his *The Plains Across: The Overland Emigrants and the Trans-Mississippi West, 1840–60* (1979; repr. Urbana: University of Illinois Press, 1993), 193–197 and the map on p. 172 for his treatment of Mormons. On William Smith see D. Michael Quinn, "The Mormon Succession Crisis of 1844," *BYU Studies* 16 (Winter 1976): 187–233.

51. "The Salt Lake Banditti," *Melchisedek & Aaronic Herald* (Covington, KY), February 1850.

52. "The Mormons of Deseret or Salt Lake," *State Gazette* (Trenton, NJ), 13 March 1850; John M. Bernhisel, Washington DC to Brigham Young, Salt Lake City, 21 March 1850, BYC, CR1234/1, box 60, folder 9 (reel 70), CHL; "The Mormons of Deseret, or Salt Lake" *New York Herald*, 8 March 1850.

53. Pauline Wonderly, *Reminiscences of a Pioneer*, ed. John Barton Hassler (Placerville, CA: El Dorado Country Historical Society, 1965), 3, California State Library, California History Room, Sacramento, California.

54. Alfreda Eva Bell, *Boadicea; The Mormon Wife: Life-Scenes in Utah* (New York: Arthur R. Orton, 1855), 81.

55. Bell, *Boadicea*, 81.

56. Garland Hurt to George W. Manypenny, 2 May 1855, in *Report of the Commissioner of Indian Affairs, Accompanying the Annual Report of the Secretary of the Interior for the Year 1857* (Washington, DC: William A. Harris, Printer, 1858), 305–306.

57. Hurt to Manypenny, 2 May 1855.

58. Charles E. Mix to Robert McClelland, 10 July 1855, in *Report of the Commissioner*, 306–307; Charles E. Mix, "Memoranda for Secretary of the Interior," 13 August 1855, in *Report of the Commissioner*, 307–308.

59. "The Mormons in Utah," *National Era* (Washington, DC), 28 June 1855.

60. Garland Hurt to George W. Manypenny, 30 August 1856, "The Utah Expedition," House Ex. Doc. 72 (35-1), 1858, Serial 956, 179.

61. Richard S. Van Wagoner, *The Complete Discourses of Brigham Young*, vol. 2 (Salt Lake City: The Smith-Pettit Foundation, 2009), 8 April 1855, 930.

62. Hurt to Manypenny, 2 May 1855, 305.

63. Jesse Smith, "Journal," 320, 341, 347 (25 March 1883, 18 January, 17 May 1884), Jesse N. Smith Papers, LTPSC.

64. Daniel Justin Herman, *Hell on the Range: A Story of Honor, Conscience, and the American West* (New Haven, CT, and London: Yale University Press, 2010), 80, 85; John Henry Standifird, diaries, 29 March 1885, MS 1192, typescript, microfilm, CHL. Standifird was working on the Manti, Utah Temple at the time he made this entry. See also Scott Christensen, *Sagwitch*, p. 130, for an example of the Shoshone attempting to induce Mormon missionary George W. Hill to join them in fighting soldiers as a part of their Book of Mormon destiny.

65. Young to Brown, 14 June 1855.

66. Diary of Helen McCowen Carpenter, 1856, 20–21, 43, California State Library, California History Room, Sacramento, California.

67. Emily McCowen Horton, *My Scrapbook* (Seattle, WA: n.p. 1927), 22–23; Diary of Helen McCowen Carpenter, 1856, 43.

68. William Smith, "Mormonism. A Letter from William Smith, Brother of Joseph, the Prophet," *New York Daily Tribune*, 28 May 1857; "Mormonism," *National Era*, 11 June 1857.

69. Dimick B. Huntington, Journal, 1857–1859, 9–14, MS 1419 2, CHL.

70. Huntington, Journal, 9–14; Bigler, *Fort Limhi*; Walker, et al., *Massacre at Mountain Meadows*, 146–148. Compton, *A Frontier Life*, 67–68, chronicles an incident in 1854 where Southern Paiutes offered to help the Mormons if "the Americans ever came here to fight the Mormons" and replace Young as "Captain."

71. Horace Bucklin to Brigham Young, November 1857, BYC, CR1234/1, box 25, folder 12 (reel 35), CHL.

72. A. R. Burbank, Portland, Oregon Territory, to Alfred Cumming, 12 December 1857, BYC, CR1234/1, box 25, folder 12 (reel 35), CHL.

73. "Mormon and Indian Alliance," *The National Era*, 3 December 1857.

74. *Message from the President of the United States, to the Two Houses of Congress at the Commencement of the First Session of the Thirty-Fifth Congress* House of Representatives, Ex. Doc. No. 2, 35th Cong., 1st Sess. (Washington DC: Cornelius Wendell, Printer, 1857), 7–8.

75. *Message from the President*, 8.

76. "Remarks," Alfred Cumming, Tabernacle, 25 April 1858, BYC, CR1234/1, Letterbook 4, 157–160 (Romney typescript), CHL.

77. "Remarks," Gilbert Clements, Tabernacle, 25 April 1858, BYC, CR1234/1, Letterbook 4, 168–188 (Romney typescript), CHL.

78. Brigham Young, Salt Lake City to Jacob B. Bigler, Nephi, Utah, 17 July 1858, BYC, CR1234/1, Letterpress copybook 3, 300 (Romney typescript), CHL.

79. Brigham Young, Salt Lake City, to George Q. Cannon, Philadelphia, Pennsylvania, 23 June 1859, BYC, CR1234/1, box 18, folder 18 (reel 26), CHL.

80. "Defiant Attitude of Brigham Young and ye Indians towards ye Uncle Sam," *Yankee Notions*, April 1858.

81. "Public Meeting," *Los Angeles Star*, 13 October 1857.

82. "Later from the South," *Daily Alta California* (San Francisco, CA) 27 October 1857; "More Outrages on the Plains!!" *Los Angeles Star*, 24 October 1857.

83. "The Mormons in the Capacity of Savages," *San Joaquin Republican* (Stockton, CA) 29 October 1857 (I am indebted to Michael Landon for sharing this source with me). Argus [Charles Wesley Wandell], "An Open Letter to Brigham Young," *Daily Utah Reporter* (Corinne, UT) 12 September 1870.

84. "The Federal Government and Utah," *Southern Vineyard* (Los Angeles, CA), 29 May 1858. This may be the first post-massacre account of Mormons dressed as Indians, an assessment arrived at after doing key word searches of 139 newspaper accounts and nineteen government documents digitized at *Horrible Massacre of Emigrants!!: The Mountain Meadows Massacre in Public Discourse*, a digital history project <http://mountainmeadows.unl.edu/index.html> established by Dr. Douglas Seefeldt at the University of Nebraska, Lincoln. It is impossible to be exhaustive in such an endeavor, and therefore it is distinctly possible that earlier accounts exist of Mormons disguised as Indians.

85. "The Mountain Meadows Massacre," *San Francisco Daily Evening Bulletin* (San Francisco, CA), 31 May 1859; "Revolution of Affairs in Mormondom," *San Francisco Daily Evening Bulletin*, 25 August 1859.

86. "The Massacre at Mountain Meadows," *Christian Observer* (Philadelphia, PA), 8 September 1859.

87. James Henry Carleton, *Special Report of the Mountain Meadow Massacre, by J. H. Carleton, Brevet Major, United States Army, Captain, First Dragoons*, US House. 57th Cong., 1st sess.

(Washington, DC: GPO, 1902), House Doc. 605, Serial 4377; James Lynch, "James Lynch Affidavit, Utah Territory, Cedar County," in James Buchanan, *Message of the President of the United States, communicating, in compliance with a resolution of the Senate, information in relation to the Massacre at Mountain Meadows, and other Massacres in Utah Territory*, US Senate. 36th Cong., 1st Sess. (Washington, DC: GPO, 1860), Senate Exec. Doc. 42, Serial 1033, 81–85; John Cradlebaugh, *Utah and the Mormons: Speech of Hon. John Cradlebaugh, of Nevada, on the Admission of Utah as a State. Delivered in the House of Representatives, February 7, 1863*, (Washington, DC: L Towers and Co., Printers, 1863); James Henry Carleton. "Camp at Mountain Meadows, Utah Territory, May 25, 1859," in *McGrorty v. Hooper, July 9, 1868—laid on the table and ordered to be printed*, US House. 40th Cong., 2nd Sess. (Washington, DC: GPO, 1868), House Exec. Report 79, 26–40.

88. C. V. Waite, *The Mormon Prophet and His Harem; or, an Authentic History of Brigham Young, His Numerous Wives and Children*. 5th ed. (Chicago: J. S. Goodman and Co., 1868), 74–76.

89. Twain, *Roughing It*, xxvii, 550–551. Historians continue to contest the validity of such accounts. Ronald Walker, Richard Turley, and Glenn Leonard include in their book on the massacre at least two Mormons, Willden and Clewes, who dressed as Indians during the five-day siege, but not at the massacre itself. They also leave open the possibility that Lee painted his face for the initial attack (Walker, et al., *Massacre at Mountain Meadows*, 158, 172–173, 205–206). Will Bagley's version threads the charge throughout his narrative. "In the moonlit darkness," Mormons "stripped for battle and donned war paint to disguise themselves as Indians" as they prepared for the initial attack on 7 September. At the massacre itself, Bagley moves the stories from rumor and innuendo to specified fact, with "some fifteen whites," some of whom he identified by name, "donned war paint and hid in the grass and brush" waiting for the signal to commence their butchery (Bagley, *Blood of the Prophets*, 122, 143; see also 120, 125, 130, 147, 154, 193, 227, 228, 230, and 327). Anthropologist Shannon A. Novak relies uncritically upon Bagley and then takes the accusation beyond fact to academic analysis. She incorrectly writes that Mormon participant Nephi Johnson later "admitted that some of the 'Indians' who attacked the women and children 'were Mormons in disguise,'" a statement not found in any of Johnson's known accounts to date. For her, Mormons who "played" Indians at the massacre did so as a way to cross the "boundaries of civilized behavior," a type of "performance" for them that "must have been liberating" (Novak, *House of Mourning*, 176–177). While Novak contemplated what Mormons "playing Indian" at the massacre may have meant to the Mormons, none of the scholars who have studied the massacre have yet considered what the accusations meant to the various peoples who repeated them. On Nephi Johnson see, Nephi Johnson, testimony, *United States v. John D. Lee,* second trial, Rogerson and Boreman transcripts and shorthand notes; Francis M. Lyman, "Diary Excerpts of Francis M. Lyman, 1892–1896," typescript, in *New Mormon Studies CD-ROM: A Comprehensive Resource Library* (Salt Lake City, UT: Smith Research Associates, [1998]), September 19, 21, 1895; Nephi Johnson, affidavit, 22 July 1908, First Presidency, Cumulative Correspondence, 1900–1949, CHL, also in Turley and Walker, *Mountain Meadows Massacre: The Andrew Jenson Collection* (Provo, UT: BYU Press, 2009), 328–331; Nephi Johnson, affidavit, 30 November 1909 in Turley and Walker, *Mountain Meadows Massacre: The Andrew Jenson Collection* (Provo, UT: BYU Press, 2009), 332–334, also quoted (with some differences) in Juanita Brooks, *The Mountain Meadows Massacre* (1950; repr. Norman: University of Oklahoma Press, 1991), 224–226; Nephi Johnson, letter to Anthon H. Lund, March 1910, CHL; Nephi Johnson, conversation with Anthony W. Ivins, 2 September 1917, typescript, Anthony W. Ivins Collection, USHS. I am indebted to Michael Shamo for his assistance with the Nephi Johnson references.

90. Rebecca Dunlap: "Mountain Meadow Massacre: The Butchery of a Train of Arkansans by Mormon and Indians While on their Way to California," *Fort Smith Elevator*, 20 August 1897; Martha Elizabeth Baker: Clyde R. Greenhaw, "Survivor of a Massacre," *Arkansas Gazette*, 4 September 1938.

91. Tom and Holt, "The Paiute Tribe of Utah," 134–135, for other Southern Paiute accounts see 135–139; Bigler and Bagley, *Innocent Blood,* 453–460; and Logan Hebner, *Southern Paiute: A Portrait* (Logan: Utah State University Press, 2010).

92. Bigler and Bagley, *Innocent Blood,* 434.

93. Gary Tom and Ronald Holt, concluded that "there is certainly some evidence that Indians with base camps on the Muddy and Santa Clara Rivers were involved at least in the initial siege of the wagon train," while historians David Bigler and Will Bagley likewise believe that there is "enough historical evidence to argue that a few Paiutes were more than mere spectators at Mountain Meadows." Tom and Holt, "The Paiute Tribe of Utah," 134–135, 138; Bigler and Bagley, *Innocent Blood,* 460.

94. "Territory of Nevada," 35th Cong., 1st Sess., House Report No. 375, 12 May 1858, serial set 966, 4.

95. Dwight Eveleth, San Francisco, to Brigham Young, Salt Lake City, 28 May 1860, BYC, CR1234/1, box 27, folder 12 (reel 37), CHL; Phineas W. Cook, Stockton, California, to Brigham Young, Salt Lake City, 8 June 1860, BYC, CR1234/1, box 27, folder 11 (reel 37), CHL.

96. Argus [Charles Wesley Wandell], "An Open Letter," 12 September 1870.

97. Smoak, *Ghost Dances and Identity,* 121–134; Brigham D. Madsen, *Corinne: The Gentile Capital of Utah* (Salt Lake City: Utah State Historical Society, 1980), 272–289; "At Deep Creek U.T." *Daily Inter-Ocean* (Chicago, IL) 20 June 1874.

98. Madsen, *Corinne,* 285–287; "Do the Mormons Mean War?" *Omaha Daily Bee* (Omaha, NE), 16 July 1874; *St. Cloud Journal* (St. Cloud, MN), 12 August 1875; "Apprehension of Trouble with the Mormon Indians," *Arizona Sentinel* (Yuma, AZ), 14 August 1875.

99. A. J. Barnes to Edward P. Smith, 11 September 1875, *Annual Report of the Commissioner of Indian Affairs* (Washington, DC: Government Printing Office, 1875), 338; C. A. Bateman, Pyramid Lake Reserve, Nev., to Hon. E. P. Smith, Commissioner of Indian Affairs, 10 September 1875, *Annual Report of the Commissioner of Indian Affairs* (Washington, DC: Government Printing Office, 1875), 342.

100. "The Indian Messiah," *Deseret Evening News,* 7 November 1890, 2. See also "Probably a Mormon Trick," *New York Times,* 8 November 1890, 5.

101. Smoak, *Ghost Dances and Identity,* 123–134, 167.

102. Smoak, *Ghost Dances and Identity,* 123–134, 165–168.

103. "The Mormons and the Edmunds Bill," *Salt Lake Daily Herald,* 18 April 1882.

104. "Brief Comment," *The Richmond Dispatch* (Richmond, VA), 8 December 1885.

Chapter 4

1. Connell O'Donovan is the leading expert on Lewis. See his "The Mormon Priesthood Ban and Elder Q. Walker Lewis: 'An Example for his More Whiter Brethren to Follow,'" *The John Whitmer Historical Association Journal* 26 (2006): 48–100, for complete biographical and contextual information. On Lewis's participation in the Baptist Church in Boston see George A. Levesque, "Inherent Reformers-Inherited Orthodoxy: Black Baptists in Boston, 1800–1873," *The Journal of Negro History* 60 (October 1975): 491–525. For the "meek humble man" assessment see William I. Appleby, Autobiography and Journal, MS 1401, folder 1, 19 May 1847, 170–171, CHL.

2. William I. Appleby, Batavia, New York to Brigham Young, 2 June 1847, BYC, CR1234/1, box 21, folder 5 (reel 30), CHL; O'Donovan, "The Mormon Priesthood Ban," 64–70.

3. O'Donovan, "The Mormon Priesthood Ban," 53.

4. O' Donovan, "The Mormon Priesthood Ban," 82–85.

5. Appleby to Young, 2 June 1847.

6. Elise Lemire, *"Miscegenation": Making Race in America* (Philadelphia: University of Pennsylvania Press, 2002), 51.

7. Appleby to Young, 2 June 1847; Appleby, Autobiography and Journal, 3 December 1847, 203–204.

8. Martha M. Ertman, "Race Treason: The Untold Story of America's Ban on Polygamy," *Columbia Journal of Gender and Law* 19, no. 2 (2010): 287–366.

9. Winthrop D. Jordan, *White Over Black: American Attitudes Toward the Negro, 1550–1812* (Baltimore, MD: Penguin Books, 1969), 150–154; George M. Fredrickson, *The Black Image in the White Mind: The Debate on Afro-American Character and Destiny, 1817–1914* (New York: Harper and Row, 1971), 253–254, 273–282.

10. On antiabolition violence in the 1830s see Leonard L. Richards, *"Gentlemen of Property and Standing": Anti-Abolition Mobs in Jacksonian America* (New York: Oxford University Press, 1970).

11. O'Donovan, "The Mormon Priesthood Ban," 55–56.

12. "Obituary," *The Deseret News Weekly* (Salt Lake City, UT), 25 May 1870.

13. "Obituary," 25 May 1870.

14. Appleby to Young, 2 June 1847; William I. Appleby, Philadelphia, to Brigham Young, 26 July 1847, BYC, CR1234/1, box 21, folder 5 (reel 30), CHL.

15. Appleby to Young, 2 June 1847.

16. On Abel see Newell G. Bringhurst, *Saints, Slaves, and Blacks: The Changing Place of Black People Within Mormonism* (Westport, CT: Greenwood Press, 1981), 37–38; and Russell W. Stevenson, "'A Negro Preacher': The Worlds of Elijah Ables," *Journal of Mormon History* 39 (Spring 2013): 165–254. On Lewis's accepted status among Mormon apostles see Newell G. Bringhurst, "An Ambiguous Decision: The Implementation of Mormon Priesthood Denial for the Black Man—A Reexamination," *Utah Historical Quarterly* 46 (Winter 1978): 45–64. The evidence for Smith ordaining Abel to the priesthood is the belated remembrance of Eunice Kenney, a woman who converted to Mormonism when she heard Elijah Abel preach in 1838. See Eunice Kenney, "My Testimony of the Latter Day Work, [*ca.* 1885]," typescript, microfilm, MS 4226, CHL; Abel himself did not claim that Joseph Smith gave him the priesthood, but he consistently argued that Smith approved.

17. Appleby to Young, 2 June 1847.

18. Peggy Pascoe, *What Comes Naturally: Miscegenation Law and the Making of Race in America* (New York: Oxford University Press, 2009), 19–22; Lemire, *"Miscegenation"*, 47.

19. Lemire, *"Miscegenation"*, 85–86.

20. Appleby, autobiography and journal, 16 June 1847, 177.

21. Terryl L. Givens and Matthew J. Grow, *Parley P. Pratt: The Apostle Paul of Mormonism* (New York: Oxford University Press, 2011), 37–63.

22. "Fanaticism," *Albany Evening Journal* (Albany, NY), 16 February 1831; "Mormonites," *The Sun* (Philadelphia), 18 August 1831; "Mormonism," *Boston Recorder*, 10 October 1832; Mark Lyman Staker, *Hearken, O Ye People: The Historical Setting of Joseph Smith's Ohio Revelations* (Salt Lake City: Greg Kofford Books, 2009), 64–65.

23. Staker, *Hearken, O Ye People*, chapters 1–8.

24. "Reuben P. Harmon," *Naked Truths about Mormonism: Also a Journal for Important, Newly Apprehended Truths, and Miscellany* (Oakland, CA), April 1888; George A. Smith, "Historical Discourse," 15 November 1864, in *Journal of Discourses* 11 (London and Liverpool: Latter-day Saints' Book Depot, 1867), 4; "Mormonites," *The Sun*, 18 August 1831; "Joel Miller's Statement," *Naked Truths about Mormonism*, April 1888; "The Golden Bible or the Book of Mormon," *American Whig* (Woodstock, VT), 14 March 1831.

25. Jesse J. Moss, "Autobiography of a Pioneer Preacher," ed. M. M. Moss, *Christian Standard* 73, no. 3 (15 January 1938), 10, 22–23, emphasis in original.

26. John Corrill, *A Brief History of the Church of Christ of Latter Day Saints* (St. Louis, MO: John Corrill, 1839), 16–17; Staker, *Hearken, O Ye People*, chap. 9.

27. "Henry Carroll's Statement," *Naked Truths about Mormonism*, April 1888; Moss, "Autobiography of a Pioneer Preacher," 10; Staker, *Hearken, O Ye People*, 43–45, 104–108, 136–139.

28. "Reuben P. Harmon," 1; "W. R. Hine's Statement," *Naked Truths about Mormonism,* January 1888; "Henry Carroll's Statement," April 1888; Staker, *Hearken, O Ye People,* 105.

29. Staker, *Hearken, O Ye People*, 181–184.

30. For evidence of other factors at play in the expulsion of Mormons from Jackson County, see Richard L. Bushman, "Mormon Persecutions in Missouri, 1833," *BYU Studies* 3 (Autumn 1960): 11–20; Warren A. Jennings, "Factors in the Destruction of the Mormon Press in Missouri, 1833," *Utah Historical Quarterly* 35 (Winter 1967): 57–76; Warren Jennings "Zion Is Fled: The Expulsion of the Mormons from Jackson County, Missouri" (PhD diss., University of Florida, 1962); Matthew J. Lund, "The Vox Populi is the Vox Dei: American Localism and the Mormon Expulsion from Jackson County, Missouri" (master's thesis, Utah State University, 2012).

31. "A Song Supposed to have been Written by the Sage of Monticello," *The Port Folio* (Philadelphia), 2 October 1802, 312; Annette Gordon-Reed, *The Hemingses of Monticello: An American Family* (New York: W. W. Norton, 2008).

32. *The Recorder; Or, Lady's and Gentlemen's Miscellany* (Richmond, VA), 22 September 1802; Lemire, *"Miscegenation"*, 1–3, 22–23.

33. Leonard L. Richards, *"Gentlemen of Property and Standing": Anti-Abolition Mobs in Jacksonian America* (New York: Oxford University Press, 1970), chap. 1, 78–79, 156–157; Lemire, *"Miscegenation"*, 51 and chap. 3.

34. Thomas Jefferson, *Notes on the State of Virginia* (Richmond, VA: J. W. Randolph, 1853), 155; P. J. Staudenraus, *The African Colonization Movement, 1816–1865* (New York: Columbia University Press, 1961); Larry E. Tise, *Proslavery: A History of the Defense of Slavery in America, 1701–1840* (Athens: University of Georgia Press, 1987), 49–51; Eric Foner, *The Fiery Trial: Abraham Lincoln and American Slavery* (New York: W. W. Norton, 2010).

35. Richards, *Gentlemen of Property and Standing*, 20–25; Lemire, *"Miscegenation"*, 56–60; Henry Mayer, *All on Fire: William Lloyd Garrison and the Abolition of Slavery* (New York: St. Martin's Press, 1998).

36. Richards, *"Gentlemen of Property and Standing"*, 43; Lemire, *"Miscegenation"*, 55–61.

37. Richards, *"Gentlemen of Property and Standing"*, 25, 38–40.

38. Lemire, *"Miscegenation"*, 59–61; Richards, *"Gentlemen of Property and Standing"* chap. 3.

39. Merton Dillon, *Elijah P. Lovejoy, Abolitionist Editor* (Urbana: University of Illinois Press, 1961); Paul Simon, *Freedom's Champion, Elijah Lovejoy* (Carbondale: Southern Illinois University Press, 1994); Richards, *"Gentlemen of Property and Standing,"* 100–111.

40. "Free People of Color," *The Evening and the Morning Star*, July 1833; Staker, *Hearken, O Ye People*, 179–184; *Evening and the Morning Star Extra*, 16 July 1833.

41. Parley P. Pratt, *History of the Late Persecution Inflicted by the State of Missouri Upon the Mormons* (Detroit, MI: Dawson and Bates, 1840), 7; Staker, *Hearken, O Ye People*, 179–188; Bringhurst, *Saints, Slaves, and Blacks*, 15–26, 36–40.

42. Colin Kidd, *The Forging of Races: Race and Scripture in the Protestant Atlantic World, 1600–2000* (New York: Cambridge University Press, 2006), 35–38; "The Gospel. No. 5," *Latter Day Saints' Messenger and Advocate* (Kirtland, OH) February 1835; "The Ancient Order of Things," *Latter Day Saints' Messenger and Advocate*, September 1835; Parley P. Pratt, *A Voice of Warning and Instruction to All People, Containing a Declaration of the Faith and Doctrine of the Church of the Latter Day Saints, Commonly Called Mormons* (New York: W. Sandford, 1837), 140; Parley P. Pratt, *The Millennium and Other Poems: To which is Annexed a Treatise on the Regeneration and Eternal Duration of Matter* (New York: W. Molineux, 1840), 58; E. S. Abdy, *Journal of a Residence and Tour in the United States of North America, From April, 1833, to October, 1834*, 3 vols. (London: John Murray, 1835), 3:58–59.

43. "Free People of Color," and "The Elders Stationed in Zion to the Churches Abroad, in Love, Greeting," *The Evening and the Morning Star*, July 1833.

44. *The Evening and the Morning Star Extra*, 16 July 1833; Staker, *Hearken, O Ye People*, 183.

45. This is a portion of the *Extra* that historians have struggled to understand. See Staker, *Hearken, O Ye People*, 182–188; Bringhurst, *Saints, Slaves, and Blacks*, 17–19, 39–40; Givens and Grow, *Parley P. Pratt*, 60–61.

46. *The Evening and the Morning Star Extra*, 16 July 1833.

47. "Regulating the Mormonites," *Erie Gazette* (Erie, PA), 5 September 1833.

48. "Regulating the Mormonites," *Daily Missouri Republican*, (St. Louis, MO) 9 August 1833; "Regulating the Mormonites," *Erie Gazette*, 5 September 1833; "Mormonism," *United States Telegraph* (Washington, DC), 21 August 1833, repr. "Mormonism!," *Times and Seasons*, 15 March 1845.

49. "To His Excellency, Daniel Dunklin, Governor of the State of Missouri," *The Evening and the Morning Star* (Kirtland, OH), December 1833; Abdy, *Journal of a Residence and Tour*, 3:41, 42.

50. "To His Excellency," 114; "Mormonism," *United States Telegraph*, 21 August 1833; "Mormonism!" *Times and Seasons*, 15 March 1845.

51. "To His Excellency," 114.

52. "Regulating the Mormonites," *Daily Missouri Republican*, 9 August 1833; "Regulating the Mormonites," *The Erie Gazette*, 5 September 1833; Brady G. Winslow, "Vienna Jacques: Eyewitness to the Jackson County Persecutions," *Mormon Historical Studies* 11 (Fall 2010): 93–98; Bringhurst, *Saints, Slaves, and Blacks*, 18; Staker, *Hearken, O Ye People*, 184; John K. Alexander, "Tarred and Feathered: Mormons, Memory, and Ritual Violence" (master's thesis, University of Utah, 2012).

53. "The Outrage in Jackson County Missouri," *Evening and the Morning Star* (Kirtland, OH), January 1834.

54. "The Outrage in Jackson County, Missouri," *Evening and the Morning Star*, February 1834.

55. W. W. Phelps, "Communications," *Latter Day Saints' Messenger and Advocate* (Kirtland, OH), March 1835, emphasis in original.

56. Parley P. Pratt, "The Science of Anti-Mormon Suckerology," *Prophet* (New York, NY), 10 May 1845; "Warsaw and Quincy," *Nauvoo Neighbor*, 2 April 1845. For other examples of Mormons depicting their enemies as degraded or black, see Bringhurst, *Saints, Slaves, and Blacks*, 44–45 and Bringhurst, "An Ambiguous Decision."

57. Donald G. Mathews, *Slavery and Methodism* (Princeton, NJ: Princeton University Press, 1965), 142; Ryan Jordan, *Slavery and the Meeting House: The Quakers and the Abolitionists Dilemma, 1820–1865* (Bloomington: Indiana University Press, 2007); Brycchan Carey and Geoffrey Plank, eds., *Quakers and Abolition* (Urbana: University of Illinois Press, 2014), 1–12, 43–55; Thomas E. Drake, *Quakers and Slavery in America* (New Haven, CT: Yale University Press, 1950), 132–33, 144–145; Tise, *Proslavery*, 267–268; Richard J. Carwardine, *Evangelicals and Politics in Antebellum America* (New Haven, CT: Yale University Press, 1993), 139.

58. Mitchell Snay, *Gospel of Disunion: Religion and Separation in the Antebellum South* (New York: Cambridge University Press, 1993); C. C. Goen, *Broken Churches, Broken Nation: Denominational Schisms and the Coming of the American Civil War* (Macon, GA: Mercer University Press, 1985).

59. Bringhurst, *Saints, Slaves, and Blacks*, 20–21; The declaration was first published in *Latter Day Saints' Messenger and Advocate* (Kirtland, OH), August 1835, under the heading "General Assembly."

60. John L. Myers, "Anti-Slavery Activities of Five Lane Seminary Boys in 1835–36," *Bulletin of the Historical and Philosophical Society of Ohio* 21 (April 1963), 99–102; "Anti-Slavery Intelligence," *Philanthropist* (Cincinnati, OH), 22 April 1836.

61. Joseph Smith Jr., "For the Messenger and Advocate," *Latter Day Saints' Messenger and Advocate* (Kirtland, OH), April 1836.

62. Warren Parrish, "For the Messenger and Advocate," *Latter Day Saints' Messenger and Advocate* (Kirtland, OH), April 1836.

63. Smith Jr., "For the Messenger and Advocate"; Richards, *Gentlemen of Property and Standing*, 12–15.

64. "The Abolitionists," *Latter Day Saints' Messenger and Advocate*, April 1836.

65. "Kirtland, May, 1836," *Latter Day Saints' Messenger and Advocate* (Kirtland, OH), May 1836.

66. For thorough discussions of Ham's curse and the ends to which it was used, see Stephen R. Haynes, *Noah's Curse: The Biblical Justification of American Slavery* (New York: Oxford

University Press, 2002); David M. Goldenberg, *The Curse of Ham: Race and Slavery in Early Judaism, Christianity, and Islam* (Princeton, NJ: Princeton University Press, 2003); Kidd, *The Forging of Races*; and Mark A. Noll, "The Bible and Slavery," in Randall M. Miller, Harry S. Stout, and Charles Reagan Wilson, eds., *Religion and the American Civil War* (New York: Oxford University Press, 1998), 43–73.

67. Goldenberg, *The Curse of Ham*, 1. See also Haynes, *Noah's Curse*, 7; and Kidd, *The Forging of Races*, 139.

68. Kidd, *The Forging of Races*, 137–139; Tise, *Proslavery*, 278; Noll, "The Bible and Slavery," 44, 50–53.

69. Smith, "For the Messenger and Advocate"; Parrish, "For the Messenger and Advocate."

70. Bringhurst, *Saints, Slaves, and Blacks*, 56–60; Richards, *"Gentlemen of Property and Standing"*, 156–170.

71. Andrew H. Hedges, Alex D. Smith, and Richard Lloyd Anderson, *The Joseph Smith Papers: Journals Volume 2: December 1841–April 1843* (Salt Lake City, UT: Church Historian's Press, 2011), 212.

72. Manuscript History, MS 155, box 1, folder 7 (8 February 1844), CHL.

73. Joseph Smith Jr., *Gen. Joseph Smith's Views of the Powers and Policy of the Government of the United States* (Philadelphia: Brown, Jacking, and Guilbert, 1844), 2–3; 8–12.

74. Andrew F. Ehat and Lyndon W. Cook, *The Words of Joseph Smith: The Contemporary Accounts of the Nauvoo Discourses of the Prophet Joseph* (Orem, UT: Grandin Book Company, 1991), 325–326. The two versions of the speech were captured by Willard Richards and Wilford Woodruff.

75. Don E. Fehrenbacher, ed., *Abraham Lincoln: Speeches and Writings, 1832–1858* (New York: The Library of America, 1989), 397–398; emphasis in original.

76. Connell O'Donovan, "'I would Confine them to their Own Species': LDS Historical Rhetoric and Praxis Regarding Marriage Between Whites and Blacks" (paper presented at Sunstone West, Cupertino, California, 2009), posted at <http://www.connellodonovan. com/black_white_marriage.html> (accessed 16 December 2011). On McCary's baptism see Robert Campbell, Journal, 1 March 1847, CHL; and on a vague reference to a possible priesthood ordination see *Voree Herald* (Voree, WI), October 1846. The *Herald* article likely refers to McCary but does not mention him by name, and it offers no indication as to how its anonymous author knew of McCary's ordination so far geographically removed from the site of the supposed event. It is a report seemingly based upon unsubstantiated information. McCary's own statements in his interview with the apostles, as described below, also seem to indicate he did not hold the priesthood. For a different version of the events regarding William (Warner) McCary see Connell O' Donovan, "Brigham Young, African Americans, and Plural Marriage: Schism and the Beginnings of Black Priesthood and Temple Denial," in Newell G. Bringhurst and Craig L. Foster, eds., *The Persistence of Polygamy: From Joseph Smith's Martyrdom to the First Manifesto, 1844-1890* (Independence, MO: John Whitmer Books, 2013), 48–86. Angela Pulley Hudson explores McCary's life outside of Mormonism and his adoption of an Indian identity under the name Okah Tubbee (Lucy Stanton became Laah Ceil) in a forthcoming book from University of North Carolina Press.

77. "Millerism Outdone," *Daily Cincinnati Commercial* (Cincinnati, OH), 27 October 1846; "Millerism Outdone," *Long Islander* (Huntington, NY) 27 November 1846; "Millerism Outside," *Jeffersonian Republican* (Stroudsburg, PA), 26 November 1846; Bringhurst, *Saints, Slaves, and Black*, 84–86. I am indebted to Ardis E. Parshall for the reports from New York and Pennsylvania.

78. Charles Kelly, ed., *Journal of John D. Lee, 1846–47 and 1859* (Salt Lake City, UT: Privately printed for Western Printing Company, 1938), 100, 103; Manuscript History, CR 100 102, vol. 17, 26 March 1847, 75.

79. Kelly, *Journal of John D. Lee*, 100, 103; Manuscript History, 26 March 1847, 75; Wilford Woodruff, journal, 1833–1898, typescript, vol. 3, ed. Scott G. Kenney (Midvale, UT:

Signature Books, 1983), 143; the journal of Lorenzo Brown, 1823–1900, typescript, 25 April 1847, 10, CHL; Nelson W. Whipple, autobiography and journal, microfilm, manuscript, MS 9995, 30–31, CHL; Juanita Brooks, ed., *On the Mormon Frontier: The Diary of Hosea Stout, 1844–1861*. vol. 1 (Salt Lake City: University of Utah Press and Utah State Historical Society, 1964), 244, 304.

80. Manuscript History, 26 March 1847, 75; Church Historian's Office, General Church Minutes, 1839–1877, CR 100 318, box 1, folder 52, 26 March 1847, CHL.

81. This reconstruction of the interview is taken from Thomas Bullock's notes contained in the General Church Minutes. Bullock frequently used abbreviations and his own system of shorthand to keep minutes, which adds to the confusion of attempting to understand an already confusing exchange. What follows is my best effort at deciphering Bullock's notes and at deducing McCarry's statements and intent. I benefited from the able assistance of Ardis E. Parshall. Silvia Ghosh, at the LDS Church History Library then provided a more thorough transcription based upon her expertise in reading Bullock's minutes. I am indebted to her and LaJean Carruth for this assistance. See Church Historian's Office, General Church Minutes, 1839–1877, CR 100 318, box 1, folder 52, 26 March 1847, CHL.

82. General Church Minutes, 26 March 1847.

83. General Church Minutes, 26 March 1847.

84. General Church Minutes, 26 March 1847.

85. General Church Minutes, 26 March 1847.

86. General Church Minutes, 26 March 1847.

87. Lemire, *"Miscegenation"*, 111–114; Kidd, *The Forging of Races*, 121–167.

88. Kidd, *The Forging of Races*, 121–167.

89. General Church Minutes, 26 March 1847.

90. General Church Minutes, 26 March 1847.

91. General Church Minutes, 26 March 1847.

92. General Church Minutes, 26 March 1847.

93. On the chronology of departures and arrivals at Winter Quarters, see Richard E. Bennett, *Mormons at the Missouri: Winter Quarters, 1846–1852* (Norman: University of Oklahoma Press, 1987), 148–167; and Givens and Grow, *Parley P. Pratt*, 261–271.

94. Kelly, journal of John D. Lee, 7 May 1847; Lorenzo Brown, journal, 25 April 1847, 10.

95. General Church Minutes, 1839–1877, CR 100 318, box 1, folder 53, 25 April 1847, CHL; for additional aspects of Pratt's speech see Givens and Grow, *Parley P. Pratt*, 263–264.

96. For a thorough and thoughtful historiographical discussion of Pratt's statement, see Newell G. Bringhurst, "The 'Missouri Thesis' Revisited: Early Mormonism, Slavery, and the Status of Black People," in Newell G. Bringhurst and Darron T. Smith, eds., *Black and Mormon* (Urbana: University of Illinois Press, 2004), 20–23. On the Book of Abraham and race see Richard Lyman Bushman, *Joseph Smith Rough Stone Rolling: A Cultural Biography of Mormonism's Founder* (New York: Alfred A. Knopf, 2005), 285–289; and Alma Allred, "The Traditions of Their Fathers: Myth versus Reality in LDS Scriptural Writings," ed. Bringhurst and Smith, *Black and Mormon*, 34–49.

97. Whipple, autobiography and journal, 30–31. O'Donovan, "The Mormon Priesthood Ban," p. 83, and Bringhurst, *Saints, Slaves, and Blacks*, p. 85, suggest that McCary was expelled from Winter Quarters in the spring of 1847 and then returned that fall and committed his sexual exploits. I believe this is a faulty timeline based upon a misreading of Whipple's autobiography and journal, written in 1863. Whipple recalls being put into a low-level ecclesiastical position at Winter Quarters in October 1847 and then mentions that "when I arrived in this branch ir [*sic*] was in rather a curious fix. A man had been there by the name of McCarry." Whipple then described McCary's activities in great detail, making it easy to assume that the events took place after Whipple assumed his leadership role in the branch. But he clearly indicates that when he arrived in the branch McCary "had been there," and by implication that he no longer was there. William Major's 16 June letter to

Brigham Young, cited below, indicates that McCarry was gone from Winter Quarters by that date. I do not believe he returned.

98. Whipple, autobiography and journal, 30–31.

99. Whipple, autobiography and journal, 30–31.

100. Lorenzo Brown, journal, 25 April 1847, 10; William W. Major, Elk Horn, to Brigham Young, 16 June 1847, BYC, CR1234/1, box 21, folder 8 (reel 30), CHL; Whipple, autobiography and journal, 30–31.

101. General Church Minutes, CR100–318, box 1, folder 59, 3 December 1847, 6–7, CHL.

102. General Church Minutes, 3 December 1847, 6–7.

103. General Church Minutes, 3 December 1847, 6–7. On violence against blacks for alleged violations of racial boundaries see Winthrop D. Jordan, *White Over Black: American Attitudes Toward the Negro, 1550–1812* (Baltimore, MD: Penguin Books, 1969), 157; Pascoe, *What Comes Naturally*, 32; Patrick Q. Mason, *The Mormon Menace: Violence and Anti-Mormonism in the Postbellum South* (New York: Oxford University Press, 2011), 10; Philip Dray, *At the Hands of Persons Unknown: The Lynching of Black America* (New York: Random House, 2002); Stewart E. Tolnay and E. M. Beck, *A Festival of Violence: An Analysis of Southern Lynchings, 1882–1930* (Urbana: University of Illinois Press, 1995).

104. General Church Minutes, 3 December 1847, 6–7.

105. General Church Minutes, 3 December 1847, 6–7.

106. General Church Minutes, 3 December 1847, 6–7.

107. Antonio J. Waring, ed., *Laws of the Creek Nation,* (Athens: University of Georgia Press, 1960), 20–21; Pascoe, *What Comes Naturally*, 22.

108. Josiah Clark Nott, *Two Lectures on the Natural History of the Caucasian and Negro Races* (Mobile, AL: Dade and Thompson, 1844), 30–35; Josiah Clark Nott, "The Mulatto a Hybrid—Probable Extermination of the Two Races If the Whites and Blacks are Allowed to Intermarry," *American Journal of the Medical Sciences* 6(1843): 252–256.

109. Nott, *Two Lectures*, 30–35.

110. Appleby, autobiography and journal, 19 May 1847, 170–171. This is a problematic entry because it is a remembrance perhaps fleshed out in hindsight in 1848 and 1849 when Appleby writes what he calls a "Compilation of my Journals" (24 May 1848, p. 234). For additional discussion of Appleby's 19 May 1847 journal entry see O'Donovan, "The Mormon Priesthood Ban," p. 84, and Bringhurst, *Saints, Slaves, and Black*, p. 104, n. 41. Both O'Donovan and Bringhurst assumed Appleby compiled his journal in the 1850s, after the priesthood ban was openly acknowledged, but historian Stephen Fleming found internal evidence otherwise. Appleby indicated, beginning 24 May 1848, that he was working on his "compilation" and continued to indicate so up through 1849. I am indebted to Stephen Fleming for these insights.

111. Appleby, autobiography and journal, 5 May 1841, 71–75; the relevant quotes from the Book of Abraham are on p. 74.

112. For evidence of Appleby compiling his journal, see entries for 24 May 1848, 234; 9 November 1848, 244; 28 January 1849, 248; 25 February 1849, 249. I am indebted to Stephen Fleming for these references. General Church Minutes, 26 March 1847.

113. Appleby, Autobiography and Journal, 3 December 1847, 203–204, 24 May 1848; General Church Minutes, 3 December 1847, 6–7.

Chapter 5

1. John Burt Colton, Council Bluffs, Iowa, to James H. Noteware, Galesburg, Illinois, 22 May 1849, holograph, HL.

2. David R. Roediger, *The Wages of Whiteness: Race and the Making of the American Working Class* (1991; repr. New York: Verso, 2007), 82–87; "The True Dignity of Labor," *The National Era* (Washington, DC), 21 May 1857.

3. "The Old Mormons Likely to Give Way," *Chicago Daily Tribune*, 10 March 1873.

4. Ariela J. Gross, *What Blood Won't Tell: A History of Race on Trial in America* (Cambridge. MA: Harvard University Press, 2008), 35–36.

5. W. G. Mills, Birmingham, England, to Brigham Young, Salt Lake City, 28 June 1861, BYC, CR1234/1, box 28, folder 11 (reel 39), CHL.

6. John Taylor and George A. Smith, New York, to Brigham Young, Salt Lake City, 17 August 1856, BYC, CR1234/1, box 43, folder 5 (reel 56), CHL; John Taylor, New York, to Brigham Young, Salt Lake City, 17 October 1856, BYC, CR1234/1, box 43, folder 5 (reel 56), CHL; John Eldridge, Youngstown, Ohio, to Brigham Young, Salt Lake City, 22 February 1861, BYC, CR1234/1, box 28, folder 4 (reel 38), CHL.

7. "From Utah," *National Era* (Washington, DC), 23 January 1851, emphasis in original.

8. "From Utah," 23 January 1851.

9. Howard Lamar, *The Far Southwest, 1846–1912: A Territorial History* (New Haven, CT: Yale University Press, 1966); Christopher B. Rich Jr., "The True Policy for Utah: Servitude, Slavery, and 'An Act in Relation to Service'" *Utah Historical Quarterly* 80 (Winter 2012): 54–74.

10. Rich, "The True Policy," 61–64; Nathaniel R. Ricks, "A Peculiar Place for the Peculiar Institution: Slavery and Sovereignty in Early Territorial Utah," (master's thesis, Brigham Young University, 2007); Dennis L. Lythgoe, "Negro Slavery in Utah," *Utah Historical Quarterly* 39 (Winter 1971): 40–54. For the estimate of blacks in Utah Territory see Newell G. Bringhurst, *Saints, Slaves, and Blacks: The Changing Place of Black People Within Mormonism* (Westport, CT: Greenwood Press, 1981), 66–67, 219, 224.

11. Ricks, "A Peculiar Place," 92–106, 157. For a timeline of events and contextual information on the 1852 legislative session see W. Paul Reeve, Christopher B. Rich Jr., and LaJean Purcell Carruth, *"Enough to Cause the Angles in Heaven to Blush": Race, Servitude, and Priesthood at the 1852 Utah Legislature,* (Salt Lake City: University of Utah Press, forthcoming).

12. Sondra Jones, *The Trial of Don Pedro Leon Lujan: The Attack against Indian Slavery and Mexican Traders in Utah* (Salt Lake City: University of Utah Press, 2000), 48–52; James F. Brooks, *Captives and Cousins: Slavery, Kinship, and Community in the Southwest Borderlands* (Chapel Hill: University of North Carolina Press, 2002); Ned Blackhawk, *Violence over the Land: Indians and Empires in the Early American West* (Cambridge, MA: Harvard University Press, 2006).

13. Jones, *The Trial of Don Pedro Leon Lujan*, 44–52.

14. Jones, *The Trial of Don Pedro Leon Lujan*, 41–44.

15. Jones, *The Trial of Don Pedro Leon Lujan*, 107–119; *Journals of the House of Representatives, Council, and Joint Sessions of the First Annual and Special Sessions of the Legislative Assembly of the Territory of Utah. Held at Great Salt Lake City, 1851 and 1852* (Salt Lake City, UT: Published by Authority of the Legislative Assembly, Brigham Young Printer, 1852), 109.

16. On Young's view of abolitionists as ignorant, see Young's sermon on 6 July 1851, in Richard S. Van Wagoner, *The Complete Discourses of Brigham Young*, vol. 1 (Salt Lake City, UT: The Smith-Pettit Foundation, 2009), 442.

17. Samuel M. Brown, "Early Mormon Adoption Theology and the Mechanics of Salvation," *Journal of Mormon History* 37 (Summer 2011): 3–52; Samuel M. Brown, "Early Mormon Chain of Belonging," *Dialogue: A Journal of Mormon Thought* 44 (Spring 2011): 1–52; Jonathan A. Stapley, "Adoptive Sealing Ritual in Mormonism," *Journal of Mormon History* 37 (Summer 2011): 53–118; Van Wagoner, *Complete Discourses*, 16 February 1847, 1:180.

18. Van Wagoner, *Complete Discourses*, 8 January 1845, 1:66; I am indebted to Jonathan Stapley for bringing this sermon to my attention.

19. Church Historian's Office, General Church Minutes, CR100 318, box 2, folder 8, 13 February 1849, CHL.

20. Bringhurst, *Saints, Slaves, and Blacks*, 84, 97; Lester E. Bush Jr., "Mormonism's Negro Doctrine: An Historical Overview," in *Neither White nor Black: Mormon Scholars Confront the Race Issue in a Universal Church*, ed. Lester E. Bush Jr. and Armand L. Mauss (Midvale, UT: Signature Books, 1984), 70.

21. The Church Historian's Office Journal in 1861 recorded Jaques's activities as "Gathering historical information for /49," "Searching books for history for 1849," "Compiling history," and "Copying & inserting items in 1849 history." By September of 1861, Jaques was "Revising and enlarging" his record for 1849 and by October he was "filling in on issues and adding matter" from additional sources. The Historian's Office Journal, CR 100/1, 1 May 1861; 13 May 1849; 31 May 1861; 19 June 1861, 10 September 1861; 17 September 1861; 20 October 1861, CHL.

22. Historian's Office, History of the Church, CR 100 102, reel 9, 1849, 17, CHL; JH, 13 February 1849, emphasis added.

23. Brigham D. Madsen, "John W. Gunnison's Letters to His Mormon Friend, Albert Carrington." *Utah Historical Quarterly* 59 (Summer 1991): 264–267.

24. John W. Gunnison, *The Mormons, or, Latter-day Saints, in the Valley of the Great Salt Lake* (Philadelphia: Lippincott, Grambo, 1852), 51, 143; Gunnison, Cleveland, Ohio, to Carrington, Salt Lake City, 19 March 1852, in Madsen, "John W. Gunnison's Letters," 272–274; See also, Gunnison, Mackinac, Michigan, to Carrington, Salt Lake City, 18 September 1852, for evidence that Gunnison's book was published, in Madsen, John W. Gunnison's Letters, 274–277.

25. Van Wagenen, *Complete Discourses*, 1 June 1851, 1:431.

26. Reeve, Rich, and Carruth,, *"Enough to Cause the Angels in Heaven to Blush."*

27. For Young's prepared remarks see *Journals of the House*, 108–110 and "Governor's Message," *Deseret News* (Salt Lake City, UT), 10 January 1852. For Young's other speeches, both the Watt and Woodruff versions, see Van Wagoner, *Complete Discourses*, 5 January 1852, 1:468–472; 23 January 1852, 1:473–474; and Papers of George D. Watt, MS 4534, box 1, folder 3, CHL.

28. *Journals of the House*, 108–110.

29. *Journals of the House*, 108–110.

30. Brigham Young, 23 January 1852, before Territorial Legislature, Papers of George D. Watt, MS 4534, box 1, folder 3, CHL, transcribed by LaJean Purcell Carruth; Van Wagoner, *The Complete Discourses*, 1: 468–472, 473–474. The George D. Watt shorthand is unpunctuated.

31. Young, 23 January 1852. For a more in depth discussion of the provisions of the bill regarding white servitude see, Reeve, Rich, and Carruth, *"Enough to cause the Angles in Heaven to Blush."*

32. Young, 23 January 1852.

33. Orson Pratt, 27 January 1852, Speech on Slavery Delivered in Territorial Legislature, Papers of George D. Watt, MS 4534, box 1, folder 3, transcribed by LaJean Purcell Carruth.

34. Orson Spencer, 27 January 1852, before the Territorial Legislature, Papers of George D. Watt, MS 4534, box 1, folder 1, transcribed by LaJean Purcell Carruth.

35. The legislative journal for this session does not include a roll call. The vote breakdown is unknown.

36. Territorial Legislative Records, 1851–1894, series 3150, microfilm, reel 1, box 1, folder 55, 704–706, Utah State Archives, Salt Lake City Utah; Rich, "The True Policy for Utah," 66–71; Ricks, "A Peculiar Place," 158–162.

37. Territorial Legislative Records, 704–706; Ricks, "A Peculiar Place," 158.

38. *Frederick Douglass' Paper* (Rochester, NY), 8 September 1854; Ricks, "A Peculiar Place," 137–145; Horace Greeley, *An Overland Journey from New York to San Francisco in the Summer of 1859* (New York: C. M. Saxton, Barker, 1860), 211–212. In the Greeley interview Young fails to distinguish between "slavery" and "servitude" but tells Greely he can read the law for himself.

39. *Journals of the House*, 125–128.

40. Van Wagoner, *The Complete Discourses of Brigham Young*, 1: 478, emphasis added; Brigham Young, 5 February 1852, before a Joint Session of the Territorial Legislature, Papers of George D. Watt, MS 4534, box 1, folder 3, CHL, transcribed by LaJean Purcell Carruth;

Van Wagoner, *The Complete Discourses of Brigham Young*, 1:468–472, includes Watt's transcribed version of the speech but misdates it to 5 January 1852. The legislative journal does not mention the speech. *Journals of the House of Representatives, Council, and Joint Sessions of the First Annual and Special Sessions of the Legislative Assembly of the Territory of Utah. Held at Great Salt Lake City, 1851 and 1852* (Salt Lake City, UT: Brigham H. Young, printer, 1852), 125–127.

41. *Acts, Resolutions, and Memorials, Passed by the First Annual, and Special Sessions of the Legislative Assembly of the Territory of Utah, Begun and Held at Great Salt Lake City, on the 22nd Day of September, A. D. 1851* (Salt Lake City, UT: Brigham H. Young, printer, 1852), 107, 178, 193; *Journals of the House*, 127–128; Juanita Brooks, ed., *On the Mormon Frontier: The Diary of Hosea Stout, 1844–1861*, 2 vols. (Salt Lake City: University of Utah Press and Utah State Historical Society, 1964), 2:423.

42. On the sometimes tense relationship between Pratt and Young, see Gary James Bergera, *Conflict in the Quorum: Orson Pratt, Brigham Young, Joseph Smith* (Salt Lake City, UT: Signature Books, 2002).

43. Van Wagoner, *Complete Discourses*, 1:468–472; Young, 5 February 1852. On Young's defense of his mixing religion with politics at the legislature, see Van Wagoner, *Complete Discourses*, 29 January 1852, 1:474–476.

44. Van Wagoner, *Complete Discourses*, 1:468–472.

45. Van Wagoner, *Complete Discourses*, 1:468–472.

46. Brigham Young, 5 February 1852; Van Wagoner, *Complete Discourses*, 1:468–472; Brigham Young, "Intelligence, Etc.," 9 October 1859, *Journal of Discourses*, vol. 7 (London: Latter-day Saints' Book Depot, 1860), 290.

47. Brigham Young, 5 February 1852; Van Wagoner, *Complete Discourses*, 1:469.

48. David M. Goldenberg, *The Curse of Ham: Race and Slavery in Early Judaism, Christianity, and Islam* (Princeton, NJ: Princeton University Press, 2003), 178–182; David Walker, *Walker's Appeal, in Four Articles; Together with a Preamble, to the Coloured Citizens of the World, but in Particular, and Very Expressly, to Those of the United States of America, Written in Boston, State of Massachusetts, September 28, 1829* (Boston: David Walker, 1830), 68.

49. Van Wagoner, *Complete Discourses*, 1:468–469; Young, 5 February 1852.

50. Young, 5 February 1852.

51. "Church History," *Times and Seasons*, 1 March 1842; Royal Skousen, *The Book of Mormon: The Earliest Text* (New Haven, CT: Yale University Press, 2009), 137.

52. Parley P. Pratt, "Heirship and Priesthood," *Journal of Discourses*, vol. 1 (London: Latter-day Saints' Book Depot, 1855), 261; George A. Smith, "The History of Mahomedanism," *Journal of Discourses*, vol. 3 (London: Latter-day Saints' Book Depot, 1856), 29. For a sermon by Young in 1845 also mentioning blood descent see Van Wagoner, *Complete Discourses*, 8 January 1845, 1:66.

53. Brigham Young, "Intelligence, Etc.," *Journal of Discourses*. Vol. 7 (London: Latter-day Saints' Book Depot, 1860), 290–291; W. W. Phelps, "Communications," *Latter Day Saints' Messenger and Advocate* (Kirtland, OH), March 1835; John Taylor, "Duties of the Saints—The Atonement, Etc.," *Journal of Discourses*, vol. 22 (London: Latter-day Saints' Book Depot, 1882), 304.

54. Van Wagoner, *Complete Discourses*, 5 January 1852, 1:469–470; Brigham Young, "The Persecutions of the Saints," *Journal of Discourses*, vol. 10 (London: Latter-day Saints' Book Depot, 1865), 110.

55. Henry Hughes, *Treatise on Sociology, Theoretical and Practical* (Philadelphia: Lippincott, Grambo, 1854), 239–240; Douglas Ambrose, *Henry Hughes and Proslavery Thought in the Old South* (Baton Rouge: Louisiana State University Press, 1996).

56. Van Wagoner, *Complete Discourses*, 1:470.

57. Van Wagoner, *Complete Discourses*, 1:468, 471. For scholars quoting Woodruff's version of Young's speech see, for example, Bush, "Mormonism's Negro Doctrine," 65; Bringhurst, *Saints, Slaves, and Blacks,* 99, although at 123 Brighurst quotes the Watt version; and

Armand L. Mauss, *All Abraham's Children: Changing Mormon Conceptions of Race and Lineage* (Urbana: University of Illinois Press, 2003), 212.

58. A. Leon Higginbotham, Jr., and Barbara K. Kopytoff, "Racial Purity and Interracial Sex in the Law of Colonial and Antebellum Virginia," in *Interracialism: Black-White Intermarriage in American History, Literature, and Law*, ed. Werner Sollors (New York: Oxford University Press, 2000), 83–89; Gross, *What Blood Won't Tell*, 43–44; John G. Mencke, *Mulattoes and Race Mixture: American Attitudes and Images, 1865–1918* (Ann Arbor, MI: UMI Research Press, 1979), 37–87.

59. Higginbotham and Kopytoff, "Racial Purity," 89–94; for a nineteenth-century discussion of the issue see Charles W. Chesnutt, "What is a White Man?" *Independent*, 30 May 1889 in *Interracialism*, ed. Werner Sollors, 37–42. The assertion regarding Young's speeches is based upon an electronic search of the five volumes in Van Wagoner, *The Complete Discourses*.

60. "To the Saints," *Deseret News*, 3 April 1852; Bringhurst, *Saints, Slaves, and Blacks*, 125; Gunnison, *The Mormons*, 51, 143.

61. Connell O'Donovan, "The Mormon Priesthood Ban and Elder Q. Walker Lewis: 'An Example for his More Whiter Brethren to Follow,'" *John Whitmer Historical Association Journal* 26 (2006), 89–98.

62. O'Donovan, "The Mormon Priesthood Ban."

63. On the announcement of polygamy see David J. Whittaker, "The Bone in the Throat: Orson Pratt and the Public Announcement of Plural Marriage," *Western Historical Quarterly* 18 (July 1987): 293–314; on the struggle over polygamy see Christine Talbot, *A Foreign Kingdom: Mormons and Polygamy in American Political Culture, 1852–1890* (Urbana: University of Illinois Press, 2013) and Sarah Barringer Gordon, *The Mormon Question: Polygamy and Constitutional Conflict in Nineteenth-Century America* (Chapel Hill: University of North Carolina Press, 2002) .

64. Alfreda Eva Bell, *Boadicea the Mormon Wife: Life Scenes in Utah* (New York and Buffalo: Arthur R. Orton, 1855), 54–55.

65. "Freaks of Popular Sovereignty in Utah," *National Era*, 2 April 1857.

66. "What Shall Be Done with the Mormons?" *Portland Transcript* (Portland, ME), 3 November 1855; "The Political Secrets of Mormonism," *New York Daily Tribune*, 7 August 1856.

67. E. D. Morgan, "Philadelphia National Convention," *National Era*, 24 April 1856; Kirk H. Porter and Donald Bruce Johnson, eds., *National Party Platforms, 1840–1956* (Urbana: University of Illinois Press, 1956), 27.

68. Stephen A. Douglas, *Remarks of the Hon. Stephen A. Douglas, on Kansas, Utah, and the Dred Scott Decision. Delivered at Springfield, Illinois, June 12th, 1857* (Chicago: Daily Times Book and Job Office, 1857), 11–15.

69. John L. Thompson, *Mormonism—Increase of the Army. Speech of Hon. John Thompson, of New York. Delivered in the House of Representatives, January 27, 1858.* (Washington, DC: Buell and Blanchard, 1858), 6–7.

70. "Polygamy and Slavery," *National Era*, 24 December 1857.

71. Samuel Salsbury, "Christianity," *Frederick Douglass' Paper*, 13 April 1855; "Mormon Cabin," *Portland Pleasure Boat* (Portland, ME), 22 June 1854; James M. Ashley, "Speech of Hon. James M. Ashley, of Ohio. Delivered in the U.S. House of Representatives, May 29, 1860," in *Duplicate Copy of the Souvenir from the Afro-American League of Tennessee to Hon. James M. Ashley of Ohio*, ed. Benjamin W. Arnett (Philadelphia: Publishing House of the AME Church, 1894), 95.

72. *Congressional Globe*, 37 Cong., 2d Sess. (Washington, DC: John C. Rives, printer, 1862), 1581, 1847, 2064, 2139, 2587, 2618, 2624, 2766, 2769, 2774, 2871, 2906, 3023, 3082; *Journal of the House of Representatives*, 37 Cong., 2d Sess. (Washington, DC: GPO, 1862), 617–618, 790, 878, 929, 949, 969; Robert F. Horowitz, *The Great Impeacher: A Political Biography of James M. Ashley* (New York: Brooklyn College Press, 1979), 77.

73. C. Vann Woodward, ed., *Mary Chesnut's Civil War* (New York: Book of the Month Club, 1994), 308, 525, 758, 793.

74. Thomas Alfred Creigh Diary, 1866, in Susan Badger Doyle ed., *Journeys to the Land of Gold: Emigrant Diaries from the Bozeman Trail, 1863–1866* (Helena: Montana Historical Society Press, 2000), 2:702.
75. "Mormonism," *New York Independent*, 14 July 1870.
76. Rev. F. A. Noble, D. D., of the Union Park Congregational Church, Chicago, IL, *The Mormon Iniquity. A Discourse Delivered Before the New West Education Commission, in the First Congregational Church, Sunday Evening, Nov. 2, 1884* (Chicago: Jameson and Morse Printers, 1884), 8, 162–164; "Affairs in Utah and the Territories," 40th Cong., 2d Sess., House of Representatives, Misc. Doc. No. 153, 17 June 1868, 27; "Mormonism," Argument of Hon. J. C. Hemingray, Delegate of the Liberal Party of Utah, Before the House Sub-Committee on Territories, on the Bill "To regulate elections and the elective franchise in the Territory of Utah," January 22, 1878 (Washington, DC: W. H. Moore, printer, 1878), 3, 30; "The Story of a Second Wife," *Anti-Polygamy Standard*, May 1880; H. D. J., "A Peep Behind the Curtain at Salt Lake," *New York Independent*, 26 August 1886.
77. "The Old Mormons Likely to Give Way," *Chicago Daily Tribune*, 10 March 1873; "Utah Polygamy," *Record of the Times* (Wilkes-Barre, PA), 1 May 1877; "The Mormon Slave Vote," *St. Louis Globe-Democrat* (St. Louis, MO) 15 August 1883; "Joseph Cook's Lectures," *The Congregationalist* (Boston, MA) 10 December 1879; "Affairs in Utah and the Territories," 27.
78. William Jarman, *U. S. A. Uncle Sam's Abscess, or Hell Upon Earth for U. S. Uncle Sam* (Exeter, UK: H. Leduc's Steam Printing Works, 1884), 6, emphasis in original.
79. *Judge*, 28 January 1882, 2, 8–9; see also Gary L. Bunker and Davis Bitton, *The Mormon Graphic Image, 1834–1914: Cartoons, Caricatures, and Illustrations* (Salt Lake City: University of Utah Press, 1983), 112–115; Chester A. Arthur, First Annual Message, 6 December 1881, *Compilation of the Messages and Papers of the Presidents*, 20 vols., James D. Richardson, ed. (New York: Bureau of National Literature, Inc., 1897–1911), 11:4644–4645; B. Carmon Hardy, *Doing the Works of Abraham: Mormon Polygamy: Its Origin, Practice, and Demise* (Norman, OK: Arthur H. Clark Company, 2007), 280–281.
80. Hardy, *Doing the Works of Abraham*, 281–285; Lorie Winder Stromberg, "Prisoners for 'The Principle': The Incarceration of Mormon Plural Wives, 1882–1890," in Newell G. Bringhurst and Craig L. Foster, *The Persistence of Polygamy: From Joseph Smith's Martyrdom to the First Manifesto, 1844–1890* (Independence, MO: John Whitmer Books, 2013), 298–325.
81. *Puck*, 30 March 1887; Hardy, *Doing the Works of Abraham*, 297–303.
82. *Puck*, 30 March 1887.

Chapter 6

1. "Later From Utah," *New York Times*, 7 February 1859.
2. "Later From Utah," 7 February 1859; Elise Lemire, *"Miscegenation": Making Race in America* (Philadelphia: University of Pennsylvania Press, 2002), 122–123.
3. Lemire, *Miscegenation*, 4, 115–117; Sidney Kaplan, "The Miscegenation Issue in the Election of 1864," *Journal of Negro History* 34 (July 1949): 274–343; [David Goodman Croly and George Wakeman], *Miscegenation: The Theory of the Blending of Races, Applied to the American White Man and Negro* (New York: H. Dexter, Hamilton, 1864), ii.
4. Lemire, *Miscegenation*, 114–118; Kaplan, "The Miscegenation Issue," 274–343; [Croly and Wakeman], *Miscegenation*, 49, 53.
5. Kaplan, "The Miscegenation Issue," 275–286, 295–298; [Croly and Wakeman], *Miscegenation*; "Miscegenation or Amalgamation. Fate of the Freedman. Speech of Hon. Samuel S. Cox of Ohio delivered in the House of Representatives, February 17, 1864," (Washington, DC: Constitutional Union, 1864), 5, 10.
6. John H. Van Evrie, *Subgenation: The Theory of the Normal Relation of the Races: An Answer to "Miscegenation"* (New York: John Bradburn, 1864), 30–32, emphasis in original.

7. Martha M. Ertman, "Race Treason: The Untold Story of America's Ban on Polygamy," *Columbia Journal of Gender and Law* 19, no. 2 (2010): 287–366; see also Ariela J. Gross, *What Blood Won't Tell: A History of Race on Trial in America* (Cambridge, MA: Harvard University Press, 2008).

8. "Immense Meeting in Indianapolis," *New York Times*, 21 July 1856.

9. "Immense Meeting in Indianapolis," *New York Times*.

10. *Frank Leslie's Budget of Fun*, (New York, NY) January 1872, 16. On black mammies see Catherine Clinton, *The Plantation Mistress: Woman's World in the Old South* (New York: Pantheon Books, 1982), 201–202; and Patricia A. Turner, *Ceramic Uncles and Celluloid Mammies: Black Images and Their Influence on Culture* (New York: Anchor Books, 1994), 43–49. On Young's arrest and eventual dismissal of charges, see Leonard J. Arrington, *Brigham Young American Moses* (Urbana: University of Illinois Press, 1986), 371–374 and John G. Turner, *Brigham Young Pioneer Prophet* (Cambridge, MA: Harvard University Press, 2012), 364–371.

11. For evidence of simian depictions of Irish, see L. Perry Curtis Jr., *Apes and Angels: The Irishman in Victorian Caricature*, Revised Edition (Washington, DC: Smithsonian Institution Press, 1997), 29–67; and on the Irish struggle for whiteness see Noel Ignatiev, *How the Irish Became White* (New York: Routledge, 1995).

12. "Negro Suffrage and Polygamy," *New York World*, 12 October 1865.

13. "Negro Suffrage and Polygamy," 12 October 1865.

14. John D. Sherwood, *The Comic History of the United States, from a Period Prior to the Discovery of America to Times long Subsequent to the Present* (Boston: Fields, Osgood, 1870), 451.

15. Sherwood, *The Comic History*, 434.

16. "The Elders' Happy Home," *Chic*, 19 April 1881.

17. George M. Fredrickson, *The Black Image in the White Mind: The Debate on Afro-American Character and Destiny, 1817–1914* (New York: Harper and Row, 1971), 275–282.

18. Patrick Q. Mason, *The Mormon Menace: Violence and Anti-Mormonism in the Postbellum South* (New York: Oxford University Press, 2011), 10–13, 15, 32, 68, 127–148; "Latter-day Saints," *Chicago Daily Tribune*, 5 November 1879. Between the end of Reconstruction and the beginning of the Great Depression, Southern mobs lynched at least 2,462 African Americans.

19. "Notes by the Way," *The Christian Recorder*, 26 June 1873; Alexander Walker Wayman, *My Recollections of African M. E. Ministers, or Forty Years' Experience in the African Methodist Episcopal Church* (Philadelphia: AME Book Rooms, 1881), 192–193.

20. "Communications," *Christian Recorder*, 25 October 1883, 1 November 1883.

21. Connell O'Donovan, "'I Would Confine Them to Their Own Species': LDS Historical Rhetoric and Praxis Regarding Marriage Between Whites and Blacks" (unpublished manuscript March 2009). Presented at Sunstone West, as posted at <http://www.connellodonovan.com/black_white_marriage.html> (accessed 26 March 2012); "The Killing of Thos. Coleman Monday Night," *Daily Union Vedette* (Salt Lake City), 15 December 1866.

22. James B. Bennett, "'Until This Curse of Polygamy is Wiped Out': Black Methodists, White Mormons, and Constructions of Racial Identity in the Late Nineteenth Century," *Religion and American Culture* 21 (Summer 2011): 167–194.

23. Alfred Trumble, *The Mysteries of Mormonism* (New York: *Police Gazette*, 1882).

24. James H. Dormon, "Shaping the Popular Image of Post-Reconstruction American Blacks: The 'Coon Song' Phenomenon of the Gilded Age," *American Quarterly* 40 (December 1988): 450–471.

25. "Latest News Items," *Daily Evening Bulletin*, (San Francisco, CA), 5 July 1879; *Hawaiian Gazette* (Honolulu, HI), 20 August 1879; "Crows' Nest Broken Up," *St. Paul Daily Globe* (St. Paul, MN), 23 December 1883.

26. "Clearing the Criminal Dock: Colored Mormonism," *St. Paul Daily Globe*, 28 June 1884; "Colored Mormon," *Sacramento Daily Record-Union* (Sacramento, California),

14 December 1889. For another example, see "Has 'Caught On,'" *The St. Johns Herald* (St. Johns, AZ), 30 April 1885; "Said to Be a Colored Mormon," *Lynchburg Virginian*, 09 May 1884.

27. Dormon, "Shaping the Popular Image," 453, 455, 458.

28. "Enterprise and Its Results," *Music Trade Review* 40, no. 5 (4 February 1905), 44; for examples of ads promoting "The Mormon Coon" see *Music Trade Review* 40, no. 1 (7 January 1905), 44; 40, no. 10 (11 March 1905), 44; 40, no. 17 (29 April 1905), 43; 41, no. 3 (22 July 1905), 39; 41, no. 14 (7 October 1905), 49.

29. "The Mormon Coon," words by Raymond A. Browne, music by Henry Clay Smith (New York: Sol Bloom, 1905).

30. "No Sentiment in It," *New York Age*, 28 November 1891; "The Census Uncertainties," *St. Louis Globe-Democrat* (St. Louis, MO), 30 January 1883.

31. "Varieties," *Deseret News*, 23 November 1864; "Senator Wilson Has Made a Speech!," *Deseret News*, 8 May 1867; "A Methodist Preacher on Miscegenation," *Deseret News*, 24 February 1869.

32. "Society in the South," *Deseret News*, 18 November 1885; see also Abraham H. Cannon Diary, 17 February 1890, LTPSC.

33. Jennie Anderson Froiseth, ed., *The Women of Mormonism; or the Story of Polygamy as Told by the Victims Themselves* (Chicago: A. G. Nettleton, 1881), iv, 25; *Georgia Weekly Telegraph, Journal and Messenger* (Macon, GA), 17 February 1882; *The Judge* (New York), 17 June 1899, 370.

34. Gross, *What Blood Won't Tell*, 138–139.

Chapter 7

1. Scipio A. Kenner, Salt Lake City, Utah, to Brigham Young, 20 November 1870, BYC, CR1234/1, box 33, folder 16 (reel 46), CHL.

2. Kenner to Young, 20 November 1870.

3. Kenner to Young, 20 November 1870.

4. Kenner to Young, 20 November 1870. I am indebted to Ardis E. Parshall for the possible link between Scipio's middle name and Agnes's suspicions.

5. Kenner to Young, 20 November 1870.

6. Kenner to Young, 20 November 1870.

7. "Scipio Africanus Kenner," New Family Search, electronic database, the Church of Jesus Christ of Latter-day Saints, Salt Lake City, Utah, accessed 26 October 2011. Kenner and Park were married at the Endowment House, a temporary structure erected to house Mormon temple rituals, including marriages or "sealings," which are ceremonies that Mormons believe bind a couple together not just for mortality, but for eternity.

8. C. Vann Woodward, *The Strange Career of Jim Crow*, 2d ed. (New York: Oxford University Press, 1966), 6–7; Edward J. Blum, *Reforging the White Republic: Race, Religion, and American Nationalism, 1865–1898* (Baton Rouge: Louisiana State University Press, 2005).

9. Peggy Pascoe, *What Comes Naturally: Miscegenation Law and the Making of Race in America* (New York: Oxford University Press, 2009), 40–46, 56–63.

10. Patrick Q. Mason, "The Prohibition of Interracial Marriage in Utah, 1888-1963," *Utah Historical Quarterly* 76 (Spring 2008): 108–131; "Letters," *Utah Historical Quarterly* 77 (Winter 2009): 99–102.

11. Pascoe, *What Comes Naturally*, 47; Ariela J. Gross, *What Blood Won't Tell: A History of Race on Trial in America* (Cambridge, MA: Harvard University Press, 2008), 43–44; A. Leon Higginbotham Jr., and Barbara K. Kopytoff, "Racial Purity and Interracial Sex in the Law of Colonial and Antebellum Virginia," in *Interracialism: Black-White Intermarriage in American History, Literature, and Law*, ed. Werner Sollors (New York: Oxford University Press, 2000), 89–94; Joshua D. Rothman, *Notorious in the Neighborhood: Sex and Families Across the Color Line in Virginia, 1787—1861* (Chapel Hill: University of North Carolina, 2003), 68.

12. Edward D. Cope, "On the Hypothesis of Evolution, Physical and Metaphysical," *Lippincott's* 6 (July 1870), 40–41. For further information on Cope and racial understanding in the last half of the nineteenth century, see John G. Mencke, *Mulattoes and Race Mixture: American Attitudes and Images, 1865–1918* (Ann Arbor, MI: UMI Research Press, 1979), 57–58.

13. Newell G. Bringhurst, *Saints, Slaves, and Blacks: The Changing Place of Black People within Mormonism* (Westport, CT: Greenwood Press, 1981); Connel O'Donovan, "The Mormon Priesthood Ban and Elder Q. Walker Lewis: 'An Example for his More Whiter Brethren to Follow,'" *John Whitmer Historical Association Journal* 26(2006): 97–100; Gross, *What Blood Won't Tell*, 139.

14. Samuel A. Woolley Diaries, microfilm, MS 1556, vol. 6, box 1, folder 2, Jan.–Jul. 1856, 66, CHL.

15. Woolley Diaries, 71–72, 116–117; Centerville, Delaware Branch Record, microfilm, Council Meeting, 16 March 1856, 35–36, FHL; Knopp's initial entry as a member of the branch, received from Essex, UK, is on pp. 12–13; his rebaptism takes place on 17 August 1856, and then he moves "to the west" the following day (see pp. 26–27). His wife does not appear in the branch record. They both arrive in Utah on 1 September 1860, in the John Smith Company. See the Mormon Pioneer Overland Travel Database <http://history.lds.org/overlandtravels/companyPioneers?lang=eng&companyId=272> (accessed 29 May 2014). Jane Knopp dies in Taylorsville, Utah, in 1881; see "Died," *Deseret News*, 2 March 1881.

16. Centerville, Delaware Branch Record, 26–27, 35–36.

17. George A. Smith Family Papers, MS 36, box 78, folder 7, Council Meeting, 26 August 1908, Manuscripts Division, Special Collections, JWML; Lester E. Bush Jr., "Mormonism's Negro Doctrine: An Historical Overview," in Lester E. Bush Jr. and Armand L. Mauss, eds., *Neither White nor Black: Mormon Scholars Confront the Race Issue in a Universal Church* (Midvale, UT: Signature Books, 1984), 60; Bringhurst, *Saints, Slaves, and Blacks*, 144–147.

18. L. John Nuttall, diary, vol. 1 (Dec. 1876–Mar. 1884), typescript, 290–293, LTPSC; Council Meeting, 4 June 1879, Lester E. Bush papers, Ms 685, box 10, folder 3, Special Collections, JWML.

19. L. John Nuttall, diary, 1: 290–291.

20. L. John Nuttall, diary, 1: 291–292.

21. L. John Nuttall, diary, 1: 292–293.

22. Council Meeting, 4 June 1879, Lester E. Bush papers, JWML; Seventies Record, Book A, CR3/51, 9–11, CHL.

23. L. John Nuttall, diary, 1: 292; US Manuscript Census, Cincinnati, Ohio, 1850; Salt Lake City, Utah, 1860, 1870, 1880.

24. Minutes of a Conference of Elders of The Church of Jesus Christ of Latter Day Saints, held in Cincinati [*sic*] 25 June 1843, CHL.

25. A Record of all the Quorums of Seventies in The Church of Jesus Christ of Latter-day Saints, CR3/51, box 3, folder 2, 5 March 1879, CHL.

26. A Record of all the Quorums of Seventies, 5 March 1879.

27. George A. Smith Family Papers, Council Meeting, 2 January 1902; 26 August 1908.

28. "Deaths," *Deseret News*, 31 December 1884; Bush, "Mormonism's Negro Doctrine," 60.

29. George A. Smith Family Papers, Council Minutes, 26 August 1908; "Deaths," *Deseret News*.

30. George A. Smith Family Papers, Council Minutes, 22 August 1895; 15 December 1897; 11 March 1900; 18 August 1900; 2 January 1902; and 26 August 1908.

31. Council Meeting, 4 June 1879, Lester E. Bush papers, JWML.

32. Jane Manning James, Salt Lake City, to John Taylor, 27 December 1884, John Taylor Papers, in Henry J. Wolfinger, "A Test of Faith: Jane Elizabeth James and the Origins of the Utah Black Community," 16–17, CHL.

33. *The Pearl of Great Price: A Selection from the Revelations, Translations, and Narrations of Joseph Smith, First Prophet, seer, and Revelator to the Church of Jesus Christ of Latter-day Saints* (Salt Lake City, UT: The Church of Jesus Christ of Latter-day Saints, 1981); General Church Minutes, 1839–1877, CR 100 318, box 1, folder 53, 25 April 1847, CHL; Dean C.

Jessee, Mark Ashurst-McGee, and Richard L. Jensen, eds., *The Joseph Smith Papers: Journals Volume 1: 1832–1839* (Salt Lake City, UT: Church Historian's Press, 2008), 152; "Report from the Presidency," *Times and Seasons*, October 1840.

34. *Pearl of Grace Price*, (Abraham 2:9, 11); Jane Manning James, Salt Lake City, to John Taylor, 27 December 1884, John Taylor papers, in Wolfinger, "A Test of Faith."

35. James to John Taylor, 27 December 1884; James to Joseph F. Smith, 7 February 1890; James to Joseph F. Smith, 31 August 1903, in Wolfinger, "A Test of Faith," 16–19; Scott G. Kenney, ed., *Wilford Woodruff's Journal*, 16 October 1894 (Midvale, UT: Signature Books, 1985), 9:322.

36. Record of Baptisms for the Dead for the Seed of Cain, Endowment House, 3 September 1875, FHL; Angus M. Cannon, Salt Lake City, to Jane E. James, 16 June 1888, Angus M. Cannon Letterpress Copybook, in Wolfinger, "A Test of Faith," 17; Salt Lake Temple, Adoptions and Sealings: living and dead, 1893–1961, book A, 18 May 1894, 26.

37. George A. Smith Family Papers, Council Minutes, 2 January 1902, 26 August 1908.

38. George A. Smith Family Papers, Council Minutes, 22 August 1895.

39. George A. Smith Family Papers, Council Minutes, 22 August 1895.

40. George A. Smith Family Papers, Council Minutes, 22 August 1895; see Connell O'Donovan, "'Tainted Blood': The Curious Cases of Mary J. Bowdidge and Her Daughter Lorah Jane Bowdidge Berry," <http://www.juvenileinstructor.org/black-history-month-at-the-ji-tainted-blood-odonovan/> (accessed 25 May 2014), for an exploration of the story of the unnamed woman and her daughters.

41. George A. Smith Family Papers, Council Minutes, 22 August 1895.

42. George A. Smith Family Papers, Council Minutes, 15 December 1897, 11 March 1900, 18 August 1900, 2 January 1902.

43. Abraham H. Cannon, diaries, 1 October 1890, LTPSC.

44. George A. Smith Family Papers, Council Minutes, 11 March 1900, 18 August 1900.

45. George A. Smith Family Papers, Council Minutes, 18 August 1900; Bush, "Mormonism's Negro Doctrine," 80–82; Alma Allred, "The Traditions of Their Fathers: Myth versus Reality in LDS Scriptural Writings," in *Black and Mormon* ed. Newell G. Bringhurst and Darron T. Smith (Urbana: University of Illinois Press, 2004), 34, 47.

46. *Pearl of Great Price* (Abraham 1:26–27); Alma Allred, "The Traditions of Their Fathers," 45–47; Bush, "Mormonism's Negro Doctrine," 81; Hugh Nibley and Michel Rhodes, *One Eternal Round* (Salt Lake City and Provo, UT: Deseret Book and Foundation for Ancient Research and Mormon Studies, Neal A. Maxwell Institute for Religious Scholarship, Brigham Young University, 2010), 162; Hugh Nibley, *Abraham in Egypt*, ed. Gary P. Gillum (Salt Lake City and Provo, UT: Deseret Book and Foundation for Ancient Research and Mormon Studies, 2000), 360–361, 428, 528.

47. George A. Smith Family Papers, Council Minutes, 18 August 1900, 26 August 1908.

48. George A. Smith Family Papers, Council Minutes, 2 January 1902; Extract from George F. Richards Record of Decisions by the Council of the First Presidency and the Twelve Apostles, (no date given but the next decision in order is dated 8 February 1907) in George A. Smith Family Papers.

49. George A. Smith Family Papers, Council Minutes, 15 December 1897.

50. *Speech of Elder Orson Hyde Delivered Before the High Priests' Quorum, in Nauvoo, April 27th, 1845, upon the course and conduct of Mr. Sidney Rigdon, and upon the merits of his claims to the presidency of the Church of Jesus Christ of Latter-day Saints* (Liverpool: James and Woodburn, 1845), 30.

51. Scott G. Kenney, ed., *Wilford Woodruff's Journal*, 25 December 1869 (Midvale, Utah: Signature Books, 1984), 6:511; "The Pre-Existence of Man," *The Seer* (Washington, DC) April 1853; B. H. Roberts, "To the Youth of Israel," *The Contributor*, May 1885; Bush, "Mormonism's Negro Doctrine," 80; Bruce R. McConkie, *Mormon Doctrine* (Salt Lake City, Utah: Bookcraft, 1958), 476–477; Bringhurst, *Saints, Slaves, and Blacks*, 125.

52. George A. Smith Family Papers, Council Minutes, 26 August 1908.

53. George A. Smith Family Papers, Council Minutes, 26 August 1908.
54. George A. Smith Family Papers, Council Minutes, 26 August 1908.
55. George A. Smith Family Papers, Council Minutes, 26 August 1908.
56. George A. Smith Family Papers, Council Minutes, 26 August 1908. For the "never corrected" instance see David McKay, Huntsville, Utah to John R. Winder, Salt Lake City, 14 March 1904, Joseph F. Smith, Stake Correspondence, CR 1/191, box 12, folder 17, CHL.
57. George A. Smith Family Papers, Council Minutes, 26 August 1908.
58. Newell G. Bringhurst, "The 'Missouri Thesis' Revisited," in Bringhurst and Smith, *Black and Mormon*, 30; Eljiah Jr. ordination, Logan 10th Ward, Record of Members, CR 375/8, part 3765; Connell O'Donovan, "'I would Confine them to their own Species': LDS Historical Rhetoric & Praxis Regarding Marriage Between Whites and Blacks," (unpublished conference paper, Sunstone West, 2009), as posted at <http://www.connellodonovan.com/black_white_marriage.html> (accessed 14 March 2012). For the difficulty the "one drop" rule presented when Mormonism spread to Brazil see Mark L. Grover, "Religious Accommodation in the Land of Racial Democracy: Mormon Priesthood and Black Brazilians," *Dialogue: A Journal of Mormon Thought* 17 (Autumn 1984): 23–34; Mark L. Grover, "The Mormon Priesthood Revelation and the Sao Paulo, Brazil Temple," *Dialogue: A Journal of Mormon Thought* 23 (Fall 1990): 39–53.
59. "Our Ticket for 1896," *Broad Ax*, 3 October 1896; "Western Union Gets Deseret Telegraph," *Deseret News*, 20 February 1900; "Local and Other Matters," *Deseret News*, 21 February 1877; "Local and Other News," *Manti Messenger*, 20 October 1900; "Local and Personal," *Manti Messenger*, 21 March 1913; "Kenner as a Peacemaker," *Salt Lake Tribune*, 12 May 1898; "Political Brevities," *Salt Lake Tribune*, 6 December 1896; "Beaver," *Salt Lake Tribune*, 31 August 1876; "Scipio A. Kenner Dies: Well Known in State," *Salt Lake Herald*, 16 March 1913; "Funeral of S. A. Kenner," *Salt Lake Herald*, 17 March 1913; "Prominent Citizens at Kenner Funeral," *Salt Lake Herald*, 24 March 1913.
60. "Death of Jane Manning James," *Deseret Evening News*, 16 April 1908; "Aged Servant is Dead," *Salt Lake Herald*, 17 April 1908; "'Aunt Jane' Laid to Rest," *Deseret Evening News*, 21 April 1908.
61. "Death of Jane Manning James," *Deseret Evening News*, 16 April 1908; "Aged Servant is Dead," *Salt Lake Herald*, 17 April 1908; "'Aunt Jane' Laid to Rest," *Deseret Evening News*, 21 April 1908.
62. Harold H. Jenson, "True Pioneer Stories," *The Instructor*, March 1930; Hannah M. Snow, "Washington County," in Kate B. Carter, comp., *Our Pioneer Heritage*, vol.5 (Salt Lake City, UT: Daughters of the Utah Pioneers, 1972), 523–524.
63. James H. Dormon, "Shaping the Popular Image of Post-Reconstruction American Blacks: The 'Coon Song' Phenomenon of the Gilded Age," *American Quarterly* 40 (December 1988), 450–451; Michael Hicks, "Ministering Minstrels: Blackface Entertainment in Pioneer Utah," *Utah Historical Quarterly* 58 (Winter 1990): 49–63.
64. Ardis E. Parshall, "Brethren in Blackface," <http://www.keepapitchinin.org/2010/11/23/brethren-in-blackface/#more-9813> (accessed 20 March 2012); Hicks, "Ministering Minstrels," 62; "Sambo's Minstrel Show—Presented by 196th Quorum of Seventy," *Church News/Deseret News*, 15 August 1948 (I am indebted to Ardis E. Parshall for this and the following articles on blackface performances in LDS units).
65. "Memphis Branch Minstrels Raise Finances for Ball," *Church Section/Deseret News*, 21 March 1951; "Minstrel Show Bolsters Mission Fund," *Church News/Deseret News*, 3 June 1961.

Chapter 8

1. "Talmadge [*sic*] on Leadville," *Lynchburg Virginian*, 16 September 1880; *The Brooklyn Tabernacle: A Collection of 104 Sermons Preached by T. DeWitt Talmage, D.D.* (New York: Funk and Wagnalls, 1884), 53–56, 375–377.

2. Terryl L. Givens, *The Viper on the Hearth: Mormons, Myths, and the Construction of Heresy* (New York: Oxford University Press, 1997), 130–137; Christine Talbot, *A Foreign Kingdom: Mormons and Polygamy in American Political Culture, 1852–1890* (Urbana: University of Illinois Press, 2013), chap. 6.

3. "Sketch of Rev. Dr. Talmage," *New York Times*, 13 April 1902; *The Brooklyn Tabernacle*, 53–56, 375–377; John Rusk, *The Authentic Life of T. DeWitt Talmage: The Greatly Beloved Divine* (Chicago and Philadelphia: Monarch Book Co., 1902), 132, 247.

4. *The Brooklyn Tabernacle*, 53–54, 375. For evidence of popular perceptions of the Chinese before and after Talmage's sermon, see Philip P. Choy, Lorraine Dong, and Marlon K. Hom, eds., *The Coming Man: 19th Century American Perceptions of the Chinese* (Seattle: University of Washington Press, 1994), 84–136, and for anti-Chinese political rhetoric in the 1880 election see Andrew Gyory, *Closing the Gate: Race, Politics, and the Chinese Exclusion Act* (Chapel Hill: University of North Carolina Press, 1998), 185–211.

5. *The Brooklyn Tabernacle*, 55–56, 375.

6. *The Brooklyn Tabernacle*, 375.

7. *The Brooklyn Tabernacle*, 375.

8. *The Brooklyn Tabernacle*, 375–376.

9. *The Brooklyn Tabernacle*, 375–376.

10. *The Brooklyn Tabernacle*, 53.

11. *The Brooklyn Tabernacle*, 54–56.

12. *The Brooklyn Tabernacle*, 55–56; on the Reynolds decision, see Sarah Barringer Gordon, *The Mormon Question: Polygamy and Constitutional Conflict in Nineteenth Century America* (Chapel Hill: University of North Carolina Press, 2002), 119–145 and Nathan B. Oman, "Natural Law and the Rhetoric of Empire: *Reynolds v. United States*, Polygamy, and Imperialism," *Washington University Law Review* 88, no. 3 (2011): 661–706.

13. *Judge*, 27 October 1883.

14. For the classic discussion of this process in a much broader context, see Edward W. Said, *Orientalism* (New York: Vintage Books, 1979).

15. "An Ordinance in Relation to Religious Societies," *Times and Seasons* (Nauvoo, IL),1 March 1841.

16. George A. Smith, "The History of Mahomedanism," 23 September 1855, *Journal of Discourses*, vol. 3 (London: Latter-day Saints Book Depot, 1856), 28–37.

17. Parley P. Pratt, "Mahometanism and Christianity," 23 September 1855, *Journal of Discourses*, 3:38–42; John Taylor, "The People of God in All Ages Led by One Spirit, and Subject to Persecution—Condition of the World," 10 January 1858, *Journal of Discourses*, vol. 7 (London: Latter-day Saints Book Depot, 1860), 118–125. On American views of Islam in the years leading up to the founding of Mormonism see Thomas S. Kidd, "'Is it Worse to Follow Mahomet than the Devil?': Early American Uses of Islam," *Church History*, 72 (December 2003): 766–790.

18. Scholars have long recognized the breadth and depth of nineteenth-century comparisons of Mormonism and Islam and especially among Joseph Smith, Brigham Young, and Mohammed. Most of the analyses to date have highlighted the parallels that nineteenth-century critics of Mormonism perceived between the American-born religion and its Eastern counterpart. The comparisons are religious, not racial; and as such they focus upon belief and practice, the ways in which Protestants used Islam and Mohammed to define Joseph Smith as an imposter, the Quran to denigrate the Book of Mormon, and the characterizations of both faiths as material and sensual. Both faiths were grounded in prophetic powers of revelation and both allegedly resorted to conversion at the point of a sword. Islam was used to construct Mormonism as a heresy, and Mormonism was used to "Islamicize" America. The analysis here highlights a blurring between the religious and racial. J. Spencer Fluhman, "An 'American Mahomet': Joseph Smith, Muhammad, and the Problem of Prophets in Antebellum America," *Journal of Mormon History* 34 (Summer 2008): 30; Timothy Marr, *The Cultural Roots of American Islamicism* (Cambridge, UK: Cambridge

University Press, 2006), 193. Marr goes as far as any scholar to date in exploring the racialization of Mormonism and Islam, see especially, 208–210. On the conflation of Mormons and Muslims in the nineteenth century see also: Givens, *The Viper on the Hearth*, 130–137; Arnold H. Green and Lawrence P. Goldrup, "Joseph Smith, an American Muhammad? An Essay on the Perils of Historical Analogy," *Dialogue: A Journal of Mormon Thought* 6 (Spring 1971): 46–58; Arnold Green, "The Muhammad-Joseph Smith Comparison: Subjective Metaphor or a Sociology of Prophethood," in *Mormons and Muslims: Spiritual Foundations and Modern Manifestations*, ed. Spencer J. Palmer (Salt Lake City, UT: Bookcraft, 1983), 63–84; Talbot, *A Foreign Kingdom*, chap. 6; Marianne Perciaccante, "The Mormon-Muslim Comparison," *Muslim World* 82, nos. 3–4 (1992): 296–314. For an exploration of the comparisons in a contemporary context, see James M. Penning, "Americans' Views of Muslims and Mormons: A Social Identity Theory Approach," *Politics and Religion* 2 (2009): 277–302. For an exploration of the ways in which Mormons and Asians were constructed as model minorities, see Chiung Hwang Chen, *Mormon and Asian American Model Minority Discourses in News and Popular Magazines*, Mellon Studies in Journalism, vol. 8 (Lewiston, NY: Edwin Mellen Press, 2004).

19. Marr, *The Cultural Roots of American Islamicism*, 189–190.

20. "Correspondence," *Valley Tan* (Corrine, UT) 12 October 1859; William Smith, Bordentown, New Jersey, to William W. Phelps, Nauvoo, Illinois, 23 November 1844, as published in *The Prophet* (New York, NY), 23 November 1844; Remonstrance of William Smith, et al., of Covington, Kentucky. Against the Admission of Deseret into the Union. 31 December 1849, US House of Representatives, 31st Cong., 1st Sess., Misc. Doc. No. 43, 2.

21. Grace Greenwood [Sarah Jane Lippincott], *New Life in New Lands: Notes of Travel* (New York: J. B. Ford and Company, 1873), 141; E. P. Hingston, ed., *Artemus Ward (His Travels) Among the* Mormons (London: John Camden Hotten, 1865), xvi, xix; Richard F. Burton, *The City of the Saints and Across the Rocky Mountains to California*, (New York: Harper and Brothers, 1862), 197–198, 287, 300, 359; Jennie Anderson Froiseth, ed., *The Women of Mormonism; or The Story of Polygamy as Told by the Victims Themselves* (Detroit: C. G. G. Paine, 1882), xvi. For a study that places such descriptions in the broader context of the American West see Richard V. Francaviglia, *Go East Young Man: Imagining the American West as the Orient* (Logan: Utah State University Press, 2011), especially chap. 3.

22. "The Political Secrets of Mormonism," *New York Daily Tribune*, 7 August 1856; Max Adeler [Chas H. Clark] *The Tragedy of Thompson Dunbar: A Tale of Salt Lake City* (Philadelphia: J. M. Stoddart and Co., 1879), 10.

23. Austin N. Ward, *The Husband in Utah; or Sights and Scenes among the Mormons: With Remarks on their Moral and Social Economy*, ed. Maria Ward (New York: Derby and Jackson, 1857), 17–18; Mrs. T. B. H. Stenhouse, *"Tell It All": The Story of a Life's Experience in Mormonism. An Autobiography: By Mrs. T. B. H. Stenhouse, of Salt Lake City, For More than Twenty Years the Wife of a Mormon Missionary and Elder.* (Hartford, CT: A. D. Worthington and Co., 1874), ix.

24. "A Traveling Frenchwoman," *Los Angeles Herald*, 29 May 1892; Grace Greenwood [Sarah Jane Lippincott], *New Life in New Lands*, 145; "Moonshine," *The Hazel Green Herald* (Hazel Green, KY) 13 July 1887; "Rev. Father Kiely and the Infidels," *The Broad Ax* (Salt Lake City, UT) 5 February 1899; "The Mormons," *Harper's Weekly*, 25 April 1857; Caleb Lyon, *Congressional Globe*, 33rd Cong., 1st Sess., 4 May 1854, 1100–1101; *Mormonism: An Address, by Hon. D. C. Haskell, M. C. of Kansas, at the National Anniversary of the American Home Missionary Society, In Chicago, June 8, 1881* (New York: American Home Missionary Society, 1881), 14; "Mrs. Stanton's Letter," *The National Republican*, (Washington, DC), 23 February 1886; "Mormonism, or the New Mohammedanism in England and America," *New York Daily Tribune*, 29 March 1843; Jules Huret, *En Amérique de San Francisco au Canada* (Paris: Bibliothèque-Charpentier, 1905), trans. Hugh MacNaughton in *On the Way to Somewhere Else: European Sojourners in the Mormon West, 1834-1930*, ed. Michael W. Homer (Spokane, WA: Arthur H. Clark Company, 2006), 345.

25. Benjamin G. Ferris, *Utah and the Mormons. The History, Government, Doctrines, Customs, and Prospects of the Latter-Day Saints. From Personal Observation During a Six Months' Residence at Great Salt Lake City* (New York: Harper and Brothers, 1854), 247; Parley P. Pratt, San Francisco, to Brigham Young, 23 August 1854, BYC, CR1234/1, box 41, folder 11 (reel 54), CHL.

26. Ferris, *Utah and the Mormons*, vii–viii, 246–247.

27. George H. Napheys, *The Physical Life of Woman: Advice to the Maiden, Wife, and Mother* (Philadelphia: H. C. Watts and Co.; Boston: G. M. Smith and Co., 1876), 64; C. V. Waite, *The Mormon Prophet and His Harem; or an Authentic History of Brigham Young, His Numerous Wives and Children* (Chicago: J. S. Goodman and Company, 1867), iii; Lyon, 4 May 1854, *Congressional Globe*, 1101; "Charge of Hon. Chas. E. Sinclair," *Valley Tan* (Corrine, UT), 26 November 1858.

28. Parley P. Pratt, "Mahometanism and Christianity," 40–41.

29. George Q. Cannon, "Celestial Marriage," 9 October 1869, *Journal of Discourses*, vol. 13 (London: Latter-day Saints' Book Depot, 1871), 202, 203.

30. Cannon, "Celestial Marriage," 202.

31. Cannon, "Celestial Marriage," 202–203.

32. Cannon, "Celestial Marriage," 204.

33. Andrea G. Radke-Moss, "Polygamy and Women's Rights: Nineteenth-Century Mormon Female Activism," in Newell G. Bringhurst and Craig L. Foster, eds., *The Persistence of Polygamy: From Joseph Smith's Martyrdom to the First Manifesto, 1844-1890* (Independence, MO: John Whitmer Books, 2014); Jessie L. Embry and Lois Kelley, "Polygamous and Monogamous Mormon Women, A Comparison," in *Women in Utah History: Paradigm or Paradox?*, ed. Patricia Lyn Scott and Linda Thatcher (Logan: Utah State University Press, 2005), 1-35; Kathryn L. MacKay, "Women in Politics: Power in the Public Sphere," in Scott and Thatcher, *Women in Utah History*, 360–393; Memorial Adopted by Citizens of Salt Lake City, Utah Territory, at a Mass Meeting Held in Said City 31 March 1870, Remonstrating Against the Passage of the Bill (H.R. No. 1089), US 41st Cong., Senate, 2d Sess., (Washington, DC: GPO, 1870).

34. Lyon, 4 May 1854, *Congressional Globe*, 1100.

35. "Scenes in an American Harem," *Harper's Weekly*, 10 October 1857; C. V. Waite, *The Mormon Prophet and His Harem; or an Authentic History of Brigham Young, His Numerous Wives and Children* (Chicago: J. S. Goodman and Company, 1867), 177, 188–189.

36. Ferris, *Utah and the Mormons*, 255, 263.

37. Ferris, *Utah and the Mormons*, 258–261.

38. Ferris, *Utah and the* Mormons, 252, 259–260.

39. "A Desperate Attempt to Solve the Mormon Question," *Puck* (New York, NY) 13 February 1884.

40. "The Mormons in the Future," *New York Daily Tribune*, 23 July 1858; "The Church's Liquor Record," *Salt Lake Tribune*, 21 February 1909.

41. [Francis Lieber], "The Mormons: Shall Utah Be Admitted to the Union?" *Putnam's Monthly* 5 (March 1855): 228, 234, 235.

42. [Lieber], "The Mormons," 230–231.

43. [Lieber], "The Mormons," 231–233.

44. "Mormonites," *The Sun* (Philadelphia, PA), 18 August 1831; Marr, *Cultural Roots*, 193–201; "Affidavit of Thomas B. March," [*sic*] 24 October 1838, and Deposition of John Corrill, in *Document Containing the Correspondence, Orders, &C. In Relation To The Disturbances With The Mormons; And The Evidence Given Before the Hon. Austin A. King* (Fayette, MO: Office of the Boon's Lick Democrat, 1841), 58, 111; on the scholarly debate see Marr, *Cultural Roots*, 200; and Green and Goldrup, "Joseph Smith, an American Muhammad?," 47.

45. "The Political Secrets of Mormonism," *New York Daily Tribune*, 7 August 1856.

46. "The Mormons in the Future," *New York Daily Tribune*, 23 July 1858.

47. "The Mormon Defiance to the Nation," *Chicago Advance,* 22 December 1881, in Froiseth, *The Women of Mormonism,* 364; "Joseph Cook's Lectures," *The Congregationalist* (Boston, MA) 10 December 1879.

48. "Mormonism," *The National Tribune* (Washington, DC) 2 May 1889, 5; "Sultans, Sulu and Utah," *San Francisco Call,* 8 August 1899.

49. *La Barbe-bleüe* in Charles Perrault, *Histoires ou Contes du Temps Passé* (Paris: Barbin, 1697); Maria Tatar, *Secrets Beyond the Door, The Story of Bluebeard and His Wives* (Princeton, NJ: Princeton University Press, 2004), chap. 1.

50. Tatar, *Secrets Beyond the Door,* 32–48; George Colman, *Blue-beard, or Female Curiosity!* (London: Cadhill and Davies, 1798); Edward H. Jeter, "Blue-bearded Mormons = Honor Code Conniptions" <http://www.juvenileinstructor.org/blue-bearded-mormons/> (accessed 11 June 2012).

51. "Joseph Cook's Lectures," *Congregationalist* (Boston, MA) 10 December 1879; Rev. Joseph Cook, "Disloyal Mormonism," in Ferdinand Vandeveer Hayden, *The Great West, Its Attractions and Resources* (Bloomington, IL: Charles R. Brodix, 1880), 330.

52. "The Modern Bluebeard," *Daily Graphic,* 21 August 1883; "The Remaining Twin," *Daily Graphic,* 15 October 1883; "Shall Not That Sword Be Drawn?" *Daily Graphic,* 25 October 1883.

53. D. Mac, "Hit 'Em Again," *Judge,* 9 January 1886.

54. "Paraguayan Affairs," *New York Sun,* 24 February 1869.

55. "Lines to Le Dook," *New York Sun,* 29 December 1880; "Misunderstood," *Kansas City Journal* (Kansas City, MO) 28 June 1897; "Prattle of the Youngsters," *Omaha Daily Bee,* (Omaha, NE), 29 July 1900; "A Cynic's Definitions," *Rich Hill Tribune* (Rich Hill, MO), 30 July 1903, and *San Juan Islander* (Friday Harbor, WA), 6 August 1903. For other examples of "Mormon and Turk" as a cultural metaphor see, "Which One, Indeed," *Washington Herald* (Washington, DC), 29 May 1910; "What Happened at Our House," *Urbana Union* (Urbana, OH), 27 April 1864, and *Edgefield Advertiser* (Edgefield, SC), 2 January 1867; "Noed their Daddy!" *The Carbon Advocate* (Lehighton, PA), 30 December 1876; and "Breeding for Sex," *St. Paul Daily Globe* (St. Paul, MN), 22 August 1888.

56. Benjamin Morgan Palmer, *Mormonism: A Lecture Delivered Before the Mercantile Library Association of Charleston, S.C.* (Columbia, SC: I. C. Morgan, 1853), 33. For Palmer's biographical information see Christopher M. Duncan, "Benjamin Morgan Palmer: Southern Presbyterian Divine," (PhD diss., Auburn University, 2008) and William Deverell, "Thoughts from the Farther West: Mormons, California, and the Civil War," *Journal of Mormon History* 34 (Spring 2008): 1–19.

57. Palmer, *Mormonism,* 33–34.

58. Palmer, *Mormonism,* 33–34.

59. Palmer, *Mormonism,* 16–17, 22–23.

60. On Chinese population and immigration see Bill Ong Hing, *Making and Remaking Asian America Through Immigration Policy, 1850–1990* (Stanford, CA: Stanford University Press, 1993), 44–49; Shih-Shan Henry Tsai, "Chinese Immigration, 1848–1882," in *Peoples of Color in the American West,* ed. Sucheng Chan, Douglas Henry Daniels, Mario T. García, and Terry P. Wilson (Lexington, MA: D. C. Heath and Company, 1994), 110–116. On anti-Chinese rhetoric and the Exclusion Act see, Stuart Creighton Miller, *The Unwelcome Immigrant: The American Image of the Chinese, 1785–1882* (Berkeley: University of California Press, 1969), 147–166, 170–188; and Andrew Gyory, *Closing the Gate: Race, Politics, and the Chinese Exclusion Act* (Chapel Hill: University of North Carolina Press, 1998).

61. *Portland Transcript* (Portland, MA), 4 November 1854, 235; for an example of similar concern in England see *The Guardian* (London, UK), 17 August 1853.

62. "The Treaty with China," *The Christian Recorder* (Philadelphia, PA) 26 September 1868.

63. "Another Solution of the 'Mormon' Problem," *Deseret Weekly News,* 13 September 1876. The *Deseret News* reprinted the article from the *Chicago Journal of Commerce.*

64. "A Prophetic Vision," *Boston Daily Advertiser* (Boston, Massachusetts) 15 March 1882.

65. Peggy Pascoe, *What Comes Naturally: Miscegenation Law and the Making of Race in America* (New York: Oxford University Press, 2009), 80–85; Patrick Q. Mason, "The Prohibition of Interracial Marriage in Utah, 1888-1963," *Utah Historical Quarterly* 76 (Spring 2008): 108–131; "Letters," *Utah Historical Quarterly* 77 (Winter 2009): 99–102.

66. "Uncle Sam's Troublesome Bedfellows," *Wasp* (San Francisco, CA) 8 February 1879; "The Three Troublesome Children," *Wasp*, 16 December 1881; "Uncle Sam's Nightmare," *Wasp*, 24 March 1882, 192; "Uncle Sam's Troublesome School," *Wasp*, 5 June 1886.

67. B. Carmon Hardy, ed., *Doing the Works of Abraham: Mormon Polygamy, Its Origin, Practice, and Demise* (Norman, OK: Arthur H. Clark Company, 2007), 73–80, 111–114, 263–266; Gordon, *The Mormon Question*, 114–116; Martha M. Ertman, "The Story of *Reynolds v. United States*: Federal 'Hell Hounds' Punishing Mormon Treason," in *Family Law Stories*, ed. Carol Sanger (New York: Foundation Press, 2008).

68. *Reynolds v. United States* (1879), 98 US 153, 161–168; [Lieber], "The Mormons," 228, 234, 235; "Charge of Hon. Chas. E. Sinclair," *Valley Tan* (Corrine, UT), 26 November 1858; Gordon, *The Mormon Question*, 119–145; Ertman, "The Story of *Reynolds v. United States*"; Oman, "Natural Law and the Rhetoric of Empire."

69. *Reynolds v. United States* (1879), 98 US 153, 161–168; "'From Ocean to Ocean'—An Inside View of Brigham Young's Harem—Lecture by the Rev. J. P. Newman, D. D.," *New York Daily Tribune*, 24 January 1871; Oman, "Natural Law and the Rhetoric of Empire"; Gordon, *The Mormon Question*, 119–145.

70. Keller, "Uncle Sam's Nightmare," *Wasp*, 24 March 1882.

71. *Milwaukee Daily Sentinel* (Milwaukee, WI) 6 November 1880; "The Indian Policy," *Idaho Avalanche* (Silver City, ID) 29 April 1882; "The Chinese and Mormon Problems," *Independent Statesman* (Concord, NH) 23 March 1882; "Missionary Work," *Daily Inter Ocean* (Chicago, IL) 3 December 1880.

72. "The Chinese and Mormon Problems," *Independent Statesman*, 194; "An Urgent Issue," *Boston Daily Advertiser* (Boston, MA) 21 July 1881; the *Louisville Post* as reprinted in "Rather Doubtful," *Deseret News*, 29 March 1882; "Chinese and Mormons," *Daily Alta California* (San Francisco, CA) 15 March 1882; "Brieflets," *Silver Reef Miner*, (Silver Reef, UT), 24 March 1882; "The Mormons in Arizona," *Sedalia Weekly Bazoo* (Sedalia, MO), 30 December 1884; O.J. Hollister, "Mormon and Chinaman," *Salt Lake Tribune*, 10 March 1883 (I am indebted to Ardis E. Parshall for sharing this reference with me); "The President's Message," *Abilene Reflector* (Abilene, KS), 17 December 1885; "All Sorts," *National Republican* (Washington, DC), 20 May 1882.

73. *Argonaut* (San Francisco, CA), 17 October 1885.

74. On Mormon missionary activity among Asians and early attitudes toward them, see Reid L. Neilson, *Early Mormon Missionary Activities in Japan, 1901–1924* (Salt Lake City: University of Utah Press, 2010), 3–34.

75. Reid L. Neilson, "Meetings and Migrations: Nineteenth-century Mormon Encounters with Asians," in *Proclamation to the People: Nineteenth-century Mormonism and the Pacific Basin Frontier*, ed. Laurie F. Maffly-Kipp and Reid L. Neilson (Salt Lake City: University of Utah Press, 2008), 260–262.

76. Hosea Stout, James Lewis, and Chapman Duncan, San Francisco, to Brigham Young, 27 August 1853, BYC, CR1234/1, box 23, folder 7 (reel 32), CHL; Hosea Stout, Hong Kong, to Brigham Young, 16 May 1853, BYC, CR1234/1, box 23, folder 7 (reel 32), CHL.

77. Pratt to Young, 23 August 1854.

78. Alexander Badlam, San Francisco, to Brigham Young, 16 September 1854, BYC, box 23, folder 9 or 10 (reel 33), CHL; Will Bagley, ed., *"Cities of the Wicked": Alexander Badlam Reports on Mormon Prospects in California and China in the 1850s* (Spokane: WA: Arthur H. Clark, 1999), 13–14, 20–21.

79. "Chinese Labor in the West," *Deseret News*, 26 May 1869; "The Inferior Race, 'Know Nothings,' on the Pacific Coast," *Deseret News*, 30 June 1869; "The Chinese Question Again," *Deseret News*, 14 July 1869. For additional discussion of Mormon attitudes toward Chinese

railroad workers in contrast to their views of Irish and other workers, see Ryan L. Dearinger, "Frontiers of Progress and Paradox: Building Canals, Railroads, and Manhood in the American West" (PhD diss., University of Utah, 2009), 197–199.

80. Nielson, "Meetings and Migrations," 271–273.

81. "Faith and Repentance," *The Young Woman's Journal* 4, no. 1 (October 1892), 28–34; "Healing of the Sick," *The Young Woman's Journal* 4, no. 4 (January 1893), 173–177.

82. G. H. Snell, "Ramblings Around the World," *Contributor* 14, no. 7 (May 1893): 335–341; 14, no. 8 (June 1893): 369–373;14, no. 9 (July 1893): 417–422;14, no. 10 (August 1893): 484–490;14, no. 11 (September 1893): 513–519;14, no. 11 (October 1893): 562–568;15, no. 1 (November 1893): 11–17;15, no. 2 (December 1893): 75–81;15, no. 3 (January 1894): 143–150;15, no. 4 (February 1894): 207–214;15, no. 5 (March 1894): 271–279;15, no. 6 (April 1894): 335–342;15, no. 7 (May 1894): 440–448;15, no. 8 (June 1894): 492–498;15, no. 9 (July 1894): 527–533;15, no. 10 (August 1894): 591–595.

83. Snell, "Ramblings Around the World," *Contributor* 14, no. 7 (May 1893), 336, 338;14, no. 10 (August 1893), 485, 489;14, no. 11 (September 1893), 513.

84. Snell, "Ramblings Around the World," *Contributor* 15, no. 6 (April 1894): 336.

85. The *Juvenile Instructor*, another publication aimed at Mormon youth, followed suit when it ran an article about Jews in 1903, which focused on physical characteristics. It highlighted the "long hooked nose," dark and "exceedingly think" eyebrows, and "cunning" eyes of Jews as evidence of their suspect character. See, "Will the Peculiar Jewish Face Ever Disappear?" *Juvenile Instructor*, 15 July 1903.

86. These shifts in attitudes notwithstanding, Mormons maintained a fairly consistent level of sympathy and defense toward Muslims. See for example, Ruby Lamont, "Time and Events of the Middle Ages," *Contributor* 14, no. 10 (August 1893): 490–496; "Afraid of Mohammed," *Deseret Evening News*, 23 April 1906; "Prof. Young on the Mormon Religion," *Evening Standard*, (Ogden, Utah) 13 January 1913.

87. Marr, *The Cultural Roots of American Islamicism*, 189–190.

Conclusion

1. Jonathan H. Moyer, "Dancing with the Devil: The Making of the Mormon-Republican Pact" (PhD diss., University of Utah, 2009), chap. 8.

2. Theodore Roosevelt, "A Premium on Race Suicide," as archived at <http://www.theodore-roosevelt.com/images/research/treditorials/o192.pdf> (accessed 23 August 2013); Thomas G. Dyer, *Theodore Roosevelt and the Idea of Race* (Baton Rouge: Louisiana State University Press, 1980), 143–167.

3. "When Roosevelt Reaches Utah," *Salt Lake Herald*, 3 May 1903.

4. "Anything But Dying," *Bisbee Daily Review* (Bisbee, AZ), 26 April 1903.

5. "Roosevelt—That's Bully! No Race Suicide There!," *Salt Lake Herald*, 10 March 1904.

6. Oscar Franklyn Davis, "Latest Word on Mormonism: A Survey of 'The Mormon Kingdom,'" (Pittsburgh, PA: National Reform Association, 1913), 6.

7. Jack London, *The Star Rover* (1915; repr. New York: Macmillan, 1963), 131.

8. Jan Shipps, *Sojourner in the Promised Land: Forty Years among the Mormons* (Urbana and Chicago: University of Illinois Press, 2000), 66–68.

9. Hans P. Freece, *The Letters of an Apostate Mormon to his Son* (Elmira, NY: Chemung Printing, 1908), 26; Elisha Brooks, *A Pioneer Mother of California* (San Francisco, CA: Harr Wagner, 1922), 29.

10. "Chinese Mormon is Being Tried," *Evening Bulletin* (Honolulu, HI) 17 October 1906; "Chinese Mormon Given Sentence," *Evening Bulletin*, 20 October 1906; "Two of His Wives Are Sisters: The Federal Grand Jury Indicts the Chinese Mormon of Maui," *Hawaiian Star* (Honolulu, HI) 19 October 1906.

11. Bruce Kinney, *Mormonism, The Islam of America* (London: Fleming H. Revell, 1912); "The Study Class for Home Missions," *Washington Herald* (Washington, DC) 28 December

1912; "Missionary Society," *Democratic Banner* (Mt. Vernon, OH) 7 February 1913; "Will Lecture on Mormonism," *Washington Herald*, 26 December 1912; "Will Discuss Mormonism," *Washington Times* (Washington, DC), 29 November 1912; "Christian Endeavor," *Washington Times*, 29 March 1913.

12. Kinney, *Mormonism*, 6–7, 109–110, 136, 163–164, 165.

13. *Congressional Record*, 59th Cong., 2d Sess., 13 December 1906 (Washington, DC: Government Printing Office, 1907), 330, 335–336; "Riis Misled President, Says a Senator's Wife," *New York Times*, 19 December 1906. I am indebted to Michael Paulos for bringing these sources to my attention. On Smoot, see Michael Harold Paulos, *The Mormon Church on Trial: Transcript of the Reed Smoot Hearings* (Salt Lake City, UT: Signature Books, 2008) and Kathleen Flake, *The Politics of Religious Identity: The Seating of Reed Smoot, Mormon Apostle* (Chapel Hill: University of North Carolina Press, 2004).

14. *Omaha Daily Bee*,(Omaha, NE), 30 April 1883; *Daily Los Angeles Herald* (Los Angeles, CA), 13 April 1882); *The Columbus Journal* (Columbus, NE), 19 December 1883; *New Ulm Weekly Review* (New Ulm, MN), 10 December 1884, 2.

15. German E. Ellsworth to Joseph F. Smith, 24 December 1909, Northern States Mission, CHL.

16. Ronald G. Coleman and Darius A. Gray, "Two Perspectives: The Religious Hopes of 'Worthy' African American Latter-day Saints before the 1978 Revelation," and Jessie L. Embry, "Spanning the Priesthood Revelation (1978): Two Multigenerational Case Studies" in *Black and Mormon*, ed. Newell G. Bringhurst and Darron T. Smith (Urbana and Chicago: University of Illinois Press, 2004), 54–57, 64–69; George Albert Smith, J. Reuben Clark Jr., and David O. McKay, Salt Lake City, UT to Virgil H. Sponberg, Long Beach, CA, 5 May 1947; Heber J. Grant, J. Reuben Clark Jr., and David O. McKay, Salt Lake City, UT to Ezra T. Benson, Washington DC, 23 June 1942, Lester E. Bush papers, Ms 685, box 10, folder 3, Special Collections, JWML.

17. George Albert Smith, J. Reuben Clark Jr., and David O. McKay, Salt Lake City, UT to Francis W. Brown, Independence, MO, 13 January 1947, Lester E. Bush papers, Ms 685, box 10, folder 3, Special Collections, JWML; Mark L. Grover, "Religious Accommodation in the Land of Racial Democracy: Mormon Priesthood and Black Brazilians," *Dialogue: A Journal of Mormon Thought* 17 (Autumn 1984): 25–36; Mark L. Grover, "The Mormon Priesthood Revelation and the São Paulo, Brazil Temple," *Dialogue: A Journal of Mormon Thought* 41 (Spring 1990): 41–53.

18. Ben E. Rich, Chattanooga, Tennessee, to L. R. Lewis, 14 July 1898, Southern States Mission, CHL.

19. Joseph F. Smith, Jr., to Alfred M. Nelson, 13 January 1907, MS 14591, microfilm, CHL.

20. Joseph Fielding Smith, "The Negro and the Priesthood," *Improvement Era* 27 (1923–1924): 564–565; Joseph Fielding Smith, *The Way to Perfection* (Salt Lake City, UT: Geneological Society of the Church of Jesus Christ of Latter-day Saints, 1931); Joseph Fielding Smith, *Answers to Gospel Questions*, 5 vols. (Salt Lake City, UT: Deseret Book Company, 1966), 5:163–164; Bruce R. McConkie, *Mormon Doctrine* (Salt Lake City, UT: Bookcraft, 1958), 476–477. See also Bryant S. Hinckley, *Sermons and Missionary Services of Melvin J. Ballard* (Salt Lake City, UT: Deseret Book Company, 1949), 248; George F. Richards sermon, in Conference Report, April 1939, 58–59. On President David O. McKay's tepid response to *Mormon Doctrine*, see Gregory A. Prince and William Robert Wright, *David O. McKay and the Rise of Modern Mormonism* (Salt Lake City, UT: University of Utah Press, 2005), 49–53. Matthew Bowman, *The Mormon People: The Making of An American Faith* (New York: Random House, 2012), 206. For additional context on LDS publications with racialized teachings see Matthew L. Harris, "Mormonism's Problematic Racial Past and the Evolution of the Divine-Curse Doctrine," *The John Whitmer Historical Association Journal* 33 (Spring/Summer 2013), 90-114.

21. Smith, *The Way to Perfection*, 101, 110; Andrew H. Hedges, Alex D. Smith, and Richard Lloyd Anderson, eds. *The Joseph Smith Papers: Journals, Volume 2: December 1841–April 1843*, 25 January 1842 (Salt Lake City, UT: Church Historian's Press, 2011), 2:30.

22 Milton R. Hunter, *Pearl of Great Price Commentary* (Salt Lake City, UT: Stevens and Wallis, 1948), 141–142.

23. First Presidency Statement, 17 August 1949, in Lester E. Bush Jr. and Armand L. Mauss, eds., *Neither White nor Black: Mormon Scholars Confront the Race Issue in a Universal Church* (Midvale, UT: Signature Books, 1984), 221.

24. First Presidency to General Authorities, Regional Representatives of the Twelve, Stake Presidents, Mission Presidents, and Bishops, 15 December 1969, in Bush and Mauss, *Neither White nor Black*, 222–224; Harris, "Mormonism's Problematic Racial Past," 102-108.

25. J. B. Haws, "Mormonism's Contested Identity" and Jan Shipps, "Non-Mormon Views of Mormonism," in *Mormonism: A Historical Encyclopedia*, ed. W. Paul Reeve and Ardis E. Parshall (Santa Barbara: ABC-CLIO, 2010), 372–383; Shipps, *Sojourner*, 68–69, 351.

26. Andrew Hamilton, "Those Amazing Mormons," *Coronet*, April 1952, 26–30; Shipps, "Non-Mormon Views of Mormonism," 381; Shipps, *Sojourner*, 100, 351; Harold H. Martin, "Elder Benson's Going to Catch It!" *Saturday Evening Post*, vol. 225 (28 March 1953), 22–23, 110, 112–113; Sheri L. Dew, *Ezra Taft Benson: A Biography* (Salt Lake City: Deseret Book, 1987), chapters 14–15.

27. First Presidency Statement, 17 August 1949; F. Ross Peterson, "Blindside: Utah on the eve of *Brown v. Board of Education*," *Utah Historical Quarterly* 73 (Winter 2005): 4–20.

28. Mark E. Petersen, "Race Problems—As They Affect the Church," Address at the Convention of Teachers of Religion on the College Level, Brigham Young University, Provo, Utah, 27 August 1954, CHL; see also Harris, "Mormonism's Problematic Racial Past," 109-111.

29. Petersen, "Race Problems."

30. This statement, approved by President David O. McKay, was drafted by Sterling M. McMurrin, professor of philosophy at the University of Utah and former US commissioner of education. Prince, *David O. McKay*, 69. See also Patrick Q. Mason, "The Prohibition of Interracial Marriage in Utah, 1888–1963," *Utah Historical Quarterly* 76, no. 2 (2008): 108–131; and J. B. Haws, *The Mormon Image in the American Mind: Fifty Years of Public Perception* (New York: Oxford University Press, 2013), chap. 3.

31. Hugh B. Brown and N. Eldon Tanner to General Authorities, Regional Representatives of the Twelve, Stake Presidents, Mission Presidents, and Bishops, 15 December 1969, CHL.

32. Edward L. Kimball, "Spencer W. Kimball and the Revelation on Priesthood," *BYU Studies* 47, no. 2 (2008), 21–22, 27; Steven Taggart, *Mormonism's Negro Policy: Social and Historical Origins* (Salt Lake City: University of Utah Press, 1970); Lester E. Bush Jr., "Mormonism's Negro Doctrine: An Historical Overview," *Dialogue: A Journal of Mormon Thought*, 8, no. 1 (Spring 1973): 11–68; Lester Bush Jr., "Writing 'Mormonism's Negro Doctrine: An Historical Overview' (1973): Context and Reflections, 1998," *Journal of Mormon History* 25, no. 1 (Spring 1999): 229–271; Harris, "Mormonism's Problematic Racial Past," 106-107; D. Michael Quinn, *The Mormon Hierarchy: Extensions of Power* (Salt Lake City: Signature Books, 1997), 13-14.

33. Edward L. Kimball, ed., *The Teachings of Spencer W. Kimball: Twelfth President of The Church of Jesus Christ of Latter-day Saints* (Salt Lake City, UT: Bookcraft, 1982), 448–449.

34. Kimball, "Spencer W. Kimball and the Revelation on Priesthood," 5–78; First Presidency, To All General and Local Priesthood Officers of the Church of Jesus Christ of Latter-day Saints Throughout the World, 8 June 1978, in Bush and Mauss, *Neither White nor Black*, 224–225.

35. Edward L. Kimball, *Lengthen Your Stride: The Presidency of Spencer W. Kimball* (Salt Lake City, UT: Deseret Book, 2005), 237. For evidence of lingering cultural attitudes see "Lesson 31: Choosing an Eternal Companion," *Aaronic Priesthood Manual* 3 (Salt Lake City: Intellectural Reserve, 1995), 128, which went out of use in 2013.

36. On Landrith, see Stephen R. Haynes, *Noah's Curse: The Biblical Justification of American Slavery* (New York: Oxford University Press, 2002), 3–4; on the Cheerios ad, see, for example, "Interracial Cheerios Ad Sparks Controversy," *The View*, ABC.com, as archived at <http://abc.go.com/shows/the-view/video/PL5554876/_m_VDKA0_nyt6luud>

(accessed 19 August 2013); "'What Matters is that the Parents are Nice, Not if They're Black or White!': The Moment a Group of Children are Told Cheerios' Mixed-race Ad Received a Torrent of Racial Abuse," *Daily Mail*, 17 July 2013, as archived at <http://www.dailymail.co.uk/femail/article-2366897/Children-react-Cheerios-ad-controversy-bira-cial-couple.html> (accessed 19 August 2013).

37. The ad campaign was featured at Mormon.org. When Love declared her candidacy, her profile and ad were removed from the website. See also Stephen Clark, "New Mormon Ad Campaign: Seeking to Dispel Myths or PR for Romney's '12 Run?" FoxNews.com, 4 September 2010, <http://www.foxnews.com/politics/2010/09/04mormons-new-ad-campaign-seeking-dispel-myths-pr-romney-run> (accessed 7 September 2010); Eric Marrapodi, "With 'I'm a Mormon' Campaign, Church Counters Lily-white Image," CNN Belief Blog, 2 November 2011, <http://religion.blogs.cnn.com/2011/11/02/with-im-a-mormon-campaign-church-counters-lily-white-image> (accessed 14 May 2013).

38. Margaret Blair Young and Darius Aiden Gray, "Mormonism and Blacks," in *Mormonism: A Historical Encyclopedia*, 278–279; Jeff Tyson, "Mission Impossible: Mormons Take Harlem," *Narratively*, 19 June 2013, <http://narrative.ly/red-state-nyc/mission-impossible-mormons-take-harlem/> (accessed 15 August 2013); Ken Driggs, "'How Do Things Look on the Ground?': The LDS African American Community in Atlanta, Georgia," in Bringhurst and Smith, *Black and Mormon*, 132–147; Lauren Wilcox, "The Saints Go Marching In," *Washington Post,* 13 May 2007, <http://www.washingtonpost.com/wp-dyn/content/article/2007/05/09/AR2007050901770.html> (accessed 6 September 2013); Betty Stevenson, "The Shining Light of Oakland," The Mormon Women Project, 6 March 2013, <http://www.mormonwomen.com/2013/03/06/the-shining-light-of-oakland/> (accessed 6 September 2013).

39. Richard L. Bushman, "Mormon Persecutions in Missouri, 1833," *BYU Studies* 3 (Autumn 1960): 11–32; Jeffrey Walker, "Mormon Land Rights in Caldwell and Daviess Counties and the Mormon Conflict of 1838: New Findings and New Understandings," *BYU Studies* 47, no 1 (2008): 4–55; Richard Lloyd Anderson, "Atchison's Letters and the Causes of Mormon Expulsion from Missouri," *BYU Studies* 26 (Summer 1986): 3–47.

40. Bruce Dain, *A Hideous Monster of the Mind: American Race Theory in the Early Republic* (Cambridge, MA: Harvard University Press, 2002), vii–viii.

41. On whiteness studies that follow a trajectory of arrival at whiteness, see Noel Ignative, *How the Irish Became White* (New York: Routledge, 1995) and Karen Brodkin, *How Jews Became White Folks and What That Says about Race in America* (New Brunswick, NJ: Rutgers University Press, 2006).

42. Arvella George, personal remembrances, November 2010, in possession of author.

43 B. Carmon Hardy, *Solemn Covenant: The Mormon Polygamous Passage* (Urbana and Chicago: University of Illinois Press, 1992), chapters 9 and 10; Martha Sonntag Bradley, *Kidnapped From That Land: The Government Raids on the Short Creek Polygamists* (Salt Lake City: University of Utah Press, 1993), chapters 2 and 3.

44. Bradley, *Kidnapped From That Land,* 18–97; Jessie L. Embry, "Expansion: 1941–Present," in *Mormonism: A Historical Encyclopedia*, 56–69.

45. Peggy Fletcher Stack, "Modern-day Mormons Disavow Polygamy," *Salt Lake Tribune*, 20 April 2008, as archived at <http://www.sltrib.com/ci_8989865> (accessed 23 April 2008); Lisa Rosetta, "Amid Confusion, LDS Clarify Faith," *Salt Lake Tribune*, 28 April 2008, as archived at <http://www.sltrib.com/news/ci_9079762> (accessed 28 April 2008).

46. Patte Comstock, Director of Public Affairs, Houston, the Church of Jesus Christ of Latter-day Saints, news release, "Improper use of the term 'Mormon' by Media," 28 April 2008; Stack, "Modern-day Mormons," 20 April 2008.

47. "Fw: Just for the record. . . .," e-mail, 26 April 2008, in possession of author.

48. "Fw: Just for the record. . . .," e-mail, 26 April 2008.

49. Jeffrey M. Jones, "Some Americans Reluctant to Vote for Mormon, 72-year-Old Presidential Candidates," Gallup News Service, 20 February 2007 <http://www.gallup.com/

poll/26611/some-americans-reluctant-vote-mormon-72yearold-presidential-candidates. aspx> (accessed 5 September 2013); Lydia Saad, "In U.S., 22% Are Hesitant to Support a Mormon in 2012," Gallup News Service, 20 June 2011, <http://www.gallup.com/ poll/148100/hesitant-support-mormon-2012.aspx> (accessed 5 September 2013); Kenneth Woodward, "The Presidency's Mormon Moment," New York Times, 9 April 2007, <http://www.nytimes.com/2007/04/09/opinion/09woodward.html?_r=0> (accessed 10 April 2007); Noah Feldman, "What Is It About Mormonism," New York Times, 6 January 2008, <http://www.nytimes.com/2008/01/06/magazine/06mormonism-t.html> (accessed 7 January 2008); Peggy Fletcher Stack, "Mitt's Bid for White House Took the Pulse of Nation on Mormonism," Salt Lake Tribune, 8 February 2008, <http://archive. sltrib.com/printfriendly.php?id=8204331&itype=ngpsid> (accessed 5 September 2013).

50. "Robotic-Looking, Special Underwear-Wearing Mormon Mitt Romney Gives Commencement Speech at Coe College in Iowa," 7 May 2006, state29.blogspot.com, <http:// state29.blogspot.com/2006/05/robotic-looking-special-underwear.html> (accessed 29 October 2007).

51. Steven Loeb, "David Letterman to Bill Maher: 'A Reliable Source Assures Me He's Pretending. It's Halloween,'" Business Insider, 26 April 2011, as archived at <http://www. businessinsider.com/letterman-bill-maher-donald-trump-video-2011-4> (accessed 23 August 2013); "Cher Upsets Mormon Leaders with Her 'Magic Underwear' Remark on Twitter," 30 June 2012, as archived at <http://www.goddiscussion.com/97949/cher-upsets-mormon-leaders-with-her-magic-underwear-remark-on-twitter-mormon-leaders-want-apology/> (accessed 23 August 2013); for Cher's tweet, see <https://twitter.com/ cher/status/218726536264687618> (accessed 23 August 2013); Jim Geraghty, "New York Times Columnist Mocks Romney's 'Magic Underwear,'" National Review Online, 23 February 2012, as archived at <http://www.nationalreview.com/campaign-spot/291858/inew-york-timesi-columnist-mocks-romneys-magic-underwear> (accessed 23 August 2013); Jack Marshall, "Ethics Dunce: NY Times Columnist Charles M. Blow, and the Times, If It Doesn't Do Something about Him," Ethics Alarms, 24 February 2012, at <http://eth-icsalarms.com/2012/02/24/ethics-dunce-ny-times-columnist-charles-m-blow-and-the-times-if-it-doesnt-do-something-about-him/> (accessed 23 August 2013).

52. See Mormon-underwear.com and the article on "Temple Garments" at <http://www. mormonnewsroom.org/article/temple-garments> (accessed 23 August 2013). See also Colleen McDannell, Material Christianity: Religion and Popular Culture in America (New Haven, CT: Yale University Press, 1995), chap. 7.

53. Mormon-underwear.com; "Temple Garments."

54. The "I'm a Mormon" campaign was hosted at Mormon.org.

55. Associated Press, "BYU Named Nation's Fittest College Campus," USA Today, 9 September 2005, as archived at <http://usatoday30.usatoday.com/news/health/2005-09-08-byu-fittest-college_x.htm> (accessed 23 August 2013).

56. Associated Press, "Princeton Review's Top 20 Party, Sober Schools," 2 August 2013, <http:// bigstory.ap.org/article/princeton-reviews-top-20-party-sober-schools> (accessed 3 August 2013); Katie Harmer, "BYU Celebrates 15th year as Stone-Cold Sober Campus Champion," Deseret News, 20 August 2012, <http://www.deseretnews.com/article/865560962/ BYU-celebrates-15th-year-as-stone-cold-sober-champion.html?pg=all> (accessed 5 August 2013); Jennifer Polland, "25 Colleges Where Students Are Both Hot and Smart," Business Insider, 20 March 2013, <http://www.businessinsider.com/colleges-where-students-are-hot-and-smart-2013-3#1-brigham-young-university-25> (accessed 3 August 2013). I am indebted to Melissa Coy for this reference.

57. Michael Otterson, "Mormons: Not Necessarily Who You Think They Are," Washington Post, 5 August 2011, as archived at <http://www.washingtonpost.com/blogs/guest-voices/ post/mormons-not-necessarily-who-you-think-they-are/2011/08/05/gIQAKFsXwI_ blog.html> (accessed 23 August 2013); Joanna Brooks, "Five Myths about Mormonism," Washington Post, 5 August 2011, as archived at <http://www.washingtonpost.com/

opinions/five-myths-about-mormonism/2011/08/03/gIQAyIhTwI_story.html> (accessed 23 August 2013).

58. Susan Saulny, "Black Mormons and the Politics of Identity," *New York Times*, 22 May 2012, as archived at <http://www.nytimes.com/2012/05/23/us/for-black-mormons-a-political-choice-like-no-other.html?_r=2&hp&>; see the embedded video "TimesCast Politics: Black Mormons" (accessed 23 August 2013).

59. Jessica Williams, "The Black Mormon Vote," as archived at <http://www.thedailyshow.com/watch/tue-october-9-2012/the-black-mormon-vote>(accessed 18 August 2013); for the perspective of one of the black Mormons interviewed see, "Sister Beehive on Black Mormons on the Daily Show with Jon Stewart," as archived at <http://www.sistasinzion.com/2012/10/sista-beehive-on-black-mormons-on-daily.html> (accessed 18 August 2013); "Jimmy Kimmel Doesn't Believe There are Black Mormons," 5 October 2012, as archived at <http://www.sistasinzion.com/2012/10/jimmy-kimmel-doesnt-believe-there-are.html> (accessed 23 August 2013).

60. Young and Gray, "Mormonism and Blacks,"278–279; "A Portrait of Mormons in the U. S.," <http://www.pewforum.org/Christian/Mormon/A-Portrait-of-Mormons-in-the-US.aspx> (accessed 16 August 2012); "Mormons in Africa: A Bright Land of Hope," <http://www.mormonnewsroom.org/article/mormons-africa-bright-land-hope> (accessed 16 August 2012). On the rise of the Church of Jesus Christ of Latter-day Saints in Africa since 1978, see Dale LeBaron: "The Church in Africa," in *Encyclopedia of Mormonism*, ed. Daniel H. Ludlow, 4 vols. (New York: Macmillan, 1992), 1:22–24; *Out of Obscurity: The LDS Church in the Twentieth Century* (Salt Lake City, UT: Deseret Books, 2000), 177–189; *All are alike unto God: Fascinating Conversion Stories of African Saints* (Salt Lake City, UT: Bookcraft, 1990).

61. "A Portrait of Mormons in the U. S.," <http://www.pewforum.org/Christian/Mormon/A-Portrait-of-Mormons-in-the-US.aspx> (accessed 16 August 2012).

62. Simon G. Whitten, La Harpe, Illinois, to Mary B. Whitten, Parsonsfield, Maine, June 22 1844, Mormon File, HL; "To His Excellency, Daniel Dunklin, Governor of the State of Missouri," *Evening and the Morning Star* (Kirtland, Ohio), December 1833; Abraham Owen Smoot, diary, 28 May 1836, MSS 896, vol. 1, LTPSC (I am indebted to Jonathan Stapley for this reference); E. S. Abdy, *Journal of a Residence and Tour in the United States of North America, From April, 1833, to October, 1834,* 3 vols. (London: John Murray, 1835), 1: 324–325; 3: 40–42, 54–59.

63. "Romney Xmas Card Represents the Melting Pot That Is Utah," 10 December 2007, <http://www.236.com/news/2007/12/10/romney_xmas_card_represents_th_2845.php> (accessed 30 April 2008).

64. Jason Horowitz, "The Genesis of a Church's Stand on Race," 28 February 2012, as archived at <http://www.washingtonpost.com/politics/the-genesis-of-a-churchs-stand-on-race/2012/02/22/gIQAQZXyfR_story.html> (accessed 2 September 2013).

65. Bruce R. McConkie, "All Are Alike Unto God," The Second Annual Church Educational System Religious Educator's Symposium, 17–19 August 1978, Brigham Young University, Provo, Utah.

66. "Church Statement Regarding 'Washington Post' Article on Race and the Church," as archived at <http://www.mormonnewsroom.org/article/racial-remarks-in-washington-post-article> (accessed 2 September 2013).

67. "Race and the Church: All Are Alike Unto God," as archived at <http://www.mormon-newsroom.org/article/race-church>(accessed 2 September 2013); "Official Declaration 2," at <http://www.lds.org/scriptures/dc-testament/od/2?lang=eng> (accessed 21 September 2013).

68. "Race and the Priesthood," <https://www.lds.org/topics/race-and-the-priesthood?lang=eng> (accessed 26 May 2014).

69. Lee Siegel, "What's Race Got to Do With It?," *New York Times*, 14 January 2012, as archived at <http://campaignstops.blogs.nytimes.com/2012/01/14/whats-race-got-to-do-with-it/?_r=0> (accessed 2 September 2013).

INDEX

Note: Page numbers in *italics* indicate photographs and illustrations.

Abdy, Edward Strutt, 23, 270, 271
Abel, 145–8, 154–8, 204–5, 208
Abel, Elijah
  baptism, 117
  and Mormon-African American relations, 109
  obituary, 199
  ordained, 109–10, 295n16
  and racial priesthood ban, 161, 193–9, 199–205, 207–10, 214
abolitionism, 106, 115–7, 122, 123–4
Abraham, 200, 255
"An Act in Relation to African Slavery," 149
"An Act in Relation to Manual Service," 149
"An Act in Relation to Service," 143, 144, 151–2
Acts, 113, 127, 131
Adam, 129–31, 145–6, 154, 156–7, 204–5, 263
adultery, 42–3
Africa, 115–9, 151, 165, 208, 261
African American Episcopal Church, 180–1
African Americans
  antimiscegenation laws, 9, 191–2, 238, 258
  and the "Elder-Berry" cartoon, 11–2
  and Mormon inclusiveness, 23
  and "one-drop" view of race, 189–93, 194–5, 203–7, 210, 254, 258
  and public perceptions of Mormons, 269–70
  and racial priesthood/temple bans, x, 12, 107, 123, 126, 133, 137–9, 145–7, 157–8, 160, 194–5, 197–200, 203, 205–8, 253, 255–6, 258–9, 270–1, 299n97, 300n110
  See also amalgamation; miscegenation; slavery
Akuna, Goo, 251–2
Allen, Charles, 120
Alta California, 5

Alvord, John Watson, 123–4
amalgamation, 82, 106–11, 111–28, 128–38, 138–9, 171–3, 186, 237. *See also* antimiscegenation laws; interracial marriage; miscegenation
An Amalgamation Polka, 171
The Amalgamation Waltz, 171
American Anti-Slavery Society, 123
American Colonization Society, 115–6
Americanization process, 4
American Revolution, 52
American school of anthropology, 136–7
Anglo Saxon triumphalism, 10–1, 39–41
animalistic depictions of Mormons, 34–8, 51
anthropology, 136–7
anti-immigrant sentiment, 7–8, 19–20, 43–50
antimiscegenation laws, 9, 80–1, 152, 191–2, 238, 258
Anti-Polygamy Standard, 86
anti-Semitism, 34
antislavery movement, 115, 127. *See also* abolitionism
apocalyptic theology, 62
Appleby, William I., 107–11, 128, 134–8, 300n110
Arabian Nights, 232
Arapaho Indians, 54
Arapeen, 78
Argonaut, 242
Arizona, 6, 238, 241, 264
Arkansas Supreme Court, 160
Arthur, Chester A., 166, 240
Ashby, Daniel, 67
Ashley, James M., 164
Audouard, Olympe de Joaral, 25
Austin Weekly Statesman, 37